Tikkun Reader

Introduction

When I and my then-wife Nan Fink started *Tikkun* magazine in 1986, we knew that the world needed healing, repair, and transformation (the English translation of the Hebrew word *tikkun*). That need is even more pressing today.

In articles printed in *Tikkun* but not included in this anthology we've presented incontrovertible proof that unless the environmental damage being done to the planet Earth is stopped and repaired soon, there will be disastrous consequences for much of humanity within the next forty years, and the possibility of the destruction of life on earth within the next eighty years.

Similarly, we've shown that the normal operations of our global economy, with its dramatically unequal distribution of wealth, food, and health care has produced a death rate of approximately 20,000 to 30,000 young children each day—from inadequate nutrition and from preventable diseases. We've focused on the irrational policies of the U.S. government and the rapaciousness of U.S. corporations, wars and the bombings of innocents, the torturing of prisoners and suspects, the erosion of civil liberties, the undermining of social supports for the poor that had been won in the twentieth century through the struggles of unions and mass movements seeking social justice, and the weakening of legislation to protect consumers and the environment—though if we had not been based here in the United States we would have given more attention to making similar arguments about the irrationalities of many other governments and societies, including those in Russia, China, the United Kingdom, Saudi Arabia, Iran, Egypt, and dozens more.

We've argued that the world simply cannot afford to be distracted from these global crises by the various entertainments of profligate consumption and media spectacles, or by endless and pointless nationalistic struggles, by escapism and denial, by defeatist forms of spirituality or religious fundamentalisms that welcome the "end of times" and ignore our communal obligation

1

to save the planet and stop the unnecessary suffering caused by wars and unequal distribution of wealth, or by immersion into a purely personal life with
all its fascinating complexities in ways that allow us to forget that we need
not be passive spectators to the unfolding drama of human history.

But I can't be much surprised that we've failed to actually achieve a tikkun
of the world in these twenty years. We already knew at the start of *Tikkun* that
we were up against a huge problem: the inability of those who might be attracted to social change (roughly what I call The Left, including the Democrats, the Greens, the antiwar movements, the women's movement, environmentalists, civil libertarians, gay and lesbian activists, the labor movement,
the civil rights movement, the various movements representing domestic minorities, the antiglobalization movement, and the human rights movement) to
fully grasp the psychological and spiritual dimensions to human experience
that make all the objective and rational arguments secondary to the healing of
the human spirit.

Tikkun actually emerged from my work as principal investigator of an
NIMH-sponsored grant that had been authorized by the Institute for Labor
and Mental Health which I worked on together with psychotherapists Peter
Gabel, Terry Kupers, Lee Schore, and many others in the late 1970s and
which has continued through the subsequent decades. That research uncov-
ered a powerful spiritual crisis in American society among middle-income
working people, particularly those moving politically to the Right.

What we learned in that research was this: There is a huge spiritual crisis
in the lives of most Americans, rooted in the ethos of selfishness and materialism that are the daily accompaniments to the "bottom line" in the world of
work, intensified by the experience of many working people that their work
offers them little opportunity to contribute to the common good or to see their
lives as connecting to some higher meaning or purpose beyond maximizing
money and power for those who control the institutions in which they work.
People learn to "look out for number one," and then bring that home into personal lives where they feel surrounded by others who have similarly brought
home the logic of the marketplace and so see others primarily in terms of
"what can you do for me?" or "how can you be of use to satisfy my needs?"

When the dynamics of the world of work are brought home into personal
life they have devastating results. People who have absorbed the rationality
of the marketplace have learned that the only way to be rational is to "look
out for number one." Unfortunately, they are surrounded by others who have
absorbed this same message. The outcome: tremendous loneliness and insecurity as friendships become weaker and loving relationships and marriages
feel increasingly insecure. People do not know who they can fully trust, and
feel unrecognized even by those closest to them, who seem to be viewing

them primarily through his framework of "Can you satisfy my needs? Else I don't want to be part of this relationship." Recognizing that at some point their partner might easily find another who would satisfy yet more of their needs, even people in families feel increasingly insecure. The culture of the world of work is massively reinforced by the media, the psychotherapeutic culture, and the marketing that tells people that their only reasonable goal is to take care of their own needs.

This is the spiritual crisis of American society—and it causes huge amounts of pain. Families no longer feel secure, and work increasingly is experienced as giving little opportunity to create a purpose-driven life. It was in light of all this that the political Right came forward and won immense political credibility by telling people that they were facing a spiritual crisis that could only be alleviated by moving into right-wing religious and political circles. The Right unfairly and mistakenly blamed the ethos of selfishness and materialism on African Americans, feminists, gays, and lesbians (and in the past few years on all secular people, all liberals, and activist judges).

The irony, of course, is that in the world of work the chief champion of the ethos of selfishness and materialism is the political Right, which consistently opposes any attempts to require social responsibility in the world of work (e.g., opposing "living wage" requirements for workers' pay, attempts to establish safety and health mandates in the workplace, attempts to monitor safety and products for the consumers, or attempts to prevent destruction of the environment by corporations).

The Right gets away with all this because the Left seems completely unable to identify the spiritual crisis as real. Born out of the struggles against feudalism in the seventeenth and eighteenth centuries, the Left adopted the emerging scientist worldview that all that was real was that which could be intersubjectively verified through sense data or which could be subject to measurement. So the Left had no intellectual tools for understanding the spiritual crisis that the globalization of capital has increasingly made a central reality of the postmodern world. As a result, tens of millions of Americans who were victims of the deprivation of meaning in their lives and of the effects of selfishness and materialism in their families, began to respond to a Religious Right that could articulate the pain that they were feeling. While the Left seemed totally tone deaf to the spiritual crisis, and assumed that these Americans were moving to the Right because of sexism, homophobia, racism, or just plain stupidity, we had discovered that they were attracted to the Right because it spoke to their well-founded fears about the loss of love and of meaning in daily life.

At first we tried to explain this to the Left. We at the Institute tried to create a progressive profamilies organization in 1980 that would take the issue of family out of the hands of the Right. But we quickly ran into powerful opposition from many in the Left. Some feminists (notably Barbara Ehrenreich) denounced any effort to create a progressive profamilies approach as inherently antifeminist, while some gay activists argued that even though we specified support for gay and lesbian families that the very assumption of monogamy underlying families represented a heterosexist bias. When we turned to the leaders of the Democratic Party and the labor movement, we found a total rejection of the notion that people were moving to the Right because of "meaning needs" or a spiritual crisis. In fact, we discovered in almost every corner of the Left a strong bias against anything that smacked of religion or connected to spiritual insights.

Stymied in our attempts to go directly to the social movements who badly needed to heed our message, we decided to create an intellectual forum that could introduce a progressive "politics of meaning" into public discourse. That forum was *Tikkun* magazine.

We realized that if we wanted to create a new political discourse in American society that included spiritual depth and wisdom, we would have to distance ourselves from the intellectually lightweight and fuzzy thinking that at the time characterized much of popular perception of the New Age spirituality that had emerged from the 1960s counterculture. While we appreciated the universalistic aspirations of the New Age, we felt little attraction to the superficiality and commercialization that characterized many of the New Age conferences and magazines or to the pop psychology that was given expression in the "take care of yourself at all costs" and "autonomy and freedom from the needs of others is the best way to live" and the underlying assumption, rooted in the capitalist marketplace, that we are fundamentally alone and the highest good is to work out our own spiritual fulfillment for ourselves. It seemed more appropriate to locate ourselves in a particular spiritual tradition with deeper roots. And since most of the founders of the Institute for Labor and Mental Health were Jewish, and Nan was in the process of converting to Judaism by that point in our relationship, it seemed most logical to make *Tikkun* a Jewish magazine with universalistic aspirations.

I had been terribly pained to watch the Jewish world move decisively toward the Right in the 1970s and 1980s. Most of my Jewish friends had watched the mainstream institutions of Jewish life abandon their previous liberalism and support for social justice and narrow their focus to self-defense against anti-Semitism and blind support for whatever policies were being pursued by the State of Israel. It became increasingly frequent to hear Jews identify Judaism with political conservatism. We hoped to reverse that trend by giving visibility to the Jewish prophetic tradition and to a Jewish universalism that recognized all human beings as equally created in the image of God and hence equally deserving of care and concern as the Jews.

We positioned ourselves as the "liberal alternative to *Commentary* magazine and the voices of Jewish conservatism and conformism." We imagined that just as *Commentary*, sponsored by the right-wing American Jewish Committee, had become the leading voice of intellectual life among American political conservatives of all different religious backgrounds, so, too, we would attempt to become a voice for a progressive social change movement that needed to rethink its current directions. But we were quickly faced with a difficult problem. Whereas Jews on the Right were happy to be identified as Jews, and conservatives on the Right seemed happy to undo their historical association with anti-Semitic causes, many Jews on the Left were insistent on their universality and unwilling to publicly claim that their intellectual life had something important to do with their Jewish cultural and intellectual inheritance, and many non-Jews on the Left felt so hostile to religious or spiritual formulations of any sort that they dismissed *Tikkun* as a "Jewish" (and hence, not for them) intellectual enterprise. Unlike non-Jewish right-wing intellectuals who flocked to *Commentary* and used it to develop their own theories about domestic and social policy, we found many left-wing intellectuals reluctant to share their theorizing in a Jewish magazine or even to subscribe to it. They often felt more comfortable in secular and often overtly-hostile-to-religion magazines like *The Nation* and *Mother Jones*, or in the slippery cynicism of *The New Republic*, than in a magazine that overtly proclaimed its commitment to a spiritual vision of hope for the possibility of fundamental transformation of American society. We were astounded to find that progressive gatherings ignored us, and that even when FAIR (the group challenging one-sided, right-wing dominance in the mainstream media) brought together a conference on alternative media, it ignored *Tikkun* just as it ignored progressive Christian magazines like *Sojourners* and *The Other Side*.

Our identification as a Jewish magazine, though we had intended to be more universalistic in public profile and in subscribers, became more pronounced with the start of the First Intifada in 1988. My editorial "The Occupation: Immoral and Stupid," which we sent to hundreds of thousands of Jews around the United States, together with our publication of an article by Hebrew University historian and researcher Benjamin Morris called "The New Historiography: Israel Confronts Its Past," in which he summarized the soon-to-be-published book in 1989 in which he would document the ways that Israel had forced from their homes tens of thousands of Palestinians who would become the core of the Palestinian refugees, caused a sensation in the Jewish world and in the mainstream media as well. Some eighteen years later critique of the policies of the State of Israel is much more widespread in the Jewish world, but when we began it in the late 1980s we faced huge opposition and public denunciations as the Jewish media (not the mainstream American media some of which has Jews in positions of power, but the weeklies written for and controlled by the American Jewish establishment and in particular the UJA/Federation world) portrayed us as "self-hating Jews." At no point since then have I gone through a month without receiving death threats or threats of violence to myself, my family, or to *Tikkun* magazine from right-wing Jews in the United States or Israel. Meanwhile, Alexander Schindler, the national president of the Union of American Hebrew Congregations (the Reform movement of Judaism), resigned from our editorial board because he disagreed with our criticisms of Israel, as did Martin Peretz and Elie Wiesel.

Our iconoclastic approach also challenged the sexism and homophobia in the Jewish world. Though twenty years later much of *Tikkun*'s insistence on the centrality of these issues may seem unnecessary in many parts of the organized Jewish community, our insistence on publishing Jewish feminists like Letty Cottin Pogrebin, Judith Plaskow, Dorothy Dinnerstein, Rabbi Laura Geller, Jo Milgrom, Lillian Rubin, Chava Weissler, Kim Chernin, Barbara Myerhoff, Sidra Dekoven Ezrahi, Rachel Adler, and our poetry editor for many years, Marge Piercy, brought them to a much wider audience than they had previously reached and gave unrelenting proof of the smarts and talents that had been given short shrift in much of the Jewish world. Similarly, *Tikkun*'s publication of the laments of a closeted gay orthodox rabbi who wished to remain both homosexual and orthodox in the rest of his practice generated a public debate that made it easier for other gays in the Jewish world to come out of the closet. *Tikkun*'s persistent critique of the homophobia in the Conservative and Orthodox movements helped create the space for many gays and lesbians to emerge into their Judaism rather than feel the need to reject it.

Meanwhile, *Tikkun*'s original intent to challenge the Right's distorted appropriation of spiritual concerns and the Left's inability to recognize the hunger for a politics of meaning was receding from public view in the first six years of our existence. But it was not lost on some of our non-Jewish readers, particularly Bill and Hillary Clinton. Bill had written to me in 1988 telling me that he felt that our analysis of politics had given him a new set of insights into America, and in the 1992 campaign he frequently quoted my editorials as he spoke to mass audiences about the selfishness and materialism of the Reagan-Bush years. When Hillary gave her first major speech following the 1993 inauguration, and unapologetically exclaimed that "what this country needs is the politics of meaning," and then invited me to the White House to strategize with her about how to implement the politics of meaning, the media had a field day denouncing her as a New Age flake and claiming that I had personally become her guru and taken over her mind. The New Republic crowd, angry that Hillary had displaced Al Gore in shaping domestic policy in the Clinton White House, claimed to be unable to understand what "meaning needs" could be about, and systematically misrepresented what she and I said, while the Left could only guffaw at a politics that they felt to be a slippery slope toward spirituality and religion.

The attempt to distance Hillary and Bill Clinton from my potential influence was intensified by some at *The New Republic* and in the White House. AIPAC supporters feared that a *Tikkun* perspective would undermine their ability to convince the public and the politicians that all American Jews would automatically support Israeli policy no matter what it would turn out to be. *The New Republic* had become a wild cheerleader for the most reactionary elements in Israel, and AIPAC, while claiming to be a representative of whatever government happened to have power, was actually acting in ways that distanced from the Rabin government once Rabin had embarked on a path toward reconciliation with Palestinians. Their supporters in the media were very effective in portraying me as a guru and Hillary as my unsophisticated student (a position that was totally at variance with the facts—no one takes over the mind of this very independent and powerful woman, and she had always made clear to me that what *Tikkun* was doing was only helping clarify and give programmatic direction to insights that she had herself brought with her from her teenage activist years in the Methodist church).

The public embrace and then subsequent distancing from the politics of meaning by the Clintons (for what appeared to be politically opportunistic reasons) coupled with the media representation of me as a guru generated a new crisis within our editorial community. There were some who argued that we had made a big mistake to embrace any form of spirituality or to give attention to religious discourse. As the magazine gave increased focus to trying to define the politics of meaning, in part to contrast it with the empty and silly versions of it that were being presented by the media to embarrass Hillary, some of our writers like Paul Berman and Todd Gitlin left the magazine, fearful that a politics of meaning was seeking to bring into the political arena spiritual or religious values that had no place there. Peter Gabel and I, on the other hand, tried to show them that there was no "values neutral" public square, that capitalist values already predominated there. In fact, as we continued to uncover in our ongoing research with middle-income working people, it was precisely the prevalence of me-firstism and materialism in the public sphere that made the Right so attractive as an alternative, and made many people open to the Religious Right's argument that the only way to stem the selfishness and materialism, the decline of families, and the prevalence of sexually exploitative media and values, would be to introduce their form of religion into the public sphere. The calls for a "Christian nation" became more prevalent. It was only by providing a more progressive values alternative in the public sphere that we could protect the first amendment and prevent the reaction against capitalist values to lead to the triumph of right-wing Christianity. The liberals, we argued, had not succeeded in keeping values out of the public sphere, they had only succeeded in keeping *their* values out of the public sphere, while right-wing values contended with capitalist values, and the Clintons seemed to vacillate between accommodations to one or the other. Gabel and I argued that if we want to protect the public sphere from dominance by right-wing Christian triumphalists, the progressive world would have to provide an alternative—a progressive spiritual or politics of meaning perspective.

Peter Gabel has been a guiding force for this magazine since its inception, and his steady guidance, originality and intellectual brilliance and creativity provided all of us with a steady compass in the many times when we've faced cynicism, ridicule, or abuse from those who felt threatened by the positions we developed. I can't begin to tell you how much I appreciate this profound thinker, loving, and ethically and spiritually evolved human being, and how much the ideas for which I am sometimes given exclusive credit actually derived from the intense intellectual bantering and arguments and sharing of our experiences that we've done together since we formed the Institute for Labor and Mental Health in 1976.

We were proud to have wide-ranging policy debates in the pages of our magazine and on our Web site (www.tikkun.org). We've consistently published views with which we don't agree—not just as letters to the editor, but as major pieces in the magazine itself and also in this anthology. This has at times made it easy for people to blame us for holding positions that actually were quite the opposite of what we were saying in our editorials, but it has kept *Tikkun* as a source of intellectually provocative material throughout our existence.

In fact, this anthology doesn't begin to touch the full richness of the ongoing discussions that continue to occur in *Tikkun*. My publisher set a severe word limit to this book, and so dozens of articles that I think made a major contribution to *Tikkun* over the years have been excluded. Among those: Thomas Cole on aging in America; Annie Dillard on writing; Jonathan Wilson on Philip Roth; Geoffrey Hartman on literary theory; Marshall Berman's arguments against postmodernism; Carol Gilligan on mothering; Anne Roiphe on Christmas; Ariel Dorfman on Chile; Sven Birkerts on George Orwell; Woody Allen on his Jewish identity; Tony Judt on the collapse of communist regimes in Eastern Europe; Carolyn Merchant, Robert Gottlieb, Anthony Westin, and Paul Wapner on environmental issues; fiction by Joyce Carol Oates, Leonard Michaels, Leslie Epstein, Rebecca Goldstein, and Francine Prose; poetry by Stanley Moss, Adrienne Rich, Primo Levi, Czeslaw Milosz, Gerald Stern, Philip Levine, Seamus Heaney, Allen Grossman, Louise Gluck, C. K. Williams, Robert Pinsky, Yehudah Amichai, and Allen Ginsberg; Estelle

Frankel on Jewish romantic relationships; Norman O. Brown on his own intellectual development; Martin Jay on Emmanuel Levinas; debates on integration and black nationalism with Gary Peller, Michael Dyson, and Thomas Byrne Edsall; David Biale on the Savage within Judaism; Paul Wellstone on the politics of the U.S. Senate; Rachel Adler on feminist theology; Sean Wilentz, Sacvan Bercovitch, and Nataline Zemon Davis on 1492; Art Spiegelman on saying goodbye to Maus; Pat Williams, Randall Kennedy, and David Kairys on race; Anne Brener on mourning; Lawrence Kushner on the unity of God; Nanette Schorr on foster care and the Liberal State; Jay Rosen on the press and its cyncism; Elliot Neaman on neo-Nazis; James Atlas on intellectuals; Sharon Kleinbaum on gays and lesbians; David Kraemer, Laurie Zoloth Dorfman. Naomi Wolf, Marie C. Wilson, Helen Alvare, and Ellen Judith Reich on abortion; Yishayahu Leibowitz, Hanan Ashrawi, Galia Golan, Abba Eban, Yithak Frankenthal, Jessica Montel, A. B. Yehoshua, Wendy Orange, Eric Yoffie, Ze'ev Sternhell, Alice Shalvi, Arnold Eisen, Elliot Dorff, Akiba Lerner, Arthur Waskow, Chaim Seidler-Feller, Azmi Bishara, Adi Ophir, Uri Avnery, Joerl Schalit, and Yossi Beilin on Israel and Palestine; David Bollier on fiber optics and community; Larry Bush and Jeffrey Dekro on the Torah of money; Amitai Etzioni and Charles Derber debating communitarianism; Meir Tamari and Judith Hauptman on economic justice; Ilan Stavans on Latino identity; Daphne Merkin on "The Song of Songs"; Svi Shapiro on meaning in education; reflections on World War II and the Holocaust by Michael Kazin, Lawrence L. Langer, Deborah E. Lipstadt, Rosemary Radford Ruether, Marla Stone, and Jon Wiener; July Lynn Felman on "Angels in America"; John Felstiner on Paul Celan; Mario von Peebles on the Black Panthers; Nicholas Bromell on Bob Dylan; Stephen Mo Hanan on why psychedelic drugs may have spiritual and liberatory value (and angry respondents); Bradley Sahvit Artson on the Torah's morally problematic passages; Linda Zisquit on the poetry of Yona Wallach; Halil Weiss on transforming the American cemetery; Michael S. Roth on desire and history; Michael Bader on the psychodynamics of cynicism; John J. Sweeney on labor's role in building a meaningful society; Jerome M. Segal on graceful simplicity; James Hillman on beauty and transformation; Jonathan Kozol on education; Jeremy Rifkin on biotech eugenics; Riane Eisler on partnership economics; prophetic visions by Andrew Weil, Fritjof Capra, Ishamael Reed, Elizabeth Lesser, Jackson Lears, Jim Wallis, Rodger Kamenetz, Alicia Ostriker, David Korten, Mordechai Gafni, Nessa Rapoport, Joseph Skibell, Aryeh Lev Stollman, Robin West, Jack Miles, Douglas Gwyn, and Roger S. Gotlieb; utopian visions from Cornel West, Henry Giroux, Zygmunt Bauman, Rami Shapiro, Roxanne Dubar Ortiz, Michael Naglar, and Deepak Chopra; Noam Chomsky on Howard Zinn; Susannah Heschel and Mathew Fox on Jesus the Jew . . . and the list goes on and on.

Our writers are rich with diversity and depth. So the one thing that has troubled me in the twenty years that I've edited this magazine is the repeated statement that *Tikkun* is really Michael Lerner. Editors of a magazine are constantly promoting others—and the list above is just a small part of the over two thousand writers that I've published in *Tikkun*. I'm proud that *Tikkun* has launched the careers of poets, writers of fiction, and many public intellectuals. So much as I appreciate the fact that in written responses to questionnaires our readers often tell us that they turn to my articles first and express high regard to my editorials (none of which are included in this volume) I hate it when people try to reduce the richness of our fare to Michael Lerner—because it ignores the powerful contributions made to *Tikkun* by so very many creative thinkers. We've been blessed with generous publishers, first Nan Fink, the cofounder with me of this magazine, then Danny Goldberg and his father Victor Goldberg, then my sister Trish Vrandenburg and her husband George Vradenburg. Without them *Tikkun* would have been buried by "market forces" as more and more young people stop reading altogether or read only on the Web or get their information through comedy shows on television. And we've been blessed by many wonderful staff people whose creativity has helped build the magazine from the start, including Joshua Henkin, Alice Chasan, Joellen Green Kaiser, Deborah Kory, and our current managing editor, Joel Schalit, plus our book editors Alan Wolfe, David Biale, Michael Kazin, and Jonathan Schorsch; our poetry editors Marge Piercy, Carolyn Forche and Josh Weiner; our literary/fiction editors Anne Roiphe, Melvin Jules Bukiet, Thane Rosenbaum, and Julian Levinson. Moreover, our whole operation has been held together by others who played an amazing role—both in the office and outside it—giving emotional, intellectual, and spiritual support, direction, guidance, and wisdom, of whom I think particularly of Craig Sumberg, Elliot Neaman, Rachel Adler, Marshall Meyer (z"l), Tsvi Blanchard, Hali Weiss, Mark Levine, Akiba Lerner, Allen Ginsberg (z"l), Cornel West, Abba Eban (z"l), Martha Mendelsohn, Susannah Heschel, Jay Rosen, Linda Zisquit, Michael Bader, Stew Albert (z"l), Svi Shapiro, Arthur Waskow, Art Green, Liz Weiner, Robyn Lundy Thomas, and Zalman Schachter Shalomi. And then there are the thousands of people who have repeatedly stretched beyond their means to donate to us as a nonprofit organization and whose generosity has kept us alive. And tens of thousands who have subscribed and read the magazine, talked about it with their friends, brought it to the attention of the media, and made many of its articles required reading in the courses that they taught in high school, college, and graduate and professional schools.

It might sound as if with all this diversity of voice that there was no unifying focus. But actually there is something very distinct about *Tikkun*, and we try to find articles that are genuinely "tikkunish." It's not only that we seek articles that highlight a hopeful approach to the possibility of healing and transforming the world (there are enough magazines reflecting cynicism to fill a library, but very few manifesting hope). It is not only that we have become the pioneers in interfaith work as a voice for the many spiritual people, including many who do not believe in God or in any higher being, but who do recognize the spiritual dimension of life. It is also that to be tikkunish is to approach the world with awe and wonder and, in the words of my teacher at the Jewish Theological Seminary A. J. Heschel, "radical amazement" at the grandeur of the universe. To be tikkunish is to assert that despite the distortions in all of us, there is a fundamental capacity for human decency, even in those whose are engaged in immoral acts or who have strayed from their own ability to recognize the God in others. A tikkunish perspective looks beneath the surface, to find the morally legitimate spiritual and psychological needs in others, the frustration of which leads some to act in ways that we see as destructive and hurtful. This is not a moral relativism—the acts are genuinely wrong and hurtful. But the tikkun task is to address those underlying needs in a more healthy way (e.g. by separating the people from racism, sexism, homophobia, anti-Semtism, xenophobia, and insensitivity to the suffering of others by providing healthier ways to achieve the fulfillment of the legitimate needs), rather than to denounce the people who have heretofore been attracted to destructive paths.

With this as our goal, we've taken on two of the most challenging tasks of the current moment: to win Jews away from a policy that is objectively oppressive to the Palestinian people, and to win Americans away from right-wing political assumptions (shared by leaders in both major parties) that rely on domination and militarism rather than on caring for others and a spirit of generosity. These goals have been particularly challenging in the first decade of the twenty-first century.

The failure of the negotiations at Camp David in 2000, the provocative visit to the Temple Mount that Ariel Sharon (accompanied by over a thousand Israeli policemen) to flaunt Israeli power at the Mosque of the Dome, and the subsequent outbreak of the second Intifada (after years of Israeli failure to withdraw from the West Bank as Israel had previously promised) led to an upsurge of violence and a distancing from hopes for peace among Israelis and American Jews alike. *Tikkun* lost many subscribers by refusing to join the Ariel Sharon-dominated media consensus in the United States and Israel that blamed this entirely on the Palestinian people. We've instead gently but firmly tried to remind Israelis and Jews that the fundamental reality of the moment is that Israel remains the powerful occupier of the West Bank and the major military and nuclear-armed force in the Middle East. The systematic violations of the human rights of Palestinians has been repeatedly documented by Israeli human rights organizations and condemned by much of the world. And while we've unequivocally condemned acts of terror against Israeli civilians, and believe that those who engage in such acts are irrational, stupid, and destructive to the possibilities of Palestinians ever achieving their rights, we've also condemned the huge numbers of acts of violence by the Israeli occupying forces that have left at least twice as many Palestinian civilians killed by Israelis as Israeli civilians killed by Palestinians. We have refused to be silent about the way that Israel treats its own Arab citizens as second-class citizens, and we have consistently challenged the way Jewish fundamentalists have been given state power to implement a religious state that not only violates our own commitment to separation between church/synagogue/mosque and state, but also destroys most of the interest in Judaism that Israelis would have otherwise shown had the religion not been linked with coercive state power.

Yet even with our consistent criticism of the current policies of the State of Israel, we've also been critics of those who have unfairly singled out Israel and tried to create the impression that it is the worst human rights violator in the world. I personally was banned from speaking at an antiwar rally before the second Iraq war began because I dared to publicly criticize one of the organizing groups which had repeatedly given excessive focus to its critique of Israel while being silent about the human rights violations of Saddam Hussein or that of other Arab regimes, and for its denying of the same rights of national self-determination to the Jewish people that it had offered to every other people on the planet.

Similarly, I've critiqued moves to single out Israel for disinvestment as a response to its oppressive policies toward Palestinians, and instead have pointed out that Israel is not even close to being the worst human rights violator on the planet, and that if we are going to disinvest in human rights violators, a concept that I support, then we ought to start by urging countries around the world to disinvest in the United States, and to do the same regarding Russia until it ends its occupation of Chechnya, China until it ends its occupation of Tibet, and other human rights violators like Pakistan, Egypt, Saudi Arabia, Syria, the Sudan in Darfur, and many others. If Israel were included in this list, it would be hard to object, but for Israel to be singled out and made the major target of anger in some Left and antiwar circles in the United States smacks of an anti-Semitism that we at *Tikkun* will continue to denounce, just as we denounce the anti-Semitism of those who blame "Jews" for the policy of Israel and then proceed to acts of violence against random Jews.

Needless to say that our "progressive middle path," which supports both Israel and Palestine, and critiques both for the ways each side has been cruel and insensitive to the legitimate needs of the other side, gets denounced by both sides. It is not infrequent for me to open my e-mails on any given day to find someone sending me a death threat or denunciation as a "self-hating Jew" or a "disgrace to the Jewish people" for my insistence that Palestinians deserve the same rights and caring that we insist upon for the Jewish people, and then to find right next to it another e-mail, often from an American leftist or Palestinian who is denouncing me for being a clever apologist for Zionist racism toward Palestinians.

Tikkun has developed a Resolution for Middle East Peace and held yearly gatherings in Washington, D.C. in which we've brought hundreds of people from Congressional districts around the United States to provide information to Congress about a "progressive middle path" that would ensure security for Israel as well as a politically and economically viable Palestinian state (along lines detailed by Yossi Beilin's Geneva Accord rather than lines imposed by Ariel Sharon's successors in the Kadima Party which would effectively annex a significant section of the West Bank to Israel). We've challenged the blindness of the Jewish establishment and the moral weakness of elements in the Jewish religious community who know that God requires us to "love the stranger" but have been unwilling to see Arabs or Palestinians as truly deserving of God's and our caring and love.

And yet beyond all political arrangements, we've continued to insist that the only path to peace is one that opens our hearts to the humanity of the other. We do not believe that any political solution based on the hidden assumption on each side that the other is fundamentally evil will be sustainable. Instead, we call for a true reconciliation of the hearts, a new spirit of openness and willingness to hear and understand the story of the other side, to be able to tell the other side's story in a convincing way, and to educate one's children with both stories being told in ways that make them plausible. To aid in this heart-opening, we've called for a Truth and Reconciliation Commission like that which had some impact in South Africa, though we know that this process can only work after Israel has withdrawn from at least 95 percent of the land of the West Bank and in an open-hearted way has helped the Palestinian people recover from the trauma of occupation and the original creation of refugees in 1947–1949. Yet here, too, we refuse to be one-sided. We reject stories that portray the Jewish people as having evil intentions or as coming to the land of Palestine as representatives of Western colonialism. The Jewish people jumped from the burning buildings of Europe, an oppressed people seeking haven, and they were not treated well by many Palestinians when it was the Jews who were powerless and homeless. Though we Jews landed on the backs of Palestinians, unintentionally hurting them, we correctly insisted that our pain was greater than theirs, and then mistakenly used that as our excuse to not notice that we had inflicted *real pain* and generated *real and legitimate anger*.

This story is told in the pages of *Tikkun*, and in my book *Healing Israel-Palestine* (North Atlantic Books, 2003), so I won't dwell on it here, except to say that if you read that book you'll see a summing up of arguments that have been made in a careful way in *Tikkun* magazine for most of the past twenty years, developing a perspective that takes the humanity of both sides seriously and respectfully.

It's this same nuanced response to America after 9/11 that won for *Tikkun* widespread respect in many non-Jewish circles when we became a major exponent of a policy of generosity toward the rest of the world. While social energy was moving toward fear, we remained a beacon of hope, challenging the cynical realists who justified war and denial of civil liberties as the only possible response to the vicious and immoral attack on the World Trade Center on September 11, 2001. We've consistently insisted that the United States would achieve genuine homeland security not by invading and occupying Iraq or Iran, not by sinking trillions of dollars into the military-industrial complex, and not by bullying the world, but rather by a politics of generosity. In particular, we've called for a Global Marshall Plan in which the United States would take the lead in bringing the other G-8 countries into a process in which each would dedicate 5 percent of their own Gross Domestic Product to ending world hunger, homelessness, poverty, inadequate education, and inadequate health care and, in the process, focusing on repairing the damage done to the environment by 150 years of irresponsible industrialization. Such a strategy of generosity flows from our spiritual commitment to a central principle: the well-being of each of us depends on the well-being of everyone else on the planet, and that there is no "private solution" that would enable the United States to do well by being successful in a world in which others suffer silently. This is just one of the many specifics of a spiritual politics that we developed in *Tikkun* and which you can also find articulated in my books *Surplus Powerlessness*, *The Politics of Meaning*, *Spirit Matters*, and most recently, *The Left Hand of God: Taking Back Our Country from the Religious Right*.

Here, then, is the essence of our spiritual commitment: to the unity of all being, to the oneness of all humanity and all life, to the well-being of the planet, and the well-being of every person alive on the planet, to its animals and its vegetables and growing things, to its minerals and to the spirit which permeates all and transcends all.

If *Tikkun* were simply a spiritual magazine we'd be well-financed by people who could recognize that we print some of the highest level, intellectually sophisticated, spiritual ideas. But, unfortunately, because we are also committed to transforming the world not just through individual meditation or working on ourselves, many spiritual people see us as "too political." If we were just a liberal or progressive Jewish magazine, we'd get support from that part of the world, but instead we appear as "too spiritual for them." If we were just Jewish we'd get support from some sections of the Jewish world, but as an interfaith enterprise we now get resistance from some who previously thought they'd be happy to fund Jewish projects. And if we were just interfaith, we might get Christian support, but in that world we are considered way too Jewish. Well, they are all right. We are a complex magazine, seeking to heal the world on the political, economic, social, intellectual, spiritual, and psychological dimensions that we see as fundamentally interconnected. Despite the fact that we have, over the years, responded to pressures to shorten some of our articles, and we've made the magazine much more visually accessible, we remain a serious intellectual and cultural voice.

And yes, we are both an interfaith enterprise and a Jewish enterprise (and if you say we can't be both, you are ALSO right, though the prophet Isaiah told us to aspire to a time when, as God is heard to have put it to Isaiah, "My house will be a house for ALL peoples"). Most people have a rich complexity of identities, and the way that some of us in the Jewish world negotiate the tensions and struggle between our different identities provide a stimulating foundation for many non-Jews who have found *Tikkun* a source of inspiration as they deal with their own conflicting identities (and why some recently created African American, Muslim, Christian Evangelical, and Buddhist journals have privately described themselves as attempting to be the African American, Muslim Evangelical or Buddist Tikkun).

Because of space constraints, you will only get a taste of what makes *Tikkun* such an exciting read and such an influential journal in contemporary cultural and political discourse. We realized, for example, that it would be impossible to give you the many nuanced articles that constitute our ongoing coverage of Israel or the war in Iraq or the problems with the strategies of Democrats and liberals in dealing with the political and Religious Right. We ask you to please subscribe to *Tikkun*—go to www.tikkun.org and subscribe online, call our office (510-644-1200), or send a check (for $29 for one year inside the U.S., US$39 in Canada, or US$43 for all others. If after reading this collection you feel moved to send us a donation to help keep this nonprofit alive, then make it to *Tikkun* and mail it to: *Tikkun*, 2342 Shattuck Ave, Berkeley, CA 94704. Even better: if you'd like to join our interfaith campaign to transform American society toward a New bottom line of love and generosity. Please join the Tikkun Community (read our vision at www.tikkun.org) or the Network of Spiritual Progressives (at www.spiritualprogressives.org).

Whatever you do, I want to bless you in the name of all that is good and all that is holy and all that is loving and all that is beautiful and for the sake of all the past generations whose goodness we've been blessed to inherit and whose wisdom we build upon, that you can join with me and the entire Tikkun Community and the Network of Spiritual Progressives to participate in the beautiful and joyous task of healing our planet, our society, and ourselves. And may you be blessed to see the fulfillment of our work together in a world that is more filled with love, kindness, compassion, generosity, peace, social justice, ecological sanity, and pleasure. And so it is. Amen.

Rabbi Michael Lerner
RabbiLerner@Tikkun.org

Tikkun Reader

Twentieth Anniversary

Edited by
Michael Lerner

ROWMAN & LITTLEFIELD PUBLISHERS, INC.
Lanham • Boulder • New York • Toronto • Plymouth, UK

ROWMAN & LITTLEFIELD PUBLISHERS, INC.

Published in the United States of America
by Rowman & Littlefield Publishers, Inc.
A wholly owned subsidiary of The Rowman & Littlefield Publishing Group, Inc.
4501 Forbes Boulevard, Suite 200, Lanham, Maryland 20706
www.rowmanlittlefield.com

Estover Road
Plymouth PL6 7PY
United Kingdom

British Library Cataloguing in Publication Information Available

Library of Congress Cataloging-in-Publication Data

Tikkun reader : Twentieth anniversary / edited by Michael Lerner.
    p. cm.
  Articles originally published in Tikkun.
  Includes bibliographical references and index.
  ISBN-13: 978-0-7425-4681-3 (cloth : alk. paper)
  ISBN-10: 0-7425-4681-0 (cloth : alk. paper)
  1. Judaism and politics. 2. Religion and politics. 3. God (Judaism) 4. Jews—United
States—Identity. 5. Holocaust, Jewish (1939-1945)—Influence. 6. Israel and the
diaspora. 7. Spiritual life—Judaism. I. Lerner, Michael, 1943- II. Tikkun. III. Title.

BM645.P64T55 2006
296.3'8—dc22   2006016983

Printed in the United States of America

⊖™ The paper used in this publication meets the minimum requirements of American
National Standard for Information Sciences—Permanence of Paper for Printed Library
Materials, ANSI/NISO Z39.48-1992.

Contents

Introduction   1
Michael Lerner

1 Approaching God

An Ocean with Many Shores   19
Jorge N. Ferrer

A God that Is More than Loving   29
Amitai Etzioni

Enchanted Agnosticism   33
Kirk J. Schneider

Pentecostalism and the Future of Christianity   39
Harvey Gallagher Cox

The God Beyond God   47
Daniel C. Matt

Redemption and Ontological Mystery   51
Robert Inchausti

2 Jewish Identity and Survival

The Kindest Un-Cut   57
Michael S. Kimmel

Making Judaism Cool   69
Jonathan Schorsch

Burning in Hell, Conservative Movement Style: Belief that
    Jews and Homosexuals Deserve Eternal Punishment   77
Judith Plaskow

Ten Ways to Recognize a Sephardic "Jew-ess": A Short Story   83
Ruth Knafo Setton

Crossing the Ethnic Divide: A Meditation on Anti-Semitism   91
Nan Fink Gefen

3 Judaism

Notes on Jewish Spirituality   99
Gershon Winkler

The Woman in the Balcony: On Reading the Song of Songs   105
Daphne Merkin

A Kabbalah for the Environmental Age   117
Arthur Green

Quantum Cosmology and Kabbalah   127
Joel R. Primack

Religious Restoration or Religious Renewal: Orthodoxy versus
    Pluralism in Judaism   139
Arthur Waskow

On the Growing Edge of Judaism: Reb Zalman at Eighty   145
Or Rose

Life as Sacred Narrative   151
Estelle Frankel

In Your Blood, Live: Re-Visions of a Theology of Purity   157
Rachel Adler

Starting on My Spiritual Path   165
Naomi Wolf

4 The Holocaust and Its Lessons

The Holocaust's Life as a Ghost—
    Lingering Psychological Effects   173
Zygmunt Bauman

Tainted Legacy: Remembering the Warsaw Ghetto   185
Lawrence L. Langer

The Paradigm Challenged—Study of the Holocaust   195
Daniel Jonah Goldhagen

5 Israel

Seven Pillars of Jewish Denial   213
Kim Chernin

We the Peacemakers   223
Mohammed Abu-Nimer

The Ideological Roots of Christian Zionism   229
Tony Campolo

Compromise for Peace   235
Yitzhak Frankenthal

Healing Israel   239
Cherie R. Brown

6 Spiritual Politics

An Interview on Spiritual Politics with Cornel West   245
Michael Lerner

Contemporary Developments in American Spirituality   253
Daniel Berrigan

Economies of Meaning   257
David C. Korten

Experts and Citizens: Rethinking Professionalism   263
William M. Sullivan

Healing Our Hearts   271
Deepak Chopra

Be Not Afraid   273
Jim Wallis

The Force of Nonviolence   277
Lama Surya Das

Confronting Evil 281
Andrew Kimbrell

Power and Cooperation 291
Jonathan Schell

Spiritualizing Foreign Policy 301
Peter Gabel

Earth Democracy 315
Vandana Shiva

A Spirituality of Resistance 323
Roger S. Gottlieb

The Challenge of the Twenty-First Century 333
Fritjof Capra

Techno-Utopia? 337
Jackson Lears

After the End of History 339
Julian Levinson

Millennial Possibilities 343
Neale Donald Walsch

Index 347

About the Contributors 363

Chapter 1

APPROACHING GOD

An Ocean with Many Shores

Jorge N. Ferrer

It's very reassuring to think that all the different religions and spiritual traditions in the world are aimed at sharing the same basic truths—and that we are all heading in the same direction. The hopes of eliminating wars and tensions between spiritual traditions is a noble goal for a humanity that has been torn apart by religious wars. No wonder it's an attractive alternative to imagine that we could all agree that there is really one basic or perennial truth—we might then find ourselves in a world with less war and less conflict. Apparent differences could be explained away: Differences between different traditions would be seen as little more than problems of translating from one spiritual language to another. Differences in behavior might be understood as reflecting different stages in the development of consciousness toward the higher rungs of this perennial truth. The task of humanity would be to find a common spiritual language and to accelerate the development of those in a "lower" place to a "higher" place. Spiritual education could solve human problems, and spiritual harmony (even the elimination of wars over religious differences) could be achieved once we developed the best techniques for facilitating or supporting people through the stages of spiritual development.

I call this a "Perennialist" position, and, though I can easily understand the appeal of such a picture, I'm afraid that it doesn't really tell an accurate story of spiritual reality. The Perennialist position ignores the way spiritual reality itself is in a process of evolution, and the role human beings and human choices play in shaping that evolution. In my view, we can't talk about people being at a certain stage of some pre-existing spiritual grid, but we can talk about the choices we make that continually shape and evolve that grid.

Despite their professed inclusivist stance, most of the prevailing universalist visions in the modern West tend to distort the essential message of various religious traditions, favoring certain spiritual paths over others and raising serious obstacles for spiritual dialogue and inquiry. Instead, I would like to suggest that spirituality emerges from human cocreative participation in an always dynamic and indeterminate spiritual power. This participatory understanding not only makes hierarchical rankings of spiritual traditions appear misconceived, but also reestablishes our direct connection with the source of our being and expands the range of valid spiritual choices that we as individuals can make.

THE PARTICIPATORY NATURE OF SPIRITUAL KNOWING

Spiritual knowing is a participatory process. What do I mean by "participatory"? First, participatory alludes to the fact that spiritual knowing is not objective, neutral, or merely cognitive. On the contrary, spiritual knowing engages us in a connected, often passionate, activity that can involve not only the opening of the mind, but also of the body, the heart, and the soul.

Although particular spiritual events may involve only certain dimensions of our nature, all of them can potentially come into play in the act of spiritual knowing, from somatic transfiguration to the awakening of the heart, from erotic communion to visionary cocreation, from contemplative knowing to moral insight, to mention only a few.

Second, the participatory nature of spiritual knowing refers to the role that our individual consciousness plays during most spiritual and transpersonal events. This relation is not one of appropriation, possession, or passive representation of knowledge, but of communion and cocreative participation.

Finally, "participatory" also refers to the fundamental ontological predicament of human beings in relation to spiritual energies and realities. Human beings are—whether we know it or not—always participating in the self-disclosure of spirit. This participatory predicament is not only the ontological foundation of the other forms of participation, but also the epistemic anchor of spiritual knowledge claims and the moral source of responsible action.

Spiritual phenomena involve participatory ways of knowing that are presential, enactive, and transformative:

1. Spiritual knowing is presential: Spiritual knowing is knowing by presence or by identity. In other words, in most spiritual events, knowing occurs by virtue of being. Spiritual knowledge can be lived as the emergence of an embodied presence pregnant with meaning that transforms both self and world. Subject and object, knowing and being, epistemology and ontology are brought together in the very act of spiritual knowing.

2. Spiritual knowing is enactive: Following the groundbreaking work of neuroscientists Francisco Varela, Evan Thompson, and Eleanor Rosch, my understanding of spiritual knowing embraces an enactive paradigm of cogni-

tion: Spiritual knowing is not a mental representation of pregiven, independent spiritual objects, but an enaction, the bringing forth of a world or domain of distinctions cocreated by the different elements involved in the participatory event. Some central elements of spiritual participatory events include individual intentions and dispositions; cultural, religious, and historical horizons; archetypal and subtle energies; and, most importantly, a dynamic and indeterminate spiritual power of inexhaustible creativity.

3. Spiritual knowing is transformative: Participatory knowing is transformative at least in the following two senses. First, the participation in a spiritual event brings forth the transformation of self and world. Second, a transformation of self is usually necessary to be able to participate in spiritual knowing, and this knowing, in turn, draws forth the self through its transformative process in order to make possible this participation.

AN OCEAN WITH MANY SHORES

Given a participatory account of human spirituality, we can begin to explore the radical plurality not only of spiritual paths, but also of spiritual liberations and spiritual ultimates.

Let us begin our story by departing from a classic Perennialist account. Perennialism generally postulates a single spiritual ultimate that can be directly known through a transconceptual, and presumably ineffable, metaphysical intuition. This insight, so the story goes, provides us with a direct access to "things as they really are," that is, the ultimate nature of reality and our innermost identity. Central to this view is the idea that once we lift the manifold veils of cultural distortions, doctrinal beliefs, egoic projections, a sense of separate existence, and so forth, the doors of perception are unlocked and the true nature of self and reality is revealed to us in a flashing, liberating insight. From a classic Perennialist perspective, every spiritual tradition leads, in practice, to this identical, single vision. Or to use one of the most popular Perennialist metaphors, spiritual traditions are "like rivers leading to the same ocean."

I do believe spiritual traditions have a common "ocean," to use the Perennialists' metaphor, but the ocean shared by most traditions does not correspond to a cross-cultural spiritual ultimate, or to "things as they really are." Perhaps more humbly, what religious and spiritual traditions share is the interest in overcoming our narrow self-centeredness and thus liberating ourselves from our correspondingly limited—and limiting—perspectives. For the sake of brevity, and mindful of the limitations of this metaphor, since most traditions identify the liberation from self-centeredness as pivotal for this transformation, I will call this common element the "Ocean of Emancipation."

I thus agree with the Perennialists that most genuine spiritual paths (be they knowledge of Brahman in Advaita Vedanta, the cleaving to God in Judaism, or the commitment to visionary service in Shamanism) involve a gradual transformation from self-centeredness toward a fuller participation in the Mystery of existence. In almost every spiritual path, we witness a liberation from self-imposed suffering, an opening of the heart, and a commitment to a compassionate and selfless life. It is in this spirit, I believe, that the Dalai Lama thinks of a common element in religion:

> "If we view the world's religions from the widest possible viewpoint, and examine their ultimate goal, we find that all of the major world religions are directed to the achievement of permanent human happiness. They are all directed toward that goal. To this end, the different world's religions teach different doctrines which help transform the person. In this regard, all religions are the same, there is no conflict."

I also concur with Perennialism in holding that the entry into the Ocean of Emancipation may be accompanied or followed by a transconceptual disclosure of reality. Due to the radical interpenetration between cognizing self and cognized world, once the self-concept is deconstructed, the world may reveal itself to us in ways that transcend our mental conceptualization. Nevertheless—and here I depart radically from Perennialism—I maintain that there are a multiplicity of transconceptual disclosures of reality. Perennialists erroneously assume that the transconceptual disclosure of reality must be necessarily One. In other words, Perennialists generally believe that plurality emerges from concepts and interpretations, and that the transcending of this sort of conceptual proliferation must then result in a single apprehension of "things as they really are."

But to enter the Ocean of Emancipation does not inevitably tie us to a particular disclosure of reality, even if it is transconceptual. In contrast, what the mystical evidence suggests is that there are a variety of possible spiritual insights and ultimates (Tao, Brahman, Sunyata, God, Kaivalyam, etc.) whose transconceptual qualities, although sometimes overlapping, are irreducible and often incompatible (personal versus impersonal, impermanent versus eternal, dual versus nondual, etc.). Perennialism typically accounts for this conflicting evidence by assuming that those qualities correspond to different interpretations, perspectives, dimensions, or levels of a single ultimate reality. As I see it, however, this interpretation is not only unfounded and problematic, but also covertly posits a pregiven spiritual ultimate that is then hierarchically situated over other spiritual goals.

A more fertile way to approach the diversity of spiritual claims is to hold that the various traditions lead to the enactment of different transconceptual disclosures of reality. Although these different spiritual realities may apparently share some qualities (e.g., nonduality in Sunyata and Brahmajñana), they constitute independent religious aims whose conflation may prove to be a serious mistake. In terms of our metaphor, we could say, then, that the Ocean of Emancipation has many shores.

Whereas Ken Wilber and other transpersonalists have rightly identified certain parallels across contemplative paths, contextualist scholars of mysticism have correctly emphasized that the enaction of different spiritual insights requires specific mystical teachings, trainings, and practices. Or, put in traditional terms, particular "rafts" are needed to arrive at particular spiritual "shores": If you want to reach the shore of Nirvana, you need the raft of the Buddhist Dharma, not the one provided by Christian praxis. And if you want to realize knowledge of Brahman (Brahmajñana), you need to follow the Advaitin path of Vedic study and meditation, and not the practice of Tantric Buddhism, devotional Sufi dance, or psychedelic Shamanism and so forth. In this account, the Dalai Lama is straightforward about the uniqueness of each tradition when he states: "Liberation in which a mind that understands the sphere of reality annihilates all defilements in the sphere of reality is a state that only Buddhists can accomplish. This kind of *moksa* or Nirvana is only explained in the Buddhist scriptures, and is achieved only through Buddhist practice."

What is more, different liberated awarenesses can be encountered not only among different religious traditions, but also within a single tradition itself. Listen once again to the Dalai Lama:

> Questioner: "So, if one is a follower of Vedanta, and one reaches the state of *satcitananda*, would this not be considered ultimate liberation?"
>
> His Holiness: "Again, it depends upon how you interpret the words, ultimate liberation. The *moksa* which is described in the Buddhist religion is achieved only through the practice of emptiness. And this kind of nirvana or liberation, as I have defined it above, cannot be achieved even by Svatantrika Madhyamikas, by Cittamatras, Sautrantikas, or Vaibhasikas. The follower of these schools, though Buddhists, do not understand the actual doctrine of emptiness. Because they cannot realize emptiness, or reality, they cannot accomplish the kind of liberation I defined previously."

What the Dalai Lama is suggesting here is that the various spiritual traditions and schools cultivate and achieve different contemplative goals. He is adamant in stressing that adherents to other religions, and even to other Buddhist schools, cannot attain the type of spiritual liberation cultivated by his own. Alternative understandings of emptiness exist even among the various Buddhist schools. To lump together these different awarenesses into one single spiritual referent reachable by all traditions may be profoundly distorting. Each spiritual shore is independent and needs to be reached by its appropriate raft.

Although the metaphor of an ocean with many shores is helpful to illustrate the variety of spiritual realities, it is ultimately inadequate to convey the participatory and enactive nature of spiritual knowing. As with all geographical metaphors, one can easily get the mistaken impression that these shores are pre-given, somehow waiting out there to be reached or discovered. That view, of course, would automatically catapult us back to a kind of perspectival Perennialism, which accounts for the diversity of religious goals in terms of different perspectives or dimensions of the same pregiven Ground of Being. This participatory account should not then be confused with the view that mystics of the various kinds and traditions simply access different dimensions or perspectives of a ready-made single ultimate reality. Such a view merely allows that the same pregiven spiritual referent can be approached from different vantage points. In contrast, the view I am advancing here is that no pre-given ultimate reality exists, and that different spiritual realities can be enacted through intentional or spontaneous cocreative participation in an indeterminate spiritual power or Mystery.

Admittedly, to postulate that human intentionality and creativity may influence or even affect the nature of the Divine—understood here as the source of being—may sound somewhat heretical, arrogant, or even inflated. It is heretical from a conventional standpoint. Why, however, are we so convinced that the Divine is an isolated and independent entity disconnected from human agency? When we understand the relationship between the divine and the human as reciprocal and interconnected, we can, humbly but resolutely, reclaim our creative spiritual role in the divine self-disclosure.

The idea of a reciprocal relationship between the human and the divine finds precedents in the world of mystical literature. Perhaps its most compelling articulation can be found in the writings of ancient Jewish and Kabbalistic theurgical mystics. For the theurgic mystic, human religious practices have a profound impact, not only in the outer manifestation of the divine, but also in its very inner dynamics and structure. Through the performance of the commandments (*mizvot*), the cleaving to God (*devekut*), and other mystical techniques, the theurgic mystic conditions divine activities such as the restoration of the sphere of the *sefirot*, the unification and augmentation of God's powers, and even the transformation of God's own indwelling. As Moshe Idel puts it, the theurgic mystic "becomes a cooperator not only in the maintenance of the universe but also in the maintenance or even formation of some aspects of the Deity."

As scholars Louis Dupré and Bernard McGinn observe, this understanding is not absent in Christian mysticism. In the so-called affective mystics (Richard of

Saint Victor, Teresa of Avila, Jan van Ruusbroec, etc.), for example, we find the idea that the love for God substantially affects divine self-expression and can even transform God himself. In relation to Ruusbroec's mysticism, Dupré points out: "In this blissful union the soul comes to share the dynamics of God's inner life, a life not only of rest and darkness but also of creative activity and light. The contemplative accompanies God's own move from hiddenness to manifestation within the identity of God's own life." And he adds: "By its dynamic quality the mystical experience surpasses the mere awareness of an already present, ontological union. The process of loving devotion realizes what existed only as potential in the initial stage, thus creating a new ontological reality." The idea of a spiritual cocreation—"one that many have assumed but few have dared to express" (Dupré)—is also present in devotional Sufism, as well as in many Indian traditions such as Shaivism and Buddhism. The point is not, however, that spiritual cocreation is a universally accepted notion (clearly that is not the case), but merely to show that it has been maintained by a variety of mystics from different times and traditions.

Once enacted in a cocreative process, spiritual shores do become more easily accessible and, in a way, "given" to some extent for individual consciousness to participate in. Once we enter the Ocean of Emancipation, spiritual forms that have been enacted so far are more readily available and tend more naturally to emerge (from *mudras* to visionary landscapes, from liberating insights to ecstatic types of consciousness, etc.). But the fact that enacted shores become more available does not mean that they are predetermined, limited in number, or that no new shores can be enacted through intentional and cocreative participation. Like trails cleared in a dense forest, spiritual pathways traveled by others can be more easily crossed, but this does not mean that we cannot open new trails and encounter new wonders (and new pitfalls) in the always inexhaustible Mystery of being.

It is fundamental to distinguish clearly this position not only from perspectival Perennialism but also from spiritual relativism and anarchy. While I have argued that there is no one spiritual reality, I do believe there is a spiritual power or Mystery out of which everything arises. Although indeterminate, this Mystery does impose restrictions on human visionary participation. As Varela, Thompson, and Rosch suggest in relation to evolution, the key move "is to switch from a prescriptive logic to a proscriptive one, that is, from the idea that what is not allowed is forbidden to the idea that what is not forbidden is allowed." That is, although certain enactions, like killing people for religious purposes, are invalid, an indefinite number of spiritual enactions are still feasible. We do not have to define the sphere of possible enactions; we only need to agree on the very few which are prohibited.

A central task for spiritual inquirers and participants in the interreligious dialogue, then, is the identification of these restrictive conditions for the enaction of valid spiritual realities. If I were to speculate, I would suggest that the nature of these parameters may have to do not so much with the specific contents of visionary worlds, but with the moral values emerging from them—for example, the saintly virtues in Christianity, the perfections (*paramitas*) in Buddhism, and so forth. In this regard, it is noteworthy that, although there are some areas of tension, religions have usually been able to find more common ground in their ethical prescriptions than in doctrinal or metaphysical issues. In any event, the regulative role of such parameters can not only free us from falling into spiritual anarchy, but also pave the way for making qualitative distinctions among spiritual insights and traditions.

CONCLUSION

In sum, the common ocean to which most spiritual traditions lead may not be a pre-given spiritual ultimate, but the Ocean of Emancipation, a radical overcoming of self-centeredness that can be accompanied by a variety of transconceptual disclosures of reality. Some of these disclosures have been enacted already by the world's spiritual traditions, while an indeterminate number have not yet come into being and will require a more creative participation, a cocreation with the divine, to come into being. Although there are certain constraints on their nature, the number of feasible enactions of spiritual worlds may be, within these boundaries, virtually limitless.

While I cannot consistently maintain the superiority of this account over others, I can highlight its advantages. In brief, the participatory understanding of spiritual realities is more generous than other metaperspectives in terms of recognizing the infinite creativity of Spirit, contributing therefore to the actual generativity of spiritual unfolding (e.g., allowing, impelling, and catalyzing Spirit's creative urges through human-embodied participation). Participatory understanding better honors the diversity of spiritual traditions, insights, and realities than other approaches, affirming, supporting, and legitimizing the largest number of spiritual perspectives on their own terms. A participatory understanding provides a more fertile ground for a constructive and egalitarian interreligious dialogue, as well as for greater respect and harmony among people holding different religious beliefs. Finally, participatory understanding has emancipatory consequences for our individual participation in the self-disclosure of reality—for example, in terms of expanding the range of creative viable options to cultivate, embody, and express the sacred.

In such a participatory cosmos, human intentional participation creatively channels and modulates the self-disclosing of Spirit through the bringing forth of visionary worlds and spiritual realities. Spiritual inquiry then becomes a journey beyond any pregiven goal, an endless exploration and disclosure of the inexhaustible possibilities of an always dynamic and indeterminate Mystery.

A God that Is More than Loving

Amitai Etzioni

Everybody seems to love a spirit that fills us with joy, raises us to a higher level of consciousness, and inspires us. But such a spirit has a touch of self-centeredness. We need a spirit that will make us nobler than we would be otherwise—whether or not this fills us with cheer.

Recently, I have been rereading the most-often quoted work of my first sociology teacher, Martin Buber. In *I and Thou*, Buber depicts God as a super I and Thou, a source of great light and enjoyment, a sea into which all the rivers of smaller, diadic human I and Thou flow. It is a God of "metaphysical love," but not one who makes claims on us.

Buber's God is not the angry deity of the Old Testament, whose true prophets keep admonishing the people to refrain from doing that which offends the Lord. Neither is it the God of the New Testament, who sacrificed His son to bring His love to the people, to redeem humanity from its sins. According to Buber, one's relation to God is, first and foremost, an expression of the I and Thou relationship. Indeed, Buber describes the I-God relationship as a sort of super I-Thou, the ultimate I-Thou relationship, though all other I-Thous have a touch of Godliness. As he writes: "Extended, the lines of relationships intersect in the eternal Thou. Every single Thou is a glimpse of that." More poetically, Buber writes that the relation between man and God "is not one relation among others; it is the universal relation into which all rivers pour without drying up for that reason."

Part of the originality of Buber's I-Thou is his assertion that God relates to us as we relate to Him (or Her). Not only does each "I" need God to form this essential relationship, but, in Buber's words, "Don't you also know that God needs you?" Yet the very nature of this bond raises my communitarian concerns, because Buber's super-Thou makes no claims on us, demands no charity for the poor, nor beseeches us to love our enemies.

29

True, at one point Buber refers to our relationship with God (and to one another) as one of metaphysical love which entails responsibility for the other, and of the other—for the I. Some have read into this a closeness of Buber to Christian ideals of love or "agape." It is important to note, though, that Buber stresses that one cannot endeavor or labor to achieve an I-Thou relationship. He writes, "The Thou encounters me by grace—it cannot be found by seeking." Discussing God, he notes that "One does not find God if one remains in the world; one does not find God if one leaves the world. Whoever goes forth to his You with his whole being and carries to it all the beings of the world, finds him whom one cannot seek." Malcolm Diamond, in his book *Martin Buber: Jewish Existentialist*, writes, "One cannot plan to experience an I-Thou encounter any more than one can plan to fall in love."

This issue is a familiar one to students and followers of other religions, in which there is often a tension between the passive notion that we may rely on God's grace to shine upon us, and the active notion that we will only be ready to be embraced by God once we have worked to become more virtuous. Many religions combine both concepts, although they differ sharply with regard to which element they emphasize. In terms of this continuum from the passive to the active, Buber's treatment of God clearly falls somewhere near the rather passive pole. Buber uses very few "should" statements—no "love others the way you wish others to love you" or other powerful prescriptions. In this sense Buber is closer to the Protestant than to the Catholic interpretation of virtue: we can find out if we are the chosen ones but we cannot become so by working to be good.

When Buber does briefly mention responsibility for the other in I and Thou (he dedicates a particularly opaque passage to it in *Between Man and Man*), it provides rather little moral guidance. On the whole, he lines up with the old communitarians in that he has no concept of individual rights to balance the call of social responsibilities, a litmus test for new or responsive communitarians. Here, Buber seems to be influenced by the Jewish tradition, which, like Islam, stresses responsibility for others (like the poor among us) but basically has no concept of the rights of others that may make claims on us. At one point Buber does refer, uncharacteristically, to "sacrifice." But it is found in the instrumental realm of economics and politics, in the realm of the It, and not the elevated, cherished realm of the Thou.

In the world of persons, the It-world has a legitimate, indeed essential, role. But just as the human I-Thou is pulled toward the I-It and must constantly be nourished, so we must recognize our tendency to "reduce the eternal Thou ever again to an It, to something, turning God into a thing, in accordance with our nature." For Buber, God is a pure Thou. So, for example, Buber adds that relations to God, around which we may form a true We, must not be institutionalized. Institutionalized religion can become a barrier, while "true" prayer is personal. When we are successful in making this super-connection to God, what we have is a mysterious hyper-experience of an indescribable joy, but one that provides no external guidance or affirmation of our own values. Values, let alone the stronger term "virtues," are not part of Buber's basic vocabulary as laid out in *I and Thou*.

This is not merely a limitation I find in Buber. It reflects the reluctance of an age we are leaving behind to pass judgment and to lay claims.

I wish we could merely accentuate and celebrate achievements without passing judgment. I wish a social world could be composed that would function that way. Maybe one day it will. But in this day and age, and in the foreseeable future, such a benign spirit will not heal the wounded, feed the poor, establish a just social order or ensure peace.

Our weakness invites a spirit that is not merely joyous and enlightening, but also one that calls on us to be better than we would be otherwise.

Enchanted Agnosticism

Kirk J. Schneider

Let's face it: with regard to faith and ethics today, we're between a rock and a hard place. The rock is extremist-fundamentalist religion and the hard place is postmodern free-market anarchy.

Fortunately, there is an alternative to these debilitating excesses which have the world in a vise grip; I call it "enchanted agnosticism." Agnosticism has a long and many-layered history. In recent times it has come to be associated with scientific doubt (or the unverifiable); but there is another kind of agnosticism that takes doubt, and particularly the mystery of being, a step further. I call this alternative *enchanted* agnosticism.

By enchanted agnosticism, I mean bedazzled uncertainty, exhilarated discernment, and enraptured curiosity; I mean the openness and skepticism of science wedded to the zeal and exaltation of religion; I mean the veneration of mystery wedded to the solemnity of responsibility. To put all this in philosophic terms, I mean our existential faith in the inscrutable.

Enchanted agnostics believe that behind every institutionalized religion is a transcendent question, "But what is beyond that?" Our answer is that behind every bounded faith resides an evolving, indefinite faith. Beyond every bounded god resides an expanding, indecipherable god. Captivating as they may be, gods and goddesses, idols and icons, obsessions and fixations are but pale stand-ins for the inscrutable. Even concepts like the Absolute or Atman or the Void—to the degree they are decipherable—are but veneers of this mysterious power. As Paul Tillich put it in *The Courage to Be*, veneers (or pieces) of the holy must not be identified with the holy itself, which is a "God beyond God."

This radically new view of God, being, or creation is a view that trumps nihilism as it does dogma; purposelessness as it does certitude. It is a view that basks not in particular things, but in the amazement, astonishment, and bewilderment *of* things. Whereas definable gods (such as those in the Old and

New Testaments, ancient myth, and popular culture) tend to polarize us, either by containing and belittling us on the one hand, or inflating and exaggerating us on the other, the inscrutable fosters wholeness—not puritan or absolute wholeness, but dynamic, paradoxical wholeness. The inscrutable evokes our humility and our possibility at the same time, but instead of dictating these conditions from on high, it inspires *us* to negotiate them, to find our way *within* them. The result of this understanding is that devotees of the inscrutable are more inclined to see *through* their investments and be less driven by them. They are less entrapped—either by false hope or false despair—and they are enlivened by a poignancy to life, an overview, that heightens each attendant moment. Enchanted agnostics are the leaders-to-be of a new spiritual consciousness.

THREE PRINCIPLES

Faith in the inscrutable combines three intertwining perspectives: the magnificence of creation, the mystery of creation, and our responsibility to creation.

MAGNIFICENCE

We don't need a directive or a definable god to feel the presence of divinity. The magnificence of creation demands it. That creation exists at all is magnificent, amazing, incomprehensible. So too, all that partakes in creation must be seen as equally amazing, equally magnificent—death as well as life. This magnificence measures the span of humanity's hope, and demands the tolerance that comes from being open to awe.

As Whitman reminds us:

> Grand is the seen, the light, to me—grand are the stars,
> Grand is the earth, and grand are lasting time and space,
> And grand are their laws, so multiform, puzzling, evolutionary,
> But grander far the unseen soul of me, comprehending, endowing all those. . . .

(Leaves of Grass, n.d.)

MYSTERY

The flip side of magnificence is mystery. One of the greatest dangers of our age is jadedness. The more jaded we become, the less we acknowledge Mystery; the less we acknowledge Mystery, the more we lose touch with its current and with the inscrutable itself.

Magnificence and Mystery are a pair. We cannot have magnificence without uncertainty, and we cannot have mystery without hope. This paradox is often overlooked in mystical circles, which sometimes emphasize magnificence to the detriment of mystery, but was familiar to Paul Tillich, who points out in *The Dynamics of Faith* that mysticism neglects "the separation of man from the ultimate. There is no faith without separation."

With separation comes anxiety; faith must live with this sense of unease. Uncertainty reminds us of our fragility, but it also reminds us of our possibility. Again, Tillich:

> [F]or man is finite, and he can never unite all elements of truth in complete balance. On the other hand, he cannot rest on the awareness of his finitude, because faith is concerned with the ultimate and its adequate expression. Man's faith is inadequate if his whole existence is determined by something that is less than ultimate. Therefore, he must always try to break through the limits of his finitude and reach what never can be reached, the ultimate itself. (p. 57)

RESPONSIBILITY

Creation's magnificence leads us to such foundational religious concepts as respecting the stranger, venerating God, and so on. Mystery, however, leads us to responsibility, the challenge to respond. The call of magnificence can be answered by reflexive, even passive, approaches to worship. Mystery, however, calls us to what Ernest Becker describes as reflective, even dialectical worship (see his 1974 interview with Sam Keen in *Psychology Today*). Once we understand the mystery of the inscrutable, we understand that each of us, as individuals, must bear the brunt of decision making.

We enchanted agnostics cannot passively defer to authority, because there is no certain authority to accept our surrender. There is no marked path, no "highway to heaven," no inviolable canon. It is *we* who must sanctify the scripts, *we* who must find the path. But we are not rudderless when it comes to this process either; faith in the inscrutable does provide landmarks. The first, following Magnificence, is an appreciation for all being; the second, following Mystery, is an openness to what evolves; and the third, following Responsibility, is a challenge to respond to or discern what evolves. That which Tillich calls "listening love" (which is akin to depth therapy as well as Martin Buber's philosophy dialogue) is a concrete realization of the aforementioned principles. "Listening love," elaborates Tillich in *My Search for Absolutes*, is a whole-bodied immersion in a dilemma or concern. "It is a listening to and looking at the concrete situation in all its concreteness, which includes the deepest motives of the other person." Tillich concludes, "The more seriously one has considered all the factors in a moral decision, the more one can be certain that there is a power of acceptance in the depth of life"—and in our own lives, I might add, for the decision we risk.

The responsibility to respond compels a mutable respect, a respect that leans on humanity. Just as one can't apply a "fits all" product to a diverse and opinionated populace, one can't force a "fits all" ethic to a complex and changing existence. Instead, the principle of responsibility that is at the heart of enchanted agnosticism calls upon the deepest energies of democracy, the fullest engagements of dialogue, and the keenest perceptions of context.

Nor is the principle of responsibility a kind of "situational" ethics, as that approach is conventionally understood. Enchanted agnosticism advocates an "awe-based" situational ethics, an ethics infused by the thrill and anxiety of living and the reverence, humility, and wonder of living. While other situational ethics tend to resort to intellectual or consensus-based criteria, an awe-based ethics is ever attuned to the whole, the embodied, and the relational in its deliberations (as in listening love, or person-to-person encounter).

THE WAY TO THE INSCRUTABLE

Enchanted agnosticism is thus very different from the reflexive faith of disciples, or the expedient faith of marketers, or the obsessive faith of fanatics (or even G. W. Bush's faith-based education!). Faith in the inscrutable is wrought from our *encounter* with these and other, singular faiths. It is a faith wrought from the encounter with the myopic, the fleeting, and the one-dimensional— a faith wrought from pain but not confined by pain. It is a faith born of deep self-inquiry, deep presence to the results of that inquiry, and deep trust in the unfolding of the results. It is a faith born of confidence that one can survive one's own intense grappling, but it is not just a faith in survival; it is a faith in that which permits survival to occur.

Awe-based faith entails a "giving up when there's nothing left," as Ernest Becker put it in 1974, a placing of one's trust in the "tremendous creative energies of the universe" to work through and with us when we are spent.

The key here is that such faith often requires that we struggle until we are spent. Struggle jolts the system, dents the armor, and jars the rails. But struggle is only the beginning. The shock and the awakening we experience are only preparatory. The next crucial question is how we pursue, engage with, and emerge from this struggle. We must learn to acknowledge, identify with, and yet somehow be more than that with which we contend.

Expediency, the catch-word of our time, is not a route to the inscrutable. It is a route to the definable, the consolable, and the delimiting. One cannot partake of the fruits of vibrancy, of the profound and the emancipating, through gimmickry. There are no tricks to cultivating awe. The danger today is that we delude ourselves into believing in such tricks; that we mistake Isaiah Berlin's jigsaw puzzle universe for the brute and throbbing one into which we are thrust. Almost every cutting-edge technology poses this danger—virtually every designer drug, genetic manipulation, and robotic innovation holds the potential for abominable self-delusion. While we can be aided and, indeed, miraculously transformed by these developments, we must not lose touch with their partiality and their envelopment by the inscrutable.

VISION

If enchanted agnosticism were to become the norm, then, how would the world look?

I envision a time when enchanted agnosticism is echoed in schools and in temples, in boardrooms and in embassies, in bedrooms and in alleyways—in every human sphere. This would be a time when churches throw open their doors to mosques, and mosques to synagogues; when Buddhist priests can perform sacred chanting rites before Hindu congregants; and when Jewish temples sanction Protestant services. It would be a time, perhaps, when every major denomination would regularly and on a rotating basis host every other major denomination and yet maintain their respective identities; when families of all faiths and backgrounds would pray together, break bread together, and partake in each other's heritage.

This would also be a time when enchanted agnosticism—awe-based living—is practiced in business and diplomatic circles; when politicians and mediators and entrepreneurs *model* the actions they expect of others; when they partake in interfaith ceremonies, avail themselves to intimate interchange, and open to diverse folk traditions. Then, and only then, will the spirals of hate, of tit-for-tat, and of intercultural estrangement be stanched. Then, and only then, will conciliation have a chance.

Further, this would be a time when diplomatic and trade meetings are attended not only by policy makers, but also by ethical philosophers, spiritual leaders, and organizational psychologists; when, for example, attendees participate in professionally facilitated process groups and promote frank exchanges of feeling; and when the input from scientists and philosophers matches that from legislators and generals. It would be a time when representatives can broach each other's personal fears as well as state or corporate agendas; when international relations can be spoken about in terms of interpersonal relations; and when hopes and trepidations can be coupled with predictions and averages.

Finally, this would be a time when people everywhere approach each other and our world from a stance of curiosity, wonderment, and potentially even attraction, for commensurate with the rise in enchanted agnosticism would be the corresponding rise in intra- and intercultural reassessment, trust, and co-operation, and with these developments, entire worlds will unfurl. Religious and scientific types, for example, would begin to perceive not only their respective divergences, but also their respective convergences, utility, and virtues. While adherents of doctrinal faith would reassess the value of openness and skepticism, devotees of calculation would reevaluate the legitimacy of veneration and faith; while spiritualists would rethink material realities, materialists would revisit the ethereal, poetic, and felt. Although hesitant at first, each of the respective parties would become increasingly appreciative of the others' legitimacy, lucidity, and sublimity.

Sound remote? Out-of-reach? Not necessarily. Social theorists from Carl Rogers to Michael Lerner have been promoting such interchanges for years and many have partaken of their fruit. As more partake in The Great Conversation, fewer will pine for The Great Detonation, or The Holy Vindication; and as some invite deepening and widening, others will permit risking, opening. In short, enchanted agnosticism—the embrace of mystery—has tremendous potential to address the confusion and spiritual hunger of our lives.

In her illuminating study of religion, *The History of God*, Karen Armstrong concludes that we in the West have reached a developmental milestone. We have witnessed the disasters of fundamentalist tyrannies and, equally, of post-Enlightenment oligarchies, and we are in need of something different. This alternative, Armstrong suggests, just might be what she calls "mystical agnosticism," which is very akin to my "enchanted agnosticism." The problem, Armstrong cautions, is that in order for such an alternative to be viable it must be "felt upon the pulse," or as Buber put it, "hallowed in the everyday." That is precisely the challenge that I pose to *Tikkun* readers today: to feel enchanted agnosticism upon the pulse.

Pentecostalism and
the Future of Christianity

Harvey Gallagher Cox

In April of this year, I arrived for church one clear Sunday morning to find a small placard attached to the outdoor bulletin board where the sermon topic is usually announced. It notified all who passed by that the "Iglesia Pentecostal Arce de Noe," a Spanish-speaking pentecostal congregation named for Noah's ark, was now sharing our building. I was not particularly surprised. Just two months earlier I had noticed that a classic white frame Congregational church on Massachusetts Avenue two blocks from my home was now sharing its space with a Portuguese-speaking Brazilian pentecostal congregation called the "Assembliea de Deus-Monte Sion." Everywhere you go in American cities today the evidence of a radical change in the religious complexion of America is increasingly self-evident. The so-called "mainline" churches, most of which have been losing members steadily, are providing space in their own premises for vigorous new ethnic congregations, many of them pentecostal ones.

There is a sea change underway in American Christianity, a movement toward a more experiential, more emotionally expressive, organizationally less rigid form of spirituality. Pentecostalism is the generic name for this religious wave. But it is not restricted to immigrants or to North America. In fact, pentecostalism is the fastest growing religious movement in the world. From its obscure beginnings one hundred years ago in a tiny black church on Azusa Street in Los Angeles it has expanded, especially in the past two decades, until it now claims 400 million people, one out of every four Christians. It is growing faster than radical Islam.

Pentecostalism's simple, spontaneous style of worship makes it especially attractive to the poor and marginalized people of the globe. Last year more than two hundred new pentecostal churches opened their doors in the city of Rio de Janiero, while only one new Catholic parish was founded. In Korea, pentecostals have grown from a tiny minority after the Korean War to about one-third of the population. The largest single Christian congregation in the world, the Yoido Full Gospel (Pentecostal) Church is in Seoul. Recently, pentecostalism has begun to grow rapidly in China and in the former Soviet Union, and in August 1994 reports reached the West of the assassination of several Iranian pentecostal leaders in response to the increased appeal the movement has for young Iranians.

With Catholicism impaled by a crisis of authority, mainline Protestantism stalled, Christian fundamentalism slowing from its recent growth, and Eastern Orthodoxy still showing few signs of the vitality it was expected to recover after the fall of communism, pentecostalism has become the most vital expression of Christianity in the world today. If present trends continue, by two decades into the next century, well over half the Christians in the world could be pentecostals.

For the past few years I have been studying pentecostalism and trying to plumb the reasons for its remarkable appeal. I have recently completed a book, *Fire From Heaven*, which limns the history and theology of this remarkable movement and tries to discern what it may be telling the rest of us. The first thing I learned about pentecostalism is that it is a serious mistake to equate pentecostals with fundamentalists. They are not the same.

Fundamentalists vigorously opposed pentecostals when they first appeared, reviling them with such epithets as "the last vomit of Satan." And there is still opposition to pentecostalism among fundamentalists, whose obsessive attachment to the letter of the verbally inspired Scripture makes them deeply suspicious of the pentecostals" stress on the immediate experience of the Spirit of God. This should not be surprising. Text-oriented believers in any religion tend to be wary of mystics, and pentecostalism is a kind of popular, folk mysticism complete with visions, ecstatic utterance, healings, and the mystic's traditional suspicion of abstract theology.

Suspicion of formal theologies, however, does not mean that pentecostalism is devoid of a complex of religious ideas and insights. The difference is that while the beliefs of the fundamentalists, and of many other religious groups, are enshrined in formal theological systems, those of pentecostalism are imbedded in testimonies, ecstatic speech, and bodily movement. Pentecostalism indeed possesses a theology, a full-blown religious cosmos, a complex system of symbols that respond to the perennial questions of human meaning and value. But historically, pentecostals have felt more at home singing their theology than writing about it.

While I was writing *Fire From Heaven*, I sang and prayed with pentecostals on four continents. I discovered that their worship constitutes a kind of compendium of patterns and practices from virtually every Christian tradition I had ever studied. While it looks to many like a narrow cult, pentecostalism is actually a kind of ecumenical movement, an original—and highly success-ful—synthesis of elements from a number of other sources, and not all of them Christian. In fact, its capacity to absorb preexisting spiritual practices—shamanism in Korea, ancestor veneration in Africa, indigenous healing in Latin America—helps account for its astonishing growth.

Pentecostalism holds such appeal, I think, because it responds with great effectiveness to the profound changes transforming the nature of religions and religious experience in contemporary life. The causes for the changes are vast and complex, but they are linked to the massive urbanization of the world that has occurred in this century. The continued growth of megacities and the depletion of rural and small-town populations mean not only that there are more people than ever living in cities but that the majority came from some-where else.

The massive dislocation and uprooting this seismic shift has entailed have cut the nerve of many expressions of traditional religion, which are often tied to specific geographical locations and cultural patterns. And the realities of city life, its atomization and impersonality, have taken most of the glamour out of the shiny vision of modernity that once lured people to the metropolis. Vast numbers of people around the world have had to make the harrowing trek to the big city. Even where they have not physically moved to cities, the city has moved out to them through television. The culture shock has pushed these urban pioneers into the search for new forms of community and new ways to make sense of life. It is precisely among these rootless pathfinders that pentecostalism is growing fastest.

By now, the results this massive change has produced are familiar to most of us. As the twentieth century progressed, large blocs of people became in-creasingly skeptical about inherited religious dogmas, and ecclesiastical in-stitutions steadily lost their power to shape cultures or provide personal meaning. This is the part of the story many scholars expected, and I was once one of those who accepted their appraisal. Twenty-five years ago, Western so-cieties' widespread and growing alienation from religious institutions gave the talk about secularization and the "death of God" a certain plausibility.

But simultaneously, something else was afoot in contemporary life, a phe-nomenon undetected by the scholars busy tracking religion's demise. A few years ago, the British rock singer Sting had a hit song whose sentiments res-onated with millions of young people. "You could say I lost my faith in science and progress," he sang, "you could say I lost my faith in holy church." The mes-sage of the song's first line was the one the scholars had missed. Not only were large numbers of people becoming alienated from traditional religion, they were also losing confidence in the bright promises of science and progress, which—despite their dazzling prowess in some matters—could not provide a source of values or significance.

What had developed was actually a double-barreled disillusionment, both with religion in its traditional institutional expression and with the pseudo-religions of technical advancement and rational enlightenment. Consequently, what large numbers of these newly urbanized masses did was to settle neither for secularization nor for the "old-time religion," but to strike out toward a third option. They felt a desperate need for credible values and a personal spiritual center. Intrigued by the shards and fragments of traditional religions but deeply suspicious of ecclesial hierarchies, millions of young urban no-mads began to construct new spiritual identities using bits and pieces from the old faiths but without buying the whole package of a philosophy, a religion, or an ideology.

The jarring cultural changes had generated a radically new religious situation. Most churches and synagogues fumbled badly in their efforts to respond to it. Conservative Christians and Jews dug in and insisted that traditions were immutable and hierarchies indispensable. Liberal Christians and Reform Jews tried to adjust to contemporary sensibilities, but ended up absorbing so much of the culture of technical rationality they no longer had any spiritual appeal.

But the pentecostals, seemingly almost by accident, found a third way. They rebelled against creeds but retained the mystery. They abolished hierarchies but kept ecstasy. They rejected both scientism and traditionalism. They returned to the raw inner core of human spirituality and thus provided just the new kind of "religious space" many people needed. They have been able to speak to the spiritual emptiness of our time by reaching below the levels of creed and institution into the core of human religiousness, into what might be called "primal spirituality," that largely unprocessed nucleus of the human psyche in which the unending struggle for a sense of meaning always goes on.

During the odyssey I traveled in order to answer my questions about the pentecostals, I came to admire them. I saw clearly in their religious practice something that I had always vaguely known: that the imagery and mood and tempo of a religious service are not just add-ons. They are not superfluous. Human beings are physical as well as mental creatures, and therefore these more tactile elements are part of the substance of worship. And since life it-self is so full of conflict and craving, of wild hopes and dashed expectations, any religion that does not resonate with the full range of these experiences and provide ways of wrestling with them is not worth much. Whatever else I might say about pentecostalism, it imparts to its people not just an idiom re-plete with lakes of fire and a city without tears, but the jubilant gestures and heartrending wails to go with it.

Pentecostals also have a kind of utopian social vision. They take their name from a story recounted in chapter two of the Acts of the Apostles. The plot describes how the confused followers of the recently crucified rabbi they believed was the messiah gathered in Jerusalem to mark the Jewish holiday of "Pentecost" (which is the Greek term used for the Feast of Weeks) that occurs fifty days after Passover. Suddenly there came a sound from heaven "like the rush of a mighty wind." The Holy Spirit filled them, tongues "as of fire" rested on their heads, and to their amazement each began to understand what the other was saying even though they came from "every nation under heaven" and spoke many different languages. It seemed that the ancient curse of Babel—the confounding of languages—had been reversed and that God was creating a new inclusive human community in which "Parthians and Medes and Elamites and residents of Mesopotamia" could all live together.

It is a powerful vision, and the early pentecostals really lived by it. They preached simplicity and rejected the blandishments of consumer culture. Their celebration of the reunification of divided peoples through the power of the Spirit made them suspicious of nationalism (and even today pentecostalism does not combine with nationalism as, for example, Islam often does).

The first decade of the twentieth century was a period of increasing racial separation. But at the early pentecostal gatherings, visitors were astonished to see blacks and whites kneeling and praying together. Since God could speak through anyone regardless of education, race, or gender, women assumed positions of leadership. In the 1920s and 1930s, Aimee Semple McPherson, a pentecostal healer and teacher, became one of the best-known religious figures in America. When some of her male colleagues questioned her calling, she founded a new church, Angelus Temple in Los Angeles, and started her own denomination, the International Church of the Foursquare Gospel, which now has more than 25,000 churches and nearly two million members worldwide.

Elizabeth Brusco, an anthropologist who has studied pentecostals in Latin America, believes their rapid growth there could undermine the cult of machismo and replace it with a sense of partnership in marriage. I have also noticed that pentecostals are quite willing to make use of family-planning techniques, and this could eventually make an enormous difference in population curves in poor countries.

But I am also worried about the future of the pentecostal movement, especially the political alliances some of its members have recently entered into. I first became acquainted with pentecostals fifty years ago when I was a teenager and accompanied my high school girlfriend to her pentecostal church, a small stucco building on the edge of town. At that time, pentecostalism was little more than a sect, popularly known as "holy rollers." Lois was not allowed to go to the movies because they were "worldly." Today, at least in America, many pentecostals have become terribly comfortable with "this world." They started out as a faith that brought hope to society's losers and rejects. Today some of their most visible representatives have become ostentatiously rich, and some even preach a gospel of wealth.

Pentecostals also started out teaching that the "signs and wonders" that took place in their congregations were not some kind of spectral fireworks, but harbingers of God's new day. Yet today, some pentecostal preachers seem so obsessed with the techniques of rapture that they have forgotten the original message.

There have been other changes, not all of them good. Pentecostals started out as rebellious antagonists of the status quo, refusing to serve in the armies of this fallen age, but many have now become impassioned super-patriots, easy marks for the high rollers of the new religious Right. They started out as a radically inclusive spiritual fellowship in which race and gender discrimination virtually disappeared. That is hardly the case today, at least in the white pentecostal churches. In short, as I came to know the pentecostal movement in its present incarnation, I discovered that the pentecostals themselves are facing a dilemma they may not survive, at least not without betraying their original vision.

But there are also signs of hope. A special experience with the "Holy Spirit" or the "Spirit of God" was the crux of the early pentecostal movement. But this was not just any spirit. Pentecostals believed it was the Spirit of the same God who had created the world, had called the people of Israel forth, spoken through the prophets, and whose love had walked the Earth in Jesus Christ and—most important—the same God who had begun to fulfill all His promises by creating a new Heaven and a new Earth where justice and compassion would reign. The early pentecostals saw themselves positioned "between the already and the not-yet," witnesses to the first fruits of the kingdom but not yet to its fullness, living in the light that precedes the dawn. In other words, the Spirit they testified to had a purpose for history and was calling people to be part of that purpose. That purpose, for the unemployed janitors and domestic servants who gathered at Azusa Street, was no less than the coming of the kingdom of God as it had been taught by the prophets and demonstrated by Jesus. And when it came, the poor would be lifted up, the hungry fed, and the brokenhearted comforted; while the mighty would be brought low and the rich sent away empty. It is hard to imagine a more radical vision of the future than the one this life-changing experience of the Spirit awakened in them.

As I got to know pentecostal people in America and elsewhere, I was pleased to find among the younger generation of their ministers a serious effort to retrieve this original pentecostal vision. These same young pentecostal leaders also realize that the fact that their movement started out among the disowned and dispossessed is not merely a historical artifact but a decisive key to what the Spirit wants them to be and to do today. A "pentecostal liberation theology" is beginning to emerge. The Puerto Rican theologian Eldin Villafane, a pentecostal himself, believes that the genius of the movement is the experience of the power of the "liberating Spirit," and he argues that this Spirit has a "project" that is being worked out within human history.

Villafane's vision of a pentecostal liberation theology is an exciting prospect. Sociologist Cecilia Maritz, who studies the Catholic "base communities" in Brazil, the groups from which liberation theology arose, has suggested that in some places they function very much like pentecostal communities. Father Pablo Richard, a Costa Rican Catholic who teaches the lay leaders of these base communities all over Latin America, claims that the difference between them and pentecostal congregations is diminishing rapidly. If these two powerful movements were somehow to combine their strengths in the coming decades, the result would be extraordinarily potent. If the pentecostals, following Villafane's lead, absorb something of the social vision of liberation theology, and the base communities shed the residual elements of vertical authority they still sometimes retain, the offspring could be more powerful than either of its parents.

Whether pentecostalism will come down on the side of the religious Right or on the side of liberation theology is an open question. There are vigorous forces pulling both ways. But, whatever happens, given the nature of the pentecostal impulse, I doubt that it will be settled through theological debate.

One thing I have learned from the many hours I have spent with pentecostals is that one should look for pentecostal theology not in books, but in the viscera of pentecostal spirituality. It is emotional, corporate, narrational, hopeful, and radically embodied.

Consequently, the future direction of the movement will appear first in the lives of its hundreds of thousands of congregations. Answers to questions about what the Spirit is doing in history and how human beings should respond will not appear in scholarly journals, but in the way these little outposts of the Kingdom of God live in a world that is both hostile and hungry. I wish them well.

The God Beyond God

Daniel C. Matt

How can you name the Oneness, the Unnamable? The Jewish mystical tradition, Kabbalah, offers a number of possibilities. One is *Ein Sof*, which translates literally as, "there is no end." Ein Sof is the Infinite, the God beyond God. This name sounds so different from the personal divine names that populate the texts of the tradition: YHVH, Elohim, Shaddai, the Holy One, blessed be He. As an anonymous kabbalist observed, neither the Bible nor the Talmud even hints of Ein Sof. This remark is both obvious and revealing, an acknowledgment of the radical originality of this mystical formula.

By calling God "Ein Sof," Jewish mystics imply that everything is divine. The kabbalist Moses Cordovero, writing in the sixteenth century, put it this way: "The essence of divinity is found in every single thing—nothing but It exists. Since It causes every thing to be, no thing can live by anything else. It enlivens them. Ein Sof exists in each existent. Do not say, 'This is a stone and not God.' God forbid! Rather, all existence is God, and the stone is a thing pervaded by divinity."

There is nothing but Ein Sof. Even a stone in a field, even a slab of concrete in a downtown parking lot, is an expression of divine energy. The entire world is God in myriad forms and disguises.

The name Ein Sof opens with a negative: Ein, "there is no." This accords with the view of the philosopher Moses Maimonides that it is more accurate to say what God is not than what God is. Calling God "powerful" conjures up the image of a muscleman. Calling God "wise" puts Him in the category of a sage. Better to say that God is neither "weak" nor "stupid." Even the bland statement "God exists" is misleading because divine existence is unlike anything that humans can conceive. A more precise formulation is: "God exists but not through existence."

47

The best theology, in Maimonides' view, is negative theology. "Know that the description of God by means of negations is the correct description, a description that is not affected by an indulgence in facile language. Negative attributes conduct the mind toward the utmost reach that one may attain in the apprehension of God. You come nearer to the apprehension of God with every increase in negations."

The kabbalists adopt Maimonides' negative style of theology and take it to an extreme. Among their names for God, Ein Sof is the most famous, but not the most radical. Having carved away all that is false, they discover a paradox of a name: Ayin, Nothingness. We encounter this bizarre term among Christian mystics as well: John Scotus Erigena calls God, nihil; Meister Eckhart, nichts; St. John of the Cross, nada.

To call God "Nothingness" does not mean that God does not exist. Rather, it conveys the idea that God is no thing: God animates all things and cannot be contained by any of them. In the words of a fourteenth-century kabbalist, David ben Abraham ha-Lavan, "Nothingness (ayin) is more existent than all the being of the world. But since it is simple, and all simple things are complex compared with its simplicity, in comparison it is called ayin." David ben Abraham's Christian contemporary, Meister Eckhart, concurred: "God's nothingness fills the entire world; His something though is nowhere."

Ayin is a name for the nameless. The paradox is that ayin embraces "nothing" and "everything." This nothingness is oneness: undifferentiated, overwhelming the distinctions between things. God is the oneness that is no particular thing. No thingness. Nothingness with a capital N.

This mystical nothingness is neither empty nor barren; it is fertile and overflowing, engendering the myriad forms of life. Medieval philosophers—Jewish, Christian, and Muslim—had taught that God created the world "out of nothing." The mystics turn this formula on its head, reinterpreting it to mean that the universe emanated from divine nothingness. Similarly, cosmologists speak of the quantum vacuum, teeming with potential, engendering the cosmic seed. This vacuum is anything but empty—a seething froth of virtual particles, constantly appearing and disappearing. According to quantum field theory, pairs of these virtual particles, one positive and one negative, appear together in the primordial vacuum, move apart, then come together again and annihilate each other. Even if cooled to absolute zero, the vacuum still shimmers with a residual hidden energy: what physicists call "zero-point energy," an energy that is infinite.

As we will discover, Kabbalah also describes a primordial vacuum, at the heart of Ein Sof. Like its quantum counterpart, this vacuum is not absolutely empty, but rather coated with a trace of divine light.

How did the universe emerge out of prolific nothingness? According to classical Kabbalah and classical big bang theory, this transition was marked by a single point. Recall the singularity: an infinitely dense point in space-time. Like ayin, a singularity is destructive and creative. Anything falling into a singularity merges with it and loses its identity, while energy emerging from a singularity can become anything. The laws of physics do not apply to the split second in which energy or mass emerges.

According to the thirteenth-century kabbalist Moses de Leon, "The beginning of existence is the secret concealed point. This is the beginning of all the hidden things, which spread out from there and emanate, according to their species. From a single point you can extend the dimensions of all things. Similarly, when the concealed arouses itself to exist, at first it brings into being something the size of the point of a needle; from there it generates everything."

In Kabbalah, this point is identified with divine wisdom, which emerges from nothingness into being. The Zohar, the masterpiece of Kabbalah, opens by disclosing the origin of the point:

A blinding spark flashed within the concealed of the concealed, from the mystery of the Infinite, a cluster of vapor in formlessness. . . . Under the impact of breaking through, one high and hidden point shone. Beyond that point nothing is known. So it is called Beginning.

As emanation proceeds, as God begins to unfold, the point expands into a circle. Similarly, ever since the big bang, our universe has been expanding in all directions. We know it is still expanding thanks to Edwin Hubble, who measured the speed at which other galaxies are moving away from us.

Redemption and Ontological Mystery

Robert Inchausti

It is almost as easy to overestimate the significance of the current boom in spirituality as it is to make fun of it. And yet, there can be no doubt that we are experiencing a cultural sea change of considerable magnitude away from materialistic thinking to something quite different: to a growing respect for the insights born of introspection.

We now have a "spirituality" of warfare, a Zen of tennis, even a "psychology" of futures trading. At their best, these new "spiritual" disciplines, if we can call them that, represent a kind of instinctive flinch by humanity at large away from the commodification of the world and the obsolescence of their own inner lives. At their worst, they represent a new form of philistinism that masks itself as antiphilistine—making it even harder for us to exchange the isolation of private devotion for a truly prophetic, transformative spiritual life.

The problem with these new "spiritual" practices is that they don't fully question the ends they serve. In their emphasis upon process over product and upon the quality of the internal experience itself, they tend to elevate the practitioner's own spiritual aspirations to a near absolute. But those desires—however seemingly "spiritual" they seem to the person holding them—may simply reflect the narcissism of the culture at large—and so instead of liberating the individual from the idols of the marketplace, bind us even more profoundly to them.

For example, rethinking corporate management practices from the point of view of a Samurai warrior may, on the surface, seem an innocent enough exercise in psychological "reframing." But to actually adopt the Samurai's code of Bushido as a self-conscious strategy for making more money does a gross injustice, not only to the integrity of Japanese thought, but also to the sincere corporate manager looking for greater spiritual fulfillment.

In fact, the corporate manager is at greater risk from such practices than is the tradition of Bushido. He may "think" he needs a "spiritual" perspective on his daily financial activities when what he may really need is a whole new moral vision capable of disclosing the misguided values at the heart of his own miserly personal ambitions.

Orthodox biblical religions do a better job questioning the ends our actions serve. For one thing, they link the individual's search for meaning to the welfare of the community, and by so doing offer an explicit critique of the culture at large. The danger, of course, is that religious communities often become insular, and rather than working to transform the world in the light of their faith, they spend most of their time defending their own image of themselves as holy, set apart, and redeemed.

What these insular communities and their New Age counterparts share is a failure to recognize that our spiritual selves are not independent individual essences but that point of nothingness at the center of our being that belongs entirely to God. Transcendence can never be an object of possession or of comprehension. Our spiritual lives are never entirely at our disposal. We cannot improve them or perfect them. We can only acknowledge their fundamental truth to us: We are not our own light! God dwells within us as an absolute freedom and unknown possibility.

When the "I" of our solitude experiences the solitude of every other person, this experience of shared "aloneness" activates a wellspring of compassion that inspires us to sacrifice and service. In turn, this compassion feeds empathy and charity back into the world at large, and when this happens, all the bogus substitutes for authentic human solidarity are exposed as frauds, and all the so-called "spiritual" practices that fail to give hope to the oppressed and pause to the proud stand revealed as half-measures.

Theodore Adorno once unwittingly described the task of contemporary spirituality quite well when he said that the only philosophy that can be responsibly practiced in our time is the contemplation of all things as they would present themselves from the standpoint of redemption. "Perspectives must be fashioned," he wrote in *Minima Moralia*, "that displace and estrange the world, reveal it to be, with its rifts and crevices, as indigent and distorted as it will appear one day in the messianic light."

We may be living in a time when the Enlightenment view of the world is falling apart, and many hitherto dismissed aspects of reality are reemerging into human consciousness. But simply renaming these aspects "spiritual" realities is not the same thing as posing a prophetic standard or assessing their worth as it will one day appear in the messianic light. To do that, as Dietrich Bonhoeffer once so eloquently pointed out in his *Letters from Prison*, we shall not need geniuses or cynics or misanthropes or clever tacticians, but plain, honest, straightforward men. "Will our inward power or resistance be strong enough," he asked, "for us to win our way back to simplicity and straightforwardness?"

Gandhi, Martin Luther King Jr., Thomas Merton, and Abraham Joshua Heschel model a complex, tragic response to contemporary history built upon the premise of a deeper ontological mystery. In their flawed experimental lives, they demonstrate how we too might cease identifying with the prevailing social order, including its shiny new "spiritualities," so we might reidentify with the persons lost within it, and by so doing, serve God's own longing for healing and reconciliation.

Before we can live in faith, we must have a faith to live—which is something quite different than having "spiritual" thoughts. It means humbly acknowledging the reality of a Self deeper than our own conscious ideals and personal identities—a Self that becomes more apparent the greater our self-effacement. Faith is really more a capacity for having spiritual second thoughts, a capacity for laying down occupations and preoccupations in order to listen to the voice of a God who speaks from within our own solitude and suffering to unite us with others who also thirst for justice and mercy.

"Though our iniquities testify against us," cried Jeremiah, "Act, O Lord, for Thy name's sake." I can think of no finer prayer in this age of hype and spiritual oversell to protect us from ourselves.

Chapter 2

JEWISH IDENTITY AND SURVIVAL

The Kindest Un-Cut

Michael S. Kimmel

FEMINISM, JUDAISM, AND MY SON'S FORESKIN

Although it was a little late by traditional religious standards, the entire family and many friends gathered in our home three weeks after our son, Zachary, was born. We had gathered for his *bris*, the moment when a young Jewish boy is first brought into the family and the community, the moment of his formal entrance into the world of Judaism. At such symbolic moments, one feels keenly the sinews of connection to family and friends that sustain a life, animate it, give it context and meaning.

The mohel, of course, was running late. When he arrived, everyone gathered in the living room, where we had set up a table on which we had placed the various items we would use in the ceremony. A special chair had been reserved for the *sandek*, the honored family male elder, often the baby's grandfather or great-grandfather, who would hold the baby during much of the proceedings. (In our case, a godmother and godfather shared this role.)

As family and friends drew closer together, glasses of wine and champagne in their hands, the ritual began with prayers over the wine and bread. Our first toast to this new creature who had entered all our lives. Then the mohel began the naming ceremony, and some relatives and friends offered their wishes for this young life.

Amy, my wife, and I each offered a thought to the other and to Zachary as we entered this new phase of our lives as parents together. For my part, I quoted Adrienne Rich, who had written, "If I could have one wish for my own sons, it is that they should have the courage of women." I wished nothing more for Zachary than that he would have Amy's courage, her integrity, and her passion.

Then it was the moment for which we had all carefully prepared, about which we had endlessly talked, debated, argued, discussed. We took a pitcher of water and a bowl to the door of the house. Amy and I carried Zachary over to the threshold. With one hand I held his little body and with the other held his tiny legs over the bowl. Amy poured some water over his feet and rubbed it in. Then she held him and I did the same. Throughout, the mohel chanted in prayer. And in that way, we welcomed Zachary into our home and into our lives.

By now you are, of course, waiting for the "real" *bris* to begin, for the mohel to stuff a wine-soaked handkerchief into our son's mouth to muffle his cries and slightly anesthetize him, and then circumcise him, cutting off his foreskin in fulfillment of God's commandment to Abraham that he mark his son, Isaac, as a sign of obedience.

Sorry to disappoint, but that's the end of our story. Or at least the end of the story of Zachary's *bris*. There was no circumcision on that day. We had decided not to circumcise our son. Although he enters a world filled with violence, he would enter it without violence done to him. Although he will no doubt suffer many cuts and scrapes during his life, he would not bleed by our hand.

This was not an easy decision, but we had plenty of time to prepare—nine months to be exact. From the moment we saw the sonogram and read the results of the amniocentesis, the debate had been joined. Would we or wouldn't we? How would we decide? The remainder of this chapter charts that process.

First, we talked. Constantly. Just when we thought the issue settled, we'd open it again. Each time one of us would read something, think something, pull something new off the Internet, we would reopen the discussion anew. We talked with friends, family members, religious authorities, doctors, and nurses. We asked our heterosexual women friends whether they had a preference for cut or uncut men. We each sought counsel from the e-mail discussion groups to which we belonged, and we consulted organizations like the American Academy of Pediatrics and the American Medical Association. We ordered and read more than a dozen books and pamphlets.

We contacted advocacy groups like National Organization of Circumcision Information Resource Centers (NOCIRC), National Organization to Halt the Abuse and Routine Mutilation of Males (NOHARMM), and Doctors Opposing Circumcision (DOC). But these organizations, while eager, were too one-sided, and tended to minimize the difficulty of our decision.

And we didn't even bother calling the organizations like Brothers United for Future Foreskins (BUFF), National Organization of Restoring Men (NORM), and RECover a Penis (RECAP) that encourage men who might "feel victimized by the unnecessary loss of their natural anatomical wholeness," as Joseph

Zoske writes in *Journal of Men's Studies* (1998), to undergo penile reconstructive surgery to "correct" the circumcised penis. Such procedures (involving either attaching a new flap or pulling the remaining tissue down over the glans to create a pseudo-foreskin) seem as unnecessary as circumcision, and no doubt attend to psychological distress that has only the most tenuous connection to a small flap of penile tissue.

PROS AND CONS

We heard a lot of arguments, for and against. To be sure, there is no shortage of arguments in favor of circumcision. Some are aesthetic, and offer a psychological theory based on that aesthetic. Without circumcision, we heard, our son will look different from his father, and thus develop shame about his body. Our son will look different from other Jewish boys, especially in our heavily Jewish neighborhood, thus be subject to ridicule and teasing, and develop a sense that he does not belong. As one man on an e-mail list to which I posed the question wrote, "I don't want my kid to be an object of interest while taking public showers, such as in gym class or in athletic clubs" (David Garnier, personal communication).

Other arguments are medical. After all, male circumcision is the most common surgical procedure in the United States and medical insurance carriers routinely cover hospital circumcision (which raises the incentives of medical practitioners to advocate the procedure). Our son's risks of penile infection, STD, and especially penile cancer would be significantly lower if he were to be circumcised. The likelihood of uterine cancer in his female sexual partners would be higher if he were not.

In addition, there were conflicting reports on the effects of circumcision on sexual functioning. There is some evidence from sex surveys that circumcised men are more sexually active and more sexually adventurous, especially as regards oral and anal sex. Circumcised men masturbate more often. And because circumcised men have less sexual sensitivity—after all, the foreskin contains about one thousand nerve endings, fully one-third of the organ's pleasure receptors—there is some evidence that circumcision delays ejaculation somewhat.

And, of course, the weight of family, history, and culture do not rest lightly on the shoulders of the new parent. As Jews we knew full well the several-thousand-year-old tradition of following one of the most fundamental of God's commandments to Abraham—that "every male among you shall be circumcised . . . and that shall be a sign of the covenant between Me and you."

In the end, none of the arguments in favor of circumcision was fully persuasive. Taken together, however, they raised issues that spoke to the core of our identities as a man and a woman, as parents, as feminists, and as Jews. Each of the points of contention seems worth discussing in a bit more detail.

THE PSYCHOLOGICAL AESTHETICS OF DIFFERENCE

That our son would look different from his father was easily negotiated. We decided that we will simply tell him that Daddy had no choice about his own body and especially his penis, but that now, as parents, we loved him so much that we decided we didn't want to hurt him like that—turning something that could be a cause of embarrassment into a source of pride.

And he will look more and more *like* the other boys rather than different. Circumcision of newborns is decreasingly popular, performed routinely only in the United States (as a medical procedure in the hospital) and in Israel, where it remains a significant religious ceremony. (Adolescent circumcision remains the norm in most Islamic nations.) After these two countries, only Canada (25 percent) and Australia (10 percent) have rates of newborn circumcision in double digits; in European nations it is virtually nonexistent among non-Jews. Over four-fifths of all men in the world are uncircumcised.

Here in the United States, rates have fallen from well over 85 percent in 1960 to about 66 percent in 2000, so there was every reason to believe that more and more boys would look like Zachary and that he had little to fear by way of social ostracism. In our own neighborhood in heavily Jewish Brooklyn, about half the baby boys born in our local hospital are circumcised in the hospital (though there is no information about those who have it performed as a religious ceremony in their homes or elsewhere).

MEDICAL AMBIVALENCE

While it is true that the risk of penile cancer or infection is virtually nonexistent among circumcised men, rates among uncircumcised men, though higher, are still minuscule. In 1991, the American Academy of Pediatrics finally lifted its long-time advocacy of routine hospital circumcision for health reasons, and now takes no position on the question, thus leaving the decision entirely up to the parents' aesthetic or religious beliefs. They concluded that there were no medical benefits to circumcision as long as the boy was instructed in proper cleanliness.

Even the redoubtable Benjamin Spock changed his mind over the years. Having always stood for the conventional wisdom that parents know best, Spock told *Redbook* in an interview in 1989 that his preference, "If I had the good fortune to have another son, would be to leave his little penis alone." In a pamphlet, "Circumcision: A Medical or Human Rights Issue?" one doctor went so far as to suggest that removing the foreskin for strictly hygienic purposes was analogous to removing the eyelid for a cleaner eyeball.

Future sexual functioning didn't weigh particularly heavily in our minds either. For one thing, sexual functioning is so profoundly variable; we expect that if we teach Zachary to develop respect for his and others' bodies as well as their personal integrity, sexual pleasure will not be an issue for him or his partners. Second, the evidence is inconsistent. While circumcised men in the United States seem to have more sex, more varied sex, and masturbate more often, this may be more of a function of race, class, education, and religion than with whether or not the man is circumcised. It's middle-class white men—who tend to be the most secular and the most sexual—who still compose the majority of circumcised men. Among blacks and Hispanics, rates of oral sex and masturbation are significantly lower than among white men, and middle-class men are more sexually active and adventurous than working-class men. "People with graduate degrees are the most likely to masturbate," noted Ed Laumann, a sociologist and one of the principal researchers in the University of Chicago sex survey in the early 1990s.

Nor were we ultimately concerned about the eventual effect on potential women partners. An informal poll among heterosexual women friends yielded a mixed anecdotal response. Most said they preferred circumcised men, and one or two indicated significant aesthetic discomfort with intact men. But an article in the January 1999 *British Journal of Urology* reported that women who had slept with both circumcised and intact men preferred sex with men who were not circumcised. The article reported that the women achieved orgasm faster, and were more likely to achieve multiple orgasms.

THE BURDEN OF HISTORY

Actually, the historical record of medical opinion consistently pushed us further into the anti-circumcision camp. The more we learned about the medical history, the more we were convinced that concerns other than the health of the baby led doctors to make circumcision a routine practice. Before the 1870s, in the United States, routine medical circumcision was quite rare, hovering around 5 to 6 percent of all newborn baby boys. Subscribers to the new Victorian sexual morality sought to reduce what critics perceived to be rampant sexual promiscuity, and especially masturbation, which, they believed, resulted in all sorts of debilities and even death. Masturbation was said to cause all manner of emotional, psychological, and physiological problems, from bed-wetting to adolescent insolence, acne to mental retardation, insanity, psychological exhaustion, and neurasthenia.

Circumcision's well-established ability to curb sexual appetite and pleasure was prescribed as a potential cure for sexual profligacy. Lewis Sayre, a prominent New York physician, hailed as "the Columbus of the prepuce" by his colleagues, experimented with circumcision as a cure for paralysis and other muscular ailments. Sayre's colleagues also noted that Jews had a lower rate of STDs than non-Jews, and hypothesized that this had to do with circumcision. (Actually, this had to do with the fact that Jews had very little sexual contact with non-Jews.)

Another physician, Dr. Peter Remondino, advocated universal male circumcision since the foreskin, which he labeled "an unyielding tube," left the intact male "a victim to all manner of ills, sufferings . . . and other conditions calculated to weaken him physically, mentally, and morally; to land him, perchance, in jail, or even in a lunatic asylum." And Robert Tooke's popular *All About the Baby* (1896) recommended circumcision to prevent "the vile habit of masturbation."

J. H. Kellogg, pioneering health reformer, cereal inventor, and general medical quack also sounded the alarm; his best-selling health advice book, *Plain Facts for Old and Young* (1888), included nearly one hundred pages on the dangers of masturbation. Circumcision is almost always successful in curbing masturbation, he counseled, and he suggested that the operation be performed "by a surgeon without administering anesthetic, as the brief pain attending the operation will have a salutary effect upon the mind." (Though this may have begun the tradition of not using anesthesia to perform circumcision, Kellogg did not pretend that the baby feels no pain during the procedure. Anyone who has ever witnessed a routine medical circumcision performed without anesthesia knows only too well how much pain the infant does feel.)

Victorian morality was pervasive. And as waves of uncircumcised immigrants entered the United States, circumcision of newborns was a way to stake a claim for a truly "American" morality. Rates jumped to 25 percent by 1900. After World War II, when the *Journal of the American Medical Association* reported that rates of STD were higher among blacks and uncircumcised white men, circumcision rates continued to climb, and by 1980, nearly nine of every ten American boys was circumcised.

But it now appears that the rapid spread of circumcision as a routine medical procedure had more to do with Victorian hysteria about sexuality than it did with hygiene. And given the American Academy of Pediatrics' recent backpedaling on the issue—from ritual endorsement to anxious agnosticism to its most recent resigned disapproval—there seems to be no medical argument—historical or hygienic—to compel the procedure.

THE WEIGHTS OF TRADITION

The combined weights of family and religious culture were not so easily negotiated. As predicted, the future grandmothers were somewhat more sanguine about the prospect of noncircumcision than were the future grandfathers. It's ironic that it's always been women—even within Judaism—who have opposed circumcision as a violence done to their babies, and circumcised males who have supported it. Perhaps it is analogous to fraternity or military initiation ceremonies, where the salutary outcome of feeling a sense of belonging to the larger homosocial group is deemed worth any price, including the removal of a third of one's potential sexual pleasure.

In our case, neither Amy nor I felt any strong compulsion toward circumcision, but I was more strongly opposed on moral grounds. Amy's opposition would come later, when she first held Zachary in her arms and she felt a visceral rage that anyone would do anything that would ever hurt this new creature. In very gender stereotyped terms, Amy's opposition grew from her emotional, visceral connection to the baby; mine grew first from a principled opposition grounded in a sense of justice and ethics.

But equally gendered, I suppose, I felt that my Judaism had always given me the ability to stand up against injustice, that the imperative of the post-Holocaust generation of "Never Again!" impelled me to speak out against injustices wherever I saw them.

Ultimately, it came down to Judaism. Jewish law is unequivocal on the subject—it has been a time-honored tradition since the celebrated Covenant with Abraham, the founding moment of monotheism. In Genesis 17, God appears before an aged Abraham—he's 99!—and commands that Abraham circumcise himself, his son, and all male members of his household (slaves and servants included).

Today, circumcision is seen as a mitzvah, linking the family to a four-thousand-year history of a people. In his masterful compendium of Jewish law and lore, *Essential Judaism*, George Robinson writes that it is a mitzvah "one performs for its own sake as a subordination of oneself to a larger entity." What's a tiny foreskin compared to four thousand years of tradition? And so it appeared that Jewish tradition might yet extract its pound of flesh—well, more likely about a quarter of an ounce—from yet another innocent baby.

Yet Judaism today is hardly as monolithic as we once thought. Even in biblical times there seems to have been some dissent about the procedure. If one follows the ritual as prescribed by Jewish law, the baby is held during the circumcision on what is called the Chair of Elijah, named after the prophet "who railed against the Jews for forsaking the ritual of circumcision." What that says to me is that not long after circumcision was instituted, there were a lot of people who were already resisting it. Then, too, there is the law that the *brit milah* be performed on the eighth day after the birth of the son, a law so iron-clad that it is perhaps the only Jewish ritual that may not be postponed for the Sabbath or even for Yom Kippur. Those who were interested in enforcing circumcision were determined that there be no excuses—no doubt because a lot of people were trying to wiggle their way out.

In her research, Amy found that even as recently as the mid-nineteenth century, in Eastern Europe and Russia there was a widespread move to stop the practice—ironically, just when it was becoming more widespread in the United States. Led by women—what a surprise!—who thought the practice barbaric and patriarchal, the movement eventually even convinced Theodore Herzl, the founder of modern Zionism, who refused to allow his own son to be circumcised.

It is, after all, quite perplexing: why would God ask Abraham do such a thing to himself and all the males of his household—especially his son? For years, I had a little cartoon in my study that depicted Abraham, standing alone on top of a mountain, looking up at the sky, forlorn and exasperated. The caption read, "Let me see if I have this right: You want us to cut the ends of our dicks off?!?!"

SUBLIMATING PLEASURE FOR TORAH

The circumcision as ritual makes sense, however, in three ways—one sexual, one political, and one symbolic. Throughout history, commentators on circumcision have agreed that the goal was to transform men's (and women's) sexual experience, and thus make men more eager to study Torah. The only thing they disagreed on was how, exactly, circumcision would accomplish this feat of sublimation.

Most observers assumed it would make a man less sexually sensitive, reduce his sexual ardor, and constrain his sexual impulses. In his fascinating study, *Eros and the Jews*, David Biale finds two contradictory impulses leading toward the same conclusion. Ancient Jews, such as Philo, understood circumcision as "the symbol of the excision of excessive and superfluous pleasure." In *Guide to the Perplexed,* the great medieval philosopher Moses Maimonides prefigured J. H. Kellogg by nearly a millennium when he wrote that the commandment to circumcise was "not prescribed with a view to perfecting what is defective congenitally, but to perfecting what is defective morally." A chief reason for the ritual was "the wish to bring about a decrease in sexual intercourse and a weakening of the organ in question, so that this activity be diminished and the organ be in as quiet a state as possible."

After all, he continued, "the fact that circumcision weakens the faculty of sexual excitement and sometimes perhaps diminishes the pleasure is indubitable."

While Maimonides argued that the physiological loss was "the real purpose" of the ritual, others believed that the psychological impact far outweighed the physical. Biale notes that an early medieval Midrash Tadshe suggests that the "covenant of circumcision was therefore placed on the genitals so that the fear of God would restrain them from sin." Later thinkers took the physical to new extremes. The early-nineteenth-century scholar Nahman of Bratslav, great-grandson of the Baal Shem Tov, argued that circumcision symbolizes the complete excision of sexual pleasure so that the "true zaddik" (holy man) experiences pain, not pleasure, during intercourse.

On the one hand, writers were convinced that men would feel less—much less, and therefore their frustration would lead inevitably toward holier devotion to study. On the other hand, some writers were convinced that circumcised men would experience far *more* sexual excitement—so much more, in fact, that it would leave both him and his partner so frustrated that they wouldn't want to have sex again. In an astonishing passage, Isaac ben Yedaiah, a late thirteenth-century French follower of Maimonides, described the difference in such overheated prose that it borders on the salacious (which alone makes it worth quoting at length):

> [A beautiful woman] will court a man who is uncircumcised in the flesh and lie against his breast with great passion, for he thrusts inside her a long time because of the foreskin, which is a barrier against ejaculation in intercourse. Thus she feels pleasure and reaches an orgasm first. When an uncircumcised man sleeps with her and then resolves to return to his home, she brazenly grasps him, holding on to his genitals and says to him, Come back, make love to me. This is because of the pleasure that she finds in intercourse with him, from the sinews of his testicles— sinews of iron—and from his ejaculation—that of a horse—which he shoots like an arrow into her womb. They are united without separating and he makes love twice and three times in one night, yet the appetite is not filled. And so he acts with her night after night. The sexual activity emaciates him of his bodily fat and afflicts his flesh and he devotes his brain entirely to women, an evil thing.
>
> But when a circumcised man desires the beauty of a woman . . . he will find himself performing his task quickly, emitting his seed as soon as he inserts the crown. . . . He has an orgasm first; he does not hold back his strength. As soon as he begins intercourse with her, he immediately comes to a climax. She has no pleasure from him when she lies down or when she arises and it would be better for her if he had not known her . . . for he arouses her passion to no avail and she remains in a state of desire. (Cited in Biale.)

So more excitement means less pleasure—for both him and his female partner. Ancient rabbis, like Philo, had argued that not only did circumcision restrain male sexual ardor, it diminished women's pleasure. "It is hard for a woman to separate herself from an uncircumcised man with whom she has had intercourse." Everyone now seemed to agree that circumcision reduces the pleasure of the woman, which is precisely why it seems to have been prescribed. And precisely why Amy and I were growing increasingly suspicious.

There were political issues involved as well. It's interesting to observe the expansion of the ritual in terms of the relationship between Jews and their neighbors. Originally, apparently, the ritual consisted of only the *brit milah*— which is the excision of a small part of the foreskin. This enabled some Jewish men to continue to "pass" as gentiles in the ancient edition of those locker room showers that my friends continually discussed. Disgruntled rabbis then added the *brit periah* that removed the entire foreskin, making it impossible to pass as gentile. (It's an ironic twist of history that it is the *brit periah* that was adopted by modern medicine when it still prescribed routine neonatal circumcision.)

But this expansion also raised, for us, the thorniest political and moral dilemma. A close friend, a child of Holocaust survivors, told me the story of his uncle, who was not so lucky. His was the now-classic story of the young man sneaking his way onto a train leaving Germany under the watchful eyes of the Nazis. When caught, he was forced to strip in the station, and when it was discovered that he was circumcised, he was shot on the spot.

Here was a political reason *to* circumcise, a slap in the face of anti-Semitism, a way to connect my son to a history of resistance against anti-Semitism, and to recognize the ways in which physical difference (whether congenitally or culturally derived) is grounds for discrimination. In fact, some historians claim that the *brit periah*, the more extensive circumcision, was first used by the Egyptians to mark their Hebrew slaves, so that they would be readily and permanently identifiable. Ironic then, that once free, these same Hebrews made the more dramatic statement a matter of their own *inclusion*.

PENILE PATRIARCHY

But what was ultimately decisive for us was the larger symbolic meaning of circumcision, and particularly the gendered politics of the ritual. After all, it is not circumcision that makes a man Jewish; one can certainly be Jewish without it. Religious membership is passed on through the mother: if the mother is Jewish then the baby is Jewish and nothing that the baby does—or that is done to him or her—can change that basic fact. A rabbi is trained to counsel parents of mixed religious backgrounds (in which the man is Jewish and the woman is not) that circumcision does not make their son Jewish, but that only the mother's conversion will make it so.

No, circumcision means something else: the reproduction of patriarchy. Abraham cements *his* relationship to God by a symbolic genital mutilation of his son. It is on the body of his son that Abraham writes his own beliefs. In a religion marked by the ritual exclusion of women, such a marking not only enables Isaac to be included within the community of men—he can be part of a minyan, can pray in the temple, can study Torah—but he can also lay claim to all the privileges to which being a Jewish male now entitles him. Monotheistic religions invariably worship male Gods, and exhibit patriarchal political arrangements between the sexes. (Looked at this way, since both Judaism and Islam practice circumcision, it is really Christianity that is the deviant case, and it would be worth exploring how Christianity justified its evasion of the practice since it is certain that Jesus was circumcised.)

Circumcision, it became clear, is the single moment of the reproduction of patriarchy. It's when patriarchy happens, the single crystalline moment when the rule of the fathers is reproduced, the moment when male privilege and entitlement is passed from one generation to the next, when the power of the fathers is enacted upon the sons, a power which the sons will someday then enact on the bodies of their own sons. To circumcise our son, then, would be, unwittingly or not, to accept as legitimate four thousand years not of Jewish tradition, but of patriarchal domination of women.

OUR CHOICE WAS CLEAR

We welcomed Zachary into our family on that morning without a circumcision. We decided that we want him to live in a world without violence, so we welcomed him without violence. We decided that we want him to live in a world in which he is free to experience the fullness of the pleasures of his body, so we welcomed him with all his fleshy nerves intact. And we decided that we want him to live in a world in which male entitlement is a waning memory, and in which women and men are seen—in both ritual and in reality—as full equals and partners. So we welcomed him equally, his mother and I, in the time-honored way that desert cultures have always welcomed strangers to their tents: We washed his feet.

Making Judaism Cool

Jonathan Schorsch

I sit listening to the newest and skankiest dub beat, bass thumping, high reverb shimmering, cool horns sliding around the syncopation, the chorus droning:

> Slaughter, slaughter, they want to slaughter 'em
> Slaughter, slaughter, watch out murderer.

The "em" is slurred enough to be "us." The singer drawls in deep Jamaican accents, the words strobe-lighted by the heavy reverb:

> I want to tell you sometin' about my granfader,
> my granfader was a concentration camp survivor
> taken from his home in the Second World War
> separated from his family by the Nazis mister
> and herded like an animal into a cattle car.

Is this some Rasta philosemite? No, only a recent CD by a collection of New York's hottest Jewish musicians. Doing the Holocaust as Jamaican dub, it struck me, marked the quintessence of a near decade of making Judaism cool.

Already in the mid-1990s, when living in Jerusalem, I noticed that the ultra-religious radio stations played all sorts of updated songs that were little more than covers of tunes from cool genres—usually from Africa or its diaspora—with words from the Bible or the like. The last decade has also witnessed the rise of the heavy metal Hasidic rock of Yossi Piamenta, the Jewish rap of Blood of Abraham, Rebbe Soul, the New Orleans Klezmer All-Stars, and the whole Lower East Side avant-garde Jewish music scene: the Klezmatics, John Zorn, the Radical Jewish Culture/Tzadik label, and so on. A Reggae Passover disk came out a few years back, while an announcement for a Reggae Chanukah disk popped up recently in my e-mail. Even the stodgy Israeli Duo Re'emim did a hip-hop/D.J.-mix cover of the traditional Ashkenazic Rosh Hashanah melodies.

This borrowing approach has a long history in music, Jewish and otherwise, and especially so in Ladino and Hasidic music, many of whose tunes originated in secular, non-Jewish contexts (for instance, as drinking songs). The Hasidim sought to elevate the fallen sparks hidden within the melodies by attaching them to words that called forth the holiest qualities. In the twentieth century, popular Jewish music also went in search of the newest fashion, in search of making the old new and the global local, like the tangos played by Polish Jewish orchestras in the 1920s, or the American "klezmer" musicians in the first part of this century who invented "authentic" old-world Jewish music by updating it with thoroughly American instruments and styles.

Today, post-baby boomers, alive to ethnicity and the rise of religiosity since the 1980s, have come to appreciate the arts of their own ethnic culture. The movement of *ba'alei teshuvah* (those who have made *teshuvah*, "returned" to Jewish observance) has shifted the demographics of the institutional Orthodox world such that the yeshivah-bochers can groove quite easily to the secular, cool, ethnic *riddims* of their sinful youths.

Indeed, such grooves typify the general trend of making Judaism cool. Just think of Madonna and Roseanne studying Kabbalah, radical Jewish culture (Tattooed Jew, and the like), Carlebach followers and fans, the hip currency of Sephardi and Mizrahi music, the style of Chabad missionizing (not to mention the popularity of the Chabad telethon), a Jewish lounge club in New York named Makor (Source). It's not just that Judaism and things Jewish are "in," though that is part of it. No, we are being told that things Jewish—traditionally very uncool—are actually cool. Some Jews are even acting as if it's cool to be Jewish. An Upper West Side paper reported that Friday nights at shul are as popular now as discos! People are converting to Judaism right and left; in some synagogues on the West Coast, converts to Judaism make up 30 percent or more of the congregation. Indeed, if one looks closely one sees that Jewish cool signifies a kind of amusing and perverse but much needed *tikkun*, or repair, for Judaism and our culture at large.

Still, isn't there something a little wrong here? Cool marks ironic distance, detachment, and anti-establishmentarianism, an overemphasis on style. "Mama, I wanna make rhythm, don't wanna make music," crooned Cab Calloway in 1937 New York, as he slid into a mock ethnic voice and scenario (a boy playing rhapsodies on a violin), before exploding into a crescendo of scat ("noise," according to the contemporary mainstream understanding of music and taste). "Pop" music, television, and Hollywood host, if not breed, irony and sarcasm as a *weltanschaung*. Meanwhile, observant Judaism for the most part entails utter seriousness, without much room for humor, sarcasm, or irony, especially in the ultra-Orthodox world. There would seem to be some tension, to say the least, between hip-hop and *tehillim* (psalms), no? Doesn't some inherent semiotics of heavy metal preclude it from serving the seriously sacred?

According to the Jerusalem-based paper *Kol Ha-Ir* some years ago, many ultra-Orthodox rabbis of Me'ah She'arim thought so and came out against the rock-and-roll religious music that had become popular enough to keep open a large, allegedly disruptive music store on one of their neighborhood's main streets. It makes sense that many of the late-night religious D.J.s in Israel broadcast while obviously stoned. Though supposedly radically different in content, the fit between the pre- and post-teshuvah lifestyles appears stylistically continuous. The newly religious traded in their black leather for the stylistics of black suits and fedoras; mohawks for the myriad of specific pe'ot styles, each representing a different Hasidic group. The ornate, patterned, textured chintz vests of the Hasidic rebbes—the fabric origin of the derogatory adjective "chintzy"—now signified for them the height of cool. (Remember the haute-fashion rip-off of Hasidic garb from a few years back?) No surprise that the rebbes worried that the seepage of the pre-teshuvah life into the ba'al-teshuvah life would threaten to undermine the entire point of the transformation.

A close look at two recent releases provides a fascinating glimpse into the paradoxes of cool Judaism. Trumpet player Steven Bernstein's disc, *Diaspora Soul* (1999), on John Zorn's Tzadik label features a small postmodern Latin jazz ensemble belting out versions of "Ani Ma'amin," "Manishtanah," "Rock of Ages," "Roumania, Roumania," and others. The playing is both straight and ironic, funky and funny; Bernstein blows a mean trumpet. In a revealing chain of associations, Bernstein describes the sound he sought:

> Not just the rhythms, but the phrasing and air flow of the R&B players are a continuation of the [New Orleans] marching style. . . . This led me to thinking not just about a New Orleans sound, but rather the Gulf Coast sound, encompassing Texas and Cuba—and the last part of the Gulf Coast was Miami. And who retired to Miami? The most popular Cuban export of the '50s was the cha-cha . . . who loves a cha-cha more than the Jews? And the final piece of the grail—the hora bass pattern—one, two-and, and-four-and—is the first half of the clave, the heart of Afro-Cuban music.

Bernstein's music is clearly a loving tribute. Note, however, that Jews here are only the recipients, the listeners to the great ethnic musics, not their creators.

The tension between the disparate elements in Bernstein's music parallels the tension in the problematic of ethnic identity itself at play in the production of this music and the manufacture of this disk. The Cuban percussion, languid dance-groove bass, vibe-like electric piano, or swelling organ underpin the Jewish melodies which make up the horn themes. These melodies, however, are more icing than cake; Bernstein's soloing, for instance, only occasionally takes up allusions to Jewish music.

Bernstein has (purposefully? ironically?) recreated the overall feeling of exactly those 1950s and 1960s Jewish groups (Mickey Katz, the Barry Sisters) who incorporated "exotic" elements. He makes fun of (and pays respect to) them just as these groups had fun with (and made fun of) the "exotic" musics they were borrowing and even the Jewish music they were simultaneously transforming, down to the cheapo arrangements, "tacky" production values, often uninspired lounge-music tracks—amusing and almost desperate efforts to make cheesy songs cool. Is this the music that Jews who love cha-cha produced? The playing is great and the concept often works; Bernstein has forged a unified sound and it constitutes convincing Jewish music. But the effect cannot be listened to unironically. Perhaps all this has to do with Bernstein's comment about being asked to do a "Jewish" album:

> How does a Jewish musician who has spent his entire life studying "other" musical cultures make a "Jewish" record? How does one make a "Jewish" record, when by nature, all of one's music is already "Jewish"?

Another new release, on the Knitting Factory label, provides one answer to Bernstein's question. *Keter* (1999), the first disc from Zohar, an ensemble made up of eclectic pianist Uri Caine, singer/hazzan Aaron Bensoussan, and other adept players of cutting-edge music scenes in the States and Israel, presents a seamless D.J. mix of Mizrahi and Sephardi trance music over extended renditions of standards such as Eli Eli, Avraham Avinu, and many more. The Arabic improvisational singing, Ladino ballads, deep syncopated percussion, throbbing bass lines, avant-garde jazz piano, samples, and tape manipulation all come and go in the overarching mix, constituting equal, interchangeable elements from the databank of world music sounds. Yet this music does not sound ironic. The titles, intensity, and ecstasy all aim to produce a Jewish answer to Nusrat Fateh Ali Khan, Yoruba street percussion, or techno: Jewish music is the primal thang, the oldest and most up-to-date, connected to the grooves of the universe.

The disc's unintended irony resides in the degree to which the music's features come from "other" musical cultures. This shouldn't surprise: the Zohar and Kabbalah itself represent utterly miscegenated texts, a seamless mix of Hellenistic, Arabic, Christian, and Jewish elements. Another unintended irony is that normalizing Jewish music, making it just one among all other ethnic grooves/styles, is done at the cost of accepting the marketing of multicultural-ism, the manufacture of cultures. In some ways the music on *Keter* is what I imagine the just-opened Jewish "club" Makor in New York must be like—I've only heard from a sister-in-law who was there herself—with its three stories of Jewish happenings, a bar and strictly kosher food, hip world music imported via the mavens from the Lower East Side, mosh pit above, *shiurim* below, a mind-body *yosher* (balance) that would do the Maharal proud.

Convivencia, man! Judaism for the new millennium! But what does it re-ally mean when lyrics yearning for the speedy rebuilding of the Temple float over the beautiful explosions of Afro-Cuban drumming, a drumming (with its own lyrics, by the way) whose rhythms, like those of Haiti, Brazil, and else-where, derive from worship devoted to deities/heroes of Yoruba or Fon or Nago origin, and energize the Afro-Cuban religion known as Santeria? The ironies here abound. Does using this beat imply that the artists condone the Santeria practice—so controversial in parts of the United States—of animal sacrifice? They should, since they sing for the revival of the Temple-based cult of animal sacrifice in Judaism. Do they really want the speedy rebuilding of the Temple and return of the sacrificial system? (Do we, when we sing this song at wedding parties?) One can certainly dance to it, but I wonder.

The cool Jewish trip could only be American. On one side, the roots of Jewish cool lie in New-Age terminology and attitude: positivity and openness to the nonmodern, to the nonrational. But New Age was never cool. It is a pre-tend religion for people with pretend traditions. The homogenized, bound-aryless music of New Age well reflects its sanitized, denatured, fake solution to personal and world problems. New Age is goofy, yet self-serious, with *no* sense of irony. On the other side, Jewish cool derives from cool aesthetes, from the beat poets to their progeny of the Sixties. These were self-serious, adolescent rebels with a cause, goofy only unintentionally. But their extreme anti-establishment cool left no escape from alienation and anomie.

One brand of Jewish cool that seems to escape this existential angst is the ecstatic neo-Hasidic style developed by the late Shlomo Carlebach. That Carlebach style is a variety of cool can readily be seen from its staunch hip-pie anti-fashion hierarchy, its rainbow-people politics, and its ease with way-long ecstatic praying and dancing, a product of its followers' affection for way-long guitar and drum solos. Carlebach style owes much to the op-timistic, cheerful searching of New-Age religiosity, but it derives as well from working-class rebellion and from a hippie back-to-the-land spirit, with roots in serious personal and political *tikkun*: Bob Dylan, the Grateful Dead, Gil Scott-Heron. It's more a whole-person Jungian-balance, caring-people kind of trip. (This might be particularly true for Jewish boys and men, whose self-involved energies adulating cool can thus be channeled into community-oriented, world-healing activities. A great deal of overlap binds Jewish renewal with the men's movement.) Carlebach followers favor a Sephardi/kabbalistic/neo-Hasidic *nusach* for prayer, a rebellion against the insipid Protestant harmonies of American Conservative and Reform synagogues and homes. Carlebach followers are very sincere. A Carlebachy approach maintains interest in the ritual efficacy of particular traditions, all of them, and is never mocking.

Yet even Carlebach style is not free from the ironies of sincerity. The very passion of Carlebach followers can lead to sometimes amusing, sometimes unsettling results. Their search for an "authentic" Judaism has led many to embrace some less-than-savory aspects of Judaism because of their seeming "authenticity." A friend of mine, for example, an inveterate hippie carpenter, pot-smoker and all, is building a piece of the ritual furniture needed for the third Temple planned by some extreme nationalist and ultra-Orthodox groups. Friends of friends apparently hold the "contract" for making the harps to be used therein by the Levitical choirs.

Likewise, I am dismayed to hear that in Israel Rabbi Carlebach's songs and image have now been usurped by right-wing settlers. I have been told that yeshivah-bochers belted out Shlomo *niggunim* (melodies) at a recent rally against dismantling West Bank settlements. I am not surprised by this: anyone can claim pieces of discourse, and Carlebach himself had a strain of nationalism. But it's one thing to market "authentic" ancient-style weddings or biblical clothing, and quite another to make mysticism into militarism by other means. Jewish passion doesn't always lead to ugly nationalism. Without any irony, however, without some critical, skeptical attitude, Carlebachy cool readily becomes too serious, a tool for the Right, and thus no longer cool at all. Can Jewish cool be ironic and serious all at once? Can it survive if it's not?

A recently released anthology of previously untranslated stories of the Ba'al Shem Tov contains a tale in which the wonder rabbi cures a Jew who was passing as a hedonistic Polish noble of his "negativity and insidious addictions." The tale explains to some degree the relationship between cool and Judaism, at least in ba'al teshuvah circles. In his healing speech, addressed both to and not to the disguised Jew, the Besht says:

> Anybody who really wants to progress on the spiritual path must look into his very own soul and see clearly what is stopping him from getting close to God. In my experience there are two traits that obstruct one from truly proceeding on the path. The first one is irrational anger, and the other is sarcasm.

In this Hasidic view, sarcasm, a form of irony, simply must be eliminated. It is easy to understand why. Irony and especially sarcasm imply disdain, haughtiness, mockery, negation, and they act as corrosive agents. Spiritual Judaism, even of the cool variety inspired by pseudo-Kabbalah, entails a voluntary move away from irony. There is to be no more camp for Madonna, who made her name camping and vamping Catholicism. Now, I am told in all seriousness, Roseanne gives *shiurim* at the Kabbalah Learning Center. Even cool Jewish culture that is openly ironic seems to be so these days only affectionately (I'm thinking of the San Francisco Bay area group Charming Hostess' covers of Eastern European and klezmer tunes, or even of Israeli comedian Gil Kopetch).

It all makes sense. People are desperate to escape the postmodern condition, which is fundamentally marked by an ironic stance toward the world. Neo-Hasidism's vision of traditional Judaism's no-nonsense approach to the world offers Jewish kids who grew up in the most assimilated, up-to-date, worldly spheres a means of maintaining the stylistics of cool while escaping cool's alienation and disinterest. A world in which nothing matters or can be done is replaced by one in which every action makes a difference and saves worlds.

Cool Judaism has enabled young Jews to express ethnic pride in themselves and in Judaism, now that they've discovered that the "true" Judaism repressed by their bourgeois parents is ethnic, oppressed and Other. Such "ethnicity" has allowed young Jews to express sincerity in acceptable cool fashion (reggae, hip hop, cutting-edge klezmer) since, unlike whites, oppressed Others are permitted to be sincere, oppositional, searching, and positive while fighting for cultural survival. And it has allowed Jews who have discovered the transcendent in "other" cultures to be open enough to themselves and others about their finding the transcendent "at home."

Through the stylistics of cool Judaism, the rebellion manufactured and harnessed for marketing the rebel youth culture is channeled into a rebellion against the very things producing these styles and attracting young people to them in the first place: the secular culture industry, bourgeois living, individualism, emotional deadness. Hopefully. One cannot forget the extent to which even seemingly authentic efforts of cultural resistance, "the relics of counterculture," as Thomas Frank writes, "reek of affectation and phoniness, the leisure-dreams of white suburban children." All too often, cool Judaism harnesses transgression for the sake of mere posture, even for profits. It remains to be seen whether cool Judaism is just another style to consume or whether it helps leads to an authentic and lasting personal rebellion against materialism, against abused worldly power, against the destructive cult of the individual and the ego, the source of the need to be cool.

Judaism will survive cool. Cool might just survive Judaism. After all else is said, these two new CDs make fantastic music for simchas! The question of whether they can survive together, however, depends in each case on the fundamental formula contained in Pierre Bourdieu's theory of the "habitus," as articulated by Duke Ellington: "it ain't what you do but the way that you do it." Passion and the search for "authenticity" cannot become substitutes for thinking, for the eternal effort to juggle the necessary opposites of God and human, devotion and critique, self-confidence and humility. Planning for the third Temple is not merely a larger equivalent of the drumming circles of men's groups. The dangers of soul without mind continue to be very real. This said, however, the potential power of cool Jewish culture remains strong. If cool Judaism helps young people to avoid the Orwellian carelessness, ignorance, and idiocy induced by the culture industry, it makes a damn good noble lie.

Burning in Hell, Conservative Movement Style

Belief that Jews and Homosexuals Deserve Eternal Punishment

Judith Plaskow

In the late 1970s, I spent three years in the "buckle of the Bible belt" teaching religion at Wichita State University. During my time there, several students told me I was going to burn in Hell because I had not "accepted Jesus Christ as my Lord and Savior." They did not say this with any malice. On the contrary, they were simply telling me how the world works. It was because they liked and respected me that they wanted me to save myself before it was too late.

I had mixed feelings about being the recipient of such tidings. Part of me was condescendingly amused that they could believe such nonsense. Part of me sympathized with the fundamental conflict that being taught by a Jew caused them. But mainly, I was angry that the students chose to hold onto the narrow tenets of their faith against the evidence of their own feelings. I was offended that they would rather squeeze me into an anti-Semitic system than let my reality as a person serve as the starting point for rethinking their religious assumptions.

I am reminded of this experience and the feelings it evoked as I reflect on the Conservative movement's year-old decision to condemn homosexual behavior. In March 1992, the Rabbinical Assembly Law Committee voted thirteen to seven (with three abstentions) to support Joel Roth's long tshuvah (decision) arguing that traditional proscriptions against homosexuality remain valid and compelling. Fourteen months later, Roth has resigned as dean of the Jewish Theological Seminary's Rabbinical School, and the issue of homosexuality deeply divides the seminary's faculty and student body as well as the Rabbinical Assembly. Still, the tshuvah remains the official teaching of the Conservative movement, and the chancellor of the seminary insists on reading all dissent as the product of external political pressure.

The movement's stance calls to mind my Wichita experience because Roth's tshuvah is as confident about the place of "homosexuals" in the divine economy as my students were about the place of Jews. Homosexuality is not innately abominable, Roth assures gay and lesbian Jews. It is just that God has defined it as such! The Torah's blanket prohibition of homosexuality as toevah (an abomination) is so clear and binding that the force of extra-legal considerations would have to be overwhelming to compel rabbis to rethink the law. In Roth's judgment, none of the available theories concerning the origins or nature of homosexuality constitutes cogent or compelling reason to overturn precedent. The "responsible halachist," therefore, is constrained not only to oppose the acceptance of gay and lesbian rabbis and cantors, and refrain from recognizing or participating in gay and lesbian commitment ceremonies, but to counsel gay and lesbian Jews that "Jewish law would have you be celibate."

I see a number of analogies between this tshuvah and the stance of my former students at Wichita State. Both affirm a traditional understanding of religious authority and teaching. Both see themselves as doing so not on grounds of prejudice, anti-Semitism, or homophobia, but of religious necessity. And both choose religious doctrine above human beings.

By claiming that no contemporary evidence is strong enough to outweigh the words of Torah—not psychoanalytic or scientific theory, and certainly not the testimony and reality of gay and lesbian Jews—the Rabbinical Assembly Law Committee avoids having to examine the presuppositions of its religious system. Were it to begin with people rather than Torah, on the other hand, were it to entertain the possibility that homosexuality is not an abomination— that it is simply a mode of sexual expression, as loving or as alienated, as much or as little a vehicle for turning toward God as heterosexuality—then it might be forced to surrender its certainty that God's will is identical with the words of Torah. While the Conservative movement has generally rejected a fundamentalist stance, in this case it is certain that it knows the mind of God.

There is another layer to my analogy as well. Both the Conservative movement and my former students ignore the history and context of the actual power relationships between the groups in question. Thus Roth argues that his decision does not support intolerance because the Jewish community should be no more intolerant of violations of sexual prohibitions than it is of violations of other halachic norms. But in the real world, being gay or lesbian is not equivalent to other halachic violations. Sabbath desecrators are not the victims of hate crimes in every city in this country. No state has yet put a referendum on its ballot abrogating the civil rights of the religiously intermarried.

The tshuvah's inattention to political context is precisely analogous to that of my students. Jews are people, they said; we are welcome in the universities; we should have civil rights; we should just know that God says we are going to burn in Hell. And regardless of the benign intent with which the students say it, every Jew knows full well that they are reflecting and supporting two thousand years of anti-Semitism. If the Rabbinical Assembly Law Committee cannot see that it is reflecting and supporting a long history of religious homophobia (Jewish and otherwise), then it is either willfully blind or patently dishonest. The fact is that, despite its protestations to the contrary, with this tshuvah the Conservative movement allies itself with the anti-gay hate that is sweeping the country.

I do not have the space here to explore the halachic, religious, ethical, and communal implications of the full acceptance of gay and lesbian Jews. But enough has been written in the pages of *Tikkun* and elsewhere to make it clear that the question is not simply one of Halacha—there are halachic arguments for acceptance of homosexuality—but of religious authority and power. Why did the law committee vote in a way that closes off discussion of this issue, and what would make it change? Why is Chancellor Schorsch choosing to attribute deeply held moral convictions to the influence of outside agitators, and how can he be convinced he is wrong? My interest as a lesbian Jew with ties to the Conservative movement is how lesbians, gays, and our allies can seize the opportunity provided by the present debate to bring about lasting change.

It seems important to recognize, first of all, the extent of the divisions within the Conservative movement. The vote of the law committee was not unanimous, and the committee is not elected by the Rabbinical Assembly and does not necessarily represent the views of all the Rabbinical Assembly's members. The committee that passed Roth's tshuvah thirteen to seven also gave eight votes to an alternative tshuvah offered by Eliott Dorff, making it a minority opinion that can be used by congregational rabbis. Dorff provides an excellent critique of Roth's halachic formalism, labels the results of his reasoning "unbelievably cruel," and calls for the establishment of a study commission to look at homosexuality as one aspect of a broader examination of Jewish attitudes toward sexuality. At its meeting in 1992, the Rabbinical Assembly established such a commission and also passed a resolution affirming gay and lesbian rights to rabbinic services. At the 1993 Rabbinical Assembly meeting, Rabbi Harold Shulweiss gave a keynote address calling for the integrations of Halacha and ethics, using homosexuality as a prime example. B'tsalmeinu ("in our image"), a group of rabbis formed to discuss gay and lesbian issues in the Conservative movement and to effect positive change, collected well over a hundred signatures on a statement asking (among other things) that the law committee not institutionalize discrimination.

The divided rhetoric of the Conservative movement provides an excellent point of departure for those who would press for change. Soon after the law committee's decision, the United Synagogue and Rabbinical Assembly passed resolutions that, while "affirming [the] tradition's prescription for heterosexuality," supported full civil equality for gays and lesbians and welcomed them as members of synagogues. While such statements mainly seem designed to ease the movement's conscience about its halachic stance, they could provide a mandate for education and real encounter with gays and lesbians that might in turn pave the way for genuine acceptance. If the support expressed in these resolutions is serious, then all Conservative synagogues can be expected to include events on gay and lesbian Jews as a regular part of their educational programs. The Women's League might launch a series of lectures and meetings parallel to its efforts on women's issues twenty years ago. Movement camps and youth programs should initiate training programs and workshops to combat the homophobia that is as rampant among their constituents as elsewhere in the youth and adolescent populations.

Meanwhile, individual congregations and Conservative Jews are not waiting for the movement to take action. Forces for transformation were at work before the law committee's vote—which provided the impetus for its consideration of the issue in the first place—and continue despite (or because of) it. Some congregations have written letters to the Jewish Theological Seminary, the Rabbinical Assembly, and United Synagogue, protesting the decision. Individual congregants have withheld from their annual synagogue dues the $33.50 that goes to the United Synagogue—a form of resistance that is also open to congregations. Education committees have taken the initiative in setting up lectures, workshops, and other programs on gay and lesbian concerns. Some synagogues are reaching out to gay and lesbian Jews in their communities through special programs, through services for people with or touched by AIDS, and through the issues addressed from their pulpits. Since many rabbis may want to explore this issue but are afraid of lay resistance, congregants can make clear that they want to hear sermons on, and see efforts to include, gays and lesbians in the Jewish community. Congregants can also support individual rabbis who practice "civil disobedience" by participating in gay and lesbian commitment ceremonies.

Two groups of Jews are especially crucial to this process of resistance and transformation: the friends and families of gays and lesbians, and gays and lesbians themselves. Chancellor Schorsch has argued that gays and lesbians are, at most, 2 to 5 percent of the population, and that homosexuality therefore affects few people and is not of interest to the Conservative laity. Rabbis who have raised the issue with lay people, however, have a different tale to tell. They hear stories of loved ones lost to AIDS who could not be mourned publicly; they are thanked for speaking out by parents, children, brothers, and sisters of gays and lesbians who had long felt isolated and invisible. My partner's parents, for example, are long-time, prominent members of a mainstream Conservative congregation. There must be thousands of family members like them, many of whom are kept from sharing both their pain and their celebrations by the movement's homophobia. If these Conservative Jews could find concrete ways to raise with their rabbis and fellow congregants the dilemmas they face as relatives and friends of people whose behavior the movement has labeled "abominable," it would quickly become apparent that many lay people care deeply about an issue that is very close to home.

Families of gay and lesbian Jews are helped to speak out by a strong gay and lesbian witness and presence. Just as my very existence as a Jewish professor was a challenge to my students' unexamined faith, so the visible participation of gays and lesbians in Jewish life is the most effective challenge to those who pretend to accept us while at the same time insisting that God rejects our loving sexual expression. The Conservative movement has available to it solid halachic arguments for new attitudes toward lesbians and gays. Jews—especially gay and lesbian Jews—taking action to create a new reality in our individual communities will either hasten the day when the law committee finds the will to refine and apply these arguments, or they will render its work colossally irrelevant.

Ten Ways to Recognize a Sephardic "Jew-ess"

A Short Story

Ruth Knafo Setton

ONE: NAME

Often unpronounceable, unmanageable, redolent of incense and cumin. A name that twists letters into spirals the way a *djinn* emerges from a lamp. Abitbol. Afriat. Bahboul. Buzaglo. Aflalo. Dweck. Ohayon. Ben'Attar. Bensussan. Chouraqui. The Spanish echoes too, of arches and Alhambra, dusty streets and brown hoods: Cabessa, Corcos, Mendes, Pinto. But the true names are weirdly resonant, heavy, harsh, satisfying; a name you can sink your teeth into, one that emerges from dirt and mud and roots: Knafo. A certain brilliantly colored cloak, *knaf* also refers to a honey-drenched, shredded phyllo dough Middle Eastern sweet, the kind set a thousand on a large tray in Jaffa or Casablanca that you eat with your fingers, swirling the flaking pastry and syrup and nut mixture on your tongue with burning Moroccan mint tea—perfumed with a drop of orange blossom water. Knafo. Say this name aloud, every which way you can imagine. Try being called Knaf-Knuf. Knasoo—a singularly ugly aberration, Konfoo, Kanfa, Knee, or in a stroke of malevolent genius: Kohenfo. The mysterious letter "k." To pronounce or not? Arabs whisper it like an "h." Hanafo. It's a breath, a wing. Knaf in Hebrew is a wing. Legend has it that Knafo means "under God's wing," even to be protected by God because we are literally under His wing. This was especially evident for Maklouf Knafo and his family on a Thursday morning in July 1790, in the Berber village of Oufran hidden in the Anti-Atlas Mountains of Morocco.

TWO: FOOD

Feed this child. Wide-eyed and yearning. This child has never tasted a bagel! Her mother distrusts anything served in a gel. Gefilte fish? She whisks her child away from it quickly. Kugel? The dough is too heavy, sinks into the stomach. Lox and cream cheese? Mom clicks her tongue against the roof of her mouth. They don't know how to be subtle, she murmurs, wielding her knife and beginning to chop. Behind her hennaed hair—beautiful auburn waves flowing down her back—I see my American backyard. A swing set on which my little sister soars, lost in her recurring daydream of rescuing stray cats and dogs and bringing them to her doll hospital. A sandbox in which my tiny naked brother sits and throws handfuls of sand back and forth. Mom chops, cuts, slices. I lean on my elbow and watch everyone at once. Even my dad far away at work sorting produce at the A&P, struggling to make sense of English syllables—coiled and Germanic—as opposed to fluid French, guttural Arabic.

I think about my own rescue fantasy. Every night in bed I return to our little backyard. The alley behind is flooded. Help! Help! someone screams. It's *I Love Lucy*! I race from my yard to save her, bring my trusty canoe through the gate, and paddle up the hill. I pull her into the boat. Her red hair gleams in the dark. She thanks me, and I set her safely in my backyard, and return to save Desi and little Ricky. It's a dangerous world, something I can't remember ever learning and yet something I must have always known. To open the front door is to enter danger. I prefer leaving from the back, where I can ease my way into the outside world, through the yard and the gate, down the alley and around the corner past Old Man Minnich's store and his display of comic books and penny candy in the window.

See, Mom says, and gestures towards the salads: oranges and black olives, the colors alone nearly sending me on another voyage; purple beets and celery; cooked peppers red, yellow and green, drizzled with olive oil and seasoned with preserved lemon, chili peppers, and cumin. Flavors shouldn't be obvious, Mom says; mix the unexpected: chicken with sweet tomato jam and dark honey, fish with almond paste and confectioners sugar, preserves made from baby eggplants and walnuts, tagines simmered with smen, saffron and za'atar. And ma fille, remember the importance of cinnamon.

THREE: THE KNAFO WHEEL

My cousin handed it to me one night at a lecture in New York. A huge sheet of paper to revolve, separated into sections: a round graph. I look at the center: Maklouf Knafo. The one who burned to death along with the other forty-nine *nisrafim* (burnt ones) in Oufran. And the branches spread out from him. Knafos, Knafos, as far as the finger extends. Knafos in Mogador of course, because that's where his wife walked with her baby. I close my eyes and imagine her voyage. A young woman, her eight-day-old infant son (just circumcised by Maklouf that morning), walking down the mountain paths— rocky and steep. But the danger is not in the rocks and winding roads; it is in the robbers and brigands who populate these mountains. A young woman and her baby. I scan the Knafo wheel, turn it around and around, try to read between the black lines and words and letters, but find no name for this young woman. A nameless woman making her way down the mountains to save her son. Nameless—except for her husband's name, Knafo. Is she under God's wing as she stumbles down the road? Sun burns on her head. The baby is hot, hungry, crying. How does she maintain her supply of milk? Everything she owns is on her back. The baby cradled in a blanket against her breasts. Her husband left behind. Her husband, Maklouf Knafo. She walks fast, head down, afraid to breathe, to smell smoke.

FOUR: PURPLE PALESTINIANS

Now this goes back years: We all lived in a shabby apartment building on Valencia in the Mission in San Francisco—above a bar, across from a bar, next door to a bar. Stumbling over drunks and homeless—only back then we didn't call them homeless, we called them bums. And winos. And I was alone for the first time in my life, scared to death, but—here's the great mixture I can't get a handle on—high on hippie life, memories of my strange isolated family haunting me, trying with my gut to be as American as you, and to that end, sitting in my third-floor apartment in the Mission, looking down at the barmaid, at least eighty, with enormous pale tits and iridescent blue eyeshadow, walking to the bar on the corner to start her shift, and I set pen to paper and begin the American novel—as interpreted by a Moroccan Jewish immigrant girl. But I've been burned already, even though I'm barely twenty-one. The first story I sent out returns with a rejection note: You write well. Next time try writing about the real Jews.

I am frozen to my soul. Too afraid to inquire more deeply into what the editor means. So ashamed I tear the note into a thousand slivers, shred them with my fingers, and throw them down the toilet. There. It's gone.

"And the pain?" as my father would say. He's known for that final aside, the joke after the punch line that sends it spinning into another dimension. He is known for that, the ironic aside that makes people realize that no joke has an end. No story truly finishes.

And so I write about an old Polish Jewish man as I stare outside and ignore Hassan from down the hall, banging on my door and screaming: I'm going to rape you the way you raped Palestine! And Amar, his roommate, the head cabdriver (the one who gives them all purple Hafiz Cab teeshirts when they arrive in the city, and the one who cooks for me and gets high with me, and we listen to Procol Harum and wonder over "A Whiter Shade of Pale" together, and stare at each other, attracted though trying not to be). Amar, sweet Amar, with the desert eyes and the tightest purple tee-shirt of all, tells his friend: leave her alone. She's a girl, she can't rape anyone. . . .

FIVE: EXOTIC

Erotique. I line my eyes with black kohl and wear large gold hoops and long gypsy skirts and low-cut hand-embroidered Romanian blouses. Paint my toenails red and wear sandals that tie around my ankles. But my legs are always cold so I begin to wear leggings beneath my skirts—and don't realize it's the way Arab women dress until my mother tells me. I play up the exotic, pronounce words with a faint French accent, *le bagel, qu'est-ce que c'est*? Boys like me; you and your crazy name, one murmurs as he bites my ear. They see me and think of *Casablanca* and Ingrid Bergman and "play it again Sam." My first real boyfriend is black. He tells me: I am from Afrikaaa. I tell him: so am I. He tells me: I am black first, a man second. I tell him: in Paris they call me *pieds noirs*, black feet. He tells me: here, they call me nigger. I tell him: they called me *dhimmi*, or the lowest of the low. We outblack each other, and even in bed, scratch and lash and attack, until we lie back, exhausted and content. We're an odd couple: he listens to Jimi and (in secret) Sweet Baby James. I listen to James Brown and John Lee Hooker. I dance better than he does. Later, the best dancer I will ever see, a Moroccan soul-sex machine come to life, whom I watched move to James Brown for hours at a time in a Netanya club called Azazel (or Hell), died at 21 in the Yom Kippur War.

SIX: MEMORY

The years in the sunless *mellahs* and *juderias* and *quartiers juifs* have bleached our skin until it's fashionably Mediterranean, only a shade or two darker than yours. Our nomadic history has given us a variety of languages, none of which is ours, but all of which we have learned to speak—with a bite. You can recognize us by the rage we carry in us, the rage of the colonized, those who are still not permitted to meet the master class eye to eye. The bitter eyes that now refuse to stay lowered, the angry tongue that can no longer be silenced, the poet's heart that it spite of everything continues to dream and hope, the soul that cannot forget. There is no wind and the smell of burning flesh remains in the square, incapable of moving elsewhere and freeing us.

SEVEN: INVISIBLE

Even within postcolonial, third-world, border-crossing, multicultural ethnic feminist identities, I am nowhere to be found. I dare you. Look for me. Born in Morocco, raised in America, in a small town—a Jew from Africa who probably scared my Pennsylvania-Dutch neighbors as much as they scared me—a minority within a minority. Be invisible, my father told me. I tried— but my black feet peeked out from every disguise. And now when I take off my veil and let you see the scratched lines of henna crisscrossing my face, the embroidered scrolls and curlicues that lace my palms, you avert your eyes. By multicultural, I didn't mean you. Latina is hot now. Lesbian Latina even better. Caribbean, mon? Remote Indian provinces, hot as curry. Even Arab American, hotter than you. Who you anyway? Afrikaan? Arab Jew? Oriental Jew? Tied in with Israel. Israel not hot.

EIGHT: NOMAD

I believe she traveled north to Taroudant in the Grand Atlas, then wound her way down the rocky hills and ravines to the east and the breezes of the Atlantic Ocean, and north once more, following the coastline past Cap Guir and Tamanar to Mogador. Mountain air is thin and clear, but in the Anti-Atlas Mountains it is pale gray, tainted with smoke. Take a deep breath. The smoke doesn't escape. Locked in the square, over a hundred years later, it smells of death, the end of the oldest Jewish community in Morocco, with a hiss and crack.

NINE: THE CHOICE: LIFE OR DEATH?

Take a deep breath and decide if it's going to be life or death, says Bou Halassa, the sheik who owns the Jews of Oufran. Think carefully, he says. The choice is simple: Die as Jews, or live as Muslims—under my protection. All you have to do is say the words: There is no God but Allah, and Mohammed is His Prophet.

The sun is shining. It is a July morning in 1790 in the Anti-Atlas Mountains. Bou Halassa is on horseback, surrounded by his men who are already at work building the funeral pyre. The fifty Jews, merchants all, are wearing black (the only color permitted them); they are barefoot (no shoes allowed for Jews); and they are standing on the ground because they are not permitted to ride a horse. The horse is considered too noble an animal to carry a lowly Jew. Bou has interrupted the *souk el'khemiss*, the Thursday morning market. Merchants selling carpets and leather, artisans with brass trays and iron kettles. Cattle, mules, donkeys, chickens.

The leader of the Jews, Rabbi Naphtali Afriat, tells them: We have no choice. To say the words and live a lie is another form of death. To die for God is to live forever as Jews. It's the only way to carry on our faith so that our children can be Jews. So that everything doesn't die this morning.

A young man on the edge of the group is torn. Only this morning, with his own hands, he circumcised his first son. Die—for what? For Bou Halassa's whim? Bou is a tyrant, a sadist, notorious in the mountains for his hatred of Jews. Even though Bou's men have swords and are now circling the Jews, we are fifty in number—maybe we can fight back? And if they overpower us, then what? If we walk into the flames, will he then turn on our women and children?

Afriat, his gold earring glinting in the sun, announces in his quavering voice: We have decided. We choose death—in the name of God. You do not frighten us, Bou Halassa. You will answer for your brutality to God, not to us.

The young man bolts—without a thought, without hesitation—slips from the crowd of Jews and Arabs, and runs to his small cottage. Then he does— what? I'd love to see this scene: how he convinces her to take the baby and leave without him. I can almost hear her: you've already come this far! They don't know you're gone! Come with us. You'll do more good to us alive than dead. Why should you die for this sadist? Come with us!

He walks his wife and baby to the town wall, the stone wall that enclosed Oufran. She is unwieldy: the blanket that supports her baby forces her to lean forward, while the bag Maklouf stuffed with bread and dates loads down her back. He helps push her up the wall, and for a moment is caught there, in the cobblestones, between death and life—his wife's hand pulling him up, the hand of "God" pulling him back. Beneath his feet, red and purple flowers sprout in crevices between the rocks.

TEN: THE QUESTION OF HOME

The sun shines through Amar's window. The Moody Blues sing about nights in white satin. I lean over Amar's shoulder as he fries a mixture of eggs, potatoes, and meat on the stove. The violent Hassan has left San Francisco. Crazy, Amar tells me, tapping his temple and handing me a fat joint. I breathe in the harsh smoke and the pungent spices that smell like my mother's food. You have to create your own home wherever you go, he says. This sounds wise, heavy. But first you have to know what a home is, I say, and hand back the joint. With a deep sigh that echoes through me, I move to the window, sit on the edge and lean out. The sun licks my cheeks with burning tongue. The old barmaid walks down the street. I yell to her. She squints up, sees me, and waves, smiles an orange and yellow smile. Her blue-veined, speckled tits jiggle like blobs of cream cheese, like gefilte fish squashed in satin.

Crossing the Ethnic Divide

A Meditation on Anti-Semitism

Nan Fink Gefen

A few weeks after converting to Judaism, I stopped by my neighborhood fish market. I told the man behind the counter that I needed supplies to make gefilte fish for Passover.

"You?" he asked. "You're Jewish?"

"Yes, of course," I answered, sounding more sure of myself than I felt.

"That can't be," he laughed. "You don't have the right kind of nose." With a flourish, he cupped his hand over his nose to make it larger.

By this time I was used to Jews questioning whether I was Jewish, but no non-Jew had done it before. And this comment about noses? I was horrified.

"You can't identify Jews that way," I said coldly. "That's an anti-Semitic stereotype."

"Don't be offended," he replied, piling fish on the scale. His tone did not sound at all remorseful.

"Lots of us have noses that are small," I continued. When he didn't answer, I let the subject drop.

As I left the store, the man waved to me. Clearly he was not bothered by our interchange, but I was shaken. This was my first direct brush with anti-Semitism as a Jew, and it brought to the surface my feeling of insecurity in this new identity.

Afterward, I began to question myself. Why hadn't I stormed out of the store? I could have made more of a scene, but I was bound by long-standing, internalized rules of politeness. What did this say about my Jewish commitment?

More confusing, this man easily could have been my cousin. He had the solid Protestant look of many members of my family. He must have assumed that I came from his side of the ethnic line, and thus he took the liberty of making the comment about noses—one Christian talking to another, an insider's joke. Had I transmitted uncertainty about my Jewish identity, thereby giving him permission?

I was outraged, but it was easier to criticize myself for catalyzing this man's comments than to stay with my feeling of anger. In those early days after my conversion, I did not want to think about anti-Semitism. My overriding concern was finding acceptance within the Jewish community, not monitoring the actions of the people I had left behind.

As I submerged myself in my new Jewish life, I hardly remembered the man in the fish store. When I did, I explained his behavior away as an isolated example of anti-Semitism. The guy was a jerk, period. One incident didn't mean that anti-Semitism was a major problem. After all, this was the United States, a good place for Jews.

But my initial interpretation of this incident stemmed from denial, not lack of knowledge. I knew a great deal about the subject of anti-Semitism, yet it was too much for me to grasp that I, a converted Jew, was now its potential target. My WASP privilege would no longer count. Instead of realizing how vulnerable this made me feel, and how ashamed I was of this reaction, I tried to convince myself that anti-Semitism was not a serious matter.

While still in a state of denial, I had a terrifying experience of anti-Semitism. In the summer of 1987, *Tikkun* magazine organized a demonstration against Pope John Paul II during his visit to the United States. As *Tikkun*'s publisher, I was involved in this much-publicized protest. During this time, when we arrived at the *Tikkun* office in the morning, we'd listen to a spate of poisonous curses and death threats left on the answering machine. "You dirty kikes," an anonymous caller (always male, in my memory) would say in a cold voice, "You're going to die." The threats were horrifying, but what could we do? We notified the police, we were watchful, and our work continued. Finally, the callers stopped harassing us.

We had been the victims of anti-Semitism, but it was hard for me to absorb this fact. As time went by, the experience seemed increasingly unreal. When people voiced their concern about anti-Semitism, I'd want to reassure them that there was little to worry about. It was obvious that the callers at the time of the demonstration had been just a bunch of right-wing crazies.

Up to this point I had been able to minimize the existence of anti-Semitism, but I soon confronted it in a way that forced me to see how deeply embedded it is in our culture. One afternoon, when I was taping the oral history of my favorite aunt, she unexpectedly stopped the interview. "Why did you become a Jew?" she asked, her voice sharp. I answered her, but she hardly listened. Describing the "money-grubbing," "unsavory," and "clannish" Jews she had met in her lifetime, she mouthed one stereotype after another.

Anti-Semitism in my family? This was hard to take. I had heard a lot of racist talk as I grew up, but no one had spoken poorly about Jews. Somehow I had not recognized my family's anti-Semitism. But there it was, brought to the surface by my conversion. I couldn't pass it off as the irrational behavior of a group of crazy people.

I began to see the prejudice in my mother. She could hardly bear that I had converted, and she freely expressed her negative opinion of Jews. Once I allowed myself to see her anti-Semitism, I began to recognize that it can exist even in the hearts of fundamentally well-intentioned people.

My mother's attitude toward Jews has hardly changed over the last decade, despite my efforts to educate her about Judaism and share my experience with her. The anger I have about this, and her anger toward me for becoming a Jew, has created a measure of distance between us. Yet she is now in her last years, and it pains me that a breach like this exists.

Through this experience, and others, I've come to acknowledge anti-Semitism more fully. When I first converted, I wasn't sure who "we" and "they" were, regarding the question of anti-Semitism. As the offspring of a non-Jewish family, I continued to carry a feeling of responsibility. Now, however, I am firmly rooted in a Jewish "we," so that "they" are non-Jews, even if "they" are my family. As the recipient of anti-Semitism, I no longer feel responsible for it.

The issue of anti-Semitism points out my weakest link to Judaism. Through the generations, no one in my family was hurt, or killed, or discriminated against because of anti-Semitism. Quite the opposite, my original family exists on the other side. They are part of the system, part of the web of discrimination, and as their child, I have had a different life experience from other Jews. It is this that separates me, even more than blood.

Yet now that I am a Jew, I am also the object of anti-Semitism. The fact that I'm a convert doesn't matter. I've passed over the ethnic divide in the eyes of non-Jews. Some, like the man in the fish store, might momentarily assume that I am a Christian, but as soon as they know I am Jewish, I do not get special treatment.

The only people who question my Jewishness are those Jews who have difficulty accepting that I am "really" Jewish. They fear that I cut it both ways, taking the best from Judaism and enjoying the privilege of the Gentile world at the same time. But such a thing is impossible. Even if non-Jews continue to see me as one of them, dwelling in both worlds would make me schizophrenic.

Ten years after conversion, I sometimes find myself looking at all non-Jews with suspicion, searching their faces and analyzing their words for hidden meaning. I experience the cynicism and disregard for "the goyim" that many other Jews carry. Yet this is tempered by my desire to remain open. After all, not everyone in my non-Jewish family is anti-Semitic; I think especially of my children, who are very supportive of my becoming Jewish.

I remind myself that if I take every glance, every remark of uneasiness by non-Jews and label it as anti-Semitic, I am slipping into paranoia. Rather than naming trouble, I am searching for it. By doing this, I ignore the possibility that I might be wrong in my perception, and I close the door to deeper understanding.

As I look back across the ethnic divide, I recount the geography of the non-Jewish world. From my experience, I know that many non-Jews in America are ignorant about Judaism. They assume that it is just another American religious denomination, not quite Christian, but one that is along the same continuum.

These are the people who wonder why Jews don't feel comfortable in their churches, or why Jews like to associate with each other, or why Jews don't want to celebrate Christmas. They think of Jews as being pretty much like themselves, and are surprised when we are different. Because of their lack of familiarity with Jewish culture and history, they often feel rejected when we don't respond to them in the way they expect.

Comments from these people might be antagonistic, but they are often based in misunderstanding or hurt feelings, rather than maliciousness. But other non-Jews, who are more hostile, agree with the ugly stereotypes of Jews that exist in the larger culture. They are the ones who, like my aunt, make assumptions about our motives and think of us as inferior. At the far edge of this group are those who threaten and physically abuse us, the ones who write on buildings and destroy graves.

Finally, there are the non-Jews who are sister-fellow travelers. I used to be one of them: people who are attracted to and make an effort to understand Jewish culture. Fueled by a love and respect for the Jewish people, they are our allies and defenders, and a bridge to the non-Jewish world.

I do not intend here to make an exhaustive survey of non-Jews' attitudes toward Jews. Rather, I want to make the point that non-Jews differ from each other, as do Jews. An anti-Semitic-sounding remark coming from one person might be the result of ignorance, while the same remark from another might mean danger. The question, of course, is how to tell them apart. The only way I know is to see what happens when these remarks are confronted. The anti-Semitic man in the fish store, with his jeering attitude, did not seem to learn anything, or even care, when I disputed him, but another non-Jew might well apologize.

In a better world, non-Jews would take it upon themselves to eradicate anti-Semitism. Putting pressure on each other to change, they would lead the way to a shift in anti-Semitic attitudes and behavior. But we recognize that this is not happening, or at least it is happening in too small a measure to make a difference. Anti-Semitic incidences have increased worldwide, and in this country the far Right—often though not exclusively the source of anti-Semitic words and acts—has become more powerful. It is up to us as Jews to be vigilant about anti-Semitism.

In the end, like every other Jew, I am faced with a destructive, frightening force that seems to go away at times, only to resurface in other shapes, other permutations. It strikes at unlikely moments, and happens so fast that it leaves me dislocated, intimidated, and horrified. Afterward the anger remains, but also an overwhelming feeling of impotence and the desire to draw in for protection.

Like others, I try to balance this with my desire to be receptive to non-Jews. I find myself walking the fine line of relating to them, and loving some of them, but fighting anti-Semitism at the same time. This is not easy, especially for me as a convert: The conflict in loyalties never subsides. Yet what is the choice? Rather than denying anti-Semitism, or finding it everywhere, I choose this more complicated course.

Chapter 3

JUDAISM

Notes on Jewish Spirituality

Gershon Winkler

The eighteenth-century Rabbi Nachmon of Breslav taught that the body yearns to know the experience of the soul, and that the soul, in turn, yearns to know the experience of the body (Likutei MaHaRan, ch. 22, para. 5). Spirituality, then, is the practice or exercise of including the bodily senses in soul experience and the soul senses in bodily experience. Dating way back into and probably beyond talmudic times, this way of spiritual practice was pretty much integrated into everyday routine from praying to studying to sipping grape juice. When you prayed, you swayed. The Talmud records how Rabbi Akiva (second century) included his body in prayer to the point that he'd begin praying in one corner and end up in the opposite corner clear across the room (Babylonian Talmud, Tosefta Birachot 3:7).

At the same time, when you would feast your eyes on a person of beauty you would include your soul by reciting a prayer acknowledging the spiritual quality of the gift of beauty (Babylonian Talmud, Tosefta Birachot 7:7). When you would feast your body on dinner, you would recite prayers of acknowledgment of the divine source of your food, thus including the soul in the experience of the body (Babylonian Talmud, Tosefta Birachot 4:1). The kabbalists through the centuries would always prelude a physical act with an incantation that declared the act as one of unifying the Godhead with the Shechinah, Creator with Creation, God Transcendent with God Immanent. The prayer goes like this:

> For the sake of the unification of the Sacred Wellspring with its earthly manifestation/dwelling (Shechinah) by means of this act, performed in awe and love, with the intention of unifying the Name *yud hey* with *vav hey*.

Reciting this invocation is a powerful way of bringing our physical awareness and spiritual awareness into a synchronicity that spells spirituality. We can bite into an apple as a purely physical experience, or we can bite into an apple as a spiritual experience, depending upon what we are invoking when we eat. Even reciting a prayer is no guarantee of spiritual nurturance unless the recitation is done with awareness as opposed to unconscious, rote muttering.

Spirituality is as much about the body as it is about the soul. The physical universe is more than merely an arena *in which* we evolve spiritually, it is the very means *by which* we evolve spiritually. It happens here. It happens not in the Garden of Paradise, but in the Garden of Paradox. The body is not only a vehicle for soul manifestation, it is a sacred facilitator of soul realization.

No person, no retreat or workshop, no book, no teacher, can transmit spirituality to you, can unravel for you the layers of ego and id that hide your soul self. No one but you can do your own spiritual work, and no one person's spiritual work resembles in any way that of another. Each of us is here for reasons unknown to our selves, let alone to others. Each of us is a mystery unique from any other person's mystery. As Martin Buber wrote: "The mystery of another lies deep within him, and it cannot be observed from without" (*Die Stunde und die Erkenntnis*, p. 155).

We are definitely living in the Amos Era, the period predicted by our prophet Amos, pronounced Ah-moss, who saw a vision in which people were thirsting and hungering, but neither for bread nor for water but to hear the word of God. "And they shall wander from sea to sea and from the north to the east, running to and fro in search of the word of God, and they shall not find it" (Amos 8:11–12) because it isn't to be sought, it is to be experienced by stepping back from desperation and by looking at what is near to our *kishkehs* rather than at what is waving at us promisingly on distant horizons. We need to allow the voice from within to be heard above the tumult of the noise from without.

Spirituality as a blanket movement with the idealized intention of sweeping all of us up in one fell swoop of spiritual consciousness is doomed to failure. Hasidism tried this and failed dismally. There were some great rebbes but very few great Hasidim. Nowadays, Jewish renewal is refreshing, but as a movement it brings up a lot of questions around its ability to perpetuate what it had set out to achieve several decades ago when it was a little *schtiebel* on Emlen Street in Philadelphia. Rather than concentrating on creating ever-unfolding spirituality, it has become a movement concentrating more and more on defining itself, and on creating ever-unfolding organizational policies and principles.

Spirituality does not happen through fads and fashions, through instant hit-and-run processes. It happens through long, patient, step-by-step and very individualized processes. I am often asked by Jews into shamanism if Judaism has quickie methods of facilitating soul journeys like some other groups do. My response is that Judaism is into foreplay, and that the longer the foreplay the more satisfying and fulfilling is the actual spiritual experience at the time of consummation (Reishis Chochmah, Sha'ar HaAhavah, 4:4). The quickie spiritual kick is a result of our contemporary cultural accent on instantism. Everything is microwaveable, everything is available in instant form—instant coffee, instant rice, bread machines, touch-tone phones. Think about this the next time you get upset because your laptop took fifteen seconds to boot itself instead of instantly. But this is where we are at and this is what our soul selves have to contend with, a quickie mindset that has all but forgotten the concept of foreplay.

Personally, I have not subscribed or in any way been drawn to contemporary modes of spiritual realization and enhancement. The only mode that has worked for me has been the ancient teachings and examples of my predecessors, from personalities in the scriptures to personalities in my own lifetime who have taught me by the example of the quality of their consciousness and of their spiritual practice in daily life. Virtually all of the ancient teachings about how to live a spiritually rich life have been accompanied by real-life examples of real people, whether it is a story about a great Jewish master like Rabbi Shim'on ben Lakish or about a non-Jewish goat herder like Damma ben Nesina. The Talmud is nondiscriminatory about its choice of examples when it comes to teaching about spirituality because spirituality is not synonymous with religion nor is it dependent upon religion nor determined by religion nor defined by religion. It is defined by action, by how you choose to live your every moment. "I call to witness the sky and the earth," declared an ancient rabbi, "that anyone can acquire the Holy Spirit, be they man or woman, freeman or slave, Jew or non-Jew—everything is determined by one's actions" (Midrash Tana D'Bei Eliyahu, ch. 9). Joseph Campbell put it this way: "Religion often gets in the way of religious experience." Or, as Abraham Joshua Heschel wrote: "The prophets were those who in the name of God stood up against that which most people to this very day call religion" (*God in Search of Man*, pp. 230–231).

The best path to a deep Jewish spirituality is to study the rich treasure of anecdotes about the early masters that fill the pages of the Talmud and Midrash, that fill the pages of Buber's *Tales of the Hasidim*, or Elie Wiesel's *Souls on Fire*, that fill the pages of my memory of my father, of my grandmother, of my ninety-year-old Rosh Yeshiva back in Jerusalem. Their inspiration is so piercing that it lays out for me a path in a way that is far more clear to me than books and workshops and seminars. Our best teachers are our stories. Our whole faith is predicated not on creeds and principles of beliefs but on stories. Without those stories, Judaism would have been for me freeze-dried, badly needing water added and to be stirred. "More precious are the conversations of the servants of the households of the ancestors than the Torah of the descendants" (Midrash B'reishis Rabbah 60:11).

As for "commandments," I don't think God cares whether you tear toilet paper on Shabbat or not. Rabbis do. The instructions of the Torah are meant as means, not ends, guidelines, lessons, road maps. They are there to help us, not hinder us. This is not my bent on it, but the perspective of our ancient teachers, in fact the very teachers who elaborated and interpreted the "commandments." I cite myriads of samples of this in my book *The Way of the Boundary Crosser*. As Abraham Joshua Heschel put it: "The fact remains that, as central as is law, only a small part of the Bible deals with the law" (*God in Search of Man*, p. 324).

Just as some Jews get too hooked on the law, a lot of people today are hooked on the promises by contemporary spiritual salespeople of solutions, personal success, power, growth, miracles, etc. Many people want out of their immediate failures and problems, and so-called spirituality promises them exactly that. Sometimes that promise is made in brochures, sometimes it is made not by the teachers or retreats or seminars but by the seekers themselves who are under the false illusion that spirituality is some kind of magical instant cure for whatever ails them, that all they need is a sweat lodge ceremony or a shamanic drum journey, and "poof!" they're saved. This is the limit of those who talk about equanimity without addressing the larger social realities.

At the same time, the gift of contemporary spirituality is that it has reversed the trend to ignore the individual for the so-called higher good of the collective. Inner peace of mind is essential to transforming the larger social environment. My personal tumult reverberates across the planet, wreaking havoc of unimaginable proportions, sort of like the theory of the butterfly flapping its wings causing a breeze which swells into a typhoon somewhere thousands of miles away.

At least in Judaism, this form of spiritual focus has always been essential. The Torah pushes for individual awareness no less than it does for communal responsibility and participation. As a nation, we were headed for the "promised land," our land promised to our ancestors and to us. Yet, there was enough individual space in our nationhood for the tribes of Reuven and Gad to choose to not settle in Israel but to remain on the eastern bank of the Jordan (Numbers, ch. 32). In the frenzy of nationalism the individual was never to be lost. In time of war, the officers pushed through the throngs of military recruits exempting all those who had just gotten married but hadn't lived with their brides at least a year, those who'd planted vineyards but hadn't had a chance to savor the fruits of their labors, those who'd just built themselves new houses but hadn't had a chance to actually live in them, those who were afraid, and so on. "If I am not for myself," taught Hillel, "then who is for me? And if I am only for myself, then what am I?" (Babylonian Talmud, Avot 1:14). I am important, and so is my community, my planet. There is a way to dance to the music of both, a way to respond to the needs of either without neglecting neither. The tribes of Reuven and Gad settled outside of Israel, but their able-bodied men joined the nation in settling the promised land before returning to Jordan to set up house (Joshua 22:1–4 and 9–10).

In my experience in spiritual work, people can move from a focus on inner work to community social action and vice versa. For some of us, involvement in social change catapulted us into involvement in our inner spiritual life, and for others of us it was our focus on our inner spiritual life that led us to involvement in social change. Each of us needs a different kind of stimuli, a different kind of springboard to do our process.

I live in an area of the southwestern United States that has some similarities to parts of the Third World. In this area many people still remain very much connected to all life as part of a single, delicate web of balance, requiring therefore that one's inner spiritual work be deemed as critical as any external social endeavor. In the world that I live, I find that people are nurtured in their inner spiritual life very much by the land, by their very intimate relationship with the earth, which, in turn, spurs them toward social involvement in a way that is positive and compassionate. They don't seek social change necessarily, only social responsibility, and it is this that they strive to convey to their children.

Rabbi Yisroel Meir Kagan was my father's teacher back in the old days when he left the safe confines of Denmark to study Torah in Russia. Reb Yisroel put it this way: "We're only here for the weekend." That is my mantra. My spiritual practice, it follows, is then about stepping out of the whirlwind of daily routine three times a day minimum to behold the magic of the ordinary, the gift of the moment, and to live in awe of the mystery of my weekend here.

Healing the planet, I feel, cannot happen by becoming overly anxious and paranoid about global warming and global this and global that and all that doomsday stuff. That will not heal the planet. The planet is alive and as such she needs as much joyfulness and celebration for her healing as any of us. We need to spend more time celebrating her than we do lamenting her. Our story is about how the whole earth went to pot but all it took was one family's faith in life and in the world to resurrect her. It was Noah and Na'amah and their kin. It took nothing else. This is what we need to get back to today—each of us needs to become Noahides and reconstruct our arks, our faith in the preciousness of existence, and to celebrate it.

I see two forms of spirituality, internal and external. Internal spirituality is something each of us carries in our suitcase as we do our walkabout on this planet. When we find ourselves lacking it, we need only peek inside our Samsonite or remember that we're schlepping one. So when you feel burdened with a heavy heart, a weighty mind, think of it as what it is: your spirituality. Without it, life would be a breeze, completely inconsequential, superfluous, meaningless, irrelevant, and you would go desperately looking for a tree of forbidden fruit to eat from so that you could get catapulted into the real world. External spirituality is different. It's more like take-home food. You go to a retreat, a seminar, a class, a rebbe, a guru, a medicine woman, get some spark from their flame to supplement your own, but then you need to take it home and add your own spice and digest it from your own dishes and with your own utensils. Too many seekers leave their food at the restaurant or gobble it up too quickly while on the run.

Still, one can learn from others. So here is what I recommend for your spiritual diet. In film, I would highly recommend "Laurel and Hardy" films, the earliest of Woody Allen's works, and all the "Pink Panther" movies with Peter Sellers. I recommend two of my most recent books: *The Place Where You Are Standing is Holy* and *The Way of the Boundary Crosser*. I also recommend Michael Lerner's *Jewish Renewal: A Path to Healing and Transformation*, which I feel is an important guidebook to the quality of spiritual and social consciousness that is not only the kernel of what has become Jewish renewal but is also an important work that I hope will remain repeated reading for generations to come, sort of an alarm clock that comes with batteries and a built-in battery charger. Reb Zalman Schachter-Shalomi's *Paradigm Shift* is a vital backdrop for anyone attempting to spark renewal in their lives, hearts, communities, and general spiritual practice and consciousness. But still I personally prefer silly movies to any books, including my own. What contemporary spirituality lacks probably more than anything else is humor. If we can't laugh at the folly of being human and at the cosmic clowning around that goes on around us constantly, then what is the point of being spiritual? As the second-century Rabbi Shim'on bar Yochai said to Rabbi Abba: "The deepest wisdom can come only from silliness" (Zohar, vol. 3, p. 47b).

The Woman in the Balcony

On Reading the Song of Songs

Daphne Merkin

I.

Everyone lies about sex, more or less, to themselves if not to others, to others if not to themselves, exaggerating its importance or minimizing its pull.

Perfect sex is like some Platonic essence, taking place only in our heads, safe from the incursions of an always-blemished reality. Sexual reality demands that we bury our erotic disappointments and leads us to credit a moment's tremorous fulfillment with the whole earth-shaking shebang. We cannot experience sex in situ, except as it is acted upon us, and we can only imagine the erotic life of others. As befits the workings of fantasy and guesswork, the mythology of sex tends toward florid stereotypes: Men in general are supposed to prefer their sex served straight up—like a strong drink, without the diluting agent of affection. Lower-class men are supposed to be either quick and unsubtle or, like Lady Chatterly's lover and the shepherd in the Song of Songs, unexpectedly gifted in the sensual arts. Then there are rich men, gone soft with too many pleasures, men on the order of King Solomon, who chase skirts frenetically, showering gold coins, but who ultimately lose out to poorer and more potent rivals.

Women, the whole lot of us, are a mystery, insistently confounding. ("What do women want?" Even Freud threw up his hands.) Supposedly incapable of sex without intimacy—of physical ardor without at least the whisper of love—we insist from time to time on following our baser instincts and thereby put the whole tentative patriarchal order in jeopardy. Just look at Eve. Ignoring the compliant Adam's lead, she bit covetously into the infamous apple and thereby sundered carnal and spiritual desires forever.

Throughout my piece, I have referred to three translated versions of the Song of Songs: the Anchor Bible, the Soncino, and the Jewish Publication Society. In

105

each case, I chose the specific translation that struck me, purely subjectively, as most in the spirit of the original Hebrew.

When speaking of erotic matters it seems we are always at pains to guard against gender anxiety, to differentiate between subject and object, between the he and the she: who's on top and who's on bottom. From biblical times through the present secular moment, the power play of lust—frivolous but telling—remains a constant if encoded theme. A strict division of behavior along male (designated as active) and female (designated as passive) lines runs like a hidden thread in the Judeo-Christian narratives that have been passed along, pulling them tight against homosexual and/or androgynous encroachment. (This is in distinct opposition to the construction of morality put forward by the ancient Greeks and Romans, wherein boys and women were treated as interchangeable objects of male desire, with the former culture glorifying homosexuality and the latter accepting it as a matter of course.) Thus, down the slope of religious history it is unmanly to seek fulfillment where none is forthcoming, but it is just like a woman to long for what she cannot have.

Accordingly we have had in the Judaic formulation of the world which was the only one of the archaic civilizations to prohibit homosexuality per se—clearly demarcated territories: The godhead is kept rigorously unanthropomorphized, while the sexes are kept in their places at opposite ends of the seduction equation as the sorely tempted male and the dangerously blandishing female. There have naturally been some lapses or detours along the way—most notably the kabbalistic strategy of investing the Jewish concept of divinity with erotic power, leading to a "restitution of primordial androgyny," as Elliot K. Ginsburg suggests in his essay "Jewish Mysticism." But the kabbalistic mode, which embraced mysticism and its attendant sacral devices, calls attention to itself by the very audacity with which it went against the mandated principles of the religion it sought to invigorate.

Enter the Shulamite, whoever she be, love object or subject, bestride (or ridden by?) this frisky colt of a text—canonical glitch or deliberate oversight, Jewish original or Persian derivative, holiest of holies or pure, unadulterated smut—called, with arrant hyperbole, the Song of Songs. Enter the dusky-skinned Shulamite ("I am black but comely," Song of Songs 1:5) filled with boundless longing, just like a woman.

Or is she, in fact, just like a man? The pinprick of gender anxiety haunts the reader almost from the moment one begins reading this most sacrosanct piece of erotica.

Marcia Falk, a feminist biblical scholar, in the introduction to her audacious, albeit meticulously researched translation of the Song, points out that "there is hardly a trace of coherent plot" and that "the voices do not conform to masculine and feminine stereotypes." All the ordinary mooring points of identity are so tentatively established in this famous love poem—a dramatic dialogue with remarkably diffuse boundaries—that the reader is left feeling deeply uncertain as to exactly who is doing the talking, much less what sex the person is.

This first sliver of doubt brings others in its wake, revolving around the basic dyad of Self and Other upon which the enigma of amorous choice is based: Are you me, am I you, are you there, are you gone, are you worthy, are you ridiculous, who is the male (i.e., dominant-aggressive) and who is the female (i.e, subordinate-receptive)? Who is the lover and who is the loved? Indeed the emotional lability of the writing—all in a dither over the Other, but the Other as representative of aspects of the Self—is so omnipresent that one could easily imagine it being presented, in another context, as psychiatric evidence of dangerous symbiotic yearnings on the part of two mental patients, the "David and Lisa" of biblical times.

It is one of the givens of literary interpretation that there will be, inevitably, almost as many perceived contexts as readers, and what looks like signs of pathology to one reader may seem indicative of the greatest psychological health to another: Turn unhealthy symbiosis on its head, in other words, and you end up with blissful mutuality.

Feminist biblical critics, ever on the lookout for hidden textual persuaders, have been quick to adduce progressive—that is, antipatriarchal—signs from the Song's suppleness, or sexual amorphousness; there is, among this crowd, glowing talk of the narrative's "egalitarianism," as if its author, unbeknownst to him/her, was a hoary prototype of the contemporary jargon-infused orthodox-feminist redactor . . . er, reader.

So you have an academic reader like Ilana Pardes, in an essay full of opaque, Bakhtinian-inspired theoretical stratagems ("'I am a Wall, and My Breasts like Towers': The Song of Songs and the Question of Canonization"), referring to the Song's "metaphoric fluidity, whereby the lovers use the same vehicles to interpret one another in their cocourting [*sic*]." With similar pyrotechnic ease at overlooking time warps and bending a given text to her will as a reader, the French psychoanalytic critic Julia Kristeva, in an essay entitled, "A Holy Madness: She and He," comments passingly on "the listless quality of the woman lover," only to go on, rather confusingly, to hold said listless lover up as a domestic woman warrior: "The amorous Shulamite is the first woman to be sovereign before her loved one. Through such a hymn to the love of the married couple, Judaism asserts itself as a first liberation of women!"

Of course, the hunger of female Bible scholars to find some trace of their own predicament in the onion-peel layering of the Old Testament is entirely understandable. Marcia Falk, in her author's note, explains that her "growing need . . . as a woman and Jew, for sources more directly connected to my own origins led me in search of Hebrew literature that included the authentic voices of women." This need helps explain why Falk seems compelled to locate in this perplexing artifact echoes of her own concerns—although she's just gotten through admitting that the poems don't offer much in the way of gender specificity, much less validation. To this wishful end she distorts, however eruditely, parts of the original material beyond recognition on more than one occasion. There is, for instance, the implausible opening line of stanza 13 as Falk renders it—"At night in bed, I want him"—which suggests the zipless fuck was invented way before Erica Jong came along to coin the phrase. It also explains how like-minded readers have managed to hear a sanguine "collective female voice" in the "daughters of Jerusalem" to whom the Shulamite addresses her warnings about love, in spite of the fact that these unwilling soul sisters are as likely to jeer at the Shulamite's advice as to applaud it: "What is your beloved above another, / O fairest of women, / What is your beloved above another, that you thus adjure us?"

Perchance one can discern in the Shulamite's predicament an early instance of sexual harassment, replete with unconscious racist overtones. . . . So long as we are merrily throwing caution and credibility to the winds, we might as well go a step farther. Who knows but that biblical times had their wily subversives just as we do—their Princes and Madonnas who had a say along with the clean-living, God-fearing, Pat Boone types. What if this most famous of love poems, preserved in the alembic of a deeply paternalistic tradition that is yet canny enough to give the opposition its due, constitutes a stab to the heart of the very androcentric religion in which it nestles? "His hands are rods of gold / Studied with beryl; / His belly a tablet of ivory, / Adorned with sapphires." Any putatively male love object described with such a decided lack of virility and such a decidedly female sense of adornment presents ripe territory for study. Could it be that what we have before us is nothing less than a daringly prescient ode to bisexuality? "The Male Lover as Odalisque: Gender Inversion" in the Song of Songs. Chills run through one at the exegetical possibilities such a hypothesis would open up, whole graduate departments trained to spot the semiotics of kinky doings in the late biblical period.

II.

There is, patently, nothing straightforward about the Song of Songs. Even before you get to the text itself—one of the five megilot included in the Ketuvim, or writings, section of the Tanakh—you encounter controversy. While the late historian Gerson D. Cohen has argued that "the Song of Songs has suffered basic neglect in modern scholarship," Marvin Pope begins his introduction to his thickly appended translation for the Anchor Bible series with the following observation: "No composition of comparable size in world literature has provoked and inspired such a volume and variety of comment and interpretation as the biblical Song of Songs."

Then there is the vexed issue of authorship. The time-honored conservative view, which attributes the poems to King Solomon, has an undeniable (if unprovable) logic to it. Who better to pen poems with a prurient undertone than the Bible's own homegrown voluptuary? Less tradition-bound scholars have tended toward a looser theory of authorship, though there is little consensus as to which reconstruction is the most persuasive. In the past generation or two, as the field of biblical criticism has come into its own and its methodology has been refined, a wide variety of historical influences have been discerned in the poems, each in turn cast aside as soon as a tantalizing new lead presents itself. Parallels have been found with Syrian nuptial customs (specifically the mode of celebratory description known as the *wasf,*) Mesopotamian fertility cults, Tamil love poems (which feature another swarthy beauty at their center), the Gita-Govinda, Hindu hymns celebrating the dark-skinned goddess Kali, and a brief Akkadian text. Then there is the smorgasbord approach, alluded to by Pope, which views the Song as "a syncretistic torrent from a variety of springs from different cult areas, Canaanite, Byblian and Babylonian."

Along with Ecclesiastes, Proverbs, and Psalms, this slim collection of verses—also known as the Canticle—occupies a much-disputed position in the biblical canon; the book has inspired a flurry of interpretive strategies bent on controlling if not outright dousing the fiery passion contained within. These strategies have themselves been looked upon with a suspicious eye: Gershom Scholem, for instance, in his *Origins of the Kabbalah*, cites one Meir of Narbonne, who, in the 1240s, thought that "the commentary on the Song of Songs deserved to be destroyed in order to prevent simple souls from being ensnared by it."

The response of simple souls has occasionally surfaced in stray remarks—such as the one by Samuel Ibn Tibbon, who is said to have heard from his father, Moses (himself the author of an elaborate commentary on the Song, written sometime in the Middle Ages, which explained the text as representing a union of active and passive intellects), that the Song of Songs was merely a love poem. Still, fears of the common reader's misjudging the book are rife: Rabbi Akiba is quoted as saying, "He who trills his voice in chanting the Song of Songs in the banquet house and treats it as a sort of song has no part in the world to come." Staunchly defended as the "holiest of holies" by none less than Rabbi Akiba (also known for indulging himself in the farther shores of mystical speculation and emerging with his belief unscathed), the book remains a strange contender for inclusion and has generally been conceded to be a bit rich for less-than-sophisticated palates. "It is like a lock," observed Sa'adya Gaon in the early tenth century, "whose key is lost or a diamond too expensive to purchase."

Reader, in other words, beware. But who can resist a challenge? The intelligentsia least of all. Precisely because of the difficulties it poses, the Song of Songs is beloved of theorists, traditional and nouveau alike. The postmodernists, especially, warm to its "charming confusion," as Pope calls it. And with good reason: If ever there was a narrative cut to fit the current fashion in dense literary speculation, this one qualifies. Various special-interest groups—be they religious, deconstructionist, or feminist—have tried to get in on a piece of the heterodoxical action, all laying claim to a unique relationship with this avowedly independent-minded text, all attempting to fudge the question: How did so conspicuously ungodly a composition—a piece of undeniable erotica, filled with enough sexual punning ("Your lips drip honey, bride," or, "Let my love enter his garden. / Let him eat its delectable fruits," Song of Songs 4:11,16) to make Shakespeare blush—slip by the defenders of the faith, the old men with beards?

And then, like dominoes toppling, a whole slew of questions comes in the wake of that first one: How could the rabbis of the first and second centuries have failed to sound the alarms and allow the Song to secure for itself a sanctified niche, right up there with the creation of the world and the destruction of the Second Temple? Were they duped into stretching the category of sanctity wide enough to let in a bastard text? Or did they discreetly look away, recognizing that a religion based on 613 commandments could do with a little leavening, a welcome touch of sensuality?

What is clear in any event is that it is well-nigh impossible for the contemporary reader to approach the Song of Songs in a virginal spirit; the book's fame—or, more rightly, infamy—as the *I Am Curious, Yellow* of Jewish literature precedes it.

III.

The notion of the taboo in Jewish thought has always struck me as hazy, underdeveloped in its implications.

Unlike Catholicism, a religion that comes with a firmly entrenched sense of sin—and a concomitant sense of atonement—Judaism makes, perhaps, insufficient fuss about the mysteries of the flesh. In the Old Testament everything is handled in a matter-of-fact, so-called "naturalistic" fashion, from Noah's drunken near-incest with his daughters, to David's wandering eye, to Kohelet's sexual malaise. This inclination to regard the promptings of the id with a certain bemused tolerance is true of rabbinic literature as well: If a man can't handle his urges, advises the Talmud, he should go to a neighboring town and seek relief. It is important to note, in any discussion of the Judaic treatment of eros, that it is the only religion that historically had no specific sexual rites. As Gerson D. Cohen has been credited with observing, the love of the couple sanctified by the law has always been at the core of the Jewish stance toward lust and its consequences. This emphasis on demystifying the erotic by placing it in an ongoing conjugal context is a canny and subtle one; without fully disavowing its power, the focus on situating sexuality within marriage works toward weakening the hold of the unattached woman, as well as the hold of the carnal in general. Yael S. Feldman, in an essay that maps out a psychoanalytic reading of the Bible, argues along these lines: "It is therefore no accident that the domestication of the sexual drive is a major theme throughout Genesis, rivaled only by the analogous gradual sublimation of the aggressive drive." If Judaism can be said to be about the contextual-ization of problematic drives, then anything that is inherently outside the law of religion—the wild landscape of eros for instance, a region without recog-nizable markings—must be brought inside and given boundaries.

Yet with all its emphasis on the connubial satisfaction of libidinal claims, there is in Jewish tradition a shrewd recognition that marital life and the busi-ness of ritual observance will not fully tame the stirrings of desire. So it seems entirely in keeping with this sense of realpolitik to allow the unrulier passions some representation. Which goes a long way to explaining the acceptance not only of the crazy-for-your-body lyrics of the Song but the groanings of the eponymous Kohelet, who, with his nihilism and decadence, might have found greater outlet for his frustrations had he lived in the latter half of this century.

But leave it to the rabbis to gyp us hapless readers. See them wink know-ingly at one another behind their *s'forim*, their big black books of learning, getting ready to renege on their offer. Watch as they pat themselves on the back for their sense of embracing irony about the human animal, stuck for-ever between the worldly and the transcendent. The rabbis—of whom it can be said, as the critic George Steiner said of Freud, that they had "a mastering bias toward solutions"—were, after all, stuck themselves between appeasing the more absolutist among their constituency and keeping the less inflexible of their followers within the fold by attending to their wishes. And so we are handed a bill of exchange in which a Shulamite virgin is meant to stand in for Israel and a tumescent Solomon is meant to stand in for God, their passion to be acknowledged but never gratified. (Renunciation as a form of holiness is something those sniffy non-Jews Henry James and Edith Wharton would surely have cottoned to.) What at first might have appeared to be a blistering piece of amatory literature turns out to be, via the magic of hermeneutics, a dutiful homiletic; instead of gaping at a skin flick we find ourselves watching a video made for the annual synagogue dinner.

How like a people who have God in the head to insist that God is in their loins too!

IV.

I have never been a true believer, not even as a child brought up in an Orthodox Jewish family. For one thing, I never understood my role in the religiously ordained hierarchy, other than to mutely observe and admire. I think of myself on Saturday mornings, standing in the women's balcony with my mother and two sisters, at a careful remove from the men's club going great guns downstairs. All those patriarchs and their sons busily thumping around with the Torah, carrying it aloft and singing its praises, opening and closing the curtain of the Aron Hakodesh, the Holy Ark, where the Torah scrolls were stored, or officiously dispensing *aliyot*, calling up young and old to the *bima*, the raised platform in the center, for a bit of momentary glory. That club included my father and three brothers, included anyone who wasn't female and excluded anyone who was: me, for instance, blusher carefully applied (rub it in, my mother would insist on the way to *shul*), the essence of self-conscious, unblossomed girlhood.

At what point did I stop listening to the text of the service, my years of Jewish day school and immersion in Hebrew endured for naught, the better to concentrate on the subtext—the palpable sexual tensions I sensed around me in the synagogue? All those dolled-up women, dressed and made up to kill, their eyes like doves, their hair as black as goats, their teeth like a flock of ewes all shaped alike, their lips like woven threads of crimson silk, their breasts like twin fawns. Why did they gleam and glisten so, I wondered, only to be cordoned off from the objects of their ministrations: the men downstairs, who cast appreciative glances upward and then went back to their noisy activities?

The burden of sexuality—both its allure and its danger—is placed on women, this much I see. Can it be that if the men venture upstairs, come too close to the expensive scents wafting through the women's balcony, they'll be bewitched, throw their marital vows out the window? Perhaps they'll cheat or, worse yet, leave their wives and families altogether; perhaps they'll go crazy with fleshly greed. Down the corridors of my mind, doors open upon a flurry of long-ago, briefly glimpsed images, scenes from a synagogue on the Upper East Side of Manhattan: sudden divorces and shamefully short marriages; older, prosperous husbands paired with younger, blond wives; trade-ins and -ups. The doors close, and order is restored. All is once again as it should be: We are here, the matriarchs and their daughters, stuck behind the *mechitza*, that inviolable dividing wall, whether balcony or curtain, consigned to an attitude of expectant readiness.

There are other questions that go unanswered because to ask them would be to imply that the bourgeois verities of life are up for grabs and thus their very asking is taboo. How interesting, really, is fulfilled desire? What happens, that is, after you get the girl, find yourself actually bedding the Shulamite? How sustainable is erotic passion once you place a ring upon its finger? How sustainable is erotic passion, period?

The Song of Songs is read aloud in synagogue at the end of the long eight-day Passover holiday. It is doubtful I was present to hear it at an age when I could most have appreciated its uniquely untheological nature; once I had put in an appearance in my spring finery on the first two mornings of the holiday, I generally forswore further shul duty. But even if I was to be found in my seat in the women's balcony, I doubt I was listening anymore by the time I could have grasped its message, the secret it clutched to itself, behind its reputation for smuttiness.

It would be years before I stumbled upon a true consideration of what that secret was, before I teased out that sexual desire is a lie we tell ourselves, more or less. Romantic enamorment is a fabrication that serves to conceal the immense relativity of all passion and the virtual invention of the love object. "How sustainable is erotic passion?" It was a question nobody asked because nobody wanted to know the answer. Tell the truth about it and you did so at your own peril, as I discovered when I heard the tale of my great-uncle, Raphael Breuer. Simple artistic soul that he was, he undertook in 1912 to write an interpretation of the Song based on literal rather than allegorical reading: It was, as Samuel Ibn Tibbon had hinted centuries before, merely a love poem. So strong was the reaction of the German-Jewish community of which he and his family were an influential part that Breuer not only had to rescind the introduction to his commentary but the gaffe is said to have cost him one of the most prestigious chief rabbinates in Germany.

And so, burdened by my particular history as a woman, I come to reacquaint myself with this infamously titillating text. How well will it live up to its reputation as the dirty, red-hot book of Jewish literature? I must admit that, after several readings to make sure I haven't somehow missed the climactic moment as I used to do when I read the late novels of Henry James, I don't find the poem particularly sexy. Resoundingly lyrical, yes; intimate and charming, undeniably; in the nature of an aphrodisiac, hardly. Perhaps it is the over-whelming rusticity of the amorous imagery—love that is like the crocus of the plain, the lotus of the valley, the apple in the wood; love that leaps over mountains and bounds over hills—that leaves me, a constitutionally urban creature without much direct experience of flora and fauna, at a loss. Perhaps it is all those trailing flocks of goats and ewes come up from the washing that give the narrative a faint whiff of barns and cow manure. I muse upon the possibility that allusions to the bestiary once carried a greater erotic charge than they do now. At any rate a zookeeper's vision of loveliness is not mine. Nor, for that matter, is a banker's; otherwise the persistently mercantile notion of comeliness that the Song advances—the lover's beauty is compared to gold, gems, ivory, sapphires, and marble—would undoubtedly move me more.

I find myself without sufficient frame of reference in the jumble of other metaphors as well. Lebanon. The tents of Qedar. Carmel. Clusters of grapes. More Lebanon. True, there is praise for a vulva that smells, improbably, of apples, but what is one to do with that piece of information?

Which leads me to the tale itself, rather than the telling. Goethe was supposed to have viewed the Song as "the most tender and inimitable expression of passionate yet graceful love that has yet come down to us." Nice words, although they still don't help me get a grip on the story.

Like, what exactly happens in it? I look ahead a couple of centuries and come upon this, from Kristeva: "The Song of Songs gives Judaism the unique trait of being the most erotic of abstractions, the most ideal of sensualities." Nice words again, although they leave me with a blurry feeling around the edges. All this obscure, high-flying description, and I'm beginning to feel like the proverbial Hollywood philistine who prefers his literary plots pitched in one sentence or less.

Here, for better or worse, is what I've made of this "enigmatic parable," as it's been called. Once you've put the credos aside, you're left slipping around in the liquid atmosphere of the text without a foothold. Interestingly enough, what almost all of the readings of the Song have in common is a notion of union, marital or merely consensual, presumed to be implicit within the poem itself. This interpretive bias can be discerned as much in the various secularist stances as in the religious-allegorical approach, which raises the bawdy goings-on of the poem to a spiritually correct level by treating Israel as the symbolic bride and God as the symbolic husband—a familiar sacral conceit, used by the prophets Hosea and Jeremiah.

But to this reader the whole predicating idea of a union is never quite persuasive, perhaps because the Shulamite never comes across as an actual breathing specimen of womankind, just as Solomon and his lowly shepherd rival never emerge as fully embodied malehood. The verses, I propose, speak not to the idea of union, either literal or metaphorical or, God help us, "depatriarchalized," but rather to its virtual opposite: the solitary, wholly interior churn of ambivalence, expectant desire entwined with melancholy longing. Inherent in the very nature of erotic presence is absence—the looming loss of the lover even as he/she is glimpsed.

How to "own" the love object, how to pin down another beyond the fleeting moment: The possibility of sexual gratification is at least as threatening as it is pleasing, with its inevitable shadowy denouement of withdrawal and further longing.

I choose, then, to think of the Song of Songs as a story about the risks of passion—about being a fool for love and all of that. A particularly overlooked aspect of the text, to my way of thinking, is its recognition of the lover's vulnerability. To fall in love is to open oneself up to potential ridicule. The Shulamite's thrice-repeated bleak admonition about the dangers of falling in love seems most significant in this regard: "I adjure you, O / daughters of / Jerusalem, / by the gazelles, and by the hinds of the field, / That ye awaken not, nor stir up love, / Until it please" (Song of Songs 8:4). Under its Zen-like absolutism, this refrain points to the fear of rejection implicit in all extensions of self. There is, too, the implied fear that once you've gone ahead and fastened your hopes on some designated other, the world will rush in with scabrous comparisons and invidious remarks of the "Who, him?!!" variety.

Radical as its inclusion in the canon of Holy Scriptures may appear to be, I suggest it is less surprising if one sees this amorous dialogue in the form of a warning—a prophylaxis, as Gerson Cohen calls it: Caution, ye seekers of passion, lest you end up lost and wandering, in a city with no name, reduced to calling on the help of anonymous and hostile "watchmen." Caution, in other words, lest you end up lovesick, shades of Truffaut's Adele H., the woman consigned to an unfulfillable longing for the absent, ever-fleeing male.

V.

The final section of the Song begins by alluding to the yearning for a preeroticized period in life in which a young boy is free to suckle on his mother's breast and a prepubescent girl ("Our sister is young / And breasts she has none") is free to kiss her brother without risk: "none would scorn me" (Song of Songs, 8:8). It is a curious scenario for a purportedly heavy-breathing amorous dialogue to end on, but an entirely reasonable conclusion for the conflicted, push-me/pull-you recitation—a monologue in several voices— that I take this text to be. Perhaps, with just the smallest of shifts in emphasis, we might read the Song of Songs as an internalized argument preceding the taking of romantic action, a sort of amplified version of Hamlet's famously indecisive soliloquy: To love or not to love, that is the question.

At the core of the Song of Songs, under all its waffling, is an erotics of restraint, even of stasis. Someone, a woman perchance, longs; someone else, a man perchance, responds, but is ultimately unattainable. It is a game, a lie, an elaborate ruse: A case for adult heterosexual passion is presented in the guise of two amorphously defined lovers who never come close to consummating their relationship. Once the dust the poem is designed to kick up has settled, its stark secret is revealed: Stay upstairs in the balcony, Shulamite woman, for withheld consummation is the best kind.

But even as I write this, it becomes clear to me that I am writing out of my own idiosyncratic tastes. As such, it must be pointed out that my imagination is drawn more to the prospect of erotic doom than to sensual rapture, to Jean Rhys and her abandoned boardinghouse creatures than to daredevil dames astride one stallion-lover-husband after another. It is, in the end, a matter of personal accounting whether any passion is worth the price of that passion. So, too, in the end, the Song throws one—in the most parodied of postmodernist theories of reading—upon oneself as Author.

It would seem, finally, that one brings to a text about love all that one was taught to read into it, an amorous imprint stretching back for generations: unto mothers and grandmothers, and behind them ancestors galore. Some of us are destined to exalt love and others to demonize it; some rise to its occasion and others shy away for reasons unknown even to themselves. Lineage counts—Noah was the son of x, the son of xx, the son of xxx—even in matters of the flesh and heart. What you recognize as the siren call of love I may fear as the siren call of imminent abandonment. Someone must have scared off the author of the Song of Songs in the porousness of childhood, whispering sweet messages of caution: "Bolt, my love / Be like a buck, / Or a young stag, / On the spice mountain" (v. 14).

A Kabbalah for the Environmental Age

Arthur Green

A longing for Kabbalah is abroad in the land. Even people with little connection to Judaism, no knowledge of Hebrew, many of them in fact non-Jews, are seeking initiation into the secret chambers of Jewish esoteric knowledge. Differing from the interest in Hasidism that centered mostly around Chabad in the preceding decades, this turn to Kabbalah has rather little to do with Jewish observance or with nostalgia for a romanticized *shtetl* past (a past that many denizens of "Kabbalah centers" in fact do not share). The Kabbalah seekers are after the Truth, with a capital T. That this Truth might also help them to solve personal problems, to predict the future, and to win fame and fortune are claims made only by the sleaziest part of the Kabbalah sales force.

Like all the waves of spiritual search that have struck our shores (the Pacific being hit with greater force than the Atlantic, for some reason), the contemporary interest in Kabbalah contains a wide range of seekers. The most serious spend long years at it, realizing that mastery of a complex teaching and way of thought does not come easily. Eventually, they realize that they have to study Hebrew. More than any other of the world's mystical teachings, Kabbalah is itself a language, constituted by wordplays, numerical computations, and meditations on letters, on names of God, and on strange readings of biblical verses—all of them rooted in the Hebrew. Others, who lack the time or patience to master the language as well as the secret doctrine, look for teachers who will distill the wisdom of the ancients in this unique Jewish garb.

Most of these seekers discover that we are no longer really Kabbalists. The old system, qua system, does not work for us. The mythic universe of Kabbalah, for all its beauty, belongs to another age. Whether we look at the hierarchical structure, at the Jewish spiritual superiority implied by Kabbalah, or at the passive-subject role assigned to the feminine, I for one do not believe

117

that a return to the mentality of the ancients is the proper solution to our current woes. Instead, our age is very much in need of a post-Kabbalistic Jewish mysticism, one richly nourished, but not dominated, by the old language and structure. Most importantly, we need a new sort of Jewish piety, a religious attitude fitting to an environmentally-concerned future that is already upon us. Among the elements I seek is a Judaism unafraid to proclaim the holiness of the natural world, one that sees creation, including both of the world and of the human self, as a reflection of divinity and a source of religious inspiration. It is in this spirit that I turn to Kabbalah, seeking to learn from, but also to adapt and transform, its vision. The insight that God and universe are related not primarily as Creator and creature, but as deep structure and surface, a central insight of the mystical tradition, is key to the Judaism of the future. But the ways in which we develop and act upon that insight will have to be appropriate to our own age.

The magnificent architectonics of the kabbalists' vision cannot be fully articulated here. Their grand picture of the inner universe, in which the One that encompasses all being opens up to reveal itself as ten, is the beginning of the kabbalistic system. The ten *sefirot* (literally: "numbers") are stations in the flow of energy from the One into the many. The ten-in-one cosmos is a way of responding to the eternal mystical question, "How do the many proceed from the One?" The kabbalists say: "Very slowly and subtly. Let us show you the process." As one gets further into Kabbalah, it turns out that each of the ten sefirot contains all the other nine and the whole process of tenfold manifestation repeats itself four times as one journeys through various upper or inner "worlds." There is thus a basic "grid" of four hundred rungs, each discussed with great finesse in the highly refined symbolic language of Kabbalah. Other versions of the kabbalistic "map" have the ten sefirot open themselves further to reveal more decades, becoming hundreds, thousands, and so forth.

For the initiate, the sefirot also serve as rungs or marking points of the mystic's inward journey. His goal (it only also can become "hers" in very recent times) is to reverse the journey of God from unity into multiplicity, going back to make the many into one again. The kabbalist who "ascends" those rungs ideally "uplifts" the lower worlds, taking them along on the journey back to oneness. In this way they, along with the mystic's own soul, may be reincluded in the one. This is the kabbalistic concept of *tikkun*, the restoration of the worlds to their original harmony as carried out in this "uplifting" activity of the mystical life. Each person is a microcosm, also built in the same pattern of the sefirot, so that cosmology and psychology, our ways of understanding life's origins and our own innermost selves, are quite identical. God's cosmic journey into multiplicity and your inward journey into unity are mirror images of one another.

This "great chain of being" approach to spirituality can be appreciated more than ever today, not only for its beauty but for a certain dimly perceived accuracy as well. Each human being contains the entire universe, claims the ancient myth. All the rungs of descent (and potential ascent) are contained in each soul. But that is true, even in demythologized form: all of our ancestors, each stage and mini-step in the evolution of life that brought us to where we are today, are present within us. The DNA that constitutes the life-identity of each of us exists indeed *zekher le-ma'aseh bereshit*, "in memory of the act of Creation," linking us back to our most remote origins.

Part of our work as self-aware, articulate beings is converting that biological "memory" into consciousness and building a holy structure (i.e., a religion or a civilization) that articulates and sanctifies those links. In this way, the actual fact of all our past's presence within us is converted into a basis for meaning, for expression of our deep rootedness in all that is and has come before us. The memory of the entire universe lies within us. Hopefully, the values represented by that ongoing project of civilization-building will lead us forward as well, helping us realize that we must be faithful transmitters to all the many future links in the evolutionary chain, just as we are the grateful recipients of the efforts of all those who have fought the ongoing life-struggle to bring us to this moment. All of the upper and lower "worlds" of the kabbalist here become manifest in human terms, as generations that lie before and behind us but also as multiple layers of human self-awareness that we seek to peel back in search of our deepest and truest selves.

But in order to constitute Judaism, the single structure of cosmos and mind has to constitute the inner structure of Torah as well. The old rabbinic version of correspondences claimed that the 613 commandments of Torah stand parallel to the 248 limbs and 365 muscles or sinews that comprise each human body (based on the knowledge of anatomy current in fourth- or fifth-century Babylonia!). The human being is thus a microcosm of Torah, itself the blueprint through which God created the cosmos. This structure is overlaid on the tenfold sefirotic structure of Kabbalah. Torah itself, according to the kabbalists, is an elaborate construction, a cosmic weave of letters drawn wholly out of the four simple letters of the name of God. At its heart lies the barely whispered breath of the four semi-consonants Yod He Waw He, the verbal noun that tries to express the divine Self. This name is an impossible conflation of the verb "to be"; hence the God of Exodus, where the name is introduced, says: "I shall be whatever I shall be," meaning that the elusive Self of the universe will ever escape definition. Those four letters are a term for being—HaWaYaH—itself. But because they are mere breath, they also stand for the birth of language, the emergence of the word from the universal silence beyond, from what we Jews call the eternal Torah of God, the wordless truth that "was" before Creation.

God *is* Being—Y-H-W-H—when existence is seen from a fully unitive, harmonic, and all-embracing point of view—a perspective that ever eludes us mere humans, located as we are in particular identities of time and space. The small self and its limitations keep us from seeing the great Self at work both within and around us. But then the letters, like pieces in a puzzle, are mysteriously re-arranged and HaWaYaH, existence itself, reveals itself to be none other than Y-H-W-H, the great and powerful name that could be spoken only by the high priest on Yom Kippur, alone in the innermost holy chamber of the holy Temple.

To create a Kabbalah for our times, we have to reach beyond the historical Kabbalah, back to the biblical tale of origins. The kabbalists' universe depends entirely on the much older biblical creation tale, the ingenious opening chapter of Genesis that for nearly twenty-five hundred years served as chief source for the West's understanding of natural, including human, origins. The account of how God in six days spoke each order of existence into being is now of only antiquarian interest as an actual account of how the world came to be, though it remains alive for us as a liturgical text and a source of mythic creativity. But I would like to lift the veil behind Genesis 1 and ask just what it was that this magnificently penned single chapter managed to accomplish.

The old Mesopotamian and Canaanite creation myths, now barely recalled, were well known to the biblical authors. They include the rising up of the primal forces of chaos, represented chiefly by Yam or Tiamat, gods of the sea, against the order being imposed by the sky gods. The defeat of that primordial rebellion and its bloody end is well documented, as scholars have shown, in a number of passages within the Bible: in the Prophets, Psalms, Job, and, by subtle implication, even in the Genesis text itself. That tale of origins was a part of the cultural legacy of ancient Israel. The fact that it is reflected even in post-biblical midrashic sources shows that it had a long life, continuing even into the Zohar of the thirteenth century. The original readers/hearers of Genesis 1, in other words, knew of another account of creation, one of conflict, slaughter, and victory, "the survival of the fittest" among the gods. What is striking about this account is precisely the absence of those elements of conflict: Genesis 1 offers a purely harmonistic version of the origin of creatures, one where everything has its place as the willed creation of the single Deity and all conflict has mysteriously been forgotten.

Our civilization has been transformed over the past century and a half in no small part by our acceptance of a new tale of origins, one that began with Darwin and is refined daily by the work of life-scientists and physicists. Scientists are the new kabbalists of our age, claiming even to know the black hole out of which being itself came to be, speculating on the first few seconds of existence as our ancestors once did on the highest triad of the ten sefirot, or rungs, of divine Being. The history of living creatures is again depicted as a bloody and violent struggle, the implications of which for human behavior — even for the possibilities of human ethics — have hardly gone unnoticed. We too are urgently in need of a new and powerfully harmonistic vision, one that will allow even the weakest and most threatened of creatures a legitimate place in this world and protection from being wiped out at the careless whim of the creature who stands, for now, at the top of the evolutionary mound of corpses. A beautiful attempt at articulating such a vision was made by Brian Swimme and Thomas Berry a few years ago in their *The Universe Story*. Such a vision more willing to base itself in part on the biblical/Judaic mythic legacy would also be a welcome contribution.

But let us return for a moment to the biblical Creation tale. While I no longer believe it in any literal sense and do not look to it, even through rein-terpretation (each "day" is a geologic era, and so on) as a source of informa-tion about geo-history, I claim it still as a religious text for me as a Jew and for us as a people. We still read it in the synagogue and its closing section is the introductory rubric for our most precious and best-beloved sacred form: the observance of the Sabbath. "Heaven and earth were finished, and all their hosts." What then does the text mean to me? What underlies the myth, or what truth or value am I implying by so privileging this ancient text?

The text says that before there were many, there was only the One. Before the incredible variety and richness of life as we know it could come to be, there had to exist a simple Self, a source from which all the many proceeded. I refer not to some single-celled amoeba that existed in the ocean hundreds of millions of years ago. I read the text on a different level by asserting that the primacy of the one to the many is not necessarily temporal in meaning. Sa-cred myth describes a deep and ineffable reality, one so profound that it is not given to expression except through the veil of narration, through encapsula-tion in a story. And stories, given the need for a sequential plot, require time. So the precedence of the One over the many, placed into story form, comes out sounding like: "In the beginning God created. . . ." Its meaning, however, is that the One *underlies* the many, then, now, and forever. A dimly perceived but awesome, deep structure links all things and ties them to the root out of which they all emerge. Multiplicity is the garbing of the One in the coat of many colors of existence, the transformation of Y-H-W-H, singularity itself, Being, into the infinite varieties of H-W-Y-H, being as we know, encounter, and *are* it.

The Genesis "creation" story is really a tale of the origins of multiplicity, a biblical attempt to answer that eternal question of mystics to which the later account of the sefirot was also addressed: "How do the many proceed from the One?" This reality is symbolized by the beginning of the Torah with the letter bet, long a subject of speculation within Jewish tradition. Bet is numerically "two"; its position at the beginning of Torah indicates that here is the beginning of duality. From now on there is not just "God" but "God and." This meaning is dramatically reinforced by the emergence of Creation in what are repeatedly described as pairs: light and darkness, day and night, heaven and earth, upper and lower waters, sun and moon, male and female, and all the rest. Behind all these twos, however, behind the bet of *bereshit bara'* ("In the beginning God created") lies the hidden, singular, silent aleph. This One, representing the absolute oneness of being, the One after which there is no "two," is to be proclaimed at Sinai in the opening letter of *anokhi*, "I am," the very heart of revelation.

This One, I believe, is the only Being that ever was, is, or will be. It is the One that undergoes the only sacred drama that really matters: the bio-history of the universe. I believe that it does so as a conscious and willful Self. From those first seconds of existence, through the emergence of life in its earliest manifestations, and along every step, including the seeming stumblings, missteps, and blind alleys along the way of evolution, it is this single Being that is evolving, entering into each new life form, ever carrying within itself the memory of all its past. The evolutionary process is here re-visioned not as the struggle of creature against creature and species against species, but as the emergence of a single life-energy, a single cosmic Mind that uses the comparative adaptabilities of all the forms it enters as a means of ongoing striving ever forward into richer and more diverse forms of life. The formless Self, which we call in Hebrew Y-H-W-H, searches out endless forms, delighting to rediscover its own identity anew in each of them. That constant movement of the One, expansive in all directions at once, is at the same time directed movement, pointing toward the eventual emergence of a life-form that can fully know and realize the One that lives in all beings. This creature, the one in whom the self-knowledge of Being can be ultimately fulfilled, is thus the telos of existence.

In this process, the emergence of humanity with its gifts of intellect, self-awareness, and language is indeed a major step forward. Judaism has always taught a distinction between humans and other forms of life, a sense in which the human stands beyond the vegetative and animal realms out of which we emerged. Each creature embodies the life-energy and hence the presence of the One, but only humans are called "God's image" in our tradition. This means that we are the first to have the mental capacity to recapitulate the process, to be self-conscious about our roots within the One. Exactly what the implications are of that potential can indeed be debated, but surely I do not mean to say that being in the Divine image gives us license for the rapacious destruction of all so-called "lower" forms. God forbid! Of the options provided within the Bible for defining humanity's role, I much prefer Psalm 148's vision of us as part of the universal chorus of praise over Genesis 1's version of us as the final creation of Friday afternoon, with the message of "stewardship" that accompanies it. A true understanding of the unitive vision being proclaimed here would lead us beyond the demands of "stewardship," the ethic usually derived from the biblical tale. Life's meaning is to be found in discovering the One, and that means realizing the ultimate unity of all being. It is in *yihud,* discovering and proclaiming the underlying oneness of all existence, that our humanity is fulfilled.

We are of the One; each human mind is a microcosm, a miniature replica of the single Mind that conceives and becomes the universe. To know that oneness and recognize it in all our fellow beings is what life is all about. But that recognition leads us to another level of awareness. The One *delights* in each of the infinite forms in which it is manifest. To play on that lovely English verb, this means that the One sends its *light* into each of these forms. Vegetative forms indeed experience this gift most in sunlight, stretching toward it as they grow. We humans are privileged to experience that same radiating light-energy as delight or love.

The One loves the many. The coat of many colors in which Being comes to be garbed is a garment of delight. We, as the self-conscious expression of Being, are called upon to love, as well as to partake in and give human expression to, the delightfulness of existence. This is expressed in Jewish liturgy in the order of daily blessings. The blessing of God as the source of nature's light is directly followed by a blessing for God's love. The One does nothing different in the interim between these blessings. It shines in delight at the eternal procession of "creatures" it comes to inhabit. Nature experiences this shining as light; we humans receive it as love. But as recipients of love we are called upon (dare I say "commanded?") to love as well.

I am also fully willing to admit that we may be at but an early stage in an ongoing evolution of aware beings. Perhaps our period will be looked upon in the distant future by creatures no more willing to demean themselves by the word "human" than we are comfortable being called "ape" as a primitive life-stage. Surely they will not be wrong, those wise beings of the future, in seeing our age as characterized by nothing so much as pretentiousness and self-glorification on the one hand, and wanton consumption and pillage of the earth's resources on the other. Let us hope that we leave room for that wise future to emerge.

Discovering the presence of the One within the natural order and therefore the sacred quality of existence itself is exactly what our father Abraham did, according to Philo of Alexandria, the hidden grandfather of all Jewish philosophy. This One manifested itself to him in terms of law: Abraham felt that he was being taught how to live in harmony with the forces of nature. Moses' Torah, according to Philo, is the lawgiver's attempt to legislate for a whole human community the life of harmonic insight with the God of nature that Abraham had already found for himself. I have tried to show elsewhere that certain writings of the Hasidic masters, unaware of the ancient precedent, continue this trend. Levi Yizhak of Berdichev, the eighteenth-century Hasidic master, introduces his treatise on hidden miracles, or the miraculous within nature, with precisely this claim: Sinai allows the entire people to apprehend that which wise old Abraham had already long earlier discerned on his own.

The law that teaches us how to live in harmony with the natural world stands in place of the old system of 613 specific correspondences between Torah and self. As Torah, it too should be one of eternal principles and countless new applications. Its most basic teachings should demand of us that we live ever at the cutting edge of sensitivity toward the suffering we cause God's creatures. We need be aware of the rest and reinvigoration that we give to the soil, the waste of living resources, for each is the embodiment of divine presence. We may not take the endless material gifts with which we are blessed any more casually than we would take God's name in vain. We may not take the One's great gift of holy water in vain. Or air, source of *nishmat kol hai*, the sacred breath of life.

To rest on the laurels of forms our ancestors created long ago or boast of their progressivism in the tenth or sixth century BCE is very much not to the point. What is the point of observing *shemitah,* the sabbatical year, but using earth-destroying pesticides? Of insisting on the humanity of *shechitah,* kosher slaughter, but hoisting and shackling and refusing to stun animals to lessen their awareness before they die? Of washing the bugs out of our lettuce while investing our greenbacks in multinationals that daily destroy entire forests? The challenge before us is to be as aware and insightful for our times as the Torah was in its day. How can we today create a civilization and a law that will be such a *torat hayyim,* a teaching that enhances life? And what will it demand of us? Surely a return to the reverence for air, water, fire (by limiting the amount that we, including our automobiles, burn!), and soil would be a good place to start.

Another potentially useful rubric within tradition for proclaiming this insight is the parallel between the ten divine utterances (of "let there be . . .") in Creation and the ten "commandments" (the Hebrew might be better rendered as "speech-acts") of Sinai. The presence of the One that underlies all being is depicted as pure verbal energy: God is the One who ever, unceasingly, says "*Yehi!*" ("Let there be!"), speaking the world into being. At Sinai, those ten yehis are translated into imperatives for us; the inner "law" of God's presence in nature is now manifest in the form of imperatives that can govern human existence, bringing us into harmony with the ten words within ourselves as well as within all creatures. And since the ten "commandments" are the basis of all the 613 "yeas" and "nays" that comprise Torah, all of it is tied through them to the ten cosmogenerative utterances of the One. This parallel is a great favorite of certain mystical teachers. Creation and revelation are two deeply interrelated manifestations of the same divine Self, one showing us that all existence is fraught with holiness, the other instructing us on how to live in the face of that awareness.

Here the language of Kabbalah may be useful again. These two tens, the utterances and the commandments, are both versions of the ten sefirot, those primal numbers that allowed us deeper entré into the "secret" of existence. The sefirot may still serve as a vehicle for meditation and as a channel for uplift and integration, as we seek out the hidden One within all existence. We manifest that secret by turning outward and inward toward the world around us, seeing it in all its awesome beauty and recognizing how deeply we are a part of all that is. We then ask (in good Jewish fashion): "What does this awareness demand of us?" Here we have the beginning point of a new Kabbalah and a new Halachah ("path" of religious practice) as well. This praxis, one using and adapting the rich forms of Jewish tradition, should be one that leads us to a life of harmony with the natural world and maximum concern for its preservation.

All this talk must seem terribly mythical to readers of a more scientific bent of mind. Perhaps it also seems obscure and irrelevant to some of those most keenly aware of the several immediate threats to global existence. Let me assure you that I share that sense of urgency. Life has so evolved that the fate of the biosphere itself is now determined by human actions. We are masters not only over our own species but also over those we consume, as so many others have been. The very existence of our planet as a fit habitat for any living thing has now fallen into human hands.

With this increase in human power comes a manifold increase of responsibility. It is the future not only of our own offspring that we threaten each day with a million decisions weighted with political, economic, and competitive baggage. The land itself, the *adamah* from which we humans derive our name, is threatened by us, the earth and all that is upon it. The changes needed in collective human behavior in order to save us from self-destruction are stupendous. Belief in their possibility stretches our credulity as much as it is demanded by our need for hope. Our economic system, including the value we place on constant expansion and growth, will have to change. The standards of consumption, created by our wealthiest economies and now the goal of all others, will have to be diminished. Effective world government, perhaps even at the cost of some of our precious freedoms, will have to triumph over the childish bickerings and threats that currently characterize world affairs.

Hardly believable, indeed. But consider the alternative. If any of this deep-seated change is to come about, religious leaders and thinkers need to take an early lead. A seismic shift in the mythical underpinnings of our consciousness is required; nothing less will do the trick. That shift will have to come about within the framework of the religious languages now spoken by large sections of the human race. Experience tells us that newly created myths do not readily take hold; they usually lack the power to withstand great challenge. But a rerouting of ancient symbols, along channels already half-cleared by the most open-eyed thinkers of earlier centuries, might indeed enable this conversion of the human heart of which we speak.

In the emergence of a new tale of origins, we Jews, who have for so long been bearers of the old tale, have a special interest. The new tale will need to achieve its own harmony, summarized with no less genius than was possessed by the author of Genesis 1. It will need to tell of the unity of all beings and help us to feel that fellow creaturehood with trees and rivers as well as with animals and humans. As it brings us to awareness of our common source, ever present in each of us, so must it value the distinctiveness and sacred integrity of each creature on its own, even the animals, or fish, or plants we eat, even the trees we cut down. If we Jews are allowed to have a hand in it, it will also speak of a human dignity that still needs to be shared with most of our species and of a time of rest, periodic liberation from the treadmill of our struggle for existence, in which we can contemplate and enjoy our fellow feeling with all that is. This sacred time also serves as a model for the world that we believe "with perfect faith" is still to come, a world of which we have never ceased to dream.

Quantum Cosmology and Kabbalah

Joel R. Primack

Modern cosmology—the scientific study of the universe as a whole—no longer sees the universe as an infinite, changeless arena in which events take place, the way Isaac Newton did. The universe is an evolving, expanding being, and its origin is the oldest mystery. For the first time in possibly a million years of human wondering, we are not simply imagining the beginning: We are observing it, in radiation that has been traveling to us since the Big Bang, possibly bearing information generated even earlier. Theorists are piecing the data together into humanity's first verifiable creation story.

Most educated people today have an essentially Newtonian picture of the universe as a place, devoid of all human meaning, in which we happen to find ourselves. If people come to understand the emerging scientific cosmology, however, they may see from what we know of the early universe that we actually are part of an extraordinary adventure. With its mind-expanding imagery, this emerging cosmology gives us a new cosmic perspective, a powerful source of awe, and a potential source of meaning in our everyday lives.

We will present the cosmological theory first directly, and then as if it were a creation myth, which it is. But here we encounter the limitations of the English language for the task: the universe is like nothing else. It's not a thing that exists at any point in time but includes within it all time and all concepts. We will therefore turn to Kabbalah, medieval Jewish mysticism, as a possible source of language and metaphor, because certain kabbalistic concepts fit our picture amazingly well. Moreover, Kabbalah's cosmology gave meaning and purpose to the everyday lives of its adherents, which we hope may become possible with the scientific cosmology emerging today.

THE LARGE-SCALE STRUCTURE OF THE UNIVERSE

While Newton believed that stars are randomly distributed through space, we now know that stars are organized into galaxies, and distant galaxies are flying away from each other as space expands. About 10 percent of galaxies are in dense clusters, with many clusters linked by sheets or free filaments of galaxies. Our own galaxy, the Milky Way, is located in a small group of galaxies on the outskirts of the large sheet of galaxies (the local supercluster) in which the Virgo Cluster is embedded. On the scale of billions of light years, there are millions of these enormous superclusters of galaxies; between them are great voids containing hardly any visible matter. Furthermore, vast flows of galaxies have been observed as a perturbation to the overall expansion of the universe. This is what astronomers call the "large-scale structure" of the universe, and much of it has been discovered only in the past decade.

As the universe expands, our neighboring galaxies will remain our neighbors forever, but farther out the expansion of space is carrying galaxies away so fast that we see their light stretched and reddened. The greater distance of expanding space we look across to see any particular galaxy, the faster that galaxy will be moving away from us. At last there is a distance where galaxies are being carried away by expanding space at the speed of light. This is our cosmic horizon. It is a spherical wall, and we are inside. Countless galaxies no doubt exist beyond, but they are whisked away by expansion. Their light cannot reach us, so we cannot see them. Every galaxy has its own horizon, its own "visible universe."

But visible matter, on scales of individual galaxies and larger, does not move as it should if it is all that exists out there. Stars in galaxies, and galaxies themselves in groups and clusters, move too rapidly to be held together by the visible matter. Something invisible is exercising enormous gravitational effects on visible matter. After eliminating all other possibilities, astronomers have, in the last fifteen years, accepted the weird idea that over ninety percent of the mass of the universe is not stars, dust, gas or anything we know, but instead some invisible substance called "dark matter." Dark matter does not emit or absorb any kind of radiation. Most of it is probably not made of electrons, protons, neutrons, or any of the familiar elementary particles. It forms an invisible halo around every galaxy perhaps ten times the radius of the disk of visible stars, and around every cluster of galaxies.

What is the dark matter made of? How much of it is out there, and where? How does it behave? There have been several competing theories that managed for years to agree with all the reliable data, because the data were so rough and incomplete. But most theories are now being shot down by new astronomical data that are rapidly accumulating from telescopes all over the world and in space. This has drastically narrowed the range of possibilities. Accordingly, coauthor Joel R. Primack has modified the theory he pioneered and which set the agenda for much of cosmology for over a decade, called Cold Dark Matter. He is currently developing a new version of the theory, called Cold Plus Hot Dark Matter. "Cold" dark matter is some kind of hypothetical particles that were moving sluggishly in the early universe. "Hot" dark matter, which was moving relativistically then, may be composed of two kinds of neutrinos—at least, that is what is suggested by the latest data from the particle physics laboratories. Each component of dark matter has its own characteristics, and each no doubt plays a crucial role in the history of the universe.

THE BLUEPRINT CAME FIRST

In 1929, Edwin Hubble discovered the expansion of the universe by showing that the more distant a galaxy is from us, the faster it is moving away. Astrophysicists ran the movie backward and realized that the universe had to have started out extremely hot and dense. The earliest point was named—derisively by astronomer and novelist Fred Hoyle, whose steady state theory it eventually replaced—the "Big Bang." Standard Big Bang theory explains the creation of the light elements of matter in the first three minutes and seems to be right as far as it goes, but it does not explain what preceded that or what has followed.

Gravity alone could not have created the complex large-scale structures and flows of galaxies that are observed to exist. Gravity magnifies differences—that is, if one region is ever so slightly denser than average, it will expand a bit more slowly and grow relatively denser than its surroundings, while regions with less than average density will become increasingly less dense. But if matter after the Big Bang was absolutely evenly distributed, gravity would have done nothing but slow down the overall expansion. Consequently, either some unknown force acting after the Big Bang formed the giant structures we observe today—which looks increasingly dubious—or else gravity must have had some differences in density to work with from the beginning. What could have caused these differences in density? Big Bang theory is silent about its own initial conditions.

The theory of inflation, proposed in the early 1980s by Alan Guth and others, says that for an extremely small fraction of a second before the Big Bang—much less time than it would take light to cross the nucleus of an atom—the universe expanded exponentially, inflating countless random quantum events in the process. The density differences in the universe reflect these quantum events, enormously inflated. This is the best theory cosmologists have for the origin of the needed density differences.

Inflation is exponential growth—the longer it goes on, the faster it gets. An old story illustrates its blinding speed:

A SULTAN'S LIFE WAS SAVED BY THE GRAND VIZIER

Overwhelmed with gratitude, the Sultan asked him to choose his reward.

"You may give me a chessboard," said the Grand Vizier, "with one grain of wheat on the first square, two grains on the next square, four on the next, and so on. That would be enough."

"Such a modest gift for so great an act?" the Sultan exclaimed. "You shall have it today!"

But when the Sultan tried to prepare the chessboard, he discovered that the amount of wheat needed grew faster and faster. By the sixty-fourth square, he would need about ten billion metric tons—twenty years' worth of the modern world's production of wheat.

The quantum events of cosmic inflation created the needed small differences in density from place to place, leaving space slightly wrinkled (in three dimensions). The wrinkles are extraordinarily subtle, like a hill 600 feet high compared to the 21,000,000-foot radius of Earth, yet gradually they attracted particles of matter by gravity alone. The large-scale structures in the universe today—the clusters and walls built of thousands of galaxies—illuminate these ancient wrinkles like glitter tossed on invisible lines of glue.

If the theory of inflation is right, then the blueprint for the large-scale structure of the universe existed before the Big Bang created matter.

CAN INFLATION BE RIGHT?

The central predictions of the theory of inflation are: (1) that the universe has critical density (i.e., contains just enough matter to keep slowing down the expansion, but not enough to cause the universe to stop or fall together in a Big Crunch) and (2) that the wrinkles, regardless of their wavelength, all have the same amplitude when they cross the horizon. (This is called a "Zel'dovich spectrum," after the great Russian physicist and cosmologist Yacov Borisovich Zel'dovich.)

Arno Penzias and Robert Wilson discovered in 1965 that heat radiation from the Big Bang itself, called cosmic background radiation, still fills the universe. This was the first light in the universe. The radiation just reaching us now has been traveling since the universe first became transparent only about 300,000 years after the Big Bang. This primal radiation would have to bear some trace of the inflationary wrinkles that were theorized to have filled the universe at that time. If it did not, then the theory of inflation had to be wrong, and the large-scale structure of the universe could not have formed by gravity alone. Numerous observations from Earth's surface and from planes and balloons detected no irregularity in the cosmic background radiation. Except for the effects of Earth's motion, the radiation appeared to be a perfectly uniform 2.7 degrees above absolute zero in every direction, until 1992.

In 1992, NASA's Cosmic Background Explorer satellite (COBE), orbiting outside Earth's atmosphere, detected tiny differences in temperature in the background radiation. If inflation is right, these differences are a lightly traced but readable fossil record of the period before the Big Bang—from which the Big Bang emerged. This is spectacular evidence of the existence of primordial wrinkles in space. What COBE found was the equivalent of lost baby pictures of immense cosmic structures, showing that they were not created whole, but grew from these infants and revealing as well, if read backwards, very intriguing implications about the babies' parentage.

The theory of inflation thus appears to be supported by the COBE discoveries and subsequent measurements by many other instruments. If we assume—and there is increasing evidence we should—that the density of cold plus hot dark matter is critical and that there is a Zel'dovich spectrum of wrinkles, the resulting theory produces a large-scale structure like that which we actually observe. Since alternative explanations are perhaps possible, this does not prove that inflation theory plus our dark matter theory are actually right, although if the predictions led to structures unlike what we see, that would certainly prove at least one of these assumptions is wrong. There are also potential stumbling blocks, such as some preliminary results from the Hubble Space Telescope suggesting (based on assumptions that may or may not be valid) that the universe may not be as old as some of the stars in our galaxy. But on balance, the theory of inflation is so beautiful and solves so many problems that initially appeared to be unrelated that it is hard to suppress the thought that it might actually be true.

While inflation theory provides an explanation for the irregularities in the Big Bang, what about the origins of inflation itself? It turns out to be more fruitful to ask instead, why did inflation end? Because if we extrapolate backwards to find the origin of inflation, the most likely possibility is that in most of the superuniverse, inflation never stopped. It is a state of existence that goes on forever. The theory of eternal inflation, largely worked out by Russian astrophysicist Andre Linde, now at Stanford University, says that inflation stopped only in the minute part of the universe we can see—within our cosmic horizon—and some unknown distance beyond that. Everywhere else it continues forever.

WHAT DOES IT ALL MEAN?

The ideas that follow are a sort of theoretical theology, a spiritual analogue of theoretical physics. A theoretical physicist's methodology involves choosing a set of hypotheses and working out the consequences to see what kind of world they describe and how close it is to what experiment has found. Hypotheses can be eliminated as wrong but cannot be proved right. Coauthor Joel R. Primack and other cosmologists test theories by creating theoretical universes in supercomputers and then comparing them with observations of the real universe to see whether the predictions of any set of hypotheses can survive confrontation with the increasingly detailed data. Several fundamental truths about the origins and composition of the universe seem to be emerging from this process, although they are still controversial and they will be constantly tested as new data become available from the latest ground-and space-based telescopes. This is a logical game, but amazingly, sometimes the universe actually embodies a theorist's dreams. When this happens, it can have the force of a religious experience—at least for the theorist involved.

So let us suppose—in the style of theoretical physics—that the theories of inflation and eternal inflation are correct and then think through some of the possible consequences for religion and culture.

To experience the human meaning of the scientific story, we must translate it into myth, the traditional form for stories about the origin of the world. In common parlance, "myth" has come to connote the opposite of reality, or the simplistic fare of the hopelessly backward or quaint. But myths, as they function in human societies, actually are explanations of the highest order: the stories a culture communally uses in order to connect with and give meaning to its universe. Every traditional culture known to anthropology has had a cosmology—a story of how the world began and how human beings took their place within it. A functional cosmology grounds people's everyday expectations of each other in the larger patterns of the universe. Such a shared cosmology may be essential to successful human community and even to individual sanity. The understanding doesn't have to be scientifically accurate. None ever has been, until now. No description is ever totally accurate anyway, unless it is the universe itself. The map is not the terrain. What we humanly need is to know the truest story of our time.

As Plato taught, the answer to the question "What does it all mean?" can only be a myth. Unlike other myths, however, a scientific myth never stands still. As long as the universe of knowledge expands, the myth must absorb, be tossed out by, or else be enfolded in larger understandings. No myth is for all time, but myth making is an ongoing human pursuit.

A MYTH OF THE ORIGIN OF THE UNIVERSE

In the beginning there was—and almost everywhere else there still is—nothing but creativity: infinite potential, hot and dense, wildly experimenting with every possibility quantum uncertainty can come up with, expanding faster and faster for all eternity, unlimited by the speed of light or by lack of space. In this everlasting acceleration, tiny events are expanding from every "sparkpoint," which is what we call the smallest physical region that quantum physics allows.

Imagine a cosmic Las Vegas, its real estate inflating forever, lights flashing, money rolling out of slots, gamblers multiplying blindingly fast, everything hot and dense. Every point is a gambler, every gambler is flipping coins, every flip is a quantum fluctuation. But in eternal inflation, the rules are as follows: Every time a coin comes up tails, it becomes half its size; every time it comes up heads, it's suddenly twice its size and there are two of them. There are minute holes in the floor. The probability is extremely small that a coin will fall through, since the rules favor inflation. Most coins grow enormously. But once in a while a coin will get small enough to fall through the floor. At that instant, it exits eternity and the realm of those rules, and time begins for it. It will fall forever.

In a chain of events as inevitable as a losing streak to a gambler, one sparkpoint got tails every time. Each throw was a random event. A single heads could have pulled the sparkpoint back and vastly increased the probability of another speedup until it merged forever in the cauldron of eternal inflation. But that did not happen. Tails continued. The gambler had started with a trillion dollars and had lost all but one dollar. It was still possible to win back the trillion. Then the last dollar was gone. There was no turning back. The sparkpoint exited eternity. Quantum events had taken it, like Alice, through an invisible looking glass.

This was the seed of our universe: a single creative sparkpoint—an almost vanishingly small capsule of eternal creativity. This sparkpoint we name "Hokhmah," a kabbalistic term whose choice we will explain later.

Hokhmah had not lost its creative character, any more than a child changes its character upon leaving home. It was still inflating and emanating quantum fluctuations. But when it exited eternity, its inflating was destined to die out. Down the hill of potential energy Hokhmah now rolled, unable to regain eternal potential, compelled to express its finite potential now. Hokhmah had only the blaze-out we call inflation—possibly as little as 10^{-32} seconds—to create the blueprint for a cosmos. And it did so. The region that would become our present horizon inflated from the size of a thought to that of a grapefruit wildly faster than the speed of light. In the process it spawned all the quantum impulses that will continue to reverberate for hundreds of billions of years, creating the wrinkles that are becoming all the cosmic structures in the universe from galaxies to superclusters and larger.

Eternal inflation is endlessly creative and lavishly profligate. Every sparkpoint in eternal inflation has the possibility of becoming a Hokhmah. In detail, every universe will be unique because the quantum fluctuations during each one's inflationary epoch will be completely different. Each universe is a tiny bubble cut off from all other bubbles by eternal inflation. No one knows if the laws of physics are the same in other bubbles, nor do we yet have any way of testing. We may be further than ever from answering the question Einstein said was the one that really interested him: "Did God have a choice?"

On the scale of the superuniverse of eternal inflation, time begins an infinite number of times. The opening words of Genesis might be better interpreted, "In A beginning. . . ." Very, very deep inside our bubble, hemmed in by a horizon probably as minuscule compared to our bubble as a child's sandbox is to the visible universe, is the rarest of phenomena: the evolution of our universe. In eternal inflation, nothing persists. When all possibilities exist, none is realized. Time can never decide what direction to run in. Every sparkpoint can create infinite possibilities, but though those fluctuations expand at the speed of light, all other sparkpoints are expanding away so much faster that they are forever out of causal contact with each other. Our universe is vanishingly small compared to the superuniverse of eternal inflation, but in it effects reverberate! It takes time to play out the great possibilities, time to grow, to become something. The great miracle of our universe is that something is happening. Galaxies are evolving. Life is evolving. We are not just eternal potential—we are a story.

If you play a drum, the skin vibrates in waves. If you could get very close to it and slow things down considerably, you would see the skin forming troughs and crests, not just one at a time but different waves in different directions across it, the troughs and crests adding to each other. The sum of all the waves makes the "sound." The wrinkles of inflation were the primal, cosmic sound whose meaning the universe is still expanding to express. This gives a physical picture of the origin akin to the phrase at the opening of the Gospel of John: "In the Beginning was the Word."

The idea that God followed a blueprint which existed before the universe was created is also found in Jewish midrashic literature. Genesis Rabbah 1:1 says: "A ruler building a palace consults an architect's plans. The Blessed Holy One, in creating the universe, also worked from a plan—the Torah."

HOKHMAH AND KABBALAH

Kabbalah, medieval Jewish mysticism, is the only traditional cosmology we know of in which the universe was understood to have begun in a point and expanded.

We are not kabbalists, nor are we trying to promote Kabbalah. We are not arguing that Kabbalah was prescient, or that the kabbalists somehow knew mystically what science is now discovering. We are interested in Kabbalah because it developed a set of ideas describing the origin of an expanding universe and integrated these ideas into its religious worldview. Can Kabbalah help us to integrate the scientific concepts we have been describing into our own culture?

"Kabbalah" means "secret tradition," and its origins are uncertain. Though its earliest preserved writings date from the twelfth century, from Provence and later Spain, its adherents believed it derived from the secret Torah given to Moses and handed down orally through the most religious Jews ever since.

The early kabbalists were Jews living at the time when Moslem culture was transmitting the philosophy and science of Plato and Aristotle to Europe. Utterly committed to the reality of the infinite and singular God, Jews began applying Greek reasoning to long-standing problems of their religion, especially the question of the nature of God. The kabbalists used every resource they had not only reason and logic but poetry, meditation, and mystical experiences—to try to understand the nature of God. They believed that they could learn about God through contemplation of God's relationship to creation. For this reason, they strove to grasp the hidden reality behind the opening words of Genesis.

At that time, Moses Maimonides, the Aristotle of Judaism, was teaching that God could only be truly described by negatives: unknowable, incorporeal, unlimited, unchangeable. How, the kabbalists asked, could God be beyond human description, yet walk with Adam and Eve and talk with Abraham and Moses, as Torah reports? How, if God is infinite, could there have been room for anything else to be created? In answer to questions like these, the kabbalists developed a theoretical system portraying God pictorially as having ten different aspects—in Hebrew, sephirot—with complex relationships among all the aspects. Beyond the picture was Ein Sof, "Without End," the unknowable God, which emanated the light that created the aspects of God knowable to humans.

Of ten sephirot, the first three deal with creation, and they correspond fairly closely to concepts from the theories of inflation and eternal inflation, although these theories are being developed by cosmologists in response to completely different questions. The first sephirah was keter, meaning the crown, symbolic of the unknowable God's infinite potential to create—to enter into some relationship with our universe. The second was Hokhmah, the bursting through of our universe. The third was Binah, the female womb in which creation expands from Hokhmah to become what it becomes.

Keter might be a thought provoking name for the state of eternal inflation, which, like keter, is infinite, the source of all that will come, yet Nothing, because no differentiation can exist within it. Hokhmah is the exiting from eternity, the beginning of time, the instant with no instant before it. Binah is expansion or spacetime. There could probably be no more accurate name for the Big Bang as we understand it scientifically today than to call it Hokhmah-Binah.

Kabbalah is an example of a cosmology resembling our own which successfully penetrated and enriched the lives of a society. In the sixteenth century, the great kabbalist Isaac Luria developed the scheme further, teaching that in the beginning, God began to withdraw into self-exile in order to make space for the universe. God envelopes the universe, in the Lurianic view, but when God withdrew, evil became possible inside. God sent holy light into the world, but the world was too weak to hold God's glory. Its cornerstones were vessels that shattered in the light. The role of the Jews is to repair the shattered vessels by recollecting the sparks of God in the world. Tzimtzum is the name of God's self-exile. Tikkun olam is the repairing of the world. For Jews in the century or so after the expulsion from Spain in 1492, the concept of a God in exile gave cosmic meaning to their people's traumatic and seemingly endless history of expulsions and exiles. The cosmology alone, however, did not provide the meaning. It came from the circumstances of their lives and their era, but it was expressible at a deep and satisfying level with the help of their kabbalistic cosmological myth. Can the same become true with modem cosmology?

Kabbalah was a cultural outgrowth of medieval European Jewish experience. By the time of the European Enlightenment, Jews who read Descartes and Newton considered the idea of sephirot as absurd as angels dancing on the head of a pin. But Kabbalah is a metaphorical description of a set of fundamental universal relationships which in light of modern astrophysics appears closer to reality than the infinite rectangular space of the Newtonian worldview.

We do not argue that either kabbalistic cosmology or current scientific theories about the origin is "true" in some ultimate sense, but rather that by seeing each in light of the other, we begin to get some sense of what to demand of any cosmology intended to function for human society in the twenty-first century. Just as light cannot be described accurately as either a particle or a wave but only as something beyond either metaphor, the universe cannot be adequately described as either something scientifically observed or something spiritually experienced. A functional cosmology must do both. The reason kabbalistic terms are helpful to our account is that they bind together the search for truth with the search for the divine. If terms such as Hokhmah did not already exist bearing religious significance, we would have had to try to coin them—which would probably have been as successful as Esperanto. The emerging scientific cosmology and Kabbalah are two metaphor systems whose juxtaposition points toward a truth larger than either can express alone.

The theory of eternal inflation, whether or not it turns out to be true, has opened a cosmic perspective on reality and the countless threads of connection, including the spiritual, weaving through. If eternal inflation theory eventually turns out to be wrong, whatever replaces it cannot explain less and will have to do better. A new standard has been set for creation stories.

If the theory of eternal inflation is correct, then there is an eternal blizzard of universes in which our bubble is a single snowflake, an infinitesimal capsule of eternal potential, crystallized into unique patterns of matter and energy, which has set off from eternal inflation on its journey to realize itself in a universe. No one has thought of a way yet to test whether eternal inflation theory is right, but the expansion of perspective the theory requires certainly enlarges our idea of the physical universe. It may also enlarge our ideas of God, because regardless of how much reality one may ascribe to God, one can only speak metaphorically, and most metaphors are limited to the extremely narrow experience of Earth. This does not make them wrong, but they are certainly limiting. Cosmology provides utterly different metaphors—eternal inflation, endless creation from every sparkpoint—that humans could not have dreamed up had theoretical physics not led them there. It seems to be a general rule that the more metaphor systems through which we try to understand non-human-scale realities, both large and small, the closer we come to truth.

COSMOLOGY AND HUMAN MEANING
IN THE TWENTY-FIRST CENTURY

In a speech given in Philadelphia on July 4, 1994, on the state of the world and its prospects, Vaclav Havel said that the planet is in transition: as vastly different value systems collide, all consistent value systems are collapsing. We cannot foresee the results. Science, which has been the bedrock of industrial civilization for so long, he said, "fails to connect with the most intrinsic nature of reality, and with natural human experience. It is now more a source of disintegration and doubt than a source of integration and meaning. . . . We may know immeasurably more about the universe than our ancestors did, and yet it increasingly seems they knew something more essential about it than we do, something that escapes us. . . . Paradoxically, inspiration for the renewal of this lost integrity can once again be found in science . . . a science producing ideas that in a certain sense allow it to transcend its own limits. . . . Transcendence is the only real alternative to extinction."

The search for scientific truth can be a form of guidance. It is as divine as any other. The foundation-building revolution that modern cosmology is undergoing today, as it seeks a verifiable description of the origin of the universe, requires that we transcend previous notions of space, time, and reality. This is the kind of science Havel is hoping for—a science whose metaphors may allow us to comprehend terrestrial problems from a cosmic perspective.

Exponential growth—like that of the wheat on successive squares of the Grand Vizier's chessboard—is the dominant characteristic of the industrial world. Not only is the human population inflating; simultaneously, so are the technological power and the resource use of each individual. Multiply these times each other: We are now processing a substantial fraction of the Earth's entire crust. In population growth, resource use, pollution, and garbage production, the human race is addicted to exponential growth. Inflation is the controlling metaphor of our time.

In our kabbalistic creation myth, *tzimtzum*—the withdrawal of God—occurred in eternal inflation. As the notion of a God in exile gave cosmic meaning to the lives of a people in exile, understanding cosmic inflation may give a new, if sobering, meaning to the lives of a people dependent upon inflationary growth. Inflation is a taste of what it is like to be God. It cannot be considered a normal human pace. In a finite environment, inflation cannot continue, however cleverly we may postpone or disguise the inevitable. This is a consequence of natural laws.

That does not mean growth must stop, however, as many people genuinely trying to save the planet assume. The great transition model for the future of Earth may be the universe. Inflation transformed to expansion can go on for a very long time. Expansion on Earth can be sustained as long as our creativity lasts. Reality is not a zero-sum game, in which a gain one place must be paid for with a loss somewhere else. Creativity is what all tiny regions do in expressing their quantum nature. The stunning lesson of eternal inflation theory is that the fundamental nature of reality is not conservation of energy or increase in entropy but endless creativity.

The question for our time is, how can we end inflation gently on Earth? How can we slow human inflation enough that creative restoration can overtake it? When we have developed a sustainable relationship with our planet, humanity and Earth will be in balance, and the transition from inflation to stable expansion will have been achieved through the restoration of the world—*tikkun olam*.

Religious Restoration or Religious Renewal

Orthodoxy versus Pluralism in Judaism

Arthur Waskow

Jews are used to finding themselves on the front pages of major newspapers—almost always in regard to peace and war in Israel. But as the spring-fever festival of hilarious Purim came this past March, suddenly there was a different kind of front-page story: a band of Orthodox rabbis had proclaimed that what Reform and Conservative Jews do is not Judaism at all.

Unfortunately, this was not a Purim joke. The institutions of non-Orthodox Judaism did not just laugh and walk away; they issued statements bespeaking deep alarm, even though they far outnumber those who are trying to delegitimize them. They realize that a profound and historic struggle for the future of the Jewish people has begun. Behind the Orthodox rabbis' proclamation they smell the threat of a new attitude from the Israeli government—not merely ignoring liberal Judaism but actively denying their legitimacy and bonding together State power, "modern Orthodox" expansionist nationalism, and ultra-Orthodox control over Jewish identity (through control of conversions and marriages) into the emergence of a new State Orthodoxy.

Why is this struggle underway? At the level of secular historical analysis, it began when Modernity shattered most traditional religious communities, including traditional Judaism. Even before the Holocaust, the economics, science, and politics of Modernity was dissolving traditional Judaism. The Holocaust—Modernity run amok—finished the job. But in the very process of shattering the traditional communities, the Holocaust (and other products of Modernity like the H-bomb and global warming) undermined respect and honor for Modernity itself; thus the birth of a new kind of untraditional fundamentalism.

Those liberal Jews who bothered to ask a religious question about this history—to ask what God had to do with it—mostly concluded that God had nothing to do with it. That accorded with their absorption into secular Modernity.

But as we all face the fundamentalist resurgence, and more importantly as we face the partial failures of secular Modernity, we might ask again. Perhaps a serious God-centered answer will illuminate our path.

From a seriously religious perspective, this seemingly secular historical transformation is an aspect of the evolution of the God Whose Name is Ehyeh Asher Ehyeh, I Will Be Who I Will Be. "Modernity" is our description of an event in the Divine life cycle that, as some kabbalists taught, is carried forward by the flow of God into a world through a growing self-awareness that is ultimately intended to provide God with a Divine Mirror—the Conscious Universe.

This process proceeds not smoothly, but in jumps. The emergence of life on earth was one such jump. Another was the emergence of the human race and its ability to be self-reflective, to conceptualize, control, and relate to the wholeness of the universe—to learn from the past and reinvent the future. Within human history, such events as the agricultural revolution and the emergence of Biblical/Prophetic Israel, Buddhism, and other ancient faiths was another such leap into greater control over and relationship with the wider universe. So were the emergence of Hellenism and the responsive emergence of Rabbinic Judaism, Christianity, and Islam.

Now, one aspect of God—the I-It/Doing/Making aspect—has come surging far more fully into the human species than ever before, without, as yet, a commensurate surge into human action of the I-Thou/Loving/Being aspect of God. That I-It influx is what we call Modernity.

The first response: Modernity works, join it. Set up a state that is Modern though Jewish. Create a form of Judaism that cedes at least six-sevenths of life to Modernity, and preserves but shreds of traditional Judaism for at most the "religious" ghetto of Shabbat. Celebrate our entry into the larger world.

The second response: Modernity—or at least its hypertrophy—endangers the world. Fear it. Flee it. Vomit it out, and restore premodern religion. Recognize the chief dangers of Hyper-Modernity: it shatters the family, the neighborhood, the life cycle, the culture, the community. The response of religious restoration is to restore these values by restoring women and men to their separate (and dominant/ subordinate) roles, and by tightening the boundaries and barricades against other communities, cultures, and traditions.

In its fullest Jewish expression, in Israel, this restorationist response seeks to use state power to define who is a Jew by traditional tests, to enforce traditional religious law among Jews, and to enforce military control by Jewish settlers and the Israeli state over non-Jews-Palestinians—in the whole Land of Israel as anciently imagined. Note that this is not an organic continuation of traditional communities but a kind of "intentional restorationism." By some it has been called "settler Judaism," but it is broader than that. It bespeaks State Orthodoxy, a new form of Judaism in that it seeks to use State power, official violence, and, sometimes, private violence, in a way that was unavailable to traditional rabbinic Judaism.

In America, the analogous phenomenon has been the emergence of a Christian Right (with some allies among Orthodox Jews) ready to restore obedience to old doctrines by imposing governmental power over the family (ruled by a father), education (replicating old certainties), poverty (a punishment for indolence), nature (a mere tool for human benefit), and so on. These versions of religious restoration have created strong political bases and have been well publicized.

Third response: Digest Modernity, rather than vomit it out or be swallowed up by it. Absorb those aspects of modernity that are sacred, and eliminate those that are destructive. This response—religious renewal—is less widely known than religious restoration, and so far has much less political power. The renewal response recognizes Modernity as an expression of God-powers newly entering human capability as God continues to flow into the world—and sees both the holiness and the dangers in this flow. It sees as dangers not only the death of spirituality, community, culture, and the family that the new overweening power of Modernity brings about but three other dangers:

1. Hyper-Modernity poisons the earth, air, and water, thereby multiplying old diseases, meanwhile extinguishing thousands of species of life and threatening the web of life on earth through the H-bomb, ozone depletion, and global warming.
2. It threatens local and regional economies, even the very economies of industrial strength that Modernity created, in order to serve the "global economy"; for many, it expropriates jobs as well as income—the very sense of worthy work done for worthwhile recompense-while forcing others into exhausting overwork.
3. Hyper-Modernity destroys community, family, and culture, as well as the earth and the economy, depriving us of our sense that the world makes sense, that there is meaning and Wholeness in the world.

Yet the response of religious renewal springs from recognizing that there are also some sacred results of this great flow of Godly power into human hands: democracy, the equality of women, the next, close contacts with other traditions, the emergence of strong Diaspora communities with real power in the societies where they live, and responsibility for the web of life throughout the planet.

Among Jews, religious renewal means the absorption of these new sacred values into Torah, and thereby the creation of a new form of Judaism, as different from Rabbinic Judaism, and as deeply rooted in it, as Rabbinic Judaism was different from, and rooted in, Biblical Judaism.

Religious restoration or religious renewal? Vomit Modernity out, or digest it? That is the crucial question that all the ancient traditions now face. For Jews, the choice is between State Orthodoxy and a new Holistic Judaism.

Why are these the necessary choices? Because the dangers of Hyper-Modernity are real, and more and more human beings, Jews among them, are feeling the great tug. Hyper-Modernity is making the ground beneath our own feet increasingly slippery. The old forms of family are vanishing: Do we restore them by brute force, or transform them? The old ways of controlling and distancing foreign peoples and cultures are vanishing: Do we restore them by brute force, or transform our relationships with them? Should we move backward or forward? It is Elijah's old challenge: We have been walking like a bird on a branching twig, one foot on each branch. But the branch is diverging; soon we must choose one branch, or fly upward to some newer place.

For the vision of Jewish renewal is indeed new—not the same as that of the nineteenth-century, Jewish Reformers and secular Zionists who compromised with Modernity by embracing it for most of life and restricting Judaism to the privatized ghetto of "religion." The vision of Jewish renewal is a Holistic Judaism in three senses: It engages the whole person; it is shaped by the whole people (not by just a small elite of verbally adept Torah scholars, still an elite even with women among them); and it is concerned for the whole planet.

This Holistic Judaism aims toward a maximalist Judaism, infused with some elements of Modernity and, in this new synthesis, shaping all of Jewish life: new paths of work, rest, sex, food, money, health, family, and political action, as well as new forms of prayer, Torah-study, dance, art, music.

Both State Orthodoxy and Holistic Judaism are new. What is new in the amalgam of "settler Judaism/State Orthodoxy" is the possibility of using the power of the state in support of Orthodox goals, and the readiness to turn the long history of Jewish subjugation, fear, and semi-repressed rage to the service of "You shall control and dominate the stranger, because you were strangers and were dominated in all the lands of your dispersal."

In Holistic Judaism, what will be new? There will be full equality of women and men in shaping what Judaism is; willingness to learn from some of the teachings of other spiritual paths; a conviction that God intends for both families of Abraham, not just one, to live freely and in peace in what we call the Land of Israel. There will be a conviction that Judaism is internally pluralist; recognition of intermarriage as more opportunity than disaster; and a conviction that Judaism must draw on its own deepest wisdom to reach beyond itself, to contribute to the healing of the earth and of the non-Jewish societies in which we live. Holistic Judaism has more open boundaries in both directions: more open to receiving and sharing both from other peoples and from the previously excluded sectors of Jewish life, and more open to carrying the teachings of Judaism outward into "non-Jewish" territory—teaching by example and persuasion, not by domination.

Holistic Judaism may include a new willingness to extend the principles of Shabbat and the sabbatical year to protect and heal non-Jewish societies and the earth outside of the Land of Israel from uncontrolled technology; to develop a Jewish sexual ethic and ritual that defines how to make holy not only gay and lesbian sexuality but also the sexual relationships of unmarried people and the emergence of new kibbutz-like groupings to raise children in a society where one parent, or even two, cannot do the job alone; a new *ecokashrut* not for food alone but also for the "eating" of coal, oil, wood, paper, and plastics, and for the investment as well as spending of money; a new ethic about how much time to spend at work and how much in rest and true re-creation, about how to share jobs in an economy that now disemploys some and overworks others; a new readiness to use dance, body gesture, drushodrama, dialogical davening, chant, and meditation as ways of getting directly in touch with God.

It is not surprising that such a Judaism has sprouted first and grows strongest in America, where the boundaries between religious communities are very fuzzy, where the State has least control over religion and therefore encourages religious pluralism, and where the equality of women and men in every sphere grows stronger and stronger. Instead of viewing these American origins as a weakness or a sign of our own inauthenticity compared to Israel or Eastern Europe, we should view it as an asset—a way into the future. Renewal is not a version of assimilation, but at least as Jewishly authentic as is the new State Orthodoxy. Indeed, it much more honors the great strand of Torah that calls on us to love the stranger and to hear that God is One.

The choice between restoration and renewal is not merely a question of politics as we usually understand it. The web of community, of worthy work and rest, and of life on this planet is at stake. If the danger as well as the majesty of Modernity is that it has brought into human hands new powers from the inward flow of the Powerful God, the Infinite I-It, its majesty must be turned to love by bringing into human hands an inward flow of the Loving God, the Eternal I-Thou. The new God powers are too strong to be contained by the old versions of God-loving. Only new forms of I-Thouing can unify the currents. We can affirm the Unity of the One God Who is both power and love, both doing and being, both I-It and I-Thou, only by ourselves acting in that Unity.

So the task of Judaism, and Christianity, and Islam, and Buddhism, and Hinduism, and all the other spiritual traditions, is now to move forward to bring the next great wave of I-Thouing, of love and restful being, of deeper, broader, and more meaningful community, into the world.

On the Growing Edge of Judaism

Reb Zalman at Eighty

Or Rose

Raised in an Orthodox Jewish family in Vienna and educated by Lubavitch Ha-sidim in Antwerp (and later in New York), Reb Zalman arrived as a refugee to the United States in 1941. Since his arrival in this country, he has grown to be-come one of the most creative and influential figures in contemporary Jewish life. He is the spiritual founder of the Jewish Renewal Movement and a pioneer in the introduction of the Jewish mystical tradition (Kabbalah and Hasidism) into popular American culture. Reb Zalman has been an inspiration to the Tikkun community, mentoring Rabbi Michael Lerner (Tikkun's founder and ed-itor) and several other prominent Jewish spiritual leaders, including Rabbis Arthur Green, Tirzah Firestone, and Arthur Waskow. He has also been at the forefront of interreligious dialogue, working closely with such renowned figures as Howard Thurman, Thomas Merton, and His Holiness The Dalai Lama.

This interview is dedicated specifically to exploring Reb Zalman's current religious thinking.

Or Rose: What does the word "God" mean to you?

Reb Zalman: I think it is important to begin this conversation humbly, rec-ognizing that all of the ways in which I speak of God are inadequate. And yet, to avoid theological discussion is not an option, because like others I have a deep desire to understand the ways of the Divine. With that caveat, let me try to say something about the Unsayable.

In the past, many people spoke about God as an existent being, albeit "omni-omni"—the Man with the long, flowing beard sitting on His heavenly throne. The God I experience most often is not theistic, but pantheistic—God as the source of all life, as a constant, unending flow of energy that animates all of life. The terms "verb" and "process" best describe this reality.

I must say, however, that despite my pantheistic leanings there are still moments when I also experience God in more personal ways. This is particularly true when I *davven* [pray]. In saying the words *"Barukh Atah"* [Blessed are You], the God of "Thou" is present to me. While I am aware of the intellectual inconsistency this creates, I can't deny the power of these moments for the sake of absolute philosophical coherence.

Rose: While the great religious traditions of the West have developed elaborate responses to life in a "theistic" world, they have developed relatively fewer responses to life in a "pantheistic" world. How do you think we can live most meaningfully and responsibly in a pantheistic reality?

Reb Zalman: The first step is the realization that God's energy flows everywhere; it is how God "gods." We cannot control this energy; all we can do is recognize it and get in step with it, so that our very existence is in harmony with what is rather than at cross-purposes with it. This orientation should help us align ourselves to all of creation, so that we can truly see the universe: the "uni"—the single tide of energy that ebbs and flows through creation—and the "verse"—the diverse array of manifest creations.

In practical terms, being in harmony with the universe entails a commitment to such endeavors as conservation and preservation of the environment—of nature and the animal kingdom—and a heightened understanding of the organic connections between people across the usual ethnic, racial, and religious divides.

Rose: What is the specific place of Judaism in this paradigm? What particular contributions does it have to make to the ongoing process of *tikkun olam* [creating a world of wholeness]?

Reb Zalman: For all of my universalism, I strongly believe that Judaism has unique gifts to offer the world. There are several things that come to mind, but let me focus here on just one of them: the Jewish concept of time.

Unfortunately, most of us in this country have bought into a concept of time as a standardized commodity, and the price we pay is consciousness. What we lose in this exchange is organic time. And the more we lose touch with organic time, the more automated we become. Time as commodity is out of step with time as it flows in nature. The Jewish notion of time is to bring these two aspects of time into sync with each other. Judaism says: sunrise, sunset; six days of work and the Sabbath; new moon, full moon; equinox and solstice. The full moon of the vernal equinox is Passover. The full moon of the autumnal equinox is *Sukkot* [the Feast of Tabernacles]. And the last phase of the moon in the last phase of the sun is Hanukkah.

These holidays come at their organic time, coinciding with the realities of nature. The rhythm of organic time is inherent in all of life. It is not something that exists only outside of us, but is also alive within us. There is an ebb and flow in our energy levels during the day and night; there are rhythms of digestion, and of the pulse and the heartbeat. Organic time is humming inside us. It is one of the many voices of God. Rebbe Nahman of Bratslav [d. 1810] called it "the voice of my Beloved" [a play on *The Song of Songs* 5:2]—the pulse. If you want to know God, he said, "You need only listen to His voice within. You can always touch your pulse and say, 'Oh, there You are.'"

Rose: Having cited the great Hasidic master, Rebbe Nahman of Bratslav, what do you think Hasidism has to teach us today?

Reb Zalman: Again, there is far too much to say for one brief conversation, but let me make one basic point.

Of all the lessons of Hasidism, the most important one to me is the imperative to remain on the growing edge of the Jewish tradition. In its early days, Hasidism was a radical movement attempting to revitalize its relationship with God and with *Yiddishkeit* [the Jewish tradition]. The Ba'al Shem Tov [Israel b. Eliezer, d. 1760, the first great Hasidic master] modeled this passion for revitalization in his introduction into Jewish life of the quality of "*mamash*"(truly). While prior Jewish thinkers preached about God, he actually went and showed people that God's glory *mamash* fills the whole earth [Isaiah 6:3], and that people of all walks of life can experience the Divine. Conservatives want to be in the center where things are safe; but as with a tree, the center is dead matter. The Hasidim didn't abandon the tradition, but they lived on the edge, seeking to renew it. We must do the same.

Renewal requires a careful look back into the past so that we know where we have come from, where we now stand, and where we might go in the future. But this exploration is not without risk—there is always a danger of being trapped and tyrannized by the past. People sometimes fall into the assumption that whatever was done back then was the "real thing"; if it was good enough for them, it's good enough for us. Give me that old-time religion! These are sentiments of fundamentalists. When we look back at our ancestors, our aim is not to be locked into the past. We want to use their experience and wisdom as reference points, as sources of guidance. Judaism is alive, and we are responsible for continuing to animate it.

Rose: Please give me an example of how we might locate ourselves on the "growing edge" of Judaism today?

Reb Zalman: Sometimes I think we Jews exist so that in every age we will be able to ask our eternal question: Is it kosher? Kosher, as I understand it, means clean, pure, and by extension, good for the natural processes of the universe. The opposite of kosher is *treif*, which means unclean, impure, polluted, and hence polluting. Kosher is energy-efficient and productive; *treif* is wasteful and destructive.

In this conception, planetary concerns, and not simply the laws on the books, must govern the standards of *kashrut* (kosher laws). For example, eggs are generally considered kosher, but what about eggs from chickens that are imprisoned in small cages? According to traditional Jewish law, all fruits and vegetables are kosher. But what about green beans or tomatoes harvested by ill-treated, underpaid, and exploited migrant workers—are these products kosher?

This approach to *kashrut* is very demanding. It requires us to ask ourselves at every turn, "What does God want of us?" What is the best way to address the needs of the world? For this, we cannot simply look into the codes; we must attune ourselves to the ongoing revelation of Sinai.

Rose: Since leaving the traditional world of Hasidism as a young man, you have explored deeply the teachings of several non-Jewish spiritual traditions. What have you learned from these encounters?

Reb Zalman: When I was first ordained I felt that all religious *goyim* [non-Jews] were idolaters and non-Orthodox Jews heretics. In those years I still concentrated all my efforts on contributing to the restoration of traditional Judaism in America and the world. I knew that this could not happen by persuading people to outward observance. We had to meet their inner spiritual needs. Having been trained in the center of *Chabad* [Lubavitch] Hasidism with its emphasis on *hitbonenut* [contemplative meditation and prayer], I felt a missionary's drive to share these spiritual treasures with any Jew who would be interested. I sought to share this with them hoping that once I offered them spiritual nourishment, I could persuade them to live a "Torah True" lifestyle.

"Wisdom among the nations—believe it. Torah among the nations—don't believe it" (*Lamentations Rabbah* 2:13).

What of those who adhered to other religions? They were right only in as much as their religions encouraged them to observe the Seven Noahide Laws. Nonetheless, [I believed then that] all but the kernel of their religions was either *Avodat Kokhavim u'Mazalot* [Worship of Stars and Constellations], or worse, *Avodat Ellilim* [idolatry]. The true spiritual treasures were among us Jews, and even among Jews mostly with the Hasidim, and even among the Hasidim mostly with the Lubavitchers whose *rebbes* [Hasidic masters] demanded of them great inner work, lengthy and intensive *davvenen* [prayer] and meditation on Hasidic teachings.

Imagine the surprise when I discovered, while teaching at a Lubavitch *yeshiva* [academy for traditional Jewish learning], some books that taught me that the *goyim* were also *ma'aminim*, real believers in the living God, and that Trappists also did "mental prayer," and that Hindus had *rebbes* like Ramakrishna. These discoveries and a later challenge from Revered Howard Thurman, Dean of the Chapel at Boston University, my black *rebbe*, threw me into turmoil. "Do you trust in the *Ruakh Ha'Kodesh?*" [the "Holy Spirit" or "Divine inspiration"] he asked me.

Here I believed in the workings of Divine providence as Hasidism taught it—*hashgakhah pratit*, specific providence—in which even the fall of a leaf is ordained by God. And now I had to face a providential power that produced a Buddha, a Lao Tzu, great souls who were no less *neshamot klaliyot* [inclusive or root souls] than our *rebbes*. Were they an accidental "oops" of God? What about those Nazarene Hasidim who followed Jesus? Didn't the Bratslav Hasidim [followers of R. Nahman of Bratslav] also believe in a *rebbe* who no longer lived on earth?

My restoration theology started to break down and it began to reorganize itself on another level. Meeting people like Howard Thurman, Thomas Merton, Timothy Leary, Richard Alpert [also known as Ram Dass], Zen Roshis, Swamis, nuns and priests, ministers, and transpersonal therapists had a bearing on my emerging reality map. I changed from one who advocated restoration to one who instead espoused renewal: an ongoing process of staying at the growing edge of the Tree of Life [Genesis 2:9], where it is both juicy and in touch with my environment. I no longer saw the world in sectarian-ideological terms. I had been initiated into being an organismic thinker, a Gaian [from "Gaia," the Greek goddess of Earth] who is a Jew.

Rose: And what does it mean to be "a Gaian who is a Jew?"

Reb Zalman: It means, first of all, to realize that the earth is alive and that each of us has a role to play in healing it. Just as the human body cannot function to the best of its ability without the heart, the kidneys, and the liver each doing its job, so does the world need us—individuals and communities—to do our particular work. The world needs Jews to be the best possible Jews, just as it needs Muslims to be the best possible Muslims. But this also requires that we cultivate a synergistic relationship in which we are growing together, sharing the vital nutrients of our traditions with one another. Our very existence depends on it.

Rose: I want to close our conversation by thanking you for the countless gifts you have given generations of religious seekers—Jewish and non-Jewish—who have turned to you for guidance over the years. I bless you with many more years of health and creativity—*ad meah ve'esrim* ["until one hundred and twenty," the lifespan of Moses]!

Life as Sacred Narrative

Estelle Frankel

More and more in my work as a healer, I find myself venturing off the beaten track of psychodynamic psychotherapy and talking to my clients about their spiritual journeys. For many years I was reluctant, as a clinician, to come out of the closet as a religious person. Though the words of ancient sacred text would often echo between the lines of my clients' narratives, in the service of maintaining therapeutic neutrality I kept these personal musings to myself. Over time, as I gained confidence and perhaps a bit of chutzpah as a clinician, I began selectively sharing spiritual teachings from the Jewish mystical tradition with my clients. Almost invariably, these occasions have lead to a deepening of insight and occasionally to a therapeutic breakthrough. The spiritual perspective offered by Jewish mysticism has opened up new possibilities for healing and transformation.

In the work of spiritual healing, our notion of who we think we are begins to expand. In a sense we are given new eyes, the ability to see ourselves from God's perspective, as it were—from the vantage point of the Infinite. Though we may only be able to hold that expanded vision of ourselves for brief moments at a time, such sight can have a profound effect on our identity. Instead of being overly identified with our problems and pathologies, we can also begin to appreciate our perfection and purpose. And instead of feeling isolated and alone in our pain, we can begin to experience ourselves as part of a larger whole in which our individual stories reflect the larger story of which all people are a part.

One of the ways we can connect with the "larger" story is by immersing ourselves in sacred myth in a process I call "sacred narrative therapy." Jewish mystics of old understood that the stories contained in the scriptures and ancient legends—known as *midrash*—were not just meant to be taken as historical accounts of what happened to our ancestors, but as mythic renderings

of what each and every one of us undergoes as we embark on the healing journey of awakening. For the Hassidic masters, the entire cast of biblical characters lives within each and every one of us, representing dimensions of the
soul.

THROUGH THE LENS OF SACRED NARRATIVE

I have found my own spiritual narrative in the book of Esther. As I put myself in Esther's shoes, I imagine that she must have struggled for years to understand why *she*, a Jewess, was chosen to be the queen of Persia and Medea.
Taken against her will to be part of the King's harem, Esther waits nine long
years before the mysterious events of her life reveal their significance and
meaning. When the king's minister, Haman, plots to kill all the Jews in the
kingdom, Esther finds herself in the unique position of having the power to
save her people. Suddenly, the providential nature of her strange fate becomes
clear, as we hear in her uncle Mordecai's impassioned plea: "Who knows if
only for the sake of this moment in time, you were chosen as queen" (Esther
4:14). Esther's personal destiny, which had been a complete conundrum until
then, suddenly takes on a sense of historic urgency and significance. Suddenly it becomes clear that she must put her own life on the line in order to
save her people.

I love the book of Esther precisely because it is so much like our lives—full
of mystery and hidden twists in the plot. The name Esther, which implies hiddenness (*seter*), teaches us about God's hidden and mysterious pathways in
our lives. To reflect this, God's name seems to have been intentionally left out
of the narrative, appearing only as a hidden acrostic (see Esther 5:4). In the
book of Esther, what begins as bad luck is, in the end, reversed into good fortune; events that initially appear to be "by chance" turn out to be providential.
The casting of lots or *purim*, suggests a certain randomness; yet the unfolding
of events in the book of Esther reveals that nothing happens by chance alone;
even those things which appear to be arbitrary or unlucky—part of the cosmic
lottery, as it were—in the end, turn out to be deeply meaningful.

In this stage of my life I, like Esther, find myself struggling to discover the
hidden hand of the divine in the many obscure and inexplicable aspects of my
life. In particular, I often struggle to make sense of the events that led me to
return to the Diaspora after having made *aliya* to Israel in my youth. Though
I had intended to spend my life in Israel, fate brought me back to the States,
where my destiny has unfolded in ways I never could have imagined. Though
I grapple with self-doubt at times, wondering whether I made the right
choices at different turning points in my life, when I view my life as though

it were a sacred narrative—inscribed on a *megillah*—the broken pieces of the puzzle begin to come together and a coherent story emerges. This story reveals how all the conscious and unconscious choices I have made, as well as the random, chance events that have shaped my being, come together in a meaningful fashion to reveal my unique essence. Finding this sense of meaning and coherence seems to be one of the important tasks we all face in midlife, as we inevitably reflect on choices we made earlier in our lives.

As I discovered in my musings over the book of Esther, something always shifts in our experience of life when we view it through the lens of sacred narrative. Instead of the disjointed and often incomplete stories that comprise our lives, a thread of meaning begins to weave the chapters together revealing their hidden connections. In these moments we often have a sense that our lives have unfolded exactly as they were meant to, mistakes and all.

THE SHATTERED VESSELS

Another myth that I find myself repeatedly turning to in recent years is Isaac Luria's myth of the shattered vessels. This sixteenth-century creation myth, which decribes creation as originating in a cosmic catastrophe, can be understood as a mystical metaphor for the universal experience of transition.

Beginning with a paradoxical process known as *tzimtzum* (withdrawal), the *Ein Sof*, or Infinite, Boundless One, is said to have contracted itself, creating an empty space within which the finite realm might come into existence. Into this womb-like space, the Ein Sof emanated a single ray of light. This primordial light was so powerful, however, that it is said to have shattered the very vessels created to contain it. As a result of this shattering, or *shevira*, sparks of the divine light became scattered and trapped in the material world, where they await redemption. Until all these fallen sparks of divinity are restored to their source, according to Luria, the world remains in a broken state, needing tikkun. This task of tikkun is the very purpose of all existence, and each of us has a role in its fulfillment.

In addition to hinting at the redemptive possibilities that can arise from crisis, Luria's three stages of divine unfolding describe the ongoing process of how life continually renews itself through creation, disintegration, and regeneration. *Tzimtzum*, *shevira*, and *tikkun* are part of the molecular structure of the cosmos. All that are born into being pass through these three gates. And at every transition point in the life cycle, when one stage of life ends and another begins, we inevitably pass through these three gates.

Since many people seeking therapy do so at transition points in their lives, Luria's myth provides a useful paradigm for placing the universal experience of transition into a larger mythic context. For instance, when we are going through a painful "ending" in our lives, knowing we are in the *shevira* stage of a transition may make it easier to accept the feelings of disorientation and grief that arise when the very ground on which we have stood is shifting. If we feel a sense of vertigo and dread as old life structures dissolve, we can be reassured that this disintegrative stage will be followed by a time of healing and reintegration. Knowing we are on a journey that has distinct stages, and being able to "name" these stages, helps us place our personal experience within a larger context.

The shattering of the vessels can also be understood as the Kabbalah's unique idiom for talking about what Buddhists refer to as life's essential impermanence. As soon as something is created, its dissolution is already at hand. The vessels of creation, the finite forms created to house the infinite, are, by design, not only impermanent, but also essentially imperfect—for no finite vessel can ever fully contain the infinite. The shattering of the vessels is an inevitable outcome of creating an embodied universe, much as error is an inevitable part of living. In fact, it seems that God intentionally created a flawed universe in order to give every creature a role in its restoration, and so that perfection might be reached through imperfection, and wholeness through brokenness.

For those of us who, like myself, have difficulty accepting imperfection, the myth of the shattered vessels provides a comforting reminder that imperfection is inescapable since it is woven into the very fabric of creation. Each of us is given some broken piece or character flaw we will have to work with in our lives—our own inner chamber of darkness. Our job is to illuminate these "dark" and uninhabitable places within our souls so that our defects or imperfections ultimately become the cracks or openings through which our inner light can shine forth into this world.

Knowing this can help us relax into life, as imperfect as it is, so that we may take joy in doing our share of the work of tikkun. For if God can made a big mistake that ultimately gives rise to the possibility of tikkun, then perhaps each of us can find ways to be holy "fixers" in this imperfect life of ours.

MAKING PEACE WITH IMPERFECTION

This particular understanding of Luria's myth provided a potent healing metaphor for Sandy, a thirty-nine-year old woman who was struggling with depression. Though on the surface of things it seemed as though Sandy had everything people dream of—a loving marriage, children, and a successful career as a schoolteacher—she was dissatisfied with almost every area of her life. Nothing felt good enough to her. As we explored her feelings of dissatisfaction in therapy, it became clear that her unhappiness stemmed from an inability to accept the ways her "real life" failed to match up with her idealized images of life.

As the daughter of wealthy and highly successful parents, Sandy had been groomed throughout her privileged childhood and young adulthood to work hard and succeed. She had indeed been highly successful throughout her school years, graduating at the top of her class and going on to complete a graduate degree in education. So long as she was able to devote herself completely to her work and studies, Sandy felt relatively content. Things began to change, however, when she married and had children. Balancing career and family, Sandy found that she was no longer able to live up to all her ideals. She was not the kind of mother she had imagined she would be, nor was she able to progress in her career as rapidly as she had hoped. Instead of revising her goals and ideals to accommodate her current reality, she became increasingly frustrated and depressed. Sandy also harbored feelings of disappointment in her marriage. Though her husband worked hard as a teacher, he was unable to provide the kind of financial security that she had grown accustomed to in her childhood. Having to live within a tight budget was not something Sandy was prepared for.

In therapy, I challenged Sandy to confront the ways she was spoiling her "real life" by always comparing it to some imaginary "ideal life." We began to explore how her unconscious search for perfection and her clinging to idealized images from the past was a defense against accepting the real nature of existence as both impermanent and imperfect. Using the myth of the shattered vessels, I suggested to Sandy that it might be easier for her to make peace with her life if she accepted the fact that impermanence and imperfection are simply woven into the very fabric of existence. As we discussed Luria's myth, something finally began to click for Sandy. The image of the shattered vessels seemed to touch her deeply, opening up the possibility of self-forgiveness and of living more gracefully with life's inevitable changes.

As Sandy's fortieth birthday approached, we began planning a ritual together based on the imagery of the shattered vessels. The *kavanah*, or intention of the ritual, was to let go of perfection. Sandy spent the week before her fortieth birthday preparing for the ritual by writing down on a scroll all her childhood hopes and dreams for how she "imagined" her life was going to be. She then placed this scroll in a beautiful ceramic vase that she had owned for many years and had deeply treasured. Sandy brought these ritual objects to our next session, in which she planned to break the vase and burn the scroll.

We began the ritual by creating a sacred space and lighting four candles — one for each decade of her life. After sitting in silence for several minutes,

Sandy read what she had written and expressed her desire to be freed from the way her attachment to "perfection" and the past was keeping her from appreciating her current life. As Sandy proceeded to smash the ceramic vase and burn the scroll, she was overcome by a tremendous wave of grief. Through this act of *shevira* she was finally able to face her grief over the way her life had turned out. By shattering the vase, something she had been deeply attached to for a long time, Sandy was finally able to release herself from the grip of the past. And in expressing her grief she felt more ready to accept her real, though imperfect life. Sandy then took the broken pieces home with her, with the intent of using them in a mosaic that would be a visual reminder of the wisdom of the shattered vessels.

Sandy will probably continue to struggle with perfectionism all her life. Therapeutic rituals are no panacea, and certainly no substitute for long-term work on oneself. Yet, they do have the power to awaken us to new insights, and long after their enactment they continue to leave an imprint on our psyches. In discovering a sacred narrative that illuminated her personal struggles, Sandy felt confident she would be able to hold on to the insights she gained in therapy.

OPENING DOORS

When we go beyond our personal predicaments and open doors to the sacred dimension, we come to experience our lives as resonant to a much greater matrix of meaning in which any transition we undergo, whether it be a birth, death, divorce, illness, or disability, may initiate us into the larger mysteries of life. As we find reflections of our individual lives in sacred myth, we tend to feel less alone in our suffering; our personal struggles shift from being simply personal, and instead are seen as mirroring sacred processes that occur throughout creation. By locating ourselves within the crucible of sacred myth, we are midwifed on our journey of transformation by the archetypal forces embedded within the myth.

Carl Jung once said that modern man's tendency to "pathologize" stemmed from the fact that we had forgotten how to "mythologize." The gods live on in us in as symptoms rather than as living archetypes. In sacred narrative therapy we relearn the ancient art of myth making so that we can begin to view our lives as sacred stories—as living embodiments of Torah.

In Your Blood, Live

Re-Visions of a Theology of Purity

Rachel Adler

Twenty years ago, as a young Orthodox woman, I began what became an influential essay with the words "All things die and are reborn continually." I was wrong. Sometimes we cannot repeat ourselves. We can only transform ourselves. Yet our moral responsibility for that earlier self and its acts lives on. Twenty years later, as a feminist Reform theologian I continue to be faced with an essay I wrote, an essay that continues to be quoted, cited, and reproduced, promulgating opinions and prescribing actions that I now cannot in good conscience endorse.

My essay, which was published both in the first *Jewish Catalogue* and in the first Jewish feminist anthology, *The Jewish Woman*, was called "Tum'ah and Taharah: Ends and Beginnings." It dealt with the ancient laws of purity whose major surviving form is the powerfully valenced body of law and custom concerning women's menstruation. Because this legislation governs sexual and social behavior and attitudes so pervasively, it can be said that menstrual impurity is constitutive of the religious selfhood of women in Orthodox Judaism. I undertook to justify this legislation by constructing around it a feminist theology of purity.

Confronting my essay, I have had to ask myself what is the responsibility of a theologian when she no longer believes what she taught to others as Torah? Merely to recant is insufficient, because theologians are not just theorists. They exemplify ways to live out Jewish commitments with integrity. What I owe to those who read and were persuaded by my theology of purity is not merely to outline abstractly my revised conclusions but to tell a richly detailed story about a particular process of rupture and transformation in a specific time and place.

My task is complicated by the fact that the earlier essay itself represents a kind of transformation—a reframing. Even the title of that project is eloquent: "Tum'ah and Taharah: Ends and Beginnings." It signals that I had defined my topic as a theological understanding of the entire ancient category, and not just the part of it pertaining to women. The title evades the words woman, sex, *niddah* (menstrual impurity), menstruation, and *mikveh* (the ritual immersion by which purity is achieved). It also eschews the common euphemism *taharat ha-mishpacha* (the purity of the family), in which women are reduced to a nameless function whereby families are produced and maintained in purity.

In the essay I attempted to reframe the meaning of women's menstrual impurity (*niddah*) by reintegrating it with the other purity regulations stipulated in the book of Leviticus rather than focusing upon it as a unique phenomenon. I interpreted all these regulations as ritual expressions of a single theology of purity equally relevant to women and men. I see clearly now how this generalized reframing reflected my awareness of and hopefulness about egalitarianism as a value in secular society. Probably, it was the discrepancy between my sense of self-worth and entitlement as a participant in secular and in traditional Jewish contexts that heightened my experience of *niddah* as a source of gender stigma. Egalitarianism seeks to normalize women by stressing their similarity to men. That is how I sought to neutralize the stigma of *niddah*: by emphasizing its kinship with the purity laws applicable to men. I maintained that all impurity ritual enacted a common set of meanings. Implicitly, this was a denial that any special "women's meaning" distinguished menstrual impurity from impurities contractable by men. The strategy I chose has been used extensively by secular jurisprudence to neutralize discrimination: Obscure or ignore the differences on which discrimination was predicated and stress instead the commonalities all are presumed to share. That the laws of pollution had once applied to men was therefore indispensable to my argument, even though men had not observed them for many hundreds of years.

It is important to understand that my concerns were as much theological as social. Existing theological justifications of menstrual impurity did not help me to make sense of myself as a God-created creature. They treated me, to use Kantian terminology, as a means to someone else's end, rather than as an end in myself. To have the observance of *niddah* and *mikveh* justified to me as the instrumentality whereby my husband was entitled lawfully to cohabit was both inadequate and insulting.

Indeed, the otherness and the instrumentality of women were foundational presumptions of the men who wrote about these laws. What was significant about menstruation for them was that it made women uniquely capable of causing men to sin by transmitting pollution to them. They never asked themselves how it would feel to be someone to whom such a capacity had been assigned, or whether menstruation might have other meanings to those who menstruated. Their one educational goal was to persuade or terrify women to keep their pollution to themselves.

Some sources threatened nonobservers with death in childbirth or deformed children.[1] Others promised observers a honeymoon every month in compensation for the estrangement of *niddah*, on the dubious assumption that sex is most satisfying when the participants are unfamiliar.[2] The only rationale the sources did not offer was the rationale that motivates all sincere piety, the one held out to men: that observing the commandments would make one holier and bring one closer to God.

I required an explanation that acknowledged my personhood as intrinsically important and affirmed my capacity for spiritual growth. Even more urgently, I needed to understand how a body that menstruates, a body that pollutes, could be a holy body. The male writers were concerned about how women were to comport themselves in their impurity. I wanted to know what it might mean to be pure.

Intuitively, I sensed that the classical texts by themselves would yield no answers. The topic had not interested their creators because women as spiritual subjects had not interested them.[3] I took my questions into fields of secular learning: anthropology, literary criticism, comparative religion. These areas provided perspectives to focus upon the Jewish texts. They offered forms of discourse in which I could view myself as a subject and participant rather than as an object to be passively defined. The classic anthropological work of Mary Douglas taught me a new way to understand the categories of purity and pollution. Douglas argues that the body may be viewed both as a symbol and as a mirror of society. Upon it are inscribed the categories that make sense of the universe. Protecting the demarcation lines of those categories protects us from chaos or meaninglessness. Pollution is the punishment for violating those boundaries, and thus endangering the coherent world. Supplementing Douglas' theory of pollution with a literary reading of the texts in Leviticus, I theorized that the boundary crossed by all those who incurred impurity was the boundary between life and death. I maintained that all of the forms of impurity were regarded as encounters with death and were associated with conditions imaged as death-like or life-diminishing, such as the erosive skin diseases the Bible calls "leprosy" (*tsara'at*), menstruation, and seminal emission, or from nexus situations that bridge the passage between life and death, such as childbirth and the purification ritual for corpse impurity.

The comparative religion scholarship of Mircea Eliade provided me with an understanding of water as an ancient and universal symbol of regeneration

and renewal and of cycles as markers of sacred time and affirmations of return and restoration. Using his formulation, I depicted the *mikveh* as the
womb or the watery chaos from which Creation is elaborated, a life-giving
fluidity in which forms can be repeatedly dissolved and made new.

Drawing on these sources, I formulated a theology of purity in which menstrual impurity and *mikveh* were relocated within a universal cyclical process
in which all creation endlessly rehearses its death and rebirth. In the context
of this theology, menstruation was not only normalized, it acquired powerful
spiritual significance. While the theology justified the laws of menstrual impurity and supported their observance, it sought to reframe their meaning, to
remove their stigma and to discover their spiritual value.

The sources I brought to my theology of purity, however, built their arguments upon assumptions very different from my own. In fact, some of the implications of these assumptions were incompatible with Orthodoxy: that diverse religions have comparable or analogous symbols, myths, and practices;
that valuations such as pure and impure are socially constructed and not di-
vinely proclaimed; that religious meanings are derived not merely from texts,
but from how the words of the texts are lived out in communities. Rabbis who
viewed my work as merely an effective apologia for getting educated women
to use the *mikveh* had no interest in pursuing these disturbing implications.
They regarded secular sources much the way they regarded women, as instruments, rather than as ends in themselves. But the more I came to understand the scholarly sources I had utilized, the deeper and more troubling were
their implicit challenges to the work into which I had incorporated them.

What did it mean to formulate a theology of purity that was blind to gender difference and silent about gender stigma, when the only kind of impurity
with behavioral consequences in Orthodox communities is gender specific—
menstrual impurity? What did it mean to claim that the theological meaning
of niddah had to do with symbolisms of life and death, when its impact on
women's lives was obviously and concretely sexual? What did it mean to describe *niddah* as part of a cycle when, in the public life of the communities in
which it was observed, women were always treated as if they were impure?

The social facts about impurity in living communities are about the impurity of women. Sexual relations with a *niddah* are forbidden. Also forbidden
are physical contacts and expressions of affection, on the grounds that they
could lead to sexual relations.[4] In all but the most left-wing Orthodox circles,
the general presumption of *niddah* status is a reason for excluding women
from conventional social courtesies like shaking hands, and for denying
them access to the Torah.[5] In contrast, men experience themselves socially
as pure. Although they may meet the qualifications for biblical impurity
(having had a seminal emission, for instance, or contact with a corpse), there

is no behavioral consequence. The only men who have to contend with impurity laws at all are kohanim, descendants of the priestly clan, who may not expose themselves to corpse impurity. Kohanim who obey these laws, although they probably bear some second hand impurity from polluted others, experience themselves as utterly pure. Socially, then, purity and impurity do not constitute a cycle through which all members of the society pass, as I argued in my essay. Instead, purity and impurity define a class system in which the most impure people are women.

Even a more rigorous literary analysis would have called into question my reading of Biblical purity law. The word *niddah* describes a state which is neither socially nor morally neutral. *Niddah*, from the root NDD, connotes abhorrence and repulsion. In a recurring prophetic motif, it is associated with adultery, idolatry, and murder.[6] The icon for sinful Israel wallowing in its corruption is not the corpse handler or the leper but the exposed *niddah*, her skirts stained with menstrual blood, shunned by passersby.[7]

I explained that imagery away, interpreting it as an expression of prophetic despair and loathing at societal impurity that refuses to be cleansed. *Tum'ah* (impurity) is a stigma, I argued, only when it is divorced from the purification cycle. At some earlier time in Israel's history, I believed, there had been a Golden Age when the cycle had revolved smoothly and blamelessly for both women and men, and gender had not been a source of stigma. This belief informed my reading of the purity texts of Leviticus. But this belief is untenable.

In his cross-cultural anthropological study, *The Savage in Judaism*, Howard Eilberg-Schwartz argues convincingly that the stigma upon menstrual blood enables ancient Israelite religion to draw a crucial distinction between men's and women's capacities for holiness. The uncontrolled blood flowing from women's genitals is blood that has the power to contaminate. Its antithesis is the blood of circumcision deliberately drawn from men's genitals, which has the power to create covenant. Eilberg-Schwartz emphasizes that the symbolism of the body and its fluids as embedded in categories and rules does not merely reflect but is constitutive of the social structure within which it applies. The Israelite purity symbolism which associates masculinity with fertility and control and femininity with death and disorder constructs a culture in which men dominate women. This polarization of the symbolic meaning of gender is intensified by developments in rabbinic and postrabbinic Judaism, in which purity laws affecting men become atrophied, while those affecting women are elaborated and made more stringent.

My theology claimed that impurity was universal. The social reality, since the rabbinic period at least, was that impurity was feminine. My theology claimed that impurity was normal and morally neutral. Literary and anthropological evidence, as well as that of contemporary social reality, identify impurity as deviant and a source of stigma and exclusion. In particular, all the meanings of menstrual impurity asserted by my theology are explicitly disconfirmed by historical precedent, by literary analysis, by linguistic usage and by communal practice. And yet women embraced this theology with great fervor and felt transformed by it.

What I had succeeded in creating was a theology for the despised, reminiscent of certain strains of early Christianity, where worldly power went unchecked, the slave remained a slave, the poor stayed poor, the woman subject to her husband, but the meaning of indignity was inverted and transfigured: humiliation was triumph, rejection was salvation, and death, eternal life. My theology upheld the rules and practices that sustained women's impurity by holding out to the impure a never before experienced sense of purity. For women who were touched by this theology, *mikveh* became not merely the water that made one sexually accessible once more, but water that cleansed the soul.

It became acutely painful to me to meet these women at lectures and conferences and have them thank me for a theology I had come to believe both intellectually and morally unjustifiable. It seemed inadequate to tell them I had changed my mind, now that my teaching had been so strongly integrated into their spiritual praxis. I did not know how to be accountable to the people who learned from me. I had never heard a theologian say that he or she had been wrong. In addition, I was left with questions of faith and practice, some of which are still unresolved for me. Is the *mikveh* usable for women's ritual? Should we ritually acknowledge our menstruation? Can we continue to regard the Holiness Code of Leviticus as sacred text? What does it mean to be pure?

When Jewish women who were not Orthodox appropriated my reframing of immersion in the *mikveh* to mark occurrences for which no ritual expression had existed, they taught me an important lesson about the possibility of salvage. They began using the *mikveh* to purify themselves of events that had threatened their lives or left them feeling wounded or bereft or sullied as sexual beings: ovarian tumors, hysterectomies, mastectomies, miscarriages, incest, rape. In waters whose meaning they had transformed and made their own, they blessed God for renewed life. The makers have imbued these rituals with a different understanding of what purity means.

They appear to agree with the writers of the ancient texts that impurity afflicts the embodied human self; it is not a malaise of disembodied soul. But for the feminist Jew, impurity seems to mean the violation of physical or sexual integrity, death by invasion. If purity is the mirroring of God's oneness in human wholeness, it is no less fragile and transitory than humankind itself. Our flesh is gnawed by disease, eroded by age, menaced by human violence and natural disasters. Our minds and our souls are subject to intrusions, exploitations, indignities. We keep breaking or being breached. We keep knitting ourselves together, restoring ourselves, so we can once again reflect God's completeness in our female or male humanity.

When I was Orthodox, I thought that God's Torah was as complete as God: inerrant, invulnerable, invariable truth. I thought that I, the erring, bleeding, mutable creature, had to bend myself to this truth. Whatever I was or saw that did not fit had to be cut off, had to be blocked out. The eye—or the I—was alone at fault. I tried to make a theology to uphold this truth, and as hard as I tried to make it truthful, it unfolded itself to me as a theology of lies.

I do not believe the laws of purity will ever be reinstated, nor should they be. The worlds reflected in such rules are not worlds we inhabit. Neither should we seek to replicate such worlds. They are unjust.

In the mind of God, according to a midrash, is a Torah of black fire written on white fire. In the hands of Jews is a Torah written in gall on the skins of dead animals. And the miracle is that the fire of God's Torah flickers through our scroll. I continue to learn the purity texts, hoping for some yet unglimpsed spark, but that is not enough. I must learn what purity can mean in my own world and in the most human world I can envision. For if ours is a Torah of and for human beings, it may be perfected only in the way that we perfect ourselves. We do not become more God-like by becoming less human, but by becoming more deeply, more broadly, more comprehensively human.

We must keep asking the Torah to speak to us in human, this crude jargon studded with constraints and distortions, silences and brutalities, that is our only vessel for holiness and truth and peace. We must keep teaching each other, we and our study partner the Torah, all that it means to be human. Human is not whole. Human is full of holes. Human bleeds. Human births its worlds in agonies of blood and bellyaches. Human owns no perfect, timeless texts because human inhabits no perfect, timeless contexts. Human knows that what it weds need not be perfect to be infinitely dear.

Sacred need not mean inerrant; it is enough for the sacred to be inexhaustible. In the depths of Your Torah, I seek You out, Eheyeh, creator of a world of blood. I tear Your Torah verse from verse, until it is broken and bleeding just like me. Over and over I find You in the bloody fragments. Beneath even the woman-hating words of Ezekiel I hear You breathing, "In your blood, live."

NOTES

1. A traditional source for this view is B. Shabbath 31b-32a.

2. A traditional source for this view is B. Niddah 31b. Its most noted modern promulgator is Norman Larnm, *A Hedge of Roses*, 4th ed. (New York: Philip Feldheim, 1972).

3. I discuss this point more extensively in, "I've Had Nothing Yet, So I Can't Take More" *Moment* 8 (September 1983): 22–26.

4. Maimonides, Mishneh Torah, Hilchot 'Isure Bi'ah 12:18.

5. Exclusion of menstruants from access to sancta is a matter of folk piety rather than law. See Shaye J. D. Cohen, "Purity and Piety: The Separation of Menstruants from the Sancta," *Daughters of the King: Women and the Synagogue*, edited by Susan Grossman and Rivka Haut (Philadelphia: Jewish Publication Society, 1991).

6. Lam. 1:8, 17; Ezek. 7:19, 36:17-18; Zac. 13:1; Ez. 7:19-20, 9:11; II Ch. 29:5.

7. Lam. 1:8, 17.

Starting on My Spiritual Path

Naomi Wolf

I was raised in a home that was comfortable with the idea that there was a mystical dimension to life. But later, as an angry young feminist who wanted to get to the roots of women's oppression, I felt alienated from the patriarchal aspects of Judaism. For instance, once I talked to an important rabbi about the struggle I was going through. I shared some of my thinking about making the liturgy more inclusive, and cited the work of Rabbi Shira Lander, who was using the *mikva* as a healing and cleansing ritual for survivors of rape. The rabbi told me that if he had to choose between inclusivity and tradition he would choose the tradition. My heart closed down completely.

Of course, the progressive, post-Marxist world of which I was part was profoundly atheistic and hostile to religious and spiritual traditions. Not only was spirituality seen as part of what kept the masses tied to an oppressive social order, it was also seen as "not tough." There was a real macho posturing that made it seem really "wimpy" as well as "bourgeois" to be interested in spirit rather than in, say, guns for the Sandinistas and the redistribution of wealth. Additionally, some of the hostility to religion from feminists I was around at the time derived from their perception that "God language" had been so coopted by the religious right that to use it was to allow oneself to be coopted.

So it felt embarrassing, a social liability, to admit an interest in God. It mattered to me that it would feel pathetic and nerdy to tell someone I was interested in spiritual issues in the progressive circles in which I spent my time; to confess that would be more uncool than to confess to various forms of vice or addiction.

But then I gave birth two-and a-half years ago. That was such a miracle that it's hard not to try to figure out how to address it. The manifest miraculousness of having your child wake up in the morning and look at you! It's hard not to speculate about "where did you come from?" The kind of love that being a parent brings out, that donkey-like, repetitive, abject, egoless love, is closer to a spiritual notion of love than any other kind of love I've experienced. Romantic love, perhaps all other kinds of love too, seem more tied up with the ego than does the love of a parent for a child. So having this kind of experience of love made it easier for me to understand some of what the spiritual traditions were addressing.

Around the same time, I went to a consultant for writer's block (from which I was suffering at the time) and this consultant put me into a meditative state. I then had a spiritual experience, an overwhelming and inexplicable mystical encounter that turned my world upside down.

I recently read that 43 percent of Americans have had some sort of mystical experience in the past few years but have not been able to talk about it with people with whom they are otherwise intimate. So many people are having some kind of powerful spiritual encounter, but this experience is outstripping our abilities to put it into words. One of the dangers of any spiritual path is that there is a lot of self-delusion. There is a widening industry of books and tapes and gurus aimed at selling or packaging the mystical or spiritual experience, and I think we need to be very wary of that. The struggle for me was to use my critical mind to make sure that I could believe in what I had encountered.

I did a lot of reading about mysticism and spirituality after having had this experience. One of the tests that great teachers in the past have urged their disciples is to be sure that whatever mystical experience they claim to have had be reflected in the way one subsequently lives one's life.

This experience was really different for me than, for example, my accepting various political ideas or ideologies. One difference was that I really didn't want to have this experience, it was upsetting, it shook me, it scared me, it created upheaval in my life, it was painful and unwelcome (as well as joyful and liberating).

Part of what was shocking to me was getting that all the things that the world I knew tended to privilege—things like status, money, beauty, self, fame—were all stripped away and that the only reality is service, the joy and beauty of it. It was painful to realize the beside-the-pointness of the ego-needs that had previously preoccupied so much of my time and energy.

As I've moved into a spiritual path, I've come to realize that every choice matters. Before, if I was having a bad day I might have snapped at someone who was taking a long time with an airline ticket or I might have shaded some aspect of the truth in a conversation because I didn't really want to get too deeply into the truth at that moment, or I might have been lazy or sloppy with my choices because "it doesn't really count" or "no one is really looking" or "on balance I'm a pretty reasonable person so it doesn't really matter what I do in this particular instance." But now, as a result of my spiritual experience, I realize that every single choice really matters. To be careful of speech, for example, because one of my biggest vices was careless speech, gossip, or saying things that were witty that weren't really nice. ("Hey, it's a cocktail party, so what does it matter?") Now, I'm conscious of how powerful the choice of our words is. I'm conscious that every single thing I put out is going to come back to me, and that every intention I have is going to manifest in the world. So I try to live more carefully now.

One thing that came to me in my mystical experience was that there was no one right way to spiritual truth, that there was no one true religion, that many paths could lead to the Divine. So I started to read voraciously from all religions. I found important truths in Buddhism (particularly its notion that one could be an activist without anger and without demonizing the opposition). I got big truths from reading about Jesus, from Kabbalah, from twentieth century Jewish philosophers. But to try to talk to family members about the ways that my heart was being moved, for example, by Jesus' message was very distressing. I found that even to like the guy a little bit was to be seen as being totally disloyal to the tribe. I understand that his message was used in an oppressive way, but what has happened in the name of Christianity has often had so little to do with his original message.

I've had to be very cautious about the spiritual yearning that is at the center of my life now. I think it can be both trivializing and invasive to talk about these issues with people who don't yearn for a spiritual element in their lives. So I'm very wary of being seen as proselytizing. But if I get a sense that there is a hunger there, then I can feel more comfortable about sharing my own thirst for this dimension of reality. I think we have to be a lot more delicate about how we franchise God and how we bring God into the world. Part of that is to be very sensitive about the fact that my experience of God might not be yours.

Yet I also know that part of my reluctance to talk about all this is fear. Particularly as a woman. It's taken me nine years to build up enough credibility in the analytic/linear world that I can now speak and have some expectation of being heard to a certain degree. It's been a long haul, and very much a gendered haul. I've had to lay down brick after brick of linear, traditionally masculine, post-Enlightenment, rational thinking. Now if I say, "And . . . I had a mystical experience," it opens the door wide to the fear that I will lose that base of reasoned discourse that was so hard won. It's traditionally women who light candles and who see angels, so there is a fear of being dismissed as a woman. Humility and service, compassion and love, are traditionally gendered "female." This makes it hard for many men to open themselves to their own mystical or spiritual side, for fear that they will be demanned by the larger culture.

Moreover, it's embarrassing. To talk about one's spiritual life is to make oneself naked. To acknowledge the role of spirit in the world and to let your relationship to it visibly shine is to make yourself as naked as you can be in the world. You are undefended by cynicism, by ego. To be truly present and truly live from your heart is to make yourself profoundly vulnerable and at risk. That is a leap of faith. If you venture something from your heart in relationship to spirit, it's your absolute truth, so if that gets rejected it's your truth that got rejected, not just some clever thing you said on a television show.

I'm a writer. I've been trained to use very specific and pointed language to identify something real. But in talking about the spiritual realm there are places where our and my language break down. Look at how the language of "the politics of meaning" was publicly attacked because it was nonlinear, because it described parts of reality that could not be quantified, even though it described truths that we all know to be true deep down. It's profoundly frightening to me to leave the skill and the defendedness and ego-security I experience as a manipulator of language, and to go into a place where language fails me. If I were to talk about this in public, there I would be, this writer, stammering. It could be mortifying. So it's not easy to come out as spiritual.

The strange thing is that when I do take a leap of faith and talk to an audience and tell this to them and talk about spiritual truths, it often resonates very deeply with people. I haven't been ridiculed—on the contrary, what I'm finding is a hunger that people have to go to this level.

I've also noticed that it's easier to talk about these issues with most of America than it is with the people within the Washington, D.C./New York media box. Spiritual truths are more unacceptable in that media/government/policy corridor than they are anywhere else in America, and that only confirms for me how much those elites are behind the rest of America. The press and government are engaged in ways of behaving that are threatened by a spiritual approach, so they are going to be hostile to it.

I confronted this personally when I was asked to be a trial host on a TV show whose format involved getting people to argue their politics with each other, and the more argument and yelling, the more fireworks, the more we were supposedly succeeding. But after the fourth session I was getting headaches and realizing that this way of interacting was degrading to me and in conflict with why we had been put onto this planet. So I had to quit. There isn't yet room in that context to say, "Whoa, let's see if we can find some common ground here and build a different way of talking to each other." So my fears about being "out" as a spiritual person are well-founded, because I can no longer get those perks, because I can't do that kind of communication any longer. That kind of institution and the kind of heart I want to develop are increasingly out of sync with each other. So, I sometimes wonder if I might get to be so evolved that I won't have any job opportunities and won't have an income.

There is another fear: whenever you talk about God, there is always the fear that you will sound or be self-righteous or egomaniacal. A lot of people use God as a resume enhancer or to sell their products or themselves. That's why I shut down when I hear people talk about God and seem to be suggesting that they have the highest truth (I want to switch the channel). It's right to be cautious and wary, and to stress, as I want to here, that I'm only a beginner, that I have a spiritual hunger and not the spiritual truth. Even saying, as I did, that I'm more cautious than I used to be about what I say and what I do, could be heard by others as self-righteous and judgmental.

One form that my spiritual life has taken for me is to do Shabbat every week. I don't have many ways in my daily life to ask God to join what I'm doing. So it's very important to me to have a place in which I can do something with other people in which I can ask God to join me. And it's wonderful to me to be able to give this to my daughter Rosa, and to see how naturally children take to it and experience the change of the air as Shabbat comes in and the sacred enters (you can see it in their faces). It balances a week of very worldly activities.

I've moved my place in the progressive world. When I first started moving in this direction, I felt so alone and marginal. But I keep meeting people like Michael Lerner, Jim Wallis, people at the Center for Visionary Leadership, and people at the 1996 Politics of Meaning Summit hosted by the Foundation for Ethics and Meaning and *Tikkun* magazine—people who are both progressive and share a deep spiritual interest. So I am increasingly drawn to people who are doing politics from a faith center or a vision of common global family or politics that comes out of love. I'm happy to know that they are out there—I really didn't know that they were.

Chapter 4

THE HOLOCAUST
AND ITS LESSONS

The Holocaust's Life as a Ghost

Lingering Psychological Effects

Zygmunt Bauman

More than half a century has passed since the victory of the Allied troops put an abrupt end to Hitler's "final solution of the Jewish question," but the memory of the Holocaust goes on polluting the world of the living, and the inventory of its insidious poisons seems anything but complete. We are all to some degree possessed by that memory, though the Jews among us, the prime targets of the Holocaust, are perhaps more than most. For Jews especially, living in a world contaminated with the possibility of a holocaust rebounds time and again in fear and horror. To many, the world appears suspect at the core; no worldly event is truly neutral—each event is burdened with sinister undertones, each contains an ominous message for the Jews, a message that can be overlooked or played down only to the Jews' own peril. As E. M. Cioran, the incisive and bitter French philosopher, put it:

> [T]o be afraid is to think of yourself continually, to be unable to imagine an objective course of events. The sensation of the terrible, the sensation that it is all happening against you, supposes a world conceived without indifferent dangers. The frightened man—victim of an exaggerated subjectivity—believes himself to be, much more than the rest of his kind, the target of hostile events. . . . [He has attained] the extremity of a self-infatuated consciousness; everything conspires against [him]."

Self-defense calls the victim to learn the lesson of history, though in order to learn it, the victim needs to decide first what the lesson is. The precept of staying alive as the sole thing that counts, as the supreme value that dwarfs all other values, is among the most tempting, and the most common, interpretations of the lesson. As the direct experience of the victims recedes and fades, the memory of the Holocaust tapers and congeals into a precept of survival: life is about surviving, to succeed in life is to outlive the others. Whoever survives—wins.

This reading of the Holocaust's lesson has been recently displayed—to worldwide acclaim and huge box-office success—in Steven Spielberg's now well-nigh canonical image of the Holocaust. According to the *Schindler's List* version of the Holocaust experience, the sole goal of that most inhuman among human tragedies was to remain alive—while the humanity of life, and particularly its dignity and ethical value, was at best of secondary importance and was never allowed to interfere with the principal goal. The goal of staying alive took care of moral concerns. What counted in the last resort was to outlive the others—even if the escape from death required being put on a separate, unique, and exclusive list of the privileged. When offered by the commandant of Birkenau a replacement for "his Jewesses," Schindler refuses; it was not the saving of lives that counted, but the saving of specific, chosen lives. By definition, survival is selective; it is coveted because of its selectiveness.

In Spielberg's film, the value of staying alive is not diminished, but made more salient yet by the fact that others, less fortunate, traveled to the extermination camp; viewers of *Schindler's List* are invited to rejoice in the sight of Schindler's master of works pulled out in the nick of time—he alone—from the train destined for Treblinka. Through a willful travestying of the Talmud's precepts, Spielberg's film translates the issue of humanity's salvation into the decision of who is to live and who is to die. As the late Gillian Rose, a sublime philosopher and Judaic scholar, pointed out in her last public lecture, "The Talmud is ironic—the most ironic holy commentary in world literature: for no human being can save the world." Rose spoke of the "ruthlessness of saving one or one thousand" and comments that while Thomas Keneally's original book, *Schindler's Arc*, "makes clear the pitiless immorality of this in the context," Spielberg's film *Schindler's List* "depends on it as congratulation."

That elevation of survival to the rank of the supreme, perhaps the only value, is not Spielberg's invention and not at all a phenomenon confined to artistic representations of the Holocaust's experience.

Soon after the end of the war psychiatrists coined the term "survivor's guilt"—a complex psychical ailment which they ascribed to the habitual way survivors ask themselves why they stayed alive when so many of their near and dear perished. According to these psychiatrists, the joy of escaping death was permanently poisoned for the survivors by their acute moral uncertainty about the propriety of sailing safely out of the sea of perdition; that uncertainty, in turn, had disastrous consequences for the survivors' will to live and to succeed in life after their rescue. Many practicing psychiatrists acquired fame and fortune treating so-construed "survivor's syndrome." Whether the syndrome was rightly spotted and the psychiatric treatment well aimed was and remains a moot question; what is rather obvious, though, is that in the course of time the "guilt" aspect, looming prominently in the beginning, has been progressively exorcised from the model of the "survival complex," leaving the pure and unalloyed, unambiguous and uncontested approval of self-preservation for the sake of self-preservation.

Such a shift brings us dangerously close to the spine-chilling image of the survivor as painted by Elias Canetti—as the man for whom "the most elementary and obvious form of success is to remain alive." For Canetti's survivor, survival—unlike mere self-preservation—is framed in relation to the other, not the self: "They want to survive their contemporaries. They know that many die early and they want a different fate for themselves." At the far end of the survivalist obsession, Canetti's survivor "wants to kill so that he can survive others; he wants to stay alive so as not to have others surviving him." For Canetti, "The survivor's most fantastic triumphs have taken place in our own time, among people who set a great store about the idea of humanity. . . . The survivor is mankind's worst evil, its curse and perhaps its doom."

The wider repercussions of that cult of survival contain dangers of potentially formidable proportions. Time and again the lessons of the Holocaust are reduced for popular consumption to a simple formula: "who strikes first, survives"; or to an even simpler one: "the stronger lives." The awesome two-pronged legacy of the Holocaust is the tendency, on the one hand, to treat survival as the sole, or at any rate the topmost value and purpose of life, and, on the other hand, to posit the issue of survival as that of a competition for a scarce resource, and survival itself as a site of conflict between incompatible interests in which the success of some depends on the nonsurvival of others.

Sinister, pernicious, and morally destructive as it is in its own right, this is not the only avatar of the Holocaust's ghost and not its only misdeed. Another is the phenomenon dubbed by Alain Finkielkraut *le juif imaginaire*—a Jew manifesting his Jewishness, so to speak, by living on the account and at the expense of a "categorical martyrdom," basking in the fame of his ancestral martyrs without paying the price of the glory. Such "imaginary Jews," in Finkielkraut's caustic description, are the "habitues of unreality," who "have taken up residence in fiction . . . live in borrowed identities . . . have chosen to pass their time in a novelistic space full of sound and fury"—and have become, as a result, "armchair Jews, since, after the Catastrophe, Judaism cannot offer them any content but suffering, and they themselves do not suffer." For this generation, Alain Finkielkraut, the prolific and refined French writer born in 1949 and one of that generation's most illustrious and famous members, is full of contempt: they are, he says, "cowards in life, martyred in dream"—"they mask their inborn softness with the outcast's courage."

There is admittedly a specifically French flavor to Finkielkraut's analysis. When he writes of this group's "desperate striving . . . to plug into the great revolt of the day," his words may sound outlandish and exotic to the members of that generation scattered in other, particularly English-speaking, parts of the Jewish diaspora. And yet—the acid remarks about the "pastiche" that "was the governing principle of deeds," about the "frantic masquerade [that] sought to appease bad conscience," about "exorcising the vapidity of lives . . . through acts of fictive intensity," and altogether looking "at current events the way Emma Bovary read popular fiction: enraptured by escapism"—may find an echo in many memories and cause the beating of many breasts. Living on a borrowed identity—as martyrs by appointment, martyrs who never suffered— "we could only bear to face ourselves unrecognizably disguised"; this spiritual predicament was the fate that the whole generation shared, even if the disguises were locally diversified dresses.

Anne Karpf has recently reported, in a penetrating and sharply ironic survey of the thriving "Holocaust syndrome" literature, her own feelings of relief and spiritual comfort when first hearing of the inherited trauma of the survivors' children. Finding out that she "belonged to a group which might warrant being helped, rather than being purely privileged and morally obliged to help others," she "was relieved and even elated that [her] years of problems weren't necessarily the result of personal pathology but might have a shared and external source."

Karpf put her finger on an open wound, gaping in many a soul. In this hectic, chameleon-like, deregulated, and unpredictable world of privatized loners, one has a lot of problems finding and guarding one's place in life; one is indeed greatly relieved if at least the blame for one's troubles can be shifted onto something other than one's own shoulders.

Exactly seventy years ago, Sigmund Freud, in his seminal study *Civilization and Its Discontents*, suggested that "civilization" is a trade-off: one cherished value is sacrificed for another, equally close to the heart. He proposed that in the civilized society of his time a lot of personal freedom of expression had been sacrificed in exchange for a good deal of collectively guaranteed security. In my *Postmodernity and its Discontents* (1997), I have suggested that were Freud writing his book seventy years later, he would probably need to reverse his diagnosis: our present-day troubles and discontents are, like their predecessors, products of a trade-off, but this time it is security which is daily sacrificed on the altar of an ever-expanding individual freedom. On the way to whatever passes for greater individual liberty of choice and self-expression, we have lost a good deal of that security which modern civilization supplied, and even more of the security it promised to supply. Worse still, we have stopped hearing promises that this supply of security will be resumed, and instead hear more and more often that security is contrary to human dignity, much too treacherous to be sought and much too dependency-breeding, addictive, and altogether quagmireish to be desired.

And so there are good enough reasons to be nervous, anxious, and angry. It is not clear, though, where the ambient fear derives, what one is truly afraid of, where the danger lies, and what one can do to mitigate it. Anxiety seeks a peg and while searching for it may easily hang itself on a wrong one, prompting actions glaringly irrelevant to the genuine cause of trouble. When genuine reasons for agitation are difficult to locate and even less easy to control if discovered, we are powerfully tempted to construe and name putative, yet credible, culprits against whom we can wage a sensible defensive (or better still, offensive) action. We may bark up a wrong tree, but at least we are barking and cannot deprecate ourselves nor be reproached by others for taking the blows against us hands down.

Throughout the United States, "self-help" groups were formed by the "children of the Holocaust"; these self-invigorating group discussions added an extra dimension of collectively sustained interpretation (and thus the authority of numbers) to the zealous search for a collective Holocaust trauma, which would put the missing sense back into these individuals' present personal troubles. This search was also given the authority of the psychiatric profession; all over the country, psychoanalysts told their patients in no uncertain terms that the roots of their "maladjustments" were buried in the Holocaust. Some therapeutic experts, like Harvey and Carol Barocas (quoted by Karpf and prestigious enough to contribute to the International Review of Psychoanalysis), went so far as to suggest that "the children of survivors show symptoms that would be expected if they actually lived through the Holocaust." And so the ghost has been issued an official permission of domicile, recognized as the lawful plenipotentiary of the "real thing," and so (in tune with the spirit of our time) the troublesome and worrying distinction between the "real" and "virtual" reality has been declared null and void.

For those involved, the message hammered home by the psychiatrists, and sunk ever deeper in the course of the self-help sessions, could not but be richly rewarding. In Anne Karpf's words, "there's undoubtedly something satisfying in joining the ranks of unequivocally wronged, those with an irrefutably legitimate claim on our sympathy." To acquire the right to sympathy and benevolence before one earns it through personal exertions, is an opportunity few people would willingly forfeit. The side effect of all this is, however, a sort of "competition for victimhood," a "pecking order of pain" reminiscent—we may recall—of the rivalry among the tuberculous residents of Thomas Mann's *The Magic Mountain* who quickly established their own eerie hierarchy of prestige and influence measured by the size of their pulmonary caverns.

There is something else, though, to the status of a "victim by proxy"—one of belonging to a *sui generis* "aristocracy of victimhood" (that is, having a hereditary claim to sympathy and to the ethical indulgence owed to those who suffer). That status can be, and often is, brandished as a signed-in-advance and in blanco certificate of moral righteousness; whatever the offspring of the victims do must be morally proper (or at least ethically correct) as long as it can be shown that it was done in order to stave off the repetition of the lot visited on their ancestors; or as long as it can be shown to be psychologically understandable, nay "normal," in view of the super-susceptibility of the hereditary bearers of victimhood to the threat of a new victimization.

The ancestors are pitied, but also blamed for letting themselves be led, like sheep, to slaughter; how can one blame their descendants for sniffing out a future slaughterhouse in every suspicious-looking street or building and—more importantly still—for taking preventive measures to disempower the potential slaughterers? Those who are to be disempowered may not be kith and kin of the perpetrators of the Holocaust, neither bodily nor spiritually, nor in any juridical or ethically sensible way charged with responsibility for their ancestors' perdition; it is, after all, the heredity of the "hereditary victims," and not the continuity of their assumed victimizers, which makes the "connection." And yet in a world haunted by the ghost of the Holocaust, such assumed would-be persecutors are guilty in advance, guilty of being seen as inclined or able to engage in another genocide. They need commit no crime; standing accused or just being suspect, true to the message of Kafka's *The Trial,* is already their crime, the only crime needed to cast them as criminals and to justify harsh preventive/punitive measures. The ethics of hereditary victimhood reverses the logic of the Law; the accused remain criminals until they have proven their innocence—and since it is their prosecutors who conduct the hearings and decide the validity of the argument, they have slim chance of their arguments being accepted in court and every chance of staying guilty for a long time to come—whatever they do.

Thus the status of hereditary victim may take the moral reprobation off such new victimization—this time perpetrated in the name of erasing the hereditary stigma. We often say that violence breeds more violence; we remind ourselves much too rarely, though, that victimization breeds more victimization. Victims are not guaranteed to be morally superior to their victimizers, and seldom emerge from the victimization morally ennobled. Martyrdom—whether lived in a real or a virtual reality—is not a warrant for saintliness.

Memory of suffering does not assure life-long dedication to the fight against inhumanity, cruelty, and the infliction of pain as such, wherever they happen and whoever are the sufferers. At least an equally probable outcome of martyrdom is the tendency to draw an opposite lesson: that humankind is divided into the victims and the victimizers, and so if you are (or expect to be) a victim, your task is to reverse the tables ("the stronger lives"). It is this lesson that the specter of the Holocaust whispers into many ears. And for this reason we cannot be sure whether the lasting legacy of the Holocaust was not the very opposite of what many had hoped and some anticipated: the moral reawakening or ethical purification of the world as a whole or any of its sections.

The pernicious legacy of the Holocaust is that today's persecutors may inflict new pains and create new generations of victims eagerly awaiting their chance to do the same, while acting under the conviction that they avenge yesterday's pain and ward off the pains of tomorrow—while being convinced, in other words, that ethics is on their side. This is perhaps the most awesome among the Holocaust's curses and the greatest of Hitler's posthumous victories. The crowds that applauded Goldstein's massacre of the Muslim worshippers in Hebron, that flocked to his funeral and go on writing his name on their political and religious banners, are the most terminally afflicted, but not the only bearers of that curse.

The phenomenon of hereditary victimhood ought not to be confused with genetic kinship, or with family tradition preserved through parental influence over the educational setting. Heredity in this case is mainly imagined, acting through the collective production of memory and through individual acts of self-enlisting and self-identification. Thus the status of the "Holocaust children," that is of hereditary victim, is open to every Jew, whatever his or her parents might have been "doing in the war" (in fact, embracing this status has turned for many into their main vehicle of Jewish self-definition). Psychiatrists conducted ample studies of the biological descendants (and/or educational objects) of the inmates of concentration camps and the dwellers of ghettos; but the swelling numbers of the "sons and daughters of the Holocaust" who are not children of either, still await a comprehensive study. There are many clues, though, of what such a study may reveal. It may well transpire that the complexes of such "imagined children," the "children-pretenders," the "self-appointed children" (and for the same reason "children manques"—flawed, if not fraudulent, children) are more severe and vicious, and burdened with more sinister consequences, than those which the psychiatrists have described thus far.

One may say this stands to reason (whatever "reason" may mean in the world of the possessed). For the "children manques," the site which they occupy in the world, from which they view the world and in which they want to be viewed by the world, is that of martyrdom; but it so happens that they are not, nor have been, personally, the butt of anybody's wrath and wrongdoing. They do not suffer, or they suffer not enough for the victims-by-birth that they are. The world seems reluctant to harm them and make them suffer, and under the circumstances such a world is too good to be acceptable—since the reality of a harmless world means the irreality of a life which derives its sense from the harm done to it and the harm yet to be done.

Living in a not-hostile and harmless world means the betrayal of that sense-giving parentage. To reach completeness, to fulfill their destiny, to get rid of their present deficiency and to efface their vexing (and in the end humiliating) impairment, to turn from children manques into children pure and simple, they would need to reforge their own imagined continuity of victimhood into the world's real continuity of victimization. That can be done only by acting as if their present site in the world was really and truly a site of the victims; through abiding by a strategy which may gain rationality only in a victimizing world. Children manques cannot be fulfilled unless the world they live in reveals its hostility, conspires against them—and, indeed, contains the possibility of another holocaust.

The awesome truth is that, contrary to what they say and think they wish, children manques—the "flawed children" are unfit to live, and feel out of place in a world free of that possibility. They would feel more comfortable living in a world more like that other world, populated by the Jew-hating murderers who would not stop short of including them among its victims if given a chance and not having their blood-soaked hands tied. They draw a sense-giving reassurance from every sign of hostility toward them; and they are eager to interpret every move of those around them as overt or latent expression of such hostility. In their lives the ghost of the Holocaust may feel safe; in their deeds it has found a magic counterspell against other people's exorcisms.

The flawed children of the martyrs do not live in homes; they live in fortresses. And to make their homes into fortresses, they need them besieged and under fire. Where else can one come closer to their dreams than among the famished and destitute, despaired and desperate, cursing and stone-throwing Palestinians. Here, the comfortable and commodious, all-mod-con houses are unlike the houses the children manques have abandoned—those comfortable and commodious, all-mod houses over there in the stale and dull, too-safe-for-comfort American suburbs, where children would be bound to stay as they are, manques. Here, in Israel, one can tightly wrap the houses with barbed wire, one can build watchtowers in every corner and one can walk from one house to another proudly caressing the gun hanging from one's shoulder. The hostile, Jew-baiting world once forced Jews into ghettos. By making a home in the likeness of the ghetto one can make the world once more hostile and Jew-baiting. In that fully and truly flawed world, the children, at long last, would be no more flawed. The chance of martyrdom missed by the generation would have been repossessed by its chosen representatives, who want to be seen as its spokesmen as well.

Whichever way you look at it, the ghost of the Holocaust appears self-perpetuating and self-reproducing. It made itself indispensable to too many to be easily exorcised. Haunted houses have an added value, and being possessed has turned for many into a valued, meaning-bestowing life formula. In this effect one can spy out the greatest posthumous triumph of the Endlosung designers. What the latter failed to accomplish when alive they may yet hope to achieve in death. They did not manage to turn the world against the Jews, but in their graves they can still dream of turning the Jews against the world, and thus—one way or another—to make the Jewish reconciliation with the world, their peaceful cohabitation with the world, all that more difficult, if not downright impossible. The prophecies of the Holocaust are not quite self-fulfilling, but they do fulfill—render plausible—the prospect of a world in which the Holocaust may never stop being prophesied, with all the deleterious and disastrous psychical, cultural and political consequences which such prophesying is bound to bring forth and propagate.

Can one exorcise the ghost of the Holocaust? A big question and a daunting task, no doubt. And a different one from making the world Holocaust-proof, although the state of being possessed makes that other task yet more daunting. It is not easy to write out a foolproof recipe for exorcism, and even if a medicine were available, there would be no guarantee that the patient would swallow the prescribed pills.

Being possessed means seeing the world as one dimensional while being blinkered to all other dimensions, not to mention their interplay. The sole dimension which the ghost of the Holocaust renders visible to the eyes of the possessed (while effacing or removing from sight all other dimensions) is that measured by the degree of Jew-resentment. The world, though, is multidimensional.

Jean-Paul Sartre proposed that the Jew is a person whom others define as a Jew. What Sartre must have meant was that the act of such defining is also the act of reductive selectiveness; one of the manifold traits of an irretrievably multifaceted person is hereby given prominence, rendering all other traits secondary, derivative, or irrelevant. In the practice of the possessed, the Sartrean procedure is conducted once more, though in the opposite direction. To the possessed, the others, the non-Jews, emerge as one-dimensional as the Jews appear in the vision of their haters. For the possessed, the others are not benign or cruel *patri familiae*, caring or selfish husbands, benevolent or malicious bosses, good or bad citizens, peaceful or pugnacious neighbors, oppressors or oppressed, pained or pain-inflicting, privileged or dispossessed, threatening or threatened; more precisely, they may be any or all of that, but the fact that they are all that and more is but of secondary and minor importance and does not count for much. What truly counts—perhaps the only thing that counts—is their attitude toward the Jews (and let us recall that the possessed take every stance directed toward a person who happens to also be a Jew as a manifestation and derivative of the attitude taken toward the Jews as such).

That is why it is so tremendously important to accept and remember that many declared anti-Semites stoutly refused to cooperate with the perpetrators of the Holocaust, while the ranks of the executors were full of law-abiding citizens and disciplined functionaries who happened to be free of any peculiar grudge against the Jews. To accept and remember that "deportation of the Jews" (as the annihilation of European Jewry was officially defined) derived its meaning in Nazi thinking from their overall, audacious plan of wholesale *Ubersiedlung*, their vision of a European continent in which well-nigh everyone would be transported from their present, contingent site to the place where reason ordered them to be (and that could entail nothingness; as the Holocaust progressed, even Jewish graveyards were proclaimed out of order and replaced with chimney smoke). To accept and remember that extermination of the Jews was conceived in the framework of a total "cleansing of the world" operation (which included also the mentally deficient, physically handicapped, ideologically deviant, and sexually unorthodox) by a state powerful enough and sufficiently immune to all opposition to afford such total plans and to execute them without fear of effective dissent. And to accept and to remember, last but not least, that the Nazis behind the Holocaust were also "Burgers," who like all Burgers now as much as then, here as much as there, had their "problems" which they dearly wished to "resolve."

The acclaim accorded to Daniel Goldhagen's version of the Holocaust as primarily the story of the voluntary and Jew-hating helpers of Hitler adds to such risks, being itself a fruit gestated in the haunted house. That some of the participants of mass murder did enjoy their part in crime either because of their sadistic inclinations or because of their hatred of the Jews or for both reasons simultaneously is not, of course, Goldhagen's fantasy (though it is not his discovery either). Taking that fact, however, as the explanation of the Holocaust, as its central point or deepest meaning, says a lot about the ghosts haunting the house, while turning our attention away from what is the most sinister truth of that genocide and what is still the most salutary lesson which our haunted world could learn from the recent history which contains the Holocaust as its major event.

The point is that for every villain of Goldhagen's book, for every German who killed his victims with pleasure and enthusiasm, there were dozens and hundreds of Germans and non-Germans who contributed to the mass murder no less effectively without feeling anything about their victims and about the nature of the actions involved.

And the point is that while we know quite well that prejudice threatens humanity, and we know even how to fight and constrain the ill intentions of people poisoned with prejudice, we know little how to stave off the threat of a murder which masquerades as the routine and unemotional function of an orderly society. As Enzo Traverso put it recently in reference to France, the causes of the Holocaust in general, and that "wall of indifference" which surrounded the mass slaughter of the French Jews, need to be sought not in the "Jewish question," as Jean-Paul Sartre saw fit, nor even in the circumstances of the genocide itself, but in the French pre-Vichy society. A genocide of unwanted strangers cannot take place in just any society, and the presence of a quantity of Jew-haters is not the only, not even the necessary, condition which needs to be met to make that genocide a possibility.

Hannah Arendt pointed out a long time ago that the phenomenon of Holocaust anti-Semitism may explain at most the choice of the victims, but not the nature of the crime. Nothing happened since then to invalidate Arendt's verdict, while the monumental memoirs of Primo Levi, the monumental historical research of Raoul Hilberg, and the monumental documentary of Claude Lanzman, to mention but a few landmarks, did a lot to confirm and reinforce it.

This is not to say that the world we live in differs from the world of the Holocaust to an extent that makes it holocaust-proof and that holocaust fears are therefore illusory. But it does mean that the threat of such holocausts as may yet come is all too often sniffed out today and searched in the wrong places and our sight is diverted from the grounds in which genuine threats are rooted. These are the grave risks of living in a haunted house.

Tainted Legacy

Remembering the Warsaw Ghetto

Lawrence L. Langer

Does Holocaust "remembrance" have redemptive power? Although this assumption has nurtured an extensive commentary on the Holocaust, it is at odds, linguistically and ultimately factually, with the reality of the survivors' memory. In framing the Holocaust through the lens of heroic rhetoric, Holocaust chroniclers exhibit their own discomfort with the facts left to us by Holocaust victims, dead and alive, and reveal the inadequacy of our language in the face of what there is to tell.

When the German administrator of the Warsaw ghetto told Adam Czerniakow, president of the Warsaw Jewish Council, that starting on July 22, 1942 he wanted six thousand Jews daily for "resettlement" to the East, Czerniakow, undeceived, decided that he did not wish to preside over the destruction of Warsaw Jewry: The next day, he committed suicide. This is a piece of incontestable documentary evidence, but like much other evidence of this sort, it offers us no guidance.

How shall we, generations later, judge this act? Does it represent courageous defiance or a withdrawal from responsibility? Czerniakow, after all, was the leader of his community, and his voice might have summoned his fellow Jews to some act of public resistance. Decades after the war, Marek Edelman, one of the few surviving leaders of the Warsaw ghetto uprising the following spring, criticized Czerniakow for failing to make a public declaration of the truth—that the Jews were about to be murdered. "One should die only after having called other people into struggle," Edelman charged. He and his dead friends reproach Czerniakow "for having made his death his own private business."

But as Yisrael Gutman, also a member of the Jewish Fighting Organization during the uprising and today a distinguished Israeli historian and director of research at Yad Vashem in Jerusalem, points out in defense of Czerniakow, at the time "even the various underground factions were unable to concur in an appraisal of the situation, address the masses of Jews with a common appeal, or call for resistance as a means of response." We also know from Czerni- akow's diary that only two days before the deportations were to begin, he went to half a dozen Gestapo, S.S., and civilian officials seeking confirmation of the persistent rumors that a massive "resettlement" operation was about to start, and to a man they denied the rumors as utter nonsense.

Lies and deception were integral parts of the German strategy; Czerni- akow's mistake was to believe what he needed and wanted to believe, but he can hardly be blamed for that, since he shared that weakness—or naivete— with most of his fellow Jews in the ghetto. His death must have been an ad- mission to himself that he had been a tool of the Germans all along, and a sign of his refusal to accept that role any longer. Since there was no organized resistance in the ghetto in July 1942, and little possibility of any appearing, Czerniakow seemed to have had little choice. But this does not make his fi- nal act any easier to assess so many decades later.

Edelman tells another story: When the Germans entered the ground floor of the children's hospital in the Warsaw ghetto to round up the young patients for deportation to Treblinka, on the upper floor Adina Blady Szwajger, a Jew- ish doctor, was busy poisoning the sick children to "rescue" them from that doom. "She saved these children from the gas chamber," says Edelman. "Peo- ple thought she was a hero." This is perhaps the most bizarre definition of heroic behavior we will ever encounter. The issue is not whether the designa- tion is correct; the issue—here, as in the case of Czerniakow's suicide—is the poverty of traditional moral vocabulary when we address the subject of hu- man conduct during the destruction of European Jewry.

Much writing about the Holocaust, including some works of history, illus- trates the failure of language to grasp the thoroughly disruptive, not to say disintegrative impact, of that event on familiar value systems. Marek Edel- man goes so far as to call the Warsaw ghetto uprising "undramatic," because for him dramatic action depended on choice, on making a decision. The fate of every Jew in the Warsaw ghetto, including those who took part in the up- rising, was predetermined by the Germans: It had already been established that they were all to be killed; any exceptions (and there were very few) would be owing to chance and luck, not choice. As a cardiologist (after the war), Edelman knew that doctors often made decisions that might save a pa- tient's life. But in the Warsaw ghetto, he admits, "It was always death that was at stake, not life." The victims, especially those who joined the uprising, knew that they were supposed to die. If we raise that awareness to a public level, it means that historians of the period must accept the fact that they are writing of a moment in time without a future. The challenge to us is to try to suspend the privilege of having a future in order to enter sympathetically into the daily ordeal of human beings who could not share it.

Fortunately, we have the testimony of survivors and victims to help us make this transition, but we must be prepared to face a reality that cannot be normalized or sanitized by romantic references to heroes and martyrs. Most victims did not see themselves that way. Listen to the voice of Abraham Lewin, whose recently translated *A Cup of Tears: A Diary of the Warsaw Ghetto*, one of the most important sources providing us with an account of the daily struggle to stay alive. Lewin writes:

> The proportions of life and death have radically changed. Times were, when life occupied the primary place, when it was the main and central concern, while death was a side phenomenon, secondary to life, its termination. Nowadays death rules in all its majesty; while life hardly glows under a thick layer of ashes. Even this faint glow of life is feeble, miserable and weak, poor, devoid of any free breath, deprived of any spark of spiritual content. The very soul, both in the individual and in the community, seems to have starved and perished, to have dulled and atrophied. There remains only the needs of the body, and it leads merely an organic-physiological existence.

Those of us familiar with descriptions of the Warsaw ghetto as a model for heroic resistance and the resolute will to survive may have difficulty reconciling Lewin's desperate portrait with that more congenial version. The conflict leads us to consider the two planes on which the event we call the Holocaust takes place in human memory—the historical and the rhetorical, the way it was and its verbal reformation, or deformation, by later commentators.

Since the Warsaw ghetto has become the emblem of Jewish resistance for many of those commentators, we need to balance the attitude based on a rhetoric of heroism with the testimony from those who were there. Probably the most important witness, in terms of the archive of documents he collected and buried, was the historian Emmanuel Ringelblum. After the war, ten cases and two milk cans of his records, diaries, journals, and historical commentary were discovered in the ruins of the ghetto. They represent an invaluable legacy of a man who tirelessly inspired a staff of writers—Abraham Lewin was one of them—to preserve for history the narrative of their people's ruin. This was not only Ringelblum's life work; it was also his death work, since when he had an opportunity after the uprising to be smuggled out of the country by the Polish underground, he refused. He preferred to continue writing in hiding until, in March 1944, the Gestapo discovered him and his family and thirty-five others and executed them all.

One of the most famous passages in Ringelblum's notes is the entry for October 15, 1942, about a month after the great deportation was temporarily suspended. Writing as historian rather than psychologist, Ringelblum raises an issue that continues to trouble many students of the Holocaust today:

> Why didn't we resist when they began to resettle 300,000 Jews from Warsaw? Why did we allow ourselves to be led like sheep to the slaughter? Why did everything come so easy to the enemy? Why didn't the hangmen suffer a single casualty? Why could 50 SS men (some people say even fewer), with the help of a division of some 200 Ukrainian guards and an equal number of [Latvians] carry the operation out so smoothly?

Ringelblum neglects to mention at this point the role of the Jewish police in the roundups, although he was certainly aware of it. Promised exemption for themselves and the members of their families, the Jewish police in the ghetto played an active and sometimes a brutal part in helping the Germans with their plans. They did it not out of hatred, but fear—a natural, if not a particularly commendable response. Threatened by similar dangers, victims from other nations behaved in the same way. It was a human, not a Jewish, reaction, made ironic by the fact that in the closing days of the deportations, the Jewish police and their families were themselves shipped off to Treblinka. Ringelblum's rhetorical questions reflect the despair of a man who has witnessed the disappearance of hundreds of thousands of his people. But they are also a trifle naive, and if we continue to ask them today, when we know the total has risen to the millions, we share in that naivete.

The questions Ringelblum raises are troublesome and remind us that documentary evidence is only the beginning of our inquiry, since it provokes the need for interpretations that threaten our comfortable belief in the redeeming power of memory. Remembering the Holocaust is the most unredemptive task one can possibly imagine. Ringelblum clearly knew that many hungry victims went voluntarily to the trains in Warsaw because the Germans promised bread and marmalade to those who complied with their order. Pleas to the human spirit, to brotherhood and cooperation, to say nothing of physical resistance, usually fall on deaf ears when those appealed to are driven to the verge of death by hunger. And even when, some months later, the Jewish Fighting Organization was finally molded into a resistance group in the ghetto, it numbered only several hundred—estimates range from 250 to 800—from the more than 50,000 to 60,000 Jews who were still alive in Warsaw in April 1943. Of course, the lack of weapons helped to keep those figures low. Still, the majority of the ghetto residents chose to defend themselves from the resumption of deportations by building secret hiding places or bunkers.

We who from the safe vantage point of the future expect heroic gestures from a weakened and terrified people betray an innocence of the fundamental nature of the psychology of despair. The Germans understood it well, which is one reason why, as part of their plan for extermination, they deliberately reduced their victims to a bare minimum of physical and moral energy. We don't need to guess what this must have been like; we have ample testimony from the documents. Lewin himself records meticulously his response when during the mass deportations his wife is sent off to Treblinka. His remorse is genuine; but so is his paralysis. "Eclipse of the sun, universal blackness," he writes:

> My Luba [his wife] was taken away during a blockade. . . . To my anguish, there is no prospect of rescuing her. It looks like she was taken directly into the train. Her fate is to be a victim of the Nazi bestiality, along with hundreds of thousands of other Jews. I have no words to describe my desolation. I ought to go after her, but I have no strength to take such a step.

As we survey the spectacle of Lewin remembering his wife, and his inability to do anything to save her, we begin to understand how little an expression like the "redeeming power of memory" can have for him, or for us. Holocaust memory redeems only when it falsifies; Lewin's subsequent reactions to his loss document the efforts of what I call unheroic memory to wrestle with a legacy that has tainted his consciousness with an indelible stain. The following day he writes:

> I will never be consoled as long as I live. If she had died a natural death, I would not have been so stricken, so broken. But to fall into the hands of such butchers!

Lewin speaks of the tragic end of their life of twenty-one years together. But in tragedy, the victim is an agent, or at least a partial agent, in his or her own fate. We know, and as we slowly perceive, Lewin does too, that a main source of his anguish is his failure to find a role for his wife or himself in what happened to her. This fills him with an unappeasable grief: "My soul can find no peace," he records two days later, "for not having gone after her when she was in danger, even though I could also have disappeared." The heroic imagination conjures up all kinds of knightly exploits that Lewin might have attempted, but these are the stuff of romantic literature or folklore, not life, and though some of us persist in imposing such exploits on the grim reality of the Holocaust, Lewin's humble words remind us how humanly unexceptional most of us are, even in moments of extreme disaster. I think if pressed, Ringelblum might have admitted this too.

"Today is the seventh day since the great calamity that befell me," Lewin writes after a week has passed. "If only I could die and be free of the whole nightmare. But I am still tied to life and it is still difficult for me to take my own life." Whatever we may call his clinging to life, celebrating it as an affirmation of the human spirit, considering the immediate context of his loss, would be to misconstrue his situation and his attitude. Since virtually all surviving victims share a similar kind of loss, it is little wonder that they demur when we ply them with the rhetoric of heroic behavior. They know we do this to shield ourselves, not to praise them.

Lewin's own vista of what lay ahead paid homage to the limitations, not the infinite vitality, of the human spirit.

"The burden on our souls and on our thoughts has become so heavy, oppressive," he wrote, "that it is almost unbearable. I am keenly aware that if our nightmare does not end soon, then many of us, the more sensitive and empathetic natures, will break down. I feel that we are standing on the threshold of the intolerable, between existence and annihilation." One can imagine Adam Czerniakow thinking those very words before he swallowed his poison.

These are not options that endear themselves to the contemporary imagination. But if we are to teach this history faithfully, we must heed without flinching the implications of testimony such as Lewin's, written from within the cauldron. Students of the Holocaust need to know what life from the threshold of the intolerable looks like. Lewin did, and he leaves us the legacy of his vision:

> If we ever live to see the end of this cruel war and are able as free people and citizens to look back on the war-years that we have lived through, then we will surely conclude that the most terrible and unholy, the most destructive aspect for our nervous system and our health was to live day and night in an atmosphere of unending fear and terror for our physical survival, in a continual wavering between life and death—a state where every passing minute brought with it the danger that our hearts would literally burst with fear and dread.

If we ask today, sometimes with a faint if self-righteous air of disapproval, why Jews in the camps or ghettos behaved the way they did, the answer, more often than not, lies locked in a heart bursting with fear or dread. It is an answer beyond judgment—but not beyond compassion.

The language of moral evaluation simply does not serve us in situations like the ones I have been describing. Adina Blady Szwajger, the Warsaw ghetto doctor who poisoned her young patients as the Nazis arrived to seize them, survived the Holocaust and recently wrote a personal account of the episode, leaving us with the challenge of interpretation. She was not driven by her own fear or dread, she says, but by the fear and dread of the children, whose plea that she stay with them "until the end" she resolved to heed. She decided that she could best fulfill this pledge by becoming the agent of that end. She thus seized two large containers of morphine (the "poison" that Edelman spoke of), and calmly narrates how she proceeded:

I took the morphine upstairs. Dr. Margolis [head of the tuberculosis ward] was there and I told her what I wanted to do. So we took a spoon and went to the infants' room. And just as, during those two years of real work in the hospital, I had bent down over the little beds, so now I poured this last medicine down those tiny mouths. Only Dr. Margolis was with me. And downstairs there was screaming because the Szaulis [units of Lithuanian collaborators] and the Germans were already there, taking the sick from the wards to the cattle trucks.

After that we went in to the older children and told them that this medicine was going to make their pain disappear. They believed us and drank the required amount from the glass. And then I told them to undress, get into bed, and sleep. So they lay down and after a few minutes—I don't know how many—but the next time I went into that room, they were asleep. And then I don't know what happened after that.

Dr. Szwajger managed to escape from the ghetto and live with false papers on the Aryan side for two years as a courier for the Jewish Fighting Organization, but she confesses that those years "still didn't manage to wipe out any of what had happened the day I gave the children morphine." That's why, she concludes, "I was always different from everybody else. And nobody ever understood this. Everybody thought I'd forgotten about everything and didn't care any more." This is a classic example of what I elsewhere call tainted memory, a concept vital for us to understand if we are ever to assess adequately the legacy with which the Holocaust has smitten our consciousness.

Since the children, like all the other Jews in the Warsaw ghetto, were sentenced to death anyway, does it matter how they died? Knowing what they were spared, we are forced by the circumstances to view the killing of the children as an act of mercy, and this itself reminds us of what the Holocaust has done to the systems of value that we cherished before its advent. The more we immerse ourselves in the personal ordeal of victims such as Abraham Lewin, Marek Edelman, and Adina Szwajger, the more we must adapt ourselves to an idea that in its relentless harshness shares the stage with the painful notion of being sentenced to die—and that is the anguish of being sentenced to live. The postmodern replacement of the death sentence that dominated western thought from Freud to Camus is the life sentence.

What can this mean? Because, unlike other crucial episodes in history such as the French or American revolutions, the Holocaust is an event without a future—that is, nothing better for mankind grew out of it—memory is sentenced to confront it without any relief from expectation. Death is no longer a destiny to be postponed (or transcended), but a constant companion. During their ordeal in the Warsaw ghetto, inhabitants knew that daily survival was merely a respite, not a triumph. And even after the war, people like Marek Edelman and Adina Szwajger realized that little had changed. You don't remake your life after an event like the destruction of the Warsaw ghetto; you simply are sentenced to live with the memory of the ruin.

One of the laudable rhythms of public or private history is that most human beings eventually seem able to resume their lives after a disaster. Superficially, this is true of Marek Edelman and Adina Szwajger too. But if we read beneath the lines of their testimony, we hear a muted theme, and it is here, in what I have called, following Auschwitz survivor and memoirist Charlotte Delbo, the realm of deep memory, that a darker truth emerges: tainted memory leaves a tainted legacy and a tainted life. For Marek Edelman, recalling details of the Warsaw ghetto uprising leads to a bitter discovery: history is not a chronology of events; rather, "historical order turns out to be nothing more than the order of dying."

Dr. Szwajger turned to pediatrics after the war, specializing in tuberculosis in children, pursuing her belief that one becomes a doctor in order to save life. "But somewhere underneath," she admits, "I thought that I had no right to carry out my profession. After all, one does not start one's work as a doctor by leading people not to life but to death." She knows there were reasons for her behavior during that time, but memory cannot appease such knowledge. She is unable to escape the feeling that "along the way something was not as it should have been." And she concludes her formal narrative with a question that continues to echo in our own helpless minds: "Maybe it was too heavy a burden for the rest of my life?"

Possibly we can relieve that burden by adding some of it to our own consciousness. This requires us to accept and generalize Dr. Szwajger's private conclusion: in the history of the Warsaw ghetto, along the way not only something; but everything was not as it should have been. The Germans were ruthless in their plans for total destruction. The Polish underground's supply of arms to the Jewish uprising leaders was scanty and, as it later turned out, inappropriate: they provided pistols, when the Jews needed rifles and machineguns for the street fighting. Meanwhile, the outside world simply ignored pleas for help. The number of Jewish fighters engaged in the uprising was never more than between one and two percent of the remaining ghetto population. The majority of those who outlived the search and the subsequent burning of the ghetto were shipped to Sobibor or Treblinka. Few survived. On the fourth day of the uprising, the commander of the Jewish Fighting Organization, twenty-three-year-old Mordecai Anielewicz, wrote to his Jewish liaison on the "Aryan" side: "I can't begin to describe the conditions under which the Jews are living. Only an elect few will hold out under them. All the others will perish, sooner or later. Our fate is sealed. In the bunkers where our comrades are hiding, it is not even possible to light a candle at night for lack of air." Two weeks later, the Germans discovered the command bunker; most of its inhabitants, including Anielewicz, died, either through suicide or the poison gas that the Germans pumped into the bunker after blocking the exits. A handful, including Marek Edelman, managed to make their way out of the ghetto through the sewers to the "Aryan" side. The ghetto itself was doomed.

What was the Warsaw ghetto's role in the history of the Holocaust? We will go on interpreting it for decades and perhaps generations, with the help of the immense number of documents from Jewish, Polish, and German sources. Simply celebrating the exploits of its courageous, if futile, defenders seems to me a hopeless effort at self-delusion. I think Claude Lanzmann understood this as well as anyone, since he chose to end his nine-and-a-half-hour cinematic epic on the destruction of European Jewry, Shoah, with the voices of two figures who were central to the ghetto's defense. What they say allows Lanzmann to deflate the desires of his viewers, many of whom, when the subject of the Warsaw ghetto was finally raised in the film, must have expected some heroic relief from their long and dismal encounter with unnatural death. But they were to be disappointed. Lanzmann chose to let the ruins of memory prevail. One of his voices (Simha Rotem, known as "Kazik") prefers facts to heroism:

> I don't think the human tongue can describe the horror we went through in the ghetto. In the streets, if you can call them that, for nothing was left of the streets, we had to step over heaps of corpses. There was no room to get around them. Besides fighting the Germans, we fought hunger, and thirst. We had no contact with the outside world; we were completely isolated, cut off from the world. We were in such a state that we could no longer understand the very meaning of why we went on fighting.

That search for meaning was complicated by Rotem's description of the situation outside the ghetto:

> In Aryan Warsaw, life went on as naturally and normally as before. The cafes operated normally, the restaurants, buses, streetcars, and movies were open. The ghetto was an isolated island amid normal life.

And there it will remain throughout history, unless we allow it to penetrate our consciousness and shatter the rhetorical shield of heroism that protects us. The other voice with which Lanzmann ends his film is that of Itzhak Zuckerman, second-in-command of the Jewish Fighting Organization in the Warsaw ghetto and, along with Edelman, the only surviving member of the leadership. Asked by Lanzmann to comment on his memory of the event, Zuckerman succinctly replies:

> I began drinking after the war. It was very difficult. . . . You asked for my impression. If you could lick my heart, it would poison you.

If normal memory is an internal ordering of images from the past, then tainted memory is an internal disordering of those images, and Zuckerman's uncommon response to his Warsaw ghetto experience reveals the origins of that taint. It is an austere and vexing legacy, but the Holocaust, when truly faced, offers us little else.

The Paradigm Challenged

Study of the Holocaust

Daniel Jonah Goldhagen

VICTIM TESTIMONY, CRITICAL EVIDENCE, AND NEW PERSPECTIVES IN THE STUDY OF THE HOLOCAUST

Imagine a history of American slavery whose authors assert that the testimony of slaves should not be used and where the practice is not to use it, where there is no extensive investigation of whites' conceptions of the enslaved Africans, where it is said that the whites were unwilling slave holders and that few nonslave-owning southern whites supported the institutions of slavery, where it is said that those enslaving and routinely brutalizing the slaves were not at all influenced by their conceptions of the victims, where the precept and practice is not to describe the full extent and character of the slave holders' brutality, where it is said furthermore that African-American scholars today are suspect because they are African American and the motivation is imputed to them of writing about slavery solely for monetary or political gain or psychological gratification. Imagine what our understanding of American slavery would look like, how skewed it would be, if even only some of these positions prevailed. We would wonder how slavery ever could have existed.

When writing about the Holocaust, many scholars and commentators routinely adopt positions analogous to one or several of these examples. Indeed, some of these positions are a never justified, seemingly unquestioned norm among those who write about the Holocaust. These positions would seem curious—methodologically, substantively, and interpretively—even absurd, if put forward about slavery or about other genocides or mass slaughters such as those in Rwanda or Bosnia. Yet when asserted about the Holocaust, barely an eyebrow is raised. The question naturally arises as to why such manifestly false positions have been frequently adopted. Why until recently were almost no studies, especially no systematic studies, of the perpetrators—namely of those who killed Jews, guarded the camps and ghettos, and deported them to their deaths—to be found among the tens of thousands of books written about the Holocaust, despite the wealth of evidence that had long been available?

The heretofore hegemonic paradigm about the Holocaust has rendered them puppet-like actors, mere pawns whose inner world need not be investigated. It denies the moral agency and assent of the perpetrators and holds that they were compelled to act by forces external to them, such as terror, bureaucratic strictures and modes of behaving, the logic of the system, or social psychological pressure. For a long time, this paradigm diverted attention away from the perpetrators because its logic of external compulsion meant that the perpetrators' internal lives (their beliefs and values) and anything that was socio-historically particular to them (that they were members of a deeply anti-Semitic political culture) did not influence their actions and that, therefore, the study of them would not contribute much to explaining the Holocaust. The problems with this view and its construction can be indicated by comparing it to the hypothetical, fanciful rendering of slavery above.

The perpetrators are finally being discussed extensively, even if the number of empirical studies remains small. Yet in the last couple of years, a phalanx of scholars and commentators have adopted positions which would make the perpetrators of the Holocaust the only perpetrators of genocide who believed that their victims did not deserve to die, indeed that their victims were innocent. This strange view seems still stranger given that many of the German perpetrators knew explicitly that they had a choice not to kill, and that no German perpetrator was ever killed, sent to a concentration camp, jailed, or punished in any serious way for refusing to kill Jews. That it was possible for many perpetrators to avoid killing Jews, and that some of them availed themselves of this possibility, became known already at the Nuremberg Trials. The related, stunning fact that not a single German perpetrator was ever seriously punished for refusing to kill Jews has been known since 1967, when the jurist Herbert Jager published his pioneering study, "Crime Under Totalitarian Domination." (I treated both the general issue and presented the case of one man who refused to kill in "The 'Cowardly' Executioner: On Disobedience in the SS" in 1985). Yet this latter fact has remained unmentioned in virtually every work written on the perpetration of the Holocaust since Jager first established it.

Why would Martin Broszat, Raul Hilberg, Eberhard Jackel, Hans Mommsen, and other scholars who wish to explain the Holocaust not discuss these fundamental facts extensively or incorporate their significance into the explanations and interpretations which they put forward? Is it of so little import—that men and women who knew that they could avoid killing children would choose to destroy them anyway—that it is not even worth mentioning this information? Acknowledging these facts would have shaken the foundations of the paradigm to which many scholars are wedded, namely that the perpetrators were compelled by external forces to act against their will. This crucial omission of evidence, for which no justification has been offered, has for decades skewed nonexperts' and the public's understanding of the Holocaust.

Similarly, when these writers depict and analyze the events of the Holocaust and particularly when they analyze the motives of the perpetrators, they rarely, if ever, use the testimony of the victims, neither their letters, diaries, memoirs, nor oral testimonies. That is not to say this testimony is never used; certainly, it is used by those writing about the lives and plight of the victims, and by scholars like Yehuda Bauer, Saul Friedlander, and Israel Gutman. But when constructing interpretations of the perpetrators of the Holocaust, it has been the unspoken practice of so many scholars to all but ignore, and certainly not to use systematically, victims' accounts of the perpetrators' actions and the victims' understanding of perpetrators' attitudes towards them. With the sometime exception of a quotation or two from Primo Levi (or some other particularly distinguished memoirist), one searches such authors' works in vain for the instances where they use such evidence seriously or even at all.

Some authors explicitly declare that victim testimony is of little value and an impediment to understanding. Raul Hilberg, who is one of the principal exponents of the conventional paradigm and practice and who often speaks authoritatively for those who are in his school, has written roughly seven pages on survivor testimony in his recent memoir, *The Politics of Memory*, which are highly distorting and almost thoroughly disparaging. He makes not a single positive statement about the victims' testimony as a historical source, except when it shows Jews in a bad light. Even though Hilberg acknowledges in passing, in a strikingly critical vein, that the survivors' "principal subjects are deportations, concentration camps, death camps, escapes, hiding, and partisan fighting"—precisely those themes relevant to learning about and analyzing the perpetrators—his practice and that of those who follow him suggests that they believe that there is little evidentiary or interpretive value in all this testimony.

This widespread devaluation of the testimony of the Jewish victims is peculiar. I know of no other historical or contemporary instance about which it is said that the victims of genocidal onslaughts, sustained violence, or brutality have little of value to tell us about those who victimized and brutalized them. I know of no other crime (e.g., assault, kidnapping), no instance of large-scale brutal domination (e.g., slavery, serfdom), no genocide (e.g., Rwanda, Cambodia), nor any other historical instance in which the victims—in the case of the Holocaust a group of eyewitnesses numbering in the millions—are said, as a class, to have little or nothing to tell us about the deeds and attitudes of the men and women who victimized them and whose murderousness and brutalities against others they witnessed. And not only is their testimony silently ignored by many and explicitly devalued by some, it is also sometimes deprecated by writers like Istvan Deak, who began a review of several books on the Holocaust in *The New York Review of Books* (June 26, 1997) by presenting a caricature of and an attack on survivors' memoirs. He goes so far as to say that "an accurate record of the Holocaust has been endangered, in my opinion, by the uncritical endorsement, often by well-known Jewish writers or public figures, of virtually any survivor's account or related writings." How have the survivors' writings "endangered . . . an accurate record of the Holocaust"? Except to say (correctly) that personal details may be inaccurate or embellished, Deak does not justify his sweeping condemnation.

The invaluable importance of survivor testimony is attested by the crucial, indeed, indispensable part that the survivors have played in the trials of thousands of perpetrators in the Federal Republic of Germany. Many of these trials could not have been held without survivor testimony. The judgment in the most famous of these trials, that of a contingent of guards and administrators of Auschwitz held in 1963, states: "Apart from scattered and not very informative documents, the court had to rely exclusively on witness testimony to help it reconstruct the acts of the defendants." One thousand, three hundred witnesses (among them former guards) gave testimony for that trial.

The Germans' documentation of the killing institutions and operations never record the details of the hundreds or thousands of perpetrators' many actions. Typically, the documents contain, at most, the bare logistics and results of killing operations. So an entire killing operation that might have lasted a full day will appear in a document with nothing more than one line stating that on a given date, the German unit "resettled" (a euphemism) or "shot" some number of Jews.

The accounts of survivors afford a more transparent, more spacious window to the Nazi inferno than the often beclouded and distorting postwar testimonies of the perpetrators who, in order to escape punishment, frequently lie. (Still, some of the perpetrators are surprisingly forthcoming, especially about other perpetrators, and many unwittingly reveal a great deal. Such testimony is invaluable and should be used.) Who would expect to learn from the perpetrators or from contemporaneous German documents a full and accurate account of the texture and details of the Holocaust, of the daily living and dying, of the treatment of the prisoners by the German overlords, including their frequent gratuitous brutality, of the social life of the inmates, their thoughts and feelings, their suffering and their agony? Where can we more fully learn about the character of the perpetrators' actions—the degree to which the perpetrators tortured, brutalized, beat, degraded, and mocked the victims—about the perpetrators' demeanor and attitudes, about whether they acted zealously or reluctantly, about whether they expressed hatred for the victims, and gain insight into the perpetrators' willingness and motivation?

The answer is obvious: from the victims.

Could accurate histories of the Jewish ghettos and of the concentration camps be written without the accounts of the survivors contained in their depositions and memoirs? A perusal of three great books, H. G. Adler's *Theresienstadt, 1941–1945*, Israel Gutman's *The Jews of Warsaw 1939–1943*, and Hermann Langbein's panoramic analysis of Auschwitz, *People in Auschwitz*, shows that the authors have drawn heavily on the accounts of survivors. Are these historical works thereby vitiated? Do they imperil the accuracy of the historical record?

A comparison with the historiography of the Soviet Gulag is instructive. Its scholars do not cast aspersion on the memoirs and accounts of former inmates, whose narratives are indispensable. Aleksandr Solzhenitsyn writes in his preface to *The Gulag Archipelago*: "This book could never have been created by one person alone. In addition to what I myself was able to take away from the Archipelago—on the skin of my back, and with my eyes and ears— material for this book was given me in reports, memoirs, and letters by 227 witnesses . . . . This is our common, collective monument to all those who were tortured and murdered." Evidence of the kind that Hilberg, Deak, Christopher, Browning, and others dismiss, explicitly or tacitly, as unreliable and inessential forms the foundation of Solzhenitsyn's magisterial work. Would Deak argue that Solzhenitsyn has "endangered . . . an accurate record" of the Gulag? Or are only survivors of the Holocaust and those who find great value in their testimony prone to such "endangerment"?

It is not because this witness testimony is meager, imprecise, or devoid of insight that it has been ignored. It includes hundreds of memorial volumes, each one containing compilations from survivors of one destroyed Jewish community after another detailing their fates; depositions of many thousands of survivors in the trials of the perpetrators from one camp, killing unit, and ghetto after another; vast amounts of oral testimony; and thousands of memoirs. It would be hard to imagine an instance of mass slaughter, violence, or brutality that would be documented by a greater abundance of rich, detailed, often highly literate testimony that contains penetrating analyses of the events and of the people who perpetrated them. This makes the disparagement of the victims' testimony and its paltry use that much more surprising and indefensible.

Victims' accounts belie the conventional paradigm and the attendant scholarly theories about the perpetrators that have held sway, namely that the perpetrators either explicitly disapproved or at least did not approve of the mass slaughter of Jews and of other victims. The victims know differently. They have testified so again and again. If the proponents of these explanations had incorporated the voices of the victims into their own writings, then they would have undercut immediately and devastatingly their own theories, and the conventional paradigm.

The omission of the survivors' accounts has obscured, among many other aspects of the Holocaust, one of its constituent features. Scholars' failure to use victim accounts has thus, to use Deak's phraseology, "endangered" "an accurate record": the perpetrators' virtually boundless cruelty towards the Jews has been all but ignored by those who purport to explain the perpetrators' actions. If, as many authors do, one relies principally on highly partial and often unrevealing contemporaneous German documents, then, of course, one will not find frequent and detailed recitations of Germans' routine torturing of Jews. These authors construct a distorted portrait of the Holocaust in which the perpetrators' brutality—so frequent, inventive, and willful—is minimized, blurred, or absent. Consequently, it is not surprising that those few authors adhering to the conventional paradigm who do at least say something in passing about the sources of the German perpetrators' brutality to the Jews do not deem the perpetrators to have been moved by hatred of their victims.

Hilberg, for instance, in *Perpetrators, Victims, Bystanders*, puts forward the notion that the German perpetrators' brutality was "most often" an "expression of impatience" with the pace of killing operations. Browning's related view, in *Ordinary Men*, is that the perpetrators' brutality was utilitarian, the consequence of a pragmatic need to be brutal when they were under "pressure" "in terms of manpower . . . to get the job done," like rounding up Jews for deportation. When not under such pressure, in Browning's view, they were cruel when under the sway of cruel officers but seemingly not at other times. Hilberg and Browning have failed to present evidence that supports what are ultimately little more than speculations. (How does Hilberg know that they were impatient? He never says. And is the torture of defenseless people, including children, the invariable result of impatience, as Hilberg's quick and casual manner of presenting his speculation suggests?) But that is the least of their problems. Hilberg and Browning's empirical claims are falsified by evidence of the perpetrators' widespread, nonutilitarian cruelty in all manner of circumstances, even when they were not undermanned, even when they were not impatient, even when they were not undertaking killing operations at all.

For example: although the Germans of Police Battalion 101, during one of the ghetto roundups and deportations in Miedzyrzec, Poland, degraded and tortured Jews in the most gratuitous, willful manner, their deeds are entirely absent from their testimony and, therefore, also from Browning's analysis of the killing operation. The accounts of survivors tell a different, more accurate, and more revealing story. Survivors are adamant that the Germans' cruelty that day was anything but instrumental. It was wanton, at times turning into sadistic sport. At the marketplace, the Jews, who had been forced to squat for hours, were "mocked" (*khoyzek gemacht*) and "kicked," and some of the Germans organized "a game" (*shpil*) of "tossing apples and whoever was struck by the apple was then killed." This sport was continued at the railway station, with empty liquor bottles. "Bottles were tossed over Jewish heads and whoever was struck by a bottle was dragged out of the crowd and beaten murderously amid roaring laughter. Then some of those who were thus mangled [*tseharget*] were shot." Afterward, the Germans loaded the dead together with the living onto freight cars bound for Treblinka. One photograph documenting the final stage of what may be this deportation has survived.

Small wonder that in the eyes of the victims—but not in the self-serving testimony of the perpetrators, in contemporaneous German documents, or in Browning's book—these ordinary Germans appeared not as mere murderers, certainly not as reluctant killers dragged to their task against their inner opposition to genocide, but as "two-legged beasts" filled with "bloodthirstiness." (Browning claims that from survivors "we learn nothing about" Police Battalion 101 or, for that matter, about itinerant units in general.) Germans' cruelty toward Jews, as the victims (and also some of the perpetrators after the war) reveal, was voluntary, widespread, sustained, inventive, and gleeful. Such gratuitous cruelty could have been produced only by people who approved of what they were doing.

The vast corpus of the victims' testimony substantiates the conclusion that ordinary Germans degraded, brutalized, and killed Jews willingly because of their hatred of Jews. So profound and near universal was the anti-Semitism during the Nazi period that to the Jewish victims it appeared as if its hold on Germans could be captured and conveyed only in organic terms. As Chaim Kaplan, the trenchant observer and diarist of the Warsaw ghetto, concluded: "A poison of diseased hatred permeates the blood of the Nazis." Once activated, the Germans' profound hatred of Jews, which had in the 1930s by necessity lain relatively dormant, so possessed them, that it appeared to have exuded from their every pore. Kaplan observed many Germans from September 1939 until March 1940 when he penned his evaluation derived from their actions and words:

> The gigantic catastrophe that has descended on Polish Jewry has no parallel, even in the darkest periods of Jewish history. First, in the depth of hatred. This is not just hatred whose source is in a party platform, and which was invented

for political purposes. It is a hatred of emotion, whose source is some psycho-pathic malady. In its outward manifestations it functions as physiological hatred, which imagines the object of hatred to be unclean in body, a leper who has no place within the camp.

The [German] masses have absorbed this sort of qualitative hatred. They have absorbed their masters' teachings in a concrete, corporeal form. The Jew is filthy; the Jew is a swindler and an evildoer; the Jew is the enemy of Germany, who undermines its existence; the Jew was the prime mover in the Versailles Treaty, which reduced Germany to nothing; the Jew is Satan, who sows dissension between one nation and another, arousing them to bloodshed in order to profit from their destruction. These are easily understood concepts whose effect in day-to-day life can be felt immediately.

Significantly, this characterization is based on the words and acts of Germans—of S.S. men, policemen, soldiers, administrators, and those working in the economy—before the formal genocidal program of systematic killing had begun. It is the masses, the ordinary Germans, not the Nazi ideologues and theoreticians, whom Kaplan exposes. The causal link between the Germans' beliefs and actions is palpable, so that the Jews feel the effect of their "concepts . . . in day-to-day life." In the more than two-and-a-half years of subsequent concentrated observation of the Germans in Warsaw, Kaplan saw no reason to alter this evaluation, an evaluation confirmed by a German police official, who states plainly that those serving alongside him in the Cracow region of Poland "were, with a few exceptions, quite happy to take part in shootings of Jews. They had a ball!" Their killing was motivated by "great hatred against the Jews; it was revenge." The revenge was not for any real harm that the Jews had visited upon Germans, but for the figmental harms for which the perpetrators believed, in their anti-Semitically-inflamed minds, the Jews were responsible.

Effectively extinguishing the voices of the victims, and sometimes suggesting that they do little more than glorify themselves, is not only indefensible methodologically but also a deep affront to survivors. Most victims want to do nothing more than convey what the perpetrators did to them, their families, and to others. Victims of such cranes can never gain full restitution for their losses and suffering. What they generally seem to want is to have the truth be told, particularly so that the perpetrators will acknowledge their crimes. Survivors often express bewilderment that their experience has been generally ignored by the scholarship that treats the perpetration of the Holocaust. Many survivors have told me that they are thankful for my book, *Hitler's Willing Executioners* and for its detailed analysis of the German perpetrators, including their gleeful cruelty and brutality, which the survivors attest was almost always voluntary. They say my interpretation of the

Holocaust accords with what they and so many others witnessed and experienced.

A new way of approaching the study of the Holocaust is implicit in much of the unparalleled, widespread public discussion about various aspects of the Holocaust that has been taking place for the last two years. The old paradigm consists of abstract, faceless structures and institutions (bureaucracy, the greatly exaggerated "terror apparatus" that was supposedly directed at ordinary Germans, the S.S., the Nazi Party, the gas chambers) and allegedly irresistible external forces (totalitarian terror, the exigencies of war, social psychological pressure). This paradigm effaces the human actors and their capacity to judge what they were doing and to make moral choices. It is ahistorical. All of this implies that any people from any era with any set of beliefs about Jews (even non-anti-Semites) would have acted in exactly the same manner as the perpetrators, with the same brutality, zeal, and Mephistophelean laughter. This is being challenged by a view that recognizes that the Holocaust was brought about by human beings who had beliefs about what they were doing, beliefs which they developed within a highly specific historical context, and who made many choices about how to act within the institutions in which they worked and which brought them to their tasks in the first place. The human beings are finally at the center of the discussion. The heretofore dominant question of "What compelled them to act against their will?" is being replaced by the question of "Why did these people choose to act in the ways that they did?"

As a result, powerful myths are crumbling: the myth that the Swiss or the Swedes acted as they did only because of the German threat; the myth that the peoples in different occupied countries did not do more to thwart the Germans or less to help in the killing of the Jews merely because of their fear of the occupying Germans; the official Allied governmental myths that they could not reasonably have attempted to do much more to save the victims; the myth that those who procured Jewish property, including art, generally did so innocently; the myth that the perpetrators, by and large, disapproved of what they were doing but were coerced, were being blindly obedient, or were pressured to act as they did; and the three related myths that the German people more broadly (all the exceptions notwithstanding) did not know that their countrymen were killing Jews en masse, did not support the Nazi regime even though its many brutal policies (forced sterilization, so-called "euthanasia," the violent persecution of the Jews and others, the reintroduction of slavery into the European continent) were widely known, and did not approve of the general eliminationist persecution of the Jews.

Not surprisingly, many people who have either been comforted by such views or whose careers have been made by adopting positions that buttress

204 Chapter 4–Daniel Jonah Goldhagen

them, and who find the new, powerful challenges to these views to be polit-ically undesirable or personally threatening, are extremely unhappy and have let that be known. The frequent response is to attack, often in the most vitri-olic and unprincipled ways, the messengers—whether they be scholars, in-stitutions like the Hamburg Institute for Social Research which produced the exhibit, "War of Extermination: The Crime of the Wehrmacht, 1941–1944" that has been traveling around Germany, the World Jewish Congress for forcing the issue of Swiss gold onto the agenda, or the witnesses, namely Jewish survivors, whose testimony has always been a devastating threat to many of the myths.

It would be beneficial if certain basics could become widely accepted which the crumbling paradigm has obscured. They include:

1. The discarding of the caricature of individual Germans as having had no views of their own about the rightness of what they or their countrymen were doing, which included slaughtering children. We need to know how these views were distributed among Germans, and how they, singly or in interaction with other factors, influenced Germans' actions during these years. The same applies to the peoples of other countries, those where the Germans found many willing helpers and those where the populace worked to thwart (sometimes successfully) the program of extermination.

2. The rejection of the myth that the large scale, mass killing of Jews re-mained unknown to the broader German public. Germans themselves are becoming more candid: 27 percent of those who were at least fourteen years old at the end of the war now admit that they knew of the extermi-nation of the Jews when it was taking place. (The survey that determined this stunning new finding, which the chief pollster of the German wire ser-vice, dpa, says is still clearly a substantial underreporting of the real fig-ure, was conducted for the German television network ZdF in September 1996. Yet in the flood of articles written about the Holocaust since then, I have seen no mention of this finding, perhaps because it explodes a cen-tral element of the conventional paradigm—even though the survey's re-sults were announced and discussed on German national television during a panel discussion on the Holocaust and reported by the dpa.)

3. The acknowledgment that Germans who were not members of specifically targeted groups (Jews; Gays; the Sinti and Roma peoples, who are com-monly known as gypsies; the mentally infirm; the Communist and Social Democratic leadership) were not so terrorized as the totalitarian terror model posits. The enormous amount of dissent and opposition that Ger-mans expressed against so many policies of the regime and the regime's responsiveness to public sentiment and action makes this clear. So a new

understanding of the relationship between state power, regime policy, and popular consent needs to be worked out. The comparative question of why Germans expressed different degrees of dissent and opposition to different policies, yet virtually no principled dissent against the eliminationist persecution of the Jews, becomes central. More generally, all models that posit that irresistible external forces compelled people—Germans, French, Poles, Swiss, or the Allies—to act as they did need to be replaced by views that acknowledge the existence of human agency. If the vast majority of the German people had genuinely been opposed to the radical eliminationist persecution of the Jews, then Hitler would have never been able to pursue it as he did.

4. The adoption of a comparative perspective on genocide, so that those who study the Holocaust do not adopt methodological practices or causal claims that are at odds with how we study and what we know of other analogous phenomena. All available evidence (contemporaneous documents and the testimony of perpetrators, victims, and bystanders) that is not rendered suspect according to clearly articulated, standard social scientific principles is to be used. Regarding the use of the testimony of Jewish survivors, for example, the reasons given for excluding it must be defensible if one changed the word "Jews" to Tutsis, Bosnians, Cambodians, Armenians, the victims of the Gulag, or enslaved blacks in the American South. The methods of the social sciences present rules regarding research design and the structure of inference, including when generalization is allowed and even required. A major research project might be undertaken using all available evidence to catalogue what is known of the backgrounds, actions, and attitudes of every perpetrator in every ghetto, camp, and other institution of killing—those who victimized Jews and non-Jews—so that a general portrait and systematic analysis of them can be composed.

5. The recognition that the Holocaust had both universal and particular elements. Its universal aspect is that all people have the capacity to dehumanize groups of others so intensely that their hatred can impel them to commit genocide. Its particular aspect is that such views do not come to exist in equal measure in every society about every group, and when they do, it is not every society that has a state that mobilizes those who hold such views in a program of mass annihilation. The universal capacity to hate does not mean that all people actually do hate and hate all others in the same way, or that all hatreds will motivate people to treat the object of their aggression similarly. Real existing hatreds, as opposed to the capacity to hate, are primarily socially constructed and historically particular.

The Holocaust is not "beyond human comprehension." In principle, it is as explicable as every other genocide. No one says that the Rwandan or Cambodian genocide cannot be explained. What so many people simply do not want to accept is that the victims of the Holocaust have a great deal to tell us about their victimizers (no less than do the victims in Rwanda and Bosnia); and that the German perpetrators were like the perpetrators of other mass slaughters: the vast majority of these Germans were also willing executioners. That people automatically accept these facts about non-Jewish victims of genocide and about African or Asian perpetrators but not about Jews and "civilized" white Christian Europeans respectively is disturbing. Does anyone think for a moment that the Turkish, Hutu, or Serbian perpetrators did not believe that slaughtering Armenians, Tutsis, or Muslims was right? Does anyone for a moment believe that the testimony of these genocides' victims should not be used extensively in order to learn about the texture of the genocides, including the attitudes of the perpetrators? Indeed, in the Armenian genocide, in Bosnia, Cambodia, Rwanda, and other instances of mass slaughter, such testimony is eagerly used by scholars and has provided the principal knowledge of the perpetrators' deeds and attitudes.

As ever more Germans themselves have come to realize, one can acknowledge that many Germans were virulent anti-Semites during and before the Nazi period, that many supported the brutal persecution of the Jews, and that the murderers of European Jewry came from the ranks of ordinary Germans, without it leading either to the indictment of those Germans who resisted the prevailing norms and practices of the time, or to a condemnation of today's Germany. This seems so obvious that it bears mentioning only because some commentators continue to put forward two fallacies: they pretend that demonstrating that individual culpability for crimes was far more widespread in Nazi Germany than had previously been presumed is the same as maintaining that Germans are guilty as a collectivity. They also react as if plain talk about the Germany of the past defames the Germany of the present. Such notions can be maintained only by people who themselves deny individual responsibility, are beholden to the insupportable notion of a timeless "national character" (Hilberg has declared in his recent memoir that a German "national character" exists and is critical of others for not accepting this), or believe in some kind of collective, inheritable guilt. Individual Germans during the Nazi period should be judged according to the same legal and moral principles that we use for people in our own societies. The Federal Republic of Germany, like all other countries, should be assessed in the light of its own character and practices, achievements and shortcomings, and not according to a period of Germany's history that is now over fifty years in the past.

Much of what I write here finds an echo in a private letter written in 1946 by a German to a priest, in which the author was plainly speaking his mind:

> In my opinion the German people as well as the bishops and clergy bear a great guilt for the events in the concentration camps. It is perhaps true that afterwards not a lot could be done. The guilt lies earlier. The German people, including a great part of the bishops and clergy, accepted the National Socialist agitation. It allowed itself to be brought into line (gleichgeschaltet) [with Nazism] almost without resistance, indeed in part with enthusiasm. Therein lies its guilt. Moreover, even if one did not know the full extent of the events in the camps, one knew that personal freedom and all the principles of justice were being trampled underfoot, that in the concentration camps great atrocities were being perpetrated, and that the Gestapo and our S.S. and in part also our troops in Poland and Russia treated the civilian population with unexampled cruelty. The pogroms against the Jews in 1933 and in 1938 took place in full public view. The murders of the hostages in France were officially announced by us. One cannot therefore truly assert that the public did not know that the National Socialist government and army command constantly and as a matter of principle violated natural law, the Hague Convention, and the most simple laws of humanity. I believe that much could have been prevented if all the bishops together on a certain day from their pulpits had publicly protested against all this. This did not occur and for this there is no excuse. If for this the bishops had been sent to prison or concentration camp, then this would not have been a loss, on the contrary. All this did not occur, therefore it is best to be silent.

The author of this letter was no less a personage than Konrad Adenauer, the long-time and, by many, revered postwar Christian Democratic Chancellor of Germany who, more than anyone else, helped to reintegrate Germany into the community of nations. No one would accuse Adenauer of condemning every last German (even though he wrote of "the German people"), of being anti-German, of maintaining that Germans could never change and would therefore eternally share the views which led them to support Nazism, so why do some deem the speaking today of Adenauer's plain truths to be indications of such attitudes and to be impermissible?

Anyone who knows today's Germany, the Germany that Adenauer worked so steadfastly to forge, knows that it is remarkably different from Nazi Germany. Indeed, it is only by acknowledging the depths to which Germany had sunk, and not just that it somehow had the misfortune to have been captured by a brutal, murderous dictatorship, that one can appreciate the enormous accomplishments of Germans after the war. By denying how Germany really was, we will never fully understand the great effort Germans have made and the good that has occurred after the war. By being false to the past, the conventional, scholarly paradigm that denies the agency of the actors is also false to the present. When one acknowledges that it was culturally-constructed racist beliefs and values that led many Germans to take part in, and so many more—though decidedly not all Germans—to support, the annihilation of the Jews and the killing and brutalizing of many other Europeans deemed racially inferior, it becomes more comprehensible why Germany has been able to change so much. Political culture can be transformed.

Just as the beliefs that led American whites to enslave blacks and then to impose legal segregation have changed profoundly, so too—as the survey data demonstrate unequivocally—have the dominant beliefs in Germany gradually changed about Jews, humanity, and democracy. (In 1933, most Germans voted for parties openly dedicated to destroying the country's democratic institutions. Today, virtually everyone in what was West Germany sincerely supports democracy.) Such profound, positive changes in beliefs and values are hopeful—though, of course, both in the United States and in Germany prejudice and ethnic hatred have by no means been completely eradicated. Over the period of a generation or two, a society can greatly remake its prevailing views, making its people less bigoted and less prone to engaging in discrimination and violence. But this is not accomplished easily. How such changes occur are little studied and little understood. Perhaps people should devote more attention to examining such transformations, instead of working so hard to deny that in Germany any transformation was necessary.

My view of the mentality of the vast majority of Germans during the Nazi period is similar to that of one of the most esteemed of German historians of this century, Friedrich Meinecke (though our understandings of what produced this mentality differ). Meinecke remained in Germany but he kept his distance from the Nazi regime, retreating into "internal emigration" from which he observed the regime's policies and the people's attitudes, sentiments, and conduct. Soon after the war, he wrote a book, *The German Catastrophe*, seeking to explain the origins and character of Nazism. He was severely critical of Germans' conduct during the Nazi era and held that certain traits and traditions common in Germany had contributed to the emergence and success of the Nazi movement. His was a rare candor.

Meinecke acknowledged that it is a "shocking" and "shameful" fact that a "criminal gang succeeded for twelve years in compelling the allegiance of the German people and in imparting to a great part of this people the belief that it was following a great 'Idea'." Germany had fallen, but it was not beyond redemption. Its moral corruption was curable. For "the German people had not become diseased to the core with a criminal mentality but suffered only a unique grave infection caused by a poison that had been administered to it. The case could have become hopeless if the poison would have wrought its effect in the body for long." The young generation would have then become incurably afflicted with moral degeneration. "That was the gloomiest thought that tormented me during the twelve years, that the party could remain in power in perpetuity and instill in the entire younger generation its own degenerate character."

His gloomy moments notwithstanding, Meinecke knew that Germany would be defeated. The prospect of that defeat filled him with mingled trepidation and hope. Germany would suffer grievous external, material destruction but it would be liberated spiritually and mentally. The poisons which he and the Warsaw ghetto's diarist, Kaplan, each identified as having infected so many Germans—so that each one chose to write in collective, corporeal terms—would, in Meinecke's view dissipate and Germany's "soul" and "conscience" would "breathe again." A new day could and would dawn.

Meinecke's depiction of the mentality of most Germans during the Nazi period could hardly be bettered. His prophecy could hardly have been more true.

Chapter 5

ISRAEL

Seven Pillars of Jewish Denial

Kim Chernin

I am thinking about American Jews, wondering why so many of us have trouble being critical of Israel. I faced this difficulty myself when I first went to Israel in 1971. I was an ardent Zionist, intending to spend my life on a kibbutz in the Galilee and to become an Israeli citizen. Back home, before leaving, I argued almost daily with my mother, an extreme left-wing radical, about the Jews' right to a homeland in our historical and therefore inalienable setting. However, once established on my kibbutz on the Lebanese border, I began to notice things that disrupted my complacency.

We used to ride down to our orchards on kibbutz trucks with Arab workers from the neighboring villages and were occasionally invited to visit. We liked sitting on a rug on a dirt floor, eating food cooked over an open fire, drinking water from the village well. Above all, we loved the kerosene lamps that were lit and set in a half circle around us as it grew dark. But walking home it occurred to me that our kibbutz had running water, electricity, modern stoves. Our neighbors were gracious, generous, and friendly, although I had learned by then that the land the kibbutz occupied had once belonged to them. We were living on land that was once theirs, under material conditions they could not hope to equal. I found this troubling.

The path from this troubled awareness to my later ability to be critical of Israel has been long and complex. Over the years I have spoken with other Jews who have traveled this same path, and to many more who haven't. In each of us I have detected mental obstacles that make it hard, sometimes impossible, for us to see what is there before our eyes. Our inability to engage in critical thought about our troubled homeland is entangled by crucial questions about Jewish identity. Why do American Jews find it difficult to be critical of Israel? Here, set out in linear form, are seven obstacles to a Jew's ability to be critical of Israel.

213

SEVEN OBSTACLES

1. A conviction that Jews are always in danger, always have been, and therefore are in danger now.

Which leads to:

2. The insistence that a criticism is an attack and will lead to our destruction.

Which is rooted in:

3. The supposition that any negativity toward Jews (or Israel) is a sign of anti-Semitism and will (again, inevitably) lead to our destruction.

Which is enhanced by:

4. Survivor's guilt.

Which contains within itself:

5. A hidden belief that we can change the past.

Which holds:

6. An even more hidden belief that a sufficient amount of suffering confers the right to violence.

Which finally brings us to:

7. The conviction that our beliefs, our ideology (or theology), matter more than the lives of other human beings.

OBSTACLES 1–3: CONVICTION

The first three obstacles reveal a cluster of convictions about Jewish endangerment that tend to reinforce one another in insidious ways. We can trace the development of this consciousness. It goes something like this: We keep a watchful eye out, we read the signs, we detect innuendo, we summon evidence, we become, as we imagine it, the ever-vigilant guardians of our people's survival. Endangered as we imagine ourselves to be; endangered as we insist we are, any negativity, criticism, or reproach, even from one of our own, takes on exaggerated dimensions; we come to perceive such criticism as a life-threatening attack.

The path to fear is clear. But our proclivity for this perception is itself one of our unrecognized dangers. Bit by bit, as we gather evidence to establish our perilous position in the world, we are brought to a selective perception of that world. With our attention focused on ourselves as the endangered species, it seems to follow that we ourselves can do no harm. We are so busy warding off danger we become unaware that we endanger others. We fill up, we occupy all the endangerment space. When other people clamor for a portion we believe they are trying to deny us our right to this ground. At its most vehement, our sense of ever-impending Jewish peril brings down on us a willed ignorance, an almost perfect blindness, to the endangerment of others and to the role we might play in it.

When I lived in Israel I practiced selective perception. I was elated by our little kibbutz on the Lebanese border until I recognized that we were living on land that had belonged to our Arab neighbors. When I didn't ask how we had come to acquire that land, I practiced blindness.

Long before I went to Israel, my mother would bring out a rolled-up poster of a Palestinian youth. Without saying a word, she would unroll it and hold it up. It showed a very young man lying in the road in a pool of his own blood. This image had caused a major family breakdown when she showed it to her brother, who stormed out without saying goodbye and didn't speak to her again for years. On another occasion, there was an even more violent scene with the father of an old high school friend of mine. My mother unrolled the poster, he jumped up from the couch, raised his fist at her, and stormed from the room. Before slamming the door behind him, he shouted back: "This time, Rose, you've gone too far. Next thing, you'll be calling Israeli soldiers." Here he caught himself, but couldn't hold back. "You'll be calling Jewish people who defend their lives." Another break, and then, finally, the unthinkable word: "You'll be calling us *fascists*."

Slam. My friend and I looked at my mother in shock, amazed to find her silent and unperturbed. Between us, between my mother and myself, I was the one still practicing blindness. Where my mother saw martyrdom, victimization, tragedy in the image of the fallen youth, I saw a dangerous enemy stopped short in his effort to destroy our people. My friend's father, who lived in constant dread of Jewish annihilation, may have seen a necessary vengeance, an image of justice. I don't know what my friend saw. I drove her home in silence and we never met up with one another again. My mother, for her part, never said a word. When I stared at her she merely narrowed her eyes and looked back with an expression that implied: "Am I afraid of a word? Am I going to let a word keep me from seeing?"

The fixed certainty of impending Jewish destruction. Wherever we look, we see nothing but its confirmation, the same old story, always about to happen. In the grip of this persuasion, any other possibilities of meaning are swept away; we are unable to imagine things, even for a split second, from another's point of view. It took me years to overcome this blindness. My thoughts would return to the scene in my mother's living room; I would pore over the image, the outrage, the silence. One day, during an enormous inner struggle, most of what I believed about most of what mattered most to me fell apart. (Martin Buber refers to such an event as "an elemental reversal, a crisis, and a shock.")

Years of images and impressions I had kept at one remove came resoundingly together. I saw what my mother had seen: A boy gunned down by a superior military force; a very young man fighting for the survival of his people, who were far more endangered that ours.

To see a people far more endangered than ours: step one in the dismantling of blindness.

OBSTACLES 4–5: SURVIVOR'S GUILT

Guilt goes something like this: I was walking across the beautiful square in Nuremburg a couple of years ago and stopped to read a public sign. It told this story: During the Middle Ages, the town governing body, wishing to clear space for a square, burned out, burned down, and burned up the Jews who had formerly filled up the space. End of story. After that, I felt very uneasy walking through the square and I eventually stopped doing it.

I felt endangered, of course, a woman going about through Germany wearing a star of David. But more than that, I experienced a conspicuous and dreadful self-reproach at being so alive, so happily on vacation, now that I had come to think about the murder of my people hundreds of years before. After reading that plaque I stopped enjoying myself and began to look for other signs and traces of the mistreatment of the former Jewish community. If I had stayed longer in Nuremburg, if I had gone further in this direction, I might soon have come to believe that I, personally, and my people, currently, were threatened by the contemporary Germans eating ice cream in outdoor cafés in the square. How much more potent this tendency for alarm must be in the Middle East, in the middle of a war zone!

What was the reasoning underlying my fear? If we live in a world as dangerous to us as the Holocaust was to our people, we can be that much closer to the victims of the Holocaust, we can know their apprehension and terror; perhaps we may even succeed in taking their suffering upon ourselves. No one holds these beliefs knowingly. But they hold on to us: in a tragically paradoxical way, our guilt brings us to magnify our vulnerability. It seems that no victory on the Israeli side, no crushing of the perceived enemy, no destruction of their wells or complete dismantling of their infrastructure, can change our fear that they will defeat us or alter this perception of ever-present danger.

We will not let it happen again. But this claim, which seems to point exclusively into the future, is also yoked to our inability to accept the past. By keeping the past alive, by living it all over again, we attempt to alter it. Hidden within the militant "never again," is the anguished, impossible cry: "It will never have happened."

There is a widespread assumption among our people that the vanished victims of the Holocaust would approve of what we do to make sure their fate cannot again befall the Jewish people. Is it fair, however, to assume that their suffering and death would hold no other meaning for them than a recourse to violence, vengeance, and paranoia?

Some of our people, listening in on our ancestors' imagined, other-worldly discourse, hear only the endless repetition of the *never again*.

I hear, *not in my name*.

There is a new poster. It shows a single Palestinian woman facing a massive Israeli bulldozer. Looking at this image one immediately understands what Primo Levi (a survivor) meant when he claimed that the Palestinians are the Jews of the Middle East. Can we face the fact that we make use of the Holocaust as a way of refusing to see our own lamentable actions?

I hate this idea. It is, I think, the harshest moral reproach I have ever directed against myself. I can just about tolerate the idea of a survivor guilt that exaggerates my sense of vulnerability and leads me to perceive danger and an enemy where there may be instead a suffering neighbor. Can I, (can we), really face the idea that we are using the six million, hiding behind them, importing our own meanings into their suffering and death, using their victimhood for propaganda? It took me a long time to face this charge; to recognize that some part of my ever-increasing concern with Holocaust victims, Holocaust books, and first-person Holocaust accounts, was serving as a cover-up, distracting my gaze from a living struggle in which another people were enduring a victimization for which we Jews were responsible.

For which we Jews are responsible.

Arafat is not Hitler. The Palestinian terrorists are not the SS. We are no longer the victims. The world has changed, but Jewish identity has not kept up with it. If we lived in the present, we would have to acknowledge that the Jewish people of the twenty-first century are no longer the world's foremost endangered species. We would have to recognize that we, as a people, are ourselves capable of victimization.

Seeing ourselves as ordinary people, not victims: step two in the dismantling of blindness.

OBSTACLE 6. SUFFERING, VIOLENCE

The Israeli army that defends our homeland behaves brutally, uses torture, fires upon innocent civilians. What justifies the behavior of this army? We call it self-defense but this is, I suggest, only the surface of our justification. Further down, tucked carefully away in our collective psyche, we find a sense of entitlement about our violence. Our historic suffering, as a people, entitles us to the violence of our current behavior. Our violence is not horrendous and cruel like the violence of other people, but is a justified, sacred violence, a holy war. Of course, we would not want to know this about ourselves—it would make us too much like the perceived enemy whose violence against us we are deploring. When the suicide bomber blows up a hotel full of Passover celebrants, we see clearly that this is an instance of hateful, unjustifiable violence. (And it is, it is.) When we destroy a refugee camp of impoverished Palestinians, this, in our eyes, is a violence purified by our history of persecution. (And it is not, it is not.) We are puzzled that much of the world doesn't see our situation in the same way.

I think many of us hold this view of purified Jewish violence without being aware of it. Though we rarely admit it, the Torah is full of ancient stories marked by tribal violence done in the name of Jehovah. We know the story of Elijah wrangling with the prophets of Baal on Mt. Carmel. The prophet wins a clear victory for Jehovah over the Canaanite gods. We know, but don't make much of the fact as we retell the story, that after Elijah won the contest on Jehovah's behalf, he took the prophets of Baal down to the brook Kishon and slew them there. All 450 of them. I have not heard of or read a midrash that elaborates this massacre.

I recently wrote an article about the traces of Goddess worship in the Torah. When I cited this example of Elijah and prophets, my three editors, all intelligent and well-educated Jewish women, were uneasily eager to have me supply a footnote for this contentious assertion. They were as surprised as I initially had been to discover that the account of this violence was in the Bible itself. And yet they had certainly read Kings II.

In a similar vein: We celebrate the military victories of Joshua. But do we really take in what they involved? "Joshua, and all Israel with him, went on up from Elon to Hebron. They attacked it, took it and struck it with the edge of the sword, with its king, all the places belonging to it and *every living creature in it* (my italics, Josh. 10:37)." I have yet to hear a rabbi help us imagine this event in which women and children, the very young and the very old, are put to the sword.

Our sense of victimization as a people works in a dangerous and seditious way against our capacity to know, to recognize, to name and to remember. Since we have adopted ourselves as victims we cannot correctly read our own history let alone our present circumstances. Even where the story of our violence is set down in a sacred text that we pore over again and again, we cannot see it. Our self-election as the people most likely to be victimized obscures rather than clarifies our own tradition.

I can't count the number of times I read the story of Joshua as a tale of our people coming into their rightful possession of their promised land without stopping to say to myself, "but this is a history of rape, plunder, slaughter, invasion and destruction of other peoples." As such, it bears an uncomfortably close resemblance to the behavior of Israeli settlers and the Israeli army of today, a behavior we also cannot see for what it is.

We are tracing the serpentine path of our own psychology. We find it organized around a persuasion of victimization, which leads to a sense of entitlement to enact violence, which brings about an inevitable distortion in the way we perceive both our Jewish identity and the world, and involves us finally in a tricky relationship to language. That boy over there with the black face mask and a rock. That is a terrorist. That boy over here with a submachine gun, firing on the boy with the rock, he is a soldier.

A trick of language? A highly dangerous trick. I was once persuaded to show up for rifle training when I lived on my kibbutz, although as an American citizen I wasn't required to attend. And whom did I imagine I would shoot? And kill? I, who cannot kill a moth? I never imagined it had to do with killing. Because of the language I used (*I lift this rifle in defense of my beleaguered homeland*) the training became a clean act, necessary, not even in need of justification.

Accepting our own history of violence: step three in the dismantling of blindness.

OBSTACLE 7. IDEOLOGY VS. LIVING PEOPLE?

Some American Jews will soon set out to join settlements on the West Bank or to volunteer for the Israeli army. Others are going to Ramallah to help the Palestinians, hoping that their presence there will make it harder to smash through the city with tanks, randomly killing civilians. Still others are talking about a peace brigade that will be established along the border, a human buffer zone between the Israelis and the Palestinians.

Jewish identity, stretched out between these extremes, is up for grabs.

At one extreme, the decision to further occupy the West Bank is guided by a sense of Jewish destiny and by an ideology that claims Judea and Samaria as Jewish sacred ground. These claims are based on archaic conversations with God. The Orthodox families moving to the settlements will set themselves down among a hostile population, will be trained to shoot, and will participate in the further partition of Palestinian lands. They will take up a great deal of the water when there is already not enough water for their neighbors, many of whom go for days without being able to wash or even drink. In service to an archaic idea these people will see their Arab neighbors, not as a humbled, battered, impoverished, hopeless people, but as a potent enemy living illegitimately on ancient Jewish land. In the grip of ideology some things get neglected. Living people, the present, the sanctity of civilian life become less important than what, exactly? An idea? The idea of the Jewish people as chosen by God, living out a covenant with Him?

When I first went to Israel in 1971 I was on my way to a new kibbutz in the Golan Heights. It was a bleak, grim, heavily armed place with living conditions as rough as those faced by the early pioneers. There were no trees on this kibbutz, no gardens, no fields, no grazing animals. It was an armed camp made up of mud, reserve forces, and young Israelis who were there to hold the newly acquired land. I was convinced that I belonged with them, although I was not invited to stay. Today I want to ask that younger self: What can it mean to be God's people if this election does not come with a concern for all living peoples? Would it mean that the God who once spoke to our people has nothing new to say?

Our God is a God of many changes. The old warrior God who has had nothing new to say for thousands of years has been able, over time, to unfold aspects of Himself our Israelite ancestors would have found surprising. In talmudic thought the war-like, conquering diety evolves into a God of profound ethical concerns. He has revealed the *Shechinah*, his female, compassionate side, who comes to her children on the Sabbath and goes out with us into exile. She has, along the way, shown herself to be in love with a good story. She inspires midrashim, cherishing them as much as stories and teachings regarded as more sacred. She rejoices as women speak to her through their own prayers and rituals in settings that for too long excluded women. She is a God of perpetual unfolding; we, her people, inherit a tradition that asks for and imposes on us the work of continual renewal. Compassion, service, and a concern for justice are the imperative expressions of our divine worship.

Call to Prayer, Call to Action

What Judaism means and will come to mean follows from the choices we make today. Our acts, as Jews, promote or defeat the crucial purpose of Judaism—to maintain a potent, living, intimate relationship to a divine force that tears through the universe busily promoting transformation. The call of this presence, as I experience it sitting here at my desk, is toward community and action, to the awareness that if we can't do everything we can still do something.

We can clarify our vision. There is no reason we must continue to live either in survivor's guilt or in a sense of our inevitable victimization as Jews. We need not take refuge in an entitlement to violence or a remorseless emphasis upon our suffering. We can see the world as it is, not as it was or as we hope or fear it might be. We can enlarge our sense of Jewish identity to include both vulnerability and aggression. We do not have to be blind. We can see and we can act.

If we don't happen to be the people called to Ramallah we are certainly the people who can join the long march to social justice.

We can:

- take on the conservative policies of the established Jewish institutions
- incessantly pester the White House and Congress to intervene in the Middle East
- join organizations that support a Judaism of radical commitment to social justice.

Challenge, pester, join — they do not seem to have the epic scope required by events that involve so much suffering and death. But it would be a mistake to diminish their significance. They stand well within the radical challenge the prophets have always made to the conservative Jewish establishment; they direct themselves, against all odds, toward formidable obstacles and will require the staying power of a visionary, activist community. These commitments, in our time, in a world in crisis, must be recognized as an essential form of Jewish prayer.

But are we, as a people, still capable of prayer? How will we manage to pray, we who have just seen this:

Wednesday, June 19, 2002. 7:10 AM. Eyewitness. Fifteen-year-old girl:

People coming apart o my god right in front of us all over the place. O my god, o my god. Mama gets out of our car. Mama steps on a finger. Let's get out of here Mama, let's go, let's run, let's get away. If you walk in the street you will fall, you will slip in the blood, Mama says we have to help them, Mama says never take the bus, walk everywhere we have to go. Could happen, any day, any minute, look around, look over your shoulder, keep an eye out. That's me, screaming no no no no no no no. That's me shouting get them, get them, make them stop, do something, kill all of them.

We who have just seen, who know, who have witnessed, if we are to pray, we will have to call upon the highest development of our Jewish God, evoking the compassion of the Shechinah and the traditional female abhorrence for violence. We will have to imagine the *midrashim* that will, in time, inevitably be told to our ethical God about the struggles between Israel and Palestine. In this crisis we need a divine presence who is still talking to us and is closely in touch with the contemporary world of our people, so that, when we are able to pray, our prayers might sound like this:

Make it possible for us not to seek vengeance.
Help us to find the way that is not the way of violence.
Teach us to grieve without turning into those who have brought us to grief.
Help us to remember the innocence of the innocent.
Teach us to remember ourselves, a holy people.
If compassion is not possible for us,
If love is not possible for us,
Teach us not to hate.

We the Peacemakers

Mohammed Abu-Nimer

I am an Israeli citizen and also a Palestinian, I was born in the Galilee, got a Masters' degree in counseling and psychology at the Hebrew University, and am well versed in Israeli society, culture, language, and politics. Today is Israeli Independence Day, and the last time I spoke on Independence Day was in 1986, when I gave personal testimony to a group of Israeli soldiers about why the Israeli government should get out of the West Bank. And here I am, doing the same thing almost twenty years later.

So how should a Palestinian feel today on Israeli Independence Day? I usually avoid these holidays because of the emotional baggage that comes with them. Israeli officials who visit Arab villages and towns on this day expect Arab citizens to be "thankful" for what the state of Israel and the various governments of Israel have done for Palestinians living in Israel. Yet, many of the Arabs in Israel have family members in Syria, Jordan, Lebanon, the West Bank, and Gaza who are refugees of the 1948 war (or Independence Day). Palestinians in Israel have lived under the pressure of declaring and proving their loyalty to the state. Such loyalty has to be declared from the first sentence so that you're not considered a "threat" to the state. So it's hard to speak about Independence Day with pride, or loyalty, or even a sense of connection. The governmental policies of discrimination and land confiscation (among other dynamics of the Israeli-Palestinian conflict) have kept Arab citizens from associating with the symbols of the state. Even those who succeeded in developing some understanding of the symbolic meaning of independence for Jewish nationalism, still find it very hard to ignore the narrative of injustice and oppression expressed by the Palestinian community in the Occupied Territories.

Listening to the stories that have been shared this morning by several Jewish peace activists, I'm very sad to hear that there's so much pressure in the

American Jewish community these days to silence the voices of peace, or voices that seem to be critical of Israeli policy. However, we peace makers always suffer from this issue. Our respective groups tend to characterize us as traitors, disloyal, and we're ostracized. What we are facing is fear, ignorance, and lack of information from our own national and religious communities. From our past experiences in Israel and Palestine, peace activists have learned (some have paid the heavy price with their lives) that it is important in a way not to jump too far ahead of their communites and to try to understand their concerns, fears, and where they stand. However, such understanding has not, thankfully, prevented Israeli and Palestinian peace activists from meeting in times when such actions were politically taboo.

I want to share with you some of the internal dynamics within the American Muslim and Palestinian Arab communities regarding this issue of jointly working for peace with our Jewish and Israeli counterparts. Yesterday I had a conversation with a group of Muslim scholars who came from Central and Southeast Asia. We spoke about pluralism and religion. One of the Imams from Kabul took me aside afterwards and said: "Are there really Christians and Jews who recognize Islam as a religion?" I was not as surprised as some of you might be by his question. I immediately thought of the similar dehumanization and stereotypes applied to Muslims both prior to and after 9/11. I also was reminded of the same kind of stereotyping and ignorance that drives people to characterize all Palestinians as terrorists, or Palestinian mothers as killing their children and having no respect for life. In response to these negative images and the reality of the Occupation, there have always been forces in the Palestinian and Arab communities who opposed joint peace work, dialogue, or any contact with the "enemy."

Palestinians who have worked for political compromise and dialogue have also faced pressure and have even been sanctioned by their own communities. One of the mistakes we make as Palestinian and Jewish or Israeli peace workers is to say that we're on two sides. We're not on two sides. We share lots of commonalities as people who advocate for peace and justice. Palestinians who call for joint peace work go through the exact process that Jewish peace workers go through in their own communities—in terms of identity, in terms of proving their loyalty, in terms of defending the "other" side—but it's important to speak and work within our own communities. When I speak to Jewish groups they often think, "This is a nice, good Palestinian working for peace." But there's always this cognitive defense mechanism that makes people wonder if they can really trust me. What I really need is for Jews to speak in their own communities because it's harder for people to dismiss you if you're from "within." And if we continue to have people in the Arab community speaking of peace and justice in their own communities, this group of "us," who suffer from not belonging fully to either side, will grow. And it's the growth of this middle group that reflects and leads the path toward hope.

Are there American Muslims who are speaking this way in their community? This is a typical question raised by audiences when they listen to a voice from the "other side." Let me affirm and say yes, there are groups who are talking about the need for internal changes and addressing issues within the American Palestinian community, as well as the American Muslim communities, regarding coalition building with other peace groups, especially Jewish Americans.

However, it is becoming harder and more challenging to raise such issues, especially since the recent Bush-Sharon exchange of letters in which George W. Bush unequivocally supported Ariel Sharon's policies. If you're a Palestinian living under occupation, and you see the policy of assassination, and you're unemployed, and you have no political solution on the horizon and no credible Palestinian leadership to negotiate or confront the Israeli occupation, and you have Arab regimes who are basically buying time from one crisis to the other without much credibility or belief that they could bring any substantial change to Palestine, then essentially you give up on the notion that the Arab regimes will save you or end the Occupation. Then there's the final stroke: the president of the United States, the only country in the world that can challenge Sharon, steps in and says he fully supports Sharon's policies. You are a Palestinian who lives among 1.4 million people in Gaza—where would you go? There is no one single group who offers hope or confronts the Israeli occupation except Hamas.

I can certainly understand the deep frustration of the Palestinian people right now who are suffering under occupation, military attacks, and a policy of collective punishment. What is hard to understand is that certain Arabs and Palestinians (as well as certain American Jews), who live twelve thousand miles from the conflict and mostly live comfortable lives, choose to support policies of increased militarism, fanaticism, or radicalism. Jews, Palestinians, and Muslims who live in the Diaspora don't pay the heavy price directly, they're not involved on the ground, and they don't live under occupation. They're not Israelis living in Jerusalem afraid to drive beside a bus. They're not Palestinians living in Gaza getting firebombed in the middle of the night. At the end of the day they go home and watch TV.

From a place of comfort, these voices declare radical positions that actually inflame the conflict. For example, in some circles people insist on a one-state solution or insist that every Palestinian refugee must return to the historic land of Palestine, without even considering other possibilities (including recognition of the right to land but the choice of settling in other Arab and foreign countries as full citizens, or leaving the negotiations to Palestinian political leadership).

Such individuals claim the moral high ground and identify so strongly as victims that they end up adding to the process of dehumanizing the other.

But if you're going to take the moral high ground as a sympathetic outsider, you should at least do something constructive to end the conflict. I think that's the role of the Jewish-American, Muslim-American, Arab-American, and Palestinian-American communities—to act constructively to end the conflict. Many people in this conversation ask "What should we do?"

Here are four things we can do:

1. DIALOGUE

We can host dialogues to understand the perspective of the "other" and learn more about "them." Being engaged in collective and individual actions, American Arab and Jewish dialoguers can support each other and sustain and expand their forums and impact. And dialogue can be very helpful in bringing about reconciliation, particularly when it addresses and is constructed around the following three principals:

A. That Arabs and Jews have the same historical right to the land. This goes against the beliefs of many Jews, Christians, and Muslims, who say, "God gave it to *us*, but we'll share it." That's not reconciliation; that's strategic compromise. In faith, in spirituality, "God gave it to all of us"—and because we all live in this land, then historically we all have the same equal rights. An act of reconciliation is not, "I'm giving you 60 percent or 40 percent or 20 percent of the land because you've been using too many bombs and I can't defeat you." But also not, "I'll share with you because I am very generous." I've heard this among Muslims and Jews as well. People say, "We should compromise because Judaism as a religion gives us the higher moral ground." That's not reconciliation; that's ethnocentrism disguised in moral high ground language.

B. That Arabs and Jews have equal human rights. We are all human. We are born the same. Whatever we think afterward was taught to us by our rabbis and imams and priests, our teachers, our mothers, and our politicians—and we should be skeptical about what they tell us. For example, just because your mother is Jewish doesn't give you more of a right to the land—even if you come from Ethiopia or Russia or Venezuela—when you arrive in town. The same statement can be made to Muslims who claim all the land of Palestine because the holy Koran and the Prophet identify Jerusalem as a third holy city.

C. The third component that dialogue can bring is cultural and religious pluralism. I'm now finishing research on Israel, Palestine, Jordan, Egypt, and Lebanon, studying interfaith relations. I have been conducting interviews and have seen amazingly pluralistic interfaith dialogue groups; yet the majority of people in these interfaith groups actually come there to convert people (but in a nice way), or defend their faith and national positions. It is hard to achieve religious pluralism through such forums. Dialogue can bring us to religious pluralism if it's conducted with the sincere intention to understand the other and grant them the equal space to exist.

2. HUMAN RIGHTS ADVOCACY

Learning to understand the "other" and creating human bridges is extremely important. But it is equally important to move beyond the individual and collective sense of understanding of the "other" into joint or separate actions to correct injustice in our reality. Joint advocacy campaigns are an important tool for those who want to affect the course of the conflict constructively. Rabbis for Human Rights in Israel is a good example. We should be doing this work not because we want to help the Palestinians or help the Jews, but because it's the right thing to do, regardless. Advocating for equal rights for all people in this conflict is a moral stand that both Arab and Jewish Americans can and should work for. We should be advocating that U.S. government officials monitor and protect the human rights of Palestinians and Israelis equally.

3. HUMANITARIAN AID

The Palestinian community is suffering a severe human tragedy under the conditions of war and occupation. This is one of the worst periods that I remember. There are reports of starvation in Gaza, and unemployment is rampant. Even small humanitarian relief or aid can relieve much of the suffering of Palestinians — kids, families, and people living under the occupation. So if you do not want to be involved in political activism, your constructive role in the diaspora can be expressed by taking actions to reduce the suffering and tragedy of this conflict.

4. NONVIOLENT DIRECT ACTION

Nonviolent direct action is for people who really want to take an active direct stand against the occupation. Gush Shalom is a protest group engaging such action in Israel-Palestine, as are the International Solidarity Movement (ISM) and Al Mubadra (The Initiative). Nonviolent direct action is the ability to stand facing Israeli soldiers at any of the 450 checkpoints and say, "This is wrong." It's the ability to confront the Hamas narrative inside the Palestinian community and say, "Suicide bombing is wrong."

One of the people who has captured the essence of peace work is Professor Haim Gordon at Ben Gurion University, who has said: "To be a peace worker you need to be able and capable of confronting the evil in your own side." We need a coalition of Jewish peace workers critical of Israeli government policy, and American Arabs, Muslims, and Palestinians who are critical of the policies and actions of groups like Hamas, to work together (here in the United States) to move U.S. policy toward more peaceful, constructive, and engaged diplomacy. Arab and Jewish Americans owe Israelis and Palestinians who suffer from the conflict such active coalition.

The Ideological Roots of Christian Zionism

Tony Campolo

George W. Bush begins his second term with a war raging in Iraq, escalating threats against Iran from his administration, and turmoil in Israel/Palestine. What the anti-war Left may not realize is that this crisis in the Middle East is actually welcomed by many of Bush's most fervent followers. These Christians see in the current chaos in the Middle East a harbinger of the end of days, when Christ will return to Jerusalem after a long and bloody Armageddon.

The guiding ideology for this strange but increasingly influential Christian Zionist movement is a theology named dispensationalism, created by John Darby, a nineteenth-century Anglican priest from Plymouth, England. Few people have ever heard of John Darby, let alone read up on his theological perspective. Without understanding dispensationalism, however, it is almost impossible to understand how Christian Zionism has come to dominate American Evangelicalism and been so influential on the course of U.S. Middle East policy.

END TIME IN JERUSALEM

The basic tenants of Christianity have always encompassed teachings about the Second Coming. Christians have always believed that the same Jesus Christ who died on the cross for their sins was resurrected three days later. We also believe that after spending forty days providing further teaching to his disciples, he ascended into heaven. But we do not believe that Christ's involvement in history ends there. Sometime in the future, he will return to Earth, put down evil, and establish the kingdom promised by the Hebrew prophets.

For many Christians—including the ancient church fathers, from Justin Martyr through St. Augustine, and the great theologians of Christendom, including St. Thomas Aquinas, Martin Luther, Ulrich Zwingli, and John Calvin—the nature and timing of Christ's return is obscure, largely an object of faith. For Christians who read the Bible literally, however, the specificity of the Hebrew prophets' vision of a Messianic Age—particularly Isaiah's famous vision in 65:17–25 of the lion lying down with the lamb—suggests that the Bible encoded the events of world history in a way that could be deciphered.

John Darby offered to his followers a system of biblical prophesies that made the Bible harmonious with historical events. It was a scheme that also explained what he believed were God's hidden plans for the world, and offered specific details as to how those plans would be fulfilled in the future. He focused particularly on the Second Coming, offering guidance to enable astute Christians to discern "the signs of the times."

Before the Kingdom of God comes into its fullness, Darby's followers believe, the following must occur:

- The nation of Israel must be reestablished.
- The Jews must return to the Holy Land and become the sole occupiers of the land.
- The Jewish Temple that once stood on Mt. Zion must be rebuilt and the temple sacrifices of ancient Israel must be reinstated.
- Jesus will then almost return. Actually, Darby predicted that he would hover over the Earth and that "born again" Christians "would fly up to meet him in the air." As a result of this event, called "the Rapture," true bona fide Christians would leave behind all nonbelievers, along with apostate Christians (which they believe will include the liberal clergy of mainline denominations and those whom they led astray, along with unregenerate Catholics).
- Following the Rapture, there will be seven cataclysmic years marked by horrendous wars, famine, and disease. Satanic forces, led by a messianic imposter called the anti-Christ, will delude people into following him.
- Against the evil host of the anti-Christ will stand 144,000 Jews who will have by then been converted to Christianity, and who will go about evangelizing those who have been "left behind." The 144,000 will join with those they convert to Christianity in a climactic battle called Armageddon, in which the evil forces will be soundly defeated.
- At the end of these seven years, called the Great Tribulation, Jesus will return again, bind Satan and his hosts, and then establish his Messianic Kingdom here on Earth in a period called the Millennium.

There is much more to Darby's outline of history, but these few points can provide some background understanding of the rationale governing the politics of Christian Zionists.

First of all, given Darby's predictions about the "end times," it is easy to figure out why dispensationalists were so wildly excited in 1948 when the modern state of Israel was founded. To them, it was biblical prophesy unfolding before their eyes. One of their most popular spokespersons, author Hal Lindsey, contended in *The Late Great Planet Earth* that, with the founding of the state of Israel, the Rapture could not be more than forty years away. Needless to say, he has made a few revisions of his prediction since 1988.

NO CHRISTIAN LEFT BEHIND

Predictions like Lindsey's might be dismissed as ludicrous were it not for the fact that dispensationalism has become a very popular and influential stream of thought in American Christianity. Its influence comes largely through Darby's own *Scofield Reference Bible*—by far the most popular study Bible ever published—and the Left Behind Christian book series. The Scofield Reference Bible, first published in 1906, remains popular because it provides extensive notes that interpret scripture in an easy-to-understand fashion for the lay reader. Most of those who read these notes do not realize that they are being indoctrinated with a very particular theology.

The more recent Left Behind series, written by religious-right evangelist Tim La Haye and his coauthor Jerry Jenkins, have spread the dispensationalist message to an even wider audience. These books have sold more than 60 million copies in the United States, and more than 700 million worldwide. To put this into perspective, the books have sold more copies than the complete works of Stephen King and John Grisham combined.

The Left Behind books are fascinating fictional reading. They tell the story of a small group of heroic people who live through struggles that accompany the chaos in the world that dispensationalists say will accompany the Second Coming of Christ. What the unsuspecting readers do not recognize is that in reading these exciting stories they are absorbing the theology of John Darby and are being indoctrinated with his prophesies about how human history will unfold and how it will end. The readers are led, in an entertaining manner, to think that what they read is in harmony with events foretold in the Bible, especially in the Book of Revelation.

Dispensationalism, however, is not merely popular among ordinary citizens; it has achieved an unprecedented influence today because many of its followers hold high positions in government. The Secretary of the Interior during the years of the Reagan administration, James Watt, was one of them. His expectation of the imminent Rapture became his rationale for exploiting natural resources with little thought of the future. Believing that the Rapture was at hand, he saw no reason to hold back on drilling for oil in national parks, eliminating environmental policies designed to protect the Earth's atmosphere, rivers, lakes, and oceans. Why worry about the kind of planet that our grandchildren will inherit if the days for planet Earth are severely limited?

President Ronald Reagan took the dispensationalist theology fed to him by televangelists Jerry Falwell and Pat Robertson very seriously, and believed that one of his responsibilities was to promote a military buildup so America (which he believed was on God's side) would be ready for the battle of Armageddon.

It is difficult to know just how much this dispensationalist eschatology has permeated the thinking of President George W. Bush. Religious leaders who espouse these beliefs, such as Falwell, Robertson, and Franklin Graham, are among his closest spiritual advisors. Bush's reference to certain nations as being an "Axis of Evil" has Elaine Pagels, a religious studies professor at Princeton, concerned about his use of religious language. She speculates that he too may have bought into Reagan's beliefs about the coming battle of Armageddon.

MIDDLE EAST CRUSADE

When political leaders believe that they have been called by God to destroy the evil nations, there can be terrible consequences. Leaders are never so destructive as when they make war under the banner of religion. War becomes a holy crusade and those who try to make peace are considered the enemies of God. This certainly is how the Left Behind books present the United Nations, which La Haye and Jenkins describe as an instrument the anti-Christ uses to try to frustrate the will of God.

Is it any wonder, then, that President Bush received strong endorsements for brushing off of the concerns of UN leaders on the eve of the war in Iraq? The war in Iraq was, according to dispensationalists, the beginning of the struggles leading up to the Rapture and Armageddon. They almost reveled in the news of the war, pointing to it as evidence that their interpretation of scripture was being lived out in current events.

Perhaps the most dangerous influence of dispensationalism is found in the molding of American policies toward Israel and the Palestinians. Christian Zionists have become a major barrier, if not the major barrier, to peace in the Middle East. Yossi Alfer, Israel Director of the American Jewish Committee, said on CBS's *60 Minutes*, "God, save us from these people." Alfer realizes that behind their apparent support for Israel, Christian Zionists have set forth a scenario for the future that not only leaves little room for a negotiated peace with Arabs, but that in the end predicts destruction for those Jews who do not convert to Christianity.

In Washington, Christian Zionists have pressured politicians into minimizing the rights of Palestinians while yielding to expansionist policies of the Sharon government. They claim that, according to their reading of scripture, the Holy Land was promised to the Jews, and Jews alone should possess the land. The stakes for the dispensationalists are high, since in their theology the end of days cannot occur until Jews become the "sole occupiers" of the land of Israel.

What is particularly frightening is that Genesis 15:18, in which this promise of the land of Israel is made to Abraham, declares that the people of Israel should occupy all the land from the Euphrates River to the Nile. This obviously suggests that Israel should expand its borders to encompass major parts of Lebanon, Syria, parts of Iraq, part of Saudi Arabia, and part of Egypt. Is the war in Iraq actually part of a dispensationalist program? Are dispensationalists in government essentially trying to drive Arab peoples out of this entire territory so that Israel might enjoy what was promised to Abraham? These questions are not as crazy as you might think: one televangelist, John Hagee, believes that the war of the end times has already begun.

CHRISTIAN ZIONISTS AND ANTI-SEMITISM

As should be evident, Jewish people should not too readily interpret all of the Christian Zionist support for Israel as evidence of a sudden vanishing of anti-Semitism among Christians. The reality is that the commitment of Christian Zionists to the state of Israel comes primarily from their understanding of end-times prophecies. Israel is viewed mainly as a means to creating the conditions that will lead up to the Rapture.

In anticipation of the need to have 144,000 converted Jews to carry on evangelistic work during the seven years of the Great Tribulation, they have made Jews into a special target of their proselytizing. As an Evangelical Christian myself, I am desirous of proclaiming the Christian gospel to all nations, in accord with Christ's command. But, when certain Evangelicals focus on the Jews as the primary group to be evangelized, as the Southern Baptists have done, it is easy to understand why many Jews get the nervous feeling that these Christians are "out to get them." Declarations by certain Christian Zionists to go after Jews with the gospel have created some tensions between

Jews and Christians, with some Jewish leaders contending that these evangelistic efforts are a form of genocide that is aimed at obliterating Judaism.

Another cause of Jewish cynicism toward Christian Zionists comes from the fact that dispensationalists are convinced that all those Jews who do not convert to Christianity will be destroyed upon Christ's Second Coming. Gershom Gorenberg, a prominent Jewish author, was correct when he told *60 Minutes* that these Christian Zionists, "don't love real Jewish people. They love us as characters in their story, in their play, and that's not who we are. . . . If you listen to the drama that they are describing, essentially, it's a five-act play in which the Jews disappear in the fourth act."

Those of us Evangelical Christians who have not been swept into the Darby fold must not be considered anti-Zionist. Overwhelmingly and intensely, we support the right of Israel to exist within secure borders. We want to do all we can to ensure safety for the citizens of Israel, so that mothers do not have to worry about what might happen to their children when these boys and girls go off to school. This is one of the main reasons we want to challenge Christian Zionists with their dispensationalist theology.

We believe that the scenario proposed by these apostles of John Darby in the end will set Jews against Arabs, generate a war with Islam (which is now what they predict Armageddon will be all about), and even lead to the destruction of Israel. As opposed to the dispensationalists, who imagine a bloody world in which very few are saved, mainstream Christian Evangelicals believe in a God who loves Palestinians every bit as much as He loves Jews—and this is why we want justice for those people, too. We pray for a two-state solution to the crisis in the Holy Land.

I believe that George W. Bush wants a peaceful solution to Israel/Palestine, I believe most Jews want that solution, and I believe that even Sharon wants that solution. We must not allow Christian Zionists to stand in the way of the peace for which the rest of us so desperately yearn. The time has come to educate ourselves about their agenda and to stop them.

Compromise for Peace

Yitzhak Frankenthal

I have lost my eldest son, Arik. He was an Israeli soldier, just nineteen years old, on his way home. He was kidnapped and murdered by Hamas.

When I was sitting *shiva*, mourning, my best friends came to me and said, "Yitzhak, you always thought that we could find a peaceful solution, you always say that the Palestinians are human beings just like us, but look, they murdered your son. Have you woken from your dream? Do you realize that the Palestinians are your enemies, that they are not human beings?"

I said, "I lost Arik for one reason. There is no peace between us and the Palestinians."

A month before Arik was murdered, I spoke with him. I asked him, "Arik, if you were a Palestinian, what would you do to achieve a Palestinian state?" He said, "Daddy, I would do what we Israelis did to the British. I would fight against the Israelis, I would kill as many Israeli soldiers as I could, because the situation they are living in is not one any human being could accept." A month later, this boy who was also my best friend was assassinated.

I have learned that if you would like to achieve peace, don't seek justice. There is no connection between justice and peace. On the contrary, if you look for justice, you won't find peace, because what is just for the Israelis is unjust for the Palestinians, and vice versa. Peace means compromise.

I am not looking for justice. I am looking for a wise way to make peace.

The Israelis have had a dream, and the Palestinians have had a dream. The Israeli dream has been to create a country from the river to the sea in security and peace. The Palestinian dream has been to destroy the Israelis and to have all that land as a Palestinian state. Both need to compromise their dreams.

SIX WAYS TO PEACE

The first step to such a compromise, on both sides, is to understand that we have made mistakes. We Israelis have made mistakes both in the way we have dealt among ourselves and in the way we have dealt with the Palestinians. Among ourselves, we have not had the patience or the dignity to listen to each other, and without listening to each other we cannot achieve reconciliation with anyone else.

Toward the Palestinians, we Israelis have made the mistake of Occupation. Occupation is a kind of terror and leads to the terror we have in the world today.

The Palestinians, in turn, have made the mistake of using force against the Israelis. I have spoken to the Palestinians many times. Once, in Gaza, I spoke to two thousand people supporting hunger strikers. They were very hungry, very angry. I told them that using force was a mistake. I said that using force is the way of weakness. Some of them wanted to kill me. Yet others protected me. Later, I got a phone call, thanking me and apologizing for the violence against me. Now, 90 percent of the hunger strikers are for peace and reconciliation.

The second way to make peace is to understand what our Talmud says, "who gives charity makes peace." We will not make peace by closing our hand. We must be generous. If we do so, we will get back what we give.

The third way to peace is to prepare the people to make painful compromises. In Israel, you can hear many, many reasons for not compromising with Palestinians—that Israel is our holy land, that it was never a Palestinian state, that the Palestinians will fight us if we give them a state, that there is no real partner for peace, and so forth. All of those reasons are only a fig leaf for people who are not ready to understand that Palestinians are people just like us and deserve their own state.

To compromise means to be ready to pay the price. My family, the parents in our organization, we have all paid the price. If we would like to achieve reconciliation, all of us can prepare to pay the price for peace.

I have met Yasser Arafat and members of his government many times. They don't think they can destroy Israel. They don't even really want that. They want to live in peace. They are willing to pay the price.

Fourth, we need to work here in the United States, in the Jewish community. When right-wingers in Israel have argued against ending the Occupation, Jewish organizations in the United States have supported them. Then look what happened. Suddenly, in May, Ariel Sharon said, "We have to end the Occupation." Over all these years, six thousand people have been killed. Where was Sharon all these years? Where were American Jews all these years?

The message of peace and compromise must go into the ears of the people who need to hear it, the ears of American Jewish society. We need to work to turn public opinion here in America. We must find words they can hear and understand so that they will help, and not hinder, this effort.

Fifth, we need to work with the American government, both to lead them to Israeli and Palestinian partners for peace, and to also prepare the Americans to pay the price for peace.

Finally, we need to build a vocabulary for peace. For example, we need better words to define terror and terrorism. You in America suffered through September 11, a terror created by ideological people. Some Americans and Israelis have linked the Palestinians to Osama Bin Laden, but that is a mistake—these are two entirely different kinds of terror. Bin Ladin's terrorism is based on ideology, while the Palestinians are conducting acts of terror out of despair. If you would take away their despair, these acts of Palestinian terror would end.

ROAD TO PEACE

I do see many roadblocks to achieving peace. The Israeli government may change right in the middle of this peace process. There might be a new terror attack. The Israeli right wing might rebel.

We can continue the peace process, however, if we remember these ten things:

1. The Palestinians are human beings.
2. The Occupation is a kind of terror.
3. A Palestinian state is in the interest of Israelis as well as Palestinians.
4. Holy places are holy no matter what civilian authority they are under.
   5. We need to ask not what we *can* do to the Palestinians, but what we *cannot* do to the Palestinians.
6. We need to change Israeli and Palestinian attitudes.
7. We need to do this work with empathy and sympathy.
8. We need to express ourselves on events of the day through media.
9. We need to act here in the United States to change attitudes.
10. We need to give hope to the Israelis and the Palestinians.

Recently, we had a blood drive. Israeli families who had lost children went to Ramallah and donated blood to Palestinians, and Palestinian families who had lost children went to Israel and donated blood to Israelis. There were many media stories. Everywhere, people asked, "What is going on, how could these people donate blood to the people who murdered their children?" We want people to ask themselves these kinds of questions, because when they find the answer to these questions they will find a way to peace.

We give blood to our enemies because they are human beings. We give blood to our enemies because we do not want any family to suffer. We give blood to our enemies because peace is not about justice. Peace is about compromise.

Healing Israel

Cherie R. Brown

I have been working primarily with U.S. Jews since 1967 on behalf of a just solution to the Arab-Israeli conflict. Before we can organize Jews on behalf of peace, we need to recognize four obstacles to Jewish participation in the peace process. Once we face these four obstacles, we can build on eight simple principles I offer here as the basis for renewing hope in a new Middle East peace initiative.

Obstacle #1: There is still a great deal of misinformation about the real causes of the most recent breakdown in peace efforts. This misinformation has left Jews feeling hopeless and susceptible to increased mistrust of Palestinians.

Most Jews (and a large majority of the U.S. press) were led to believe that Ehud Barak had made a generous offer to the Palestinian people and that the blame therefore was primarily with Arafat and the Palestinian leadership for not accepting such a good offer. Many Jews were never given the real facts "on the ground"—that this "generous" offer meant that Palestinians were permanently saddled with Israeli military roadblocks and checkpoints throughout Palestinian-occupied land. In addition, there were no arrangements in the settlement for any compensation or even any discussion of Palestinian refugee issues. When this peace offer was rejected, many Jews decided that there was no hope for real cooperation with Palestinians. This loss of hope has been a major roadblock to reaching out to Jews and to engaging them in renewed efforts for peace.

Obstacle #2: Given the history of the Holocaust and the attempted genocide of Jews, it has been extremely difficult for many Jews to be able to see ourselves in the oppressor role with regards to another people.

I recently watched an excellent new film by an Israeli filmmaker—*The Promise*—which showed a group of young Palestinian children and young

Israeli children being brought together over a two-year trust building period. In the film, a number of hard-hitting scenes were shown about daily life for Palestinians under the Occupation, including being stopped at military checkpoints throughout the occupied territories. As I watched these scenes, I found myself hardly breathing. I wanted to scream out, "It can't be this bad. Are you sure this is balanced enough? Please don't show this picture of Israel to the world. They will just end up hating the Israeli people!" While my mind knew this was a true picture of Palestinian life under occupation—and needed to be known—my heart rebelled. I have been working for justice for Palestinians for thirty years, and I could hardly watch these scenes. And these are not the most hard-hitting scenes of Palestinian life under occupation. We are going to need to find a way to make it safe enough for Jews to remember how good we are so we are able to take an honest look at the oppressor role that Israel has been set up to play with the Palestinian people. Jews will not be able to face the oppressive things that the Israeli government does unless we know that the world still believes we are a deeply good people.

Obstacle #3: Jews continue to feel isolated and unable to reach out for allies out of a sense of terror and powerlessness.

I attended the NGO meeting of the United Nations Conference on Racism this past August in Durban, South Africa. It was, at times, a painful place to be as a Jew. Israel was unfairly singled out for condemnation in several of the proposed documents and sessions at the conference. At one point during the week, the Jewish Caucus made up T-shirts with a Jewish star and a peace symbol on the front and a quote from Martin Luther King Jr. on the back. As I walked from tent to tent at the conference, I saw groups of Jewish young people, wearing their T-shirts, huddled together with each other for support. The attacks on Israel had left these young Jews feeling vulnerable and isolated. They weren't able to reach out and build friendships with other antiracist activists from around the world. And without these friendships, it was impossible to have allies who could stand up both for Israel and for the Palestinian people. I understood in Durban, in a whole new way, how difficult it was, even for some of my closest friends, to stand up fully for Palestinians and not feel like they were somehow betraying Jews—or to stand up fully against the singling out of Israel for condemnation and not to feel like they were somehow betraying the Palestinian people. And this is what is needed—allies who will stand up clearly for both peoples no matter how much pressure there is to take sides.

Obstacle #4: There is a generation gap between progressive Jews who were born before 1967 and those who were born after the annexation of the West Bank and Gaza that is hindering the building of an effective Jewish peace coalition.

Progressive Jews who were born prior to 1967 (some who lived through World War II, others who know that there was no place for Jewish refugees to go after the war) often say in their organizing efforts that they are speaking out against the policies of the Israeli government out of a deep love of Israel and an understanding of the need for Israel as a necessary homeland for the Jewish people. Those who were born after 1967—when the Occupation was firmly in place—have little collective memory of World War II or of Jews as victims. Therefore, they often focus their efforts on ending the Occupation and the oppressive policies of the Israeli government but do not always add that their organizing efforts are based in a love of Israel or a need for a homeland for the Jewish people. Each group is going to need to be listened to fully and this "generational rift" healed if an effective new Jewish progressive peace coalition is to be built in this next period. A love of Israel (the older generation's key concern)—which is then linked to the end of the Occupation (the younger generation's key concern)—needs to be foremost in any new Middle East peace project that we set up.

How are we going to break through these obstacles and develop a new Middle East peace project? I would like to propose eight simple working principles about human beings that could form the basis of a new Middle East peace effort. These working principles are based on an understanding that what is needed now to break the current impasse is not one more analysis of the conflict (God knows—we have enough people fighting to have us agree with their analysis and perspective), but instead a simple set of guidelines about what is true about Jews and Palestinians that will give us enough hope to keep moving forward.

Principle #1: It is no longer possible to destroy the State of Israel or the Palestinian people—and their right to justice and statehood. Both peoples have too many allies worldwide. Both peoples exist and both peoples will continue to exist. The attempted destruction of any people weakens the struggle for liberation of everyone.

Principle #2: There *is* a just solution for all involved in the Palestinian-Israeli conflict and we are capable of finding it—including on the issue of Jerusalem. It must be recognized that Israel cannot have lasting peace without an economically viable nation for the Palestinian people.

Principle #3: Both sides do hurtful things and both sides have been hurt. Given the injustices that both peoples have faced, each group is going to need to be listened to far more than they have been to date. The small number of listening projects that have been organized have been important, but more resources will need to be put into expanding these listening projects in this next period.

Principle #4: There are no human enemies. Both sides have and will behave irrationally in response to having been hurt. We will never be able to undo or redress all the past mistreatment. However, when both sides have been listened to fully (Principle #3), each will be more able to think clearly about solutions. Solutions to the conflict will need to be based primarily on what will work in the present.

Principle #5: There is reason for continued hope in the present situation. What appears to be a difficult moment is, in reality, a time when the unresolved difficulties can come to the surface for further understanding. For example, the latest round of violence demonstrated that the recent peace talks did not have the clear backing of large segments of the Palestinian population or significant segments of the Israeli population. The backing of large enough portions of both populations will be necessary for any final peace settlement. The recent difficulties are providing new opportunities that, if taken, could lead to more effective solutions. And this is very hopeful.

Principle #6: None of the violence that has happened in the recent period negates any of the important and useful efforts towards cooperation that have taken place in the past. Every cooperative effort from the past has been important, no matter how much these efforts have been covered over by discouragement.

Principle #7: It does not make sense to call for an end to Palestinian violence without also calling for an end to Israeli military domination of Palestinians. The domination of one people by another—no matter how much that domination is based in a real perceived fear—will not result in an end to violence.

Principle #8: Real solutions will come when we apply our thinking to the actual issues and struggles in the present as distinct from the painful emotion that surrounds these issues and struggles. Painful emotion needs to be listened to but it should not be the basis for formulating policy.

The obstacles to organizing Jews on behalf of a just peace in the Middle East can seem overwhelming at times. But they are *not* insurmountable. Every impasse in the past has eventually given way to the next steps in the negotiation process. This period is no different. This impasse will end. And all of our continued efforts, including these eight proposed principles, will enable us to move past the current paralysis and restore hope in a permanent and just peace.

Chapter 6

SPIRITUAL POLITICS

An Interview on Spiritual Politics with Cornel West

Michael Lerner

Cornel West is cochair, with Michael Lerner and Sister Joan Chittester, of the Tikkun Community. He is University Professor of Religion at Princeton University and a prolific writer.

Michael Lerner: What were the lessons from September 11 that we should have learned, but haven't?

Cornel West: We have to recognize that America must come to terms with the painful truth—the world is not only a dangerous place, and peace delicate and fleeting, but we are interdependent. We have to acknowledge that what we do affects everyone, that we are part of one interlinked garment of destiny. America as a country began as a European slave society settling on an indigenous people's land, then it broke from the English empire, and now we are the greatest empire since the Roman Empire. We are a settler society vis-à-vis indigenous power, a colony that developed a revolutionary tradition in response to the imperial power of England, and now we are *the* imperial power of the early twenty-first century. The challenge that faces us in the post-September 11 period, as we become increasingly willing to see our central role in the world, is how do we build on the best in our democratic and libertarian traditions so that we can wield our imperial power in ways that enhance human rights and democracy around the globe?

Now, to do that, we must try to relate to the United Nations and countries around the world in a different way than we have in the past. We need to overcome our arrogance and unilateralism so that we can relate to other countries in ways that emphasize common goals and our willingness to work together to achieve them in a spirit of mutual respect. One common thread among our political, economic, and cultural elites is this thread of arrogance and the attitude that we don't have to take into account the United Nations, the World

Court, the well-being of others, and how our actions affect their destinies. More and more of the world sees this arrogance for what it is.

Lerner: What's our role?

West: One of the roles of radical democrats such as ourselves in the Tikkun Community is to help support the instincts of many Americans to challenge this arrogance and to help make mutual respect a guiding principle in shaping America's interactions with the world.

But the post-September 11 year has been difficult for radical democrats. The first casualties of the official institutions of American economic, political, and cultural power have been truth and dissent. So we in the Tikkun Community continually face the challenge of telling the painful truths about the injustices of the world system which we lead, and raising our dissenting voices. We know that we will be trashed as anti-American, though we are not one whit anti-American—we are pro-human. We stand in the tradition of people who are proudly pro-American and pro-human, but who have been critical of American policies, from Walt Whitman to Fannie Lou Hamer.

Lerner: Many people feel that this kind of pro-human voice is being increasingly marginalized in the current period.

West: Though there are attempts to marginalize us, our voices are still being heard. There is no doubt that Tikkun's voice was heard when we were arrested in Washington, D.C., in April for protesting U.S. unwillingness to constrain Ariel Sharon's invasion of West Bank cities, and that what we were saying was picked up by people in the U.S. State Department. Despite the disappointing and misguided policy announced by President Bush, we are at a moment in which many Americans are more willing to listen to our message than ever before.

The Tikkun Community's call for security for Israel and justice for the Palestinians, presented as equally important demands, would have been truly marginalized fifteen years ago, but today it is beginning to get a serious hearing, both in the media and in the corridors of American elites. We have Colin Powell echoing our call for even-handedness, and though he might not be winning the immediate battles of the moment in the elite structures of the White House, his voice is there and has been strengthened by ours. Our challenge is to continue to speak from the standpoint of prophetic witness, as Tikkun does so effectively, and to simultaneously be cautious not to take on a tone of self-righteousness and insensitivity to those whose policies we critique. We don't want to mirror the arrogance of our elites. We are against all forms of dogmatism, including left-wing dogmatism. We have to cut through all forms of provincialism, parochialism, and tribalism—this is the perennial struggle of being a progressive.

There is a reactionary movement with significant power in the White House that is consolidating right now on the domestic and military fronts—the tightening of the plutocracy and the patriarchy in ways that effect all people who have been marginalized in our society: working people, gays and lesbians, people of color. Our role as progressives is to expose the deceit and use our analytic and empathic skills to help people discern what is happening in our world, and to connect not only to the minds but to the hearts and souls of our fellow citizens.

So we have to expose the lies and the curtailments of rights and liberties that Mr. Ashcroft is carrying out (as we did in the new book *It's a Free Country* by *Tikkun*'s former publisher, Danny Goldberg). But even as we critique Bush, we have to acknowledge moments when he does something valuable, as he did when he made the distinction between gangster terrorists who happen to be Muslim and Islam as a religion. It doesn't translate on the ground in the Justice Department—that's where the hypocrisy comes in—but we can still commend Bush for being right when he was.

Similarly, we have to expose corporate criminality—the kind of thing that Ralph Nader was doing so eloquently in the 2000 election and which now is forced onto public consciousness by Enron, Global Crossing, and Worldcom. It is this corporate abuse and mendacity which has gotten to a point where people have lost faith in our capacity to maintain an economy. The trust has been undermined by corporate gangsters. For years we've had a media that has focused negative attention on gangsta rap and gangster culture in many poor ghetto communities, but meanwhile the gangsters at the top have been "getting away with murder." As a result, public trust in corporations has plunged, and now you have corporate executives rushing to discuss corporate accountability.

I had a meeting not too long ago with many of the Democrats in the U.S. Senate. I was invited to meet with them along with Kevin Phillips, Arthur Schlesinger Jr., Randy Kennedy, and Alan Brinkley. Kevin Phillips' wonderful new book *Wealth and Democracy* had just come out, explaining the way that America is a plutocracy. There was great receptivity to the discussions of the threats posed by corporate power to American democracy, but discussions of that sort rarely go beyond those rooms. At the moment, many of the senators express concern that they not be perceived as striking out against America at a time when it is under external attack from terrorists. And that's a real issue for the few remaining progressive voices in the Senate, because the truth is that America does have some real enemies. That's a real issue for all progressives. We have to recognize that some of these enemies of America are not a bit progressive. We have to be able to criticize them without demonizing them, and be sure that they are hunted down and brought to justice.

Lerner: Progressives face a difficult moment. On the one hand, the Democratic Party has become less and less courageous over the past two decades in championing progressive causes, and yet on the other hand many progressives feel that they unintentionally may have contributed to the election of Bush when they put energies into building a third party. The Democrats have done little to invite the progressives back or to open up their own institutions of decision making, so that leaves progressives in the position once again of voting for lesser-evil candidates who are only marginally better than their opponents, and who represent positions that many progressives find anathema.

West: When the Right is unified, the Left has little possibility of making significant inroads into the population because it needs to be there to support liberals who are under attack. But when the Right becomes more discredited and disunited, as it may be soon because of the current economic problems, then there is more room for the Left to assert its programs separately from the liberal forces. It is at the moment that conservatism is in deep crisis that we get our best chance.

The Democratic Party is always both indispensable and inadequate for progressives. If we want our ideas to enter the mainstream, we have to engage the Democratic Party because there are progressives in that party who have access to serious power (Sen. Paul Wellstone, Rep. Jesse Jackson Jr., Sen. Russell Feingold, and others). My heart, however, lies more with the Ralph Naders and other radical democrats—the critics of corporate power—who are more explicitly concerned about social justice both domestically and internationally. But I don't think we can abandon our attempts to engage the Democratic Party and to challenge it from within. That's one of the things that I think will emerge with Al Sharpton's possible primary challenge in the 2004 election, because he is going to be raising issues about the way the criminal justice system works in poor and third-world communities, racial profiling, the prison industrial system, as well as issues of corporate power. If we can get those issues to play a role in the primaries then we might be able to have some impact on the Democratic Party.

But if we still end up faced with a centrist Democrat winning those primaries, then we may once again have no choice but to vote for a third-party candidate. We can't just endlessly and uncritically support candidates whose views are so far from our own. But if we end up with a progressive in the Democratic Party, that would be a very different story.

Lerner: Too bad, then, to have to rely for this strategy on someone like Sharpton, who has such a problematic past which will make it so much easier for the media to divert attention from the more controversial issues that need to be addressed. Why not have one of the other progressive African-American elected officials as a candidate?

West: There aren't that many who would be willing to be a candidate and who simultaneously are willing to raise the kind of radical democratic critique that could mobilize people in a serious way. There are very few African-American politicians who would be willing to offer this kind of critique not only about the Democratic Party itself but about the larger society, and who would be willing to raise the issues not only about corporate power but about racial profiling and the criminal justice system as it operates among third-world and poor communities. There are some very talented political leaders, but they have developed ties inside the Democratic Party that make them reluctant to speak with the kind of clarity that Sharpton has. This is understandable, though not always defensible, to the extent that maintaining those ties does in fact give them some influence inside the circles of power.

Lerner: In the recent attempt by neoconservatives to throw you out of a conference planned for October at NYU on the life and works of Sidney Hook, wasn't your association with Tikkun raised privately by some of them as one reason they wanted to distance from you?

West: Absolutely. The four major conservative intellectuals from that conference—Hilton Kramer, William Kristol, Gertrude Himmelfarb, and John Dinkens—all abruptly withdrew when I was asked to replace Richard Rorty. There were three claims being made: First, that "West doesn't know anything about Sidney Hook" (apparently they were unfamiliar with my book on the American pragmatists which has an entire chapter assessing the works of Hook); that "West isn't a real intellectual"; and that "West is an anti-Semite, proved by the fact of his association with self-hating Jew Michael Lerner." And I said the third point is a compliment, because if the fact that you love not only Jews but other human beings as well and insist on the biblical message that everyone is created in the image of God and equally deserving of God's love makes you someone who is going to be demeaned, then I'm proud to be identified with you and with those other Jews who are willing to overcome tribalism.

I witness how your stance makes you the victim of attacks and put-downs by people who disagree with your willingness to stand for peace and justice and for the equal value of everyone on the planet—particularly by fellow Jews who think that the only way to love Jews is to show that they are loved more than other people on the planet. I've seen how painful that is for you, because in fact you have a passionate love for the Jewish people, and I've heard how passionately you criticize others on the Left when you feel that they are not giving the respect to Israel or Jews that is deserved. So I understand how difficult it is for you to have your actual love for the Jewish people being denied just because you think that the current policies of the State of Israel are deeply mistaken and the American Jewish alignment with those policies deeply immoral. So, I'm happy to have the chance to stand with you on these issues.

But of course these people had never read my book *The American Evasion of Philosophy*. This was a moment of ignorance in action and arrogance run amok. It reminds me of Harvard President Larry Summers and his actions toward me as a "University Professor" at Harvard. Summers summoned me to his office, critiqued me for being involved in political activity (something which is not entirely new to Harvard professors, as both former Harvard professor Henry Kissinger and current professor Samuel Huntington exemplify), critiqued me for making a spoken-word album of which he had not heard a note, then insisted that he wanted to supervise my academic work of which he had not read a page, and insisted that I come and report to him every two months on how my scholarship was coming along and present it to him. But most importantly, he falsely accused me of skipping three weeks of classes to support my dear brother, Bill Bradley.

Now a provost or dean wouldn't dare say something like this to an untenured assistant professor, much less to a tenured "University Professor," so I realized that this would not be a hospitable place for me to teach. He wouldn't say this to anyone whom he thought had even a modicum of self-respect, except if his goal was to push me out—and I had no desire to use my time to be engaged in that kind of a battle. No one should be subject to this kind of unjust treatment. It was so disrespectful. Then he posed himself as a victim after having initiated a vicious attack on my integrity, my character, and my scholarship. So he positions himself as a victim, yet he is part of the crowd of people who speak out against victimology when third-world or poor people talk about being victimized. Fortunately, I was blessed to become a part of the great humanistic conversation at Princeton University.

Lerner: To return to the issue of what progressives should be doing and saying on the anniversary of September 11: As cochair of the Tikkun Community, what is your message for this moment?

West: Well, first we have to put at the center our sadness at the fact that innocent human lives were sacrificed. Each of these precious lives was lost in a vicious way. That has to be the central point. And then, from our anguish at the loss of innocent lives we should begin to also discuss the innocent lives that are being lost every day in other parts of the world by virtue of the social, economic, and political realities that could be changed. So we root ourselves in a moral and ethical stance—rooted in the best of American traditions. And from that position we can also critique specific American policies, and the policies of other countries, that do not take seriously enough the preciousness of human life.

It was that message that led you and me to get arrested in Washington in April—our insistence that a Palestinian life is as precious as an Israeli life, because every person on the planet is equally valuable. This principle, which is the center of the Tikkun Community message, is so basic, and yet in the contemporary world it is seen as subversive when we take it seriously. It's a message that goes back to the prophets and the great leaders of many different religious and secular traditions.

Any talk about defending what is best in America and critiquing what is worst cannot be separated from a critique of what the United States is doing in the Middle East. Our criticisms of the Occupation have to be articulated clearly, though not in a way that trashes Israel or romanticizes the PLO; but neither should we pull back from our moral critique of both sides. The Tikkun Community is one of the few spaces in our entire culture where the various progressive voices come together in such a way that people who are paralyzed or who don't have a historical sense of what is happening can get educated and motivated. And that is what happens when they hear the Tikkun Community voice with its careful concern to affirm the best in both Israeli and Palestinian life and to critique the worst in both—reflecting a balanced perspective, yet a clear prophetic concern about justice that goes beyond the "accepted discourses" of both sides. When people hear your voice on television, they feel liberated from the constraints of the doctrinaire partisans on both sides, and as a result your perspective has become not only the most visible but the most significant voice articulating this middle and progressive path.

But this is the moment when progressive Jews are under severe attack and severe test. If ever there was an historical moment in which the best voices of the Jewish world should be heard, it is now. On the one hand, we must be unequivocal in our fierce opposition to the anti-Semitic voices that are escalating. On the other hand, the connection of much of American Jewish power to the most conservative elements in American elites has allowed a downplaying of the suffering of the Palestinian people and a willingness to not take the lives of Palestinians as of equal value to those of Jews or Americans. Thus we have the need to be both unequivocal in our support for the security of Israel while simultaneously being fully committed to ending the subjugation of the Palestinian people. Progressive Jews can maintain both the demand for Israeli security *and* the demand for an end to the Occupation and subjugation of the Palestinian people, and join with non-Jews like myself who are ready to walk with you. We can open up possibilities for a very important kind of progressive movement. That is one of the many things that excites me about being cochair with you of the Tikkun Community—you've made it an organization for both Jews and non-Jews. And Tikkun is uniquely well suited, not only because of its continuing ties to both secular and religious Jews and your serious commitment to Judaism, but also because Tikkun continues to be respected beyond progressive circles right into the mainstream of American politics.

Contemporary Developments in American Spirituality

Daniel Berrigan

There may be some people who think that spirituality is intrinsically antithetical to political action, but I've been privileged to meet many thousands of people of faith whose lives have been dedicated to testifying to the word of God through social protest and acts of intervention against illegitimate authority.

Most recently, some of us have been arrested repeatedly at a notorious war museum, the (Navy vessel) SS *Intrepid*, a pest house anchored in the New York Harbor. We are appalled that busloads of children from both public and parochial schools are brought to this obscenity to view the latest indiscriminate weapons—we believe that the place should be declared "pornographic" and off limits for children. We've been involved in protesting the American war machine in all its manifestations—my brother Phillip has been in prison for many years for his courageous actions against the weapons of war. We've been involved both here and in other places around the world where human rights are violated and where the obscenity of war is being waged. What sustains us in all this is our reading and study of the Bible, and our faith. We in the Catholic world see ourselves as deeply aligned with the social healing and transformation project that you at *Tikkun* magazine have been pursuing so courageously and beautifully in the Jewish world.

Religious faith has been particularly important because it seems to sustain itself in moments when society is experiencing a recession of hope. Religious faith joins us to a much longer and tested human phenomenon than American culture can offer. The enticements to get in lockstep with the dominant culture are enormous and the pressures to fit in are enhanced by icons of greed and violence. We need saints and prophets to withstand the dominant culture—and those are rarely supplied by the "alternative" streams in American culture.

A lot of people find it hard to sustain their commitment to their own high-est ideals because America has so successfully imbued its citizens with the notion that the highest goal is success. "Success" is such a weasel word. The goal of success is so very different from the dominant thrust of the Bible— there are few success stories in the Bible. The story of Jesus, in particular, is one of loss, failure, and capital punishment. The biblical message is one of sustaining faith in possibility even when the power of the forces of the cur-rent establishment seem to be overwhelming. So my brother can spend nine of the last thirty years of his life in prison, and yet still keep up his spirits, write, have a worldwide correspondence, and keep at it without being crushed by the system because he is connected to this biblical faith. I think that many of the secular social-change movements that avoid spiritual connection some-times lack this kind of basis for sustaining the individual through difficult pe-riods where there is no American-style "success" to be had.

There's a dimension to political work that I think is particularly common among spiritually-oriented folk that is not as common in the rest of the pro-gressive social-change movements: namely, some connection with the vic-tims of this society, whether they be the homeless, the poor, the sick, people with AIDS, or others who have experienced social oppression. I think that this kind of connection is very important for people who do social-change work, and yet I find it very unpopular among many social-change activists.

I often find our secular friends acting on the principle that unless a partic-ular action has a big impact, they don't want to sustain it; they are looking for a quick avenue to success, and feeding the hungry or housing the homeless doesn't really have that kind of impact. Nobody can sustain him or herself in the struggle for a nonviolent world on the basis of the criterion of immediate success. The Bible gives us a long view rather than the expectation of a quick fix. All of us are in grave danger of being infected by this American ethos that good work brings quick change, rather than the older spiritual notion that good work is its own justification and that the outcome is in other hands be-sides ours.

Of course I'm aware that there is a kind of spiritual movement growing in America today that is divorced from a *tikkun* perspective, with people unin-terested in anything outside of their own inner feelings. I've watched some of this new American spirituality fill itself with prideful psychobabble as it pro-vides a self-obsessed inner focus for people who have "made it" but who don't care much about those who have not. Some of this spirituality is aimed at claiming one's own turf and immunizing oneself against the misery of the streets. It was very upsetting to me to be in some spiritual retreat centers and experience this attitude, the radiating affluence, self-satisfaction, and isola-tion from the suffering of others. It's a form of spirituality that I find degrading and divorced from any tradition of the human that I can understand. Yet I feel great compassion for the people who buy into this form of living. The price that one pays for this kind of spirituality is being out of one's own time and place in the universe, out of the sphere of the ethical, and being part of a shrinking minority of people on this planet who can afford to be selfish and buy immunity from the lot of humanity. One of the disturbing aspects of these kinds of spiritual communities—very different from, for example, the community of spiritually-oriented social-change activists with whom I work—is that people seek out their own kind and so they look very much alike, the same color, the same kind of clothing, the same implicit American understanding about being "number one" in the world and "anything goes" in order to retain it. I've even seen people coming from this place willing to cooperate with or even support some of the most ravenous policies of the American economy without any feeling of unease. Needless to say, those who are in the command positions of the American corporations and the military have no objection to this kind of spirituality—from their standpoint it's fine.

I rarely find New Age people involved with us when we are demonstrating against militarism or when we are feeding the hungry or creating shelters for the homeless or in the hospital work we do with AIDS people, whereas I find many spiritual people who are connected to religious communities. Too often some of the New Age people are seeking a soft world, which their affluence allows them to purchase, while turning their attention from the harsh realities of a world that needs healing and repair.

Some people today argue that equanimity achieved through inner spiritual work is a necessary condition for sustaining one's ethical and political commitments. But to the prophets of the Bible, this would have been an absolutely foreign language and a foreign view of the human. The notion that one has to achieve peace of mind before stretching out one's hand to one's neighbor is a distortion of our human experience, and ultimately a dodge of our responsibility. Life is a roller coaster and one had better buckle one's belt and take the trip. This focus on equanimity is actually a narrow-minded, selfish approach to reality dressed up within the language of spirituality.

Open up the book of Jeremiah and you do not find a person looking for inner peace. What the prophet (and those inspired by the prophetic tradition) seeks is to be faithful to God in the midst of a maelstrom of suffering and setback. Jeremiah is crying out and at wit's end, and then is filled with ecstasy and sees the promise—he goes through mountains and valleys. That kind of richness I find very appealing, whereas the kind of spirituality that looks for a flat emotional landscape brought on by the endless search for inner peace and equanimity I find disturbing, a quest that goes nowhere. I once scolded Thich Nhat Hanh after I heard him speak at a church in Manhattan. I told him that from my observation his audience was composed of people seeking cheap peace of mind, and that he had not helped people understand that his own life, though having elements of inner peace, had been an enormous struggle. He didn't tell his own story and gave people the impression that life could simply be about little acts of kindness without any connection to the larger struggles for social justice. It's those struggles that lead us beyond the confines of personal life to connect with the realities of others, including others who are suffering and who do not live in our neighborhoods and with whom we would not have contact (and hence, not have an opportunity to share acts of kindness) unless we consciously chose to seek them out.

I know that the prophetic vision is not popular today in some of these spiritual circles. But our task is not to be popular or to be seen as having an impact, but to speak the deepest truths that we know. We need to live our lives in accord with the deepest truths we know even if doing so does not produce immediate results in the world.

Economies of Meaning

David C. Korten

The politics of meaning poses a challenging question: What would be the characteristics of an economy that both meets our material needs and serves to create the ethos of caring relationships and of ethical, spiritual, and ecological sensitivity essential to life in a good society? If we take this to be a twofold performance test of the good economy then it is evident that our existing economy is serving us poorly.

There is little room for ethical, spiritual, and ecological sensitivity in a global economy that defines success purely in terms of the financial bottom line, creates a growing gap between its winners and losers, and provides fabulous financial rewards to those willing to sacrifice long-term human and environmental interests for short-term financial gain.

Leading proponents of the new global economy such as Rosabeth Kanter, Harvard Business School professor and author of the business bestseller, *World Class*, counsel that in the global economy financial success belongs to those who are willing to sacrifice loyalty to community and nation in the pursuit of personal economic opportunity. The March 25, 1995 issue of *Fortune* advises young graduates to approach every job as though they are self-employed, because success will come to those who look out for number one, always using one's present job to open better opportunities with other employers.

It is abundantly clear: In the global free-market economy, caring, loyalty, and moderation are out. Individual self-interest, materialism, and opportunism are in.

Since the disintegration of the Soviet Empire in 1989, countries nearly everywhere have joined in an uncritical embrace of market-driven economic growth based on deregulating markets, privatizing public assets, scaling back social programs, and removing barriers to the free international flow of goods and finance. Political parties from across the political spectrum have converged on a commitment to variations of this agenda, leaving those who question the underlying assumptions or the moral implications of this agenda with few political alternatives.

In spite of its claims to firm theoretical and empirical foundations, the neoliberal economic policy agenda is best described as an ideology of corporate libertarianism based on the perpetuation of myths deeply embedded in our political culture and an embrace of social dysfunction as the foundation of a perverse moral philosophy. It is useful to examine a few of the more central of these myths.

The Myth That Growth in Aggregate Economic Output is a Valid Measure of Human Well-Being and Progress

To the contrary, the indicators of aggregate economic output by which economic policy managers evaluate their performance tell us nothing about the social utility of that output. Expanded use of cigarettes and alcohol increases economic output both as a direct consequence of their consumption and because of the related increase in health care needs. The need to clean up oil spills increases economic activity. Gun sales to minors generate economic activity. A divorce generates both lawyers fees and the need to buy or rent and outfit a new home, increasing real estate brokerage fees and retail sales. It is now well documented that in the United States and a number of other countries the quality of living of ordinary people has been declining as aggregate economic output increases.

The Myth That Technology Frees Us from Environmental Restraints on Economic Growth

While technology in some instances allows us to use ecosystem resources more efficiently, there is a strong historical relationship between growth in economic output and growing human demands on the earth's finite ecosystem. Furthermore, a fivefold increase in the world's economic output since 1950 has now pushed the human burden on the planet's regenerative systems, its soils, air, water, fisheries, and forestry systems beyond what the planet can sustain. Continuing to press for economic growth beyond the planet's sustainable limits accelerates the rate of breakdown of those systems, as we see so dramatically demonstrated in the case of many ocean fisheries, and intensifies the competition between rich and poor for the earth's remaining output of life-sustaining resources.

The Myth That an Open and Unregulated "Free" Market is the Fairest and Most Efficient Way to Allocate Society's Resources and Is the Foundation of Human Freedom and Democratic Citizen Sovereignty

Market economies are highly responsive to the wants of those who have money. They are blind to the needs of those who have no money. In contrast to political democracy, which is based on one person, one vote, economic democracy is about one dollar, one vote. Under conditions of relative economic equality, the market mechanism has an important role in the fair, efficient, and democratic allocation of resources. Under the conditions of extreme inequality that presently prevail, an unfettered market allocates resources in ways that are grossly unfair, inefficient, and undemocratic. Contrary to the rhetoric of ideologues from both Right and Left, markets are neither inherently good nor inherently bad. It is a question of the conditions under which a particular market functions.

The Myth That the Only Alternative To a Free Market Economy is A State-Planned, Command Economy

Our own history is one of many sources of alternative examples. During the post–World War II period, in which a large and prosperous middle class was a defining feature of the Western industrial nations, the market functioned within a framework of rules set through a democratic public process. The institutions of government, market, and civil society functioned in a reasonable pluralistic balance. A combination of deregulation and globalization have freed the market and destroyed this balance, rapidly eroding the conditions on which efficient market function depends. For example, in the absence of government intervention, successful competitors gain ever-greater monopolistic advantage through their accumulation of economic and political power. Now the competitive market economy is being steadily replaced by a centrally planned global economy managed by an ever more tightly integrated alliance of global corporations.

The Related Myths That Trade Agreements are about Trade, That Open Economic Borders Are Universally Beneficial, and That Economic Globalization is A Consequence of Immutable Historical Forces

The truth is that most trade agreements—such as NAFTA, GATT, and the European Maastricht Treaty—are really economic integration agreements intended to guarantee the rights of global corporations to move both goods and investments wherever they wish, free from public interference and accountability. Greater rights for global corporations inevitably mean fewer rights for ordinary citizens to set the rules by which their own local and national economies will function. The trend toward ever-greater global economic integration is inevitable only so long as we allow the world's largest corporations to buy our politicians and write our laws.

The Myth That Global Corporations are Benevolent Institutions that, Once Freed From Governmental Interference, Will Provide Local Prosperity, Jobs, and a Clean Environment for All

In reality, the institution of the corporation was invented to concentrate control over economic resources while shielding those who hold the resulting power from personal accountability for the public consequences of its use. In a globalized, deregulated market, the only legal public accountability of corporate management in the use of their power is to a global financial market that has one incessant demand: Maximize short-term returns to shareholders. This puts enormous pressures on management to take advantage of every available opportunity to pass the costs of production onto the community by lowering wages and working conditions, obtaining government subsidies and tax breaks, and cutting corners on environmental protection. Gains are privatized to the benefit of the power holders. Costs are socialized by passing them to those who have no political or economic voice.

These myths of our political culture are buttressed by a number of moral premises embedded in the corporate libertarian ideology that serves as the foundation for most neoliberal economic theory. These moral premises may be summarized as follows:

- People are by nature motivated primarily by greed.
- The drive to acquire material wealth is the highest expression of what it means to be human.
- The relentless pursuit of greed and acquisition leads to socially optimal outcomes.
- It is in the best interest of human societies to encourage, honor, and reward these values.

While most economists would not state these premises in such stark terms, this is the essence of the value assumptions underlying most contemporary market theory. Unfortunately, economic policies driven by these deeply flawed moral premises create a self-fulfilling prophecy by rewarding dysfunctional behaviors deeply detrimental to the healthy function of human societies, as we now see demonstrated all around us.

Our development models — and their underlying myths and values — are artifacts of the ideas and institutions of the industrial era. The corporation and the modern state have been cornerstones of that era, concentrating massive economic resources in a small number of centrally controlled institutions. They have brought the full power of capital-intensive technologies to bear in exploiting the world's natural and human resources so that a small minority of the world's people could consume far more than their rightful share of the world's real wealth.

Economic globalization has served to advance this exploitation of the earth's social and environmental systems beyond their limits of tolerance, by freeing errant corporations from restraints to their growth, their ability to monopolize ever larger markets, and the use of their economic power to win political concessions that allow them to pass on to the community ever more of the costs of their production. It has delinked corporations and financial markets from accountability to any public jurisdiction or interest, contributed to a massive concentration of financial power, and richly rewarded those who place the values of acquisition, competition, and self-interest ahead of values of simplicity, cooperation, and sharing.

We are not limited to choosing between markets or governments as the instruments of our exploitation. Nor is there need to eliminate markets, trade, private ownership, the state, or even the institution of the corporation. Rather, it is a matter of creating a new architecture for each of these institutions appropriate to the values we believe a good society should embody and nurture. This creative task belongs neither to corporations nor to states, which are incapable of questioning the assumptions on which the legitimacy of their present institutional form is based. It belongs to citizens — to the people whose interests and values the new architecture is intended to serve. It is people rather than corporations or other big-money interests that appropriately set the terms of the economic and political agenda.

Citizen groups throughout the world are already actively engaged in the experimental creation of economies of meaning aligned with life-affirming values. Powerful formative ideas are emerging from these initiatives. For example, millions of people in the voluntary simplicity movement are discovering that good living is more fulfilling than endless accumulation and consumption. In a healthy society, a life of material sufficiency and social, cultural, intellectual, and spiritual abundance can readily be sustained in balance with the environment.

Others are learning that there are alternatives to a global economy that inherently fosters inequality and global competition among local people and communities. They are demonstrating such possibilities by building strong, self-reliant, local economies that root resource management and ownership in democratically governed communities and recognize that all people have an inherent right of access to a basic means of creating a livelihood. Such economies are an essential foundation of healthy societies able to engage in cooperative and caring exchanges with their neighbors.

These are lessons with profound implications for a politics of meaning. In large measure, societies express and sustain their cultural values through their choice of economic structures. The fact that our present economic system values and rewards greed, gluttony, and disregard for the needs of others didn't just happen. It is a consequence of conscious acts of choice—poorly informed though they may be. It is equally within our means to create a globalized system of localized economies that thrive on life-affirming values of sufficiency, caring, cooperation, and reverence for life. It is a matter of adequately informed collective political choice.

Yet our existing political formations, no matter where they are positioned on the traditional Left-Right spectrum, reveal no awareness of even the possibility of replacing an economy of meanness with economies of meaning. That is one of many compelling reasons why we need a new political movement in the United States that is not defined by traditional Left-Right values and agendas. The politics of meaning movement is engaging this task. I believe that building public awareness of the potential to create economies of meaning and putting forward a policy agenda that advances this outcome must receive high priority on the movement's agenda.

Experts and Citizens

Rethinking Professionalism

William M. Sullivan

Something has gone wrong with the professions in the United States. Where law, medicine, and the other venerable "learned professions" once served as models of useful knowledge in service to the community, today's entrants to these fields find them beset by cynicism and disillusionment bred of a narrow commercialism. We no longer look to the successful lawyer or doctor for community leadership and public service. Today we worry whether their malpractice premiums are paid up.

The professions' recent record in national leadership is equally embarrassing. During several years of crucial debate over health care, the chief discernable contribution of the American Medical Association, the nation's most powerful professional organization, has been to wheel and deal to enhance its members' incomes. And as newer professions such as engineering, management, and journalism, nursing, and social work have come to the fore, they too appear unsure of their ethical vision. As the social and economic importance of professional work expands, the ethical vision within the professions appears to be contracting.

Many Americans think that there is something wrong with professionals as well. Not financially, of course. Quite the contrary. Professionals make up a large percentage of the fortunate fifth of the nation whose incomes have risen during the past decade, and the top earners among doctors, lawyers, and business executives have been doing even better than the average professional. But most of us, who have been watching our incomes stagnate and decline, now claim to see plenty of things wrong with our professional classes. From lawyer jokes to angry charges of "profscams" in the academy, to outrage at rising medical costs for declining services, professionals are finding their legitimacy threatened, their very professionalism trashed as a cloak for an arrogant ascendancy.

Everybody has good reason to worry about the state of the professions. Because professionals dominate many of the nation's most critical institutions, they play a major role in determining the fate of their fellow citizens. Whether we like it or not, we all depend upon professional competence and probity to get accurate understandings of events, to work and travel safely, to raise families, even to preserve physical and psychic health. How well professionals perform their functions is of serious, sometimes vital, concern to every American. That is why exposes of scientists who falsify crucial research data, or physicians who take financial kickbacks, or lawyers who violate conflict-of-interest codes—all of which now appear with alarming regularity—ignite public anger.

Along with the revelations of malfeasance has come the insidious erosion of morale in many fields. Teachers increasingly find their work unrewarding, doctors urge aspirants not to enter medicine, journalists find their judgment preempted by the conflicting pressures of profitable sensationalism and the constraints of libel law. The health of professionalism is a public concern, and its revival will only be possible when professionals recognize and reassert the public purposes and responsibilities at the core of their enterprise.

Today, the ethical foundation of professional life is at risk. Professionalism, the competent and ethical application of expert knowledge, traditionally has lent integrity to professional life and made the privileges and status of professionals publicly acceptable. Professionalism is vital because professions can administer their own licensing and standards only so long as they maintain the public trust. So when Americans stop trusting professionals—when they begin to doubt the integrity of the entire field of law or question the reality of professionalism in medicine and a host of other fields—the consequence is a crisis of public confidence that cannot help but determine the future of professional work.

The many manifestations of this crisis flow from a common source. We all sense that both the general public and many professionals themselves have lost can administer their own licensing and standards only so long as they maintain the public trust. So when Americans stop trusting professionals—when they begin to doubt the integrity of the entire field of law or question the reality of professionalism in medicine and a host of other fields—the consequence is a crisis of public confidence that cannot help but determine the future of professional work.

The many manifestations of this crisis flow from a common source. We all sense that both the general public and many professionals themselves have lost faith in the inherent value of what they do, beyond its immediate cash reward. Market values of unrestrained competition and profit-maximization have for some time been corrupting the professional conscience and eroding professional loyalties. The spread of the idea that the economic bottom line must determine what counts as good professional practice undermines professional self-respect even as it makes the ideals of service and public responsibility appear as mere options on a fixed menu of tough-minded self-interest. It is symptomatic of the demoralization of professional life, the decadence of professionalism.

So far, responses to these dismaying tendencies have been uncertain and ineffective. Driven by a chorus of public outrage and a plague of lawsuits, calls for "ethics" echo each other across the professions. With much fanfare, both the American Medical Association and the American Bar Association have mounted campaigns to enlist practitioners in more pro bono and community-service work—with dismal results. During the past decade, dozens of universities and professional schools have established programs and "centers" to promote more ethical practice in a variety of fields, but the effect of this focus on "ethics" is inconclusive.

These appeals to the professional conscience are not so much misguided as incomplete. What is missing is recognition of the public, indeed political, nature of the professions. Law, medicine, education, scientific research, teaching, management serve public, not simply individual values. At its core, professionalism promises that by contributing important services, individuals can make something of their talents and achieve a self-respecting place in society. The institutional vehicle for this ideal has been the publicly accountable occupational group: the bar, the health care fields, or the academic, social service, and managerial organizations.

Breakdowns in professional integrity remind us painfully of our dependence upon the work of anonymous others. They reveal how large a stake we each have in seeing that professional functions are carried out effectively. External controls—either carrots or sticks alone—cannot renew professionalism. There is finally no substitute for the engaged commitment of the persons actually involved in providing the service.

Professionalism will not survive—and it certainly cannot be renewed—unless most practitioners understand that they are in business for the common welfare as well as their own, and that their work has value in relation to that common aim. That is why it is so important to rearticulate the nature and meaning of professionalism as a public value. Articulating a standard for genuine professionalism helps people recognize that the integrity of professional life depends upon mutual trust between experts and the public. Professionals can then see how economic self-interest and technical arrogance in the professions are undermining the quality of life for everyone. This recognition can set in motion the needed counter forces of civic energy.

To renew the vigor of professionalism will take public action. The demoralization among professionals will persist so long as the lay public distrusts the experts. Healing these frayed bonds of trust will require new forms of partnership. But they are unlikely to develop unless professionals and the lay public can understand and respond to each other. They need common ground, common standards to which to hold each other accountable, and even more, a sense of common interest and purpose. That is why a clearer understanding of the full dimensions of professionalism is essential.

Even amid all the skepticism about professional integrity, to judge a person or a performance "professional" means a good deal. The term evokes technical competence, plus the genuine dedication that enables individuals to rise above self-interest to do the job well. In fact, we expect professional work to embody a sense of calling. We trust doctors and clergy to be "on call," to put our welfare first. We collectively demand uncompensated service pro bono publico from doctors and lawyers. Even though professionals are allowed and expected to pursue economic success, this high sense of mission and public responsibility is what has traditionally defined professional work.

Yet these traditions have eroded and weakened. This is particularly true in a market society that increasingly prizes career flexibility or simply the smarts to grasp the main chance over vocational integrity. Professional skills, like others, are marketed. Thus, in practice, professionalism has to manage the conflict between market opportunities, which propel calculations of individual advantage, and the defining goals of the profession, which encourage its members toward responsibility for common values. The market puts pressures on. . . . [profess]sionals are no longer the solo practitioners of popular image, but members of large bureaucratic organizations. The purposes of these organizations—their efforts to maintain their power and enhance their prestige—like the profit motive of the market, put a lot of destructive pressure on professional standards.

The advances of modern technology have also ratcheted up the tension between professional purposes and organizational imperatives such as competition and survival. Especially in the health professions, the aura of technological wizardry has redefined the healer. Less the caregiver of old and more the technician able to engineer health, the physician has become increasingly tied to the high-technology medical center, exchanging the old humble function of care for a less personal, if more effective, role as technician. At the extreme, the redefined physician in the medical center can succeed in a career defined almost entirely in terms of technical and economic success and nearly devoid of attention to the human meaning and moral ties which long gave healing its purpose and value.

In the face of this narrow conception of the professional as technician, it is especially critical to insist upon the broader moral horizon of professional responsibility. By encouraging the illusion that technology can somehow banish the vulnerability of the human condition, the technical deformation of professionalism subtly supports the conclusion that solace and care for the suffering and the unfortunate are obsolete values.

In fact, modern societies hold out to individuals many occupational choices and opportunities for personal satisfaction. Traditional ties and moral constraints have loosened, yet individual lives have become ever more intricately tied into unseen networks of interdependence, increasing the need for forethought and large-scale cooperation. This conjunction of developments provides both the exhilaration of personal freedom and an increasing burden of responsibility. Coherence and meaning in modern life are of necessity highly personal achievements and yet deeply dependent upon social relationships. Professionalism as an ideal articulates a way toward integrity in this complicated situation.

During the past decade, the young urban professional ("yuppie") lifestyle has come to exemplify the complexities of contemporary professional life. In the upper reaches of the occupational ladder among the best educated and most ambitious professionals, the allure of wealth and prestige, the pride of technical expertise, and vastly expanded opportunities for personal exploration maintain an uneasy coexistence. The conflicts of yuppie life illustrate in compressed form the clashing tendencies at work in American life as a whole.

The twin values of competence and adaptability drive professional work at its upper levels. Yet this cult of competence among young professionals engenders few lasting ties to employers, coworkers, clients, or organizations. In their outlook, status flows from hard work per se, with little corresponding sense of gratitude, few overarching loyalties, faint responsibility to others. Even when they have altruistic urges, entrants into these high-flying careers quickly discover that relentless pressure for more productivity greatly limits the possibility for more than token pro bono work or other civic involvements.

The very intensity of their work world, accentuated for many by the increasingly international scope of competition; focuses attention on staying viable, leaving little psychic energy for considering the long-term or larger significance of day-to-day decisions. All this encourages traveling light, morally as well as physically. The demands of managing a fast-paced career require incessant "networking" with similarly ambitious members of their aspiring class, but little attention to those outside the charmed circle of success.

While we look to the intimate realm of personal life to balance or at least relieve the demands and stresses of work, the race to live well can turn into an exhausting battle for psychic survival. Under this strain, relationships, including marriage and family, often become areas for great anxiety and severe disappointment.

Missing from this degenerating professionalism is any shared confidence in the public import of the work itself. Without this, there can be little honor in professional status. Without this, the effort to become one's own person through instrumental achievement cannot, for most, support satisfaction in practicing a profession over time. Shorn of the shared loyalty to public purposes that characterizes genuine professionalism, there can be no secure recognition for individual achievement, leaving individuals anxious, having to validate their self-worth through comparative ranking along an infinite scale of cleverness, wealth, and power.

By contrast, an authentic professionalism provides an escape from this unhappy consciousness by focusing a person's energies toward engagement with the challenges of society's needs. This civic—as opposed to a purely technical or commercial—professionalism unfolds as part of a cooperative civic culture. The future of professionalism depends upon the ability of professionals and their associations to rediscover their connections with their fellow citizens and the place their expertise might occupy in enhancing this shared culture.

In a democratic society, professional legitimacy is always precarious because it rests upon a general balance between the kinds and degree of professional privilege and the public's perception that professional services contribute significantly to the public welfare. The integrity of professional life, in fact its future, is bound up with the health of the larger civic culture. And that in turn depends in significant part upon widespread recognition of the need to renew and support efforts at cooperation and partnership among mutually suspicious groups.

Fortunately, experiments are underway in a variety of professional fields to reverse the deformation of professionalism by connecting professional work in new ways to the needs of democratic life. In these experiments, professionals and their organizations serve as social partners, working with other groups of citizens to address important common problems more effectively.

Long a collaborative, integrative field, public health today is expanding its purview to include the areas of juvenile violence and social decay, not by taking over other fields so much as by developing new patterns of cooperation with law enforcement through community policing, and with social work through community-based organizations for health education and prevention. The movement for civic journalism is expanding in its efforts to have journalists and the news print media recast their role beyond that of the detached observer toward partnership with government, business, education, and other major institutions in building civic culture. In a similar way, innovative planning efforts in several states have begun to bring professionals together with the business sector and citizens' groups to assume responsibility for enhancing their communities' collective resources over the long term.

As these examples suggest, professional renewal has begun to unleash creative energy, which now needs a sense of common purpose to focus and catalyze these nascent efforts. Professionalism, understood in its full, civic meaning, could provide that focus, as well as support and inspiration toward renewing civic cooperation. The benefits of such a strategy for professions and the society alike could be very great. Where civic cooperation is weak or sporadic, however, individuals and groups find it harder to accept self-restraint or to shoulder collective responsibilities. They fear that others will take advantage of them when they do so. Their public stance becomes wary and competitive, with a hard and calculating edge. This attitude makes democratic cooperation ever more difficult, reinforcing cynicism and weakening social trust still further. Everyone suffers from the lack of trust, but at the same time, everyone fears the risks necessary to reestablish cooperation. The irresponsible behavior of contemporary professionals who take all they can when they can has its source in this descending spiral of social entropy, even as it contributes to it.

Conversely, where levels of trust, self-restraint, and cooperativeness are high, where social interactions are perceived as equitable and mutually beneficial to all parties, professional organizations are more likely to behave as "good citizens," taking responsible leadership roles in civic life. In return the professions garner public support and often prestige.

The idea of civic professionalism also has implications for work beyond professionalized occupations. The ethic of professionalism addresses a central problem of modern life, the question of meaning in work. Meaning refers to the sense of value persons experience when they understand their own lives to be linked in a significant way with larger processes of intrinsic value. To discover meaning is to find a point to living by recognizing oneself as a participant in a worthwhile enterprise whose accomplishment calls out one's energies and whose purposes define and vindicate one's having lived.

To live with meaning is to have discovered the secret to fulfillment. In the modern world, the sources of meaning are plural, a significant advance over the narrow possibilities offered to most persons in traditional societies. This is in part the result of the extension of freedom to ever-greater sectors of the population, enabling women, the young, and ethnic and racial minorities to begin defining their own lives.

Meaning does not stem from work alone, but from family life, friendship, knowledge, from national, global, cultural, religious, and philosophical concerns. In modern societies, however, work plays a key role in providing the means by which individuals can develop their capacities and express their individuality. Work offers solidarity through the pursuit of shared goals and values. In its broadest sense, then, professionalism is a civic virtue, an aspiration that can unite many individual lives in the common cause of realizing human meaning in modern work.

Healing our Hearts

Deepak Chopra

We have the deepest aspirations. We want to create a new mythology that says that peace and harmony and laughter and love are possible. That says that social justice and economic parity and ecological balance and a sense for the sacred and a universal spirituality irrespective of our origins are all part of the tangled hierarchy, the interdependency chorus.

Human beings have only existed for two hundred thousand years. For most of this time, we have been surrounded by predators. In order to survive, we have had a biological response, the flight/fight response. Because we have become so good at this flight/fight response, we have become the predator on this planet. We are the most dangerous animal.

That is not our whole history, however. Something very interesting happened to us about four thousand years ago, when a few luminaries across the world appeared at once. They were the prophets of the Pentateuch, the great Greek philosophers, the sages of the Upanishads, the Eastern seers like Lao Tsu, Confucius, and Buddha, and many others. They developed the ability to get in touch with the domain of awareness that is nonlocal, that transcends the space-time energy and everything that we can perceive with our senses.

The great English poet William Blake once wrote, "We are led to believe a lie / when we see with and not through the eye / that was born in the night, to perish in the night, / while the souls slept in beams of light." When we see beyond the physical we see into our souls.

We can go a whole lifetime without getting in touch with our souls. But once we get in touch with this presence, there is no going back. This soul place is one of knowingness, of light, of love, compassion, and understanding. Intention, imagination, insight, intuition, creativity, meaning, purpose, and decision making are the attributes of this presence. When we get in touch with it, we have recourse to what is called the intuitive response, which is a form of intelligence that is contextual, relational, holistic, and nurturing. When I'm in this presence, and you are, we are in the same place.

We see that we are part of a great chain of being where we interdependently cocreate each other. There is more that we share than what separates us. We all seek love, we all seek self-esteem, we all seek creative expression, we all seek self-actualization—these are the birthright of every human being.

There is no more important task at this moment in our history than to get in touch with the sacred core of our being that is common to all of us. Our practical proposals will be effective only when we get in touch with our souls, and feel this fundamental shift in our hearts. If we can feel that shift in our hearts, if we can join together and be living examples of this shift, then the world will transform, because the world is as we are. The world is nothing other than the projection of our souls.

Just because we are part of a collective insanity, we must not assume it is normal. It is the psychopathology of the average. I am committed to the vision Michael Lerner has expressed in *Tikkun* and elsewhere that we can emancipate ourselves from this psychopathology through the realm of spirit. Even though we have interesting scientific insights, the religious traditions of the world have access to universal truths.

A friend of mine sent me an English translation of an Egyptian papyrus discovered in the 1940s. The language is pre-Babylonian. We don't know who the author is, but he or she lived in the time of Solomon. The author is talking to God and he or she says:

> You split me and you tore my heart open and you filled me with love.
> You poured your spirit into mine. I knew you as I knew myself.
> My eyes are radiant with your light. My ears delight in your music.
> My nostrils are filled with your fragrance. My face is covered with your dew.
> You have made me see all things shining. You have made me see all things new.
> You have granted me perfect ease. And I have become like Paradise.
> And having become like Paradise, my soul is healed.

At this moment, there is a rift in our collective soul. But there is one part of our evolution that says this rift can be healed. And if we heal it, we will all move into that ecstasy which is nothing other than the exaltation of spirit.

Be Not Afraid

Jim Wallis

I'm a father, so I try not to be away from home for too many days. But when I am away, I have frequent conversations with my two boys, Luke and Jack. Luke is four, but he has the phone thing down. I want to tell you about one of those phone conversations.

I was in Florida, and Luke and I had already talked twice that day. So when I got to the hotel room and heard a little voice on my hotel voice mail I smiled. Two hours had passed—lots of things had happened. I had to be caught up.

I listened and heard this little voice go through all that had happened since we last talked. He said goodbye, but he didn't hang up, and what he said next stopped me dead in my tracks. He said, "Daddy, don't be afraid."

I heard my wife, Joy, take in her breath in the background. A little four-year-old child says, "Daddy, don't be afraid."

You might know that in the Christian tradition, Jesus instructed his disciples that way, using that phrase more than any other single instruction. Over and over again, Jesus said, "Be not afraid."

Even as I speak we are on Orange Alert, high danger of threat from terrorism, just as we were throughout the war in Iraq, a war that was argued for and justified mainly on the basis of fear. A monk named Thomas Merton said many years ago, "The root of war is fear."

Since September 11, our nation has been terrified. Even now, in victory, we are still terrified.

September 11 shattered the American sense of invulnerability. That was the invitation of September 11: accept the feeling of vulnerability that most of the world's people already live with. Join the rest of us.

Most Americans don't want to join the kids of color in my urban neighborhood who already are familiar with the kind of random, senseless violence that takes loved ones away. They want something no one can give us. They want someone to erase our vulnerability. If the government says war will make it go away, they say, fine. If the government says suspending civil liberties will do that, they say, fine. If the government claims spending more and more of our tax dollars on the military and homeland security at the expense of everything else will make us once again feel invulnerable, they say, fine.

But we can't erase our vulnerability. Our vulnerability, in fact, is the source of some of our greatest creativity and best impulses. Being prudent and vigilant in the face of danger is good. But when a government offers to take away our vulnerability, I would suggest to you, theologically, that it borders on idolatry.

I am convinced that mere political action to counter policies based on fear will not be enough. We must go deeper, to the roots of our fear. Courage is not the absence of fear; it is the resistance to fear. For people of faith, that means trusting in the One we call God. For those who are not persons of faith, it means believing at some deep level that what you know, what you believe, and who you are is finally more trustworthy than that which others say you must be afraid of. We need nothing less than the healing of a nation, beginning with our fears; that healing will be essential to make peace-making possible.

Those who now lead this nation, however, believe that peace comes through unquestioned military superiority. Presidential words from battleships point the way. A new Pax Americana is being offered quite boldly. The word "empire" is no longer a dirty word—it is being used in a positive sense. Bill Kristol of the *Weekly Standard* has said, "There is nothing wrong with dominance, as long as it is in favor of the right values." Meaning ours.

In 1997, Kristol and others formed a group called the Project for the New American Century, proposing a policy to enforce American interests throughout the world. They say in "Rebuilding America's Defenses," a September, 2000 report: "The United States is the only superpower combining preeminent military power, global technological leadership and the world's largest economy. At present the United States faces no global rivals. America's grand strategy should aim to preserve and extend this advantageous position as far into the future as possible. If an American peace is to be maintained and expanded it must have a secure foundation on unquestioned U.S. military predominance. The failure to prepare for tomorrow's challenges will ensure that the current Pax Americana comes to an end" (www.newamericancentury.org).

There is another way. My favorite prophet in an era of globalization is eighth-century B.C.E. Micah. Micah says, "Ye shall judge between the nations and shall arbitrate between strong peoples far away. They shall beat their swords into plowshares and their spears into pruning hooks. Nation shall not lift up sword against nation; neither shall there be war anymore." Then he says, "They shall all sit under their own vines and their own fig trees; and no one shall make them afraid" (4:1–7).

See, Micah knew that we will not beat our swords into plowshares until everyone has their own vine and fig tree, meaning a share in this global economy. When you have a little piece of security, it is hard to make you afraid.

Micah knew there is no security for ourselves until there is security for others. There is no security for me when there is no security for my brother, my neighbor, even my adversary. There is no security when more than half the world lives on two dollars a day. There is no security when our own poor are denied a tax cut while the rich are given back thousands of dollars. There is no security when thousands are dying from AIDS without relief.

There is no security for ourselves until there is security for others. We will not be at peace until all of us can be unafraid. That is a profoundly spiritual reality and the most pragmatic, practical piece of wisdom you will hear.

The Force of Nonviolence

Lama Surya Das

The enemy can be our greatest teacher.

—Shantideva

The first anniversary of September 11 should be a time for prayer. It's a time to reflect on what is most important in our lives, and to think about what steps we might take towards nonviolence within ourselves in order to build a more peaceful world. As a Buddhist, a believer in karma, I know there are no accidents. The task before us is to cultivate a clear mind and an open heart so that we may understand as fully as possible the origins of the crisis in the world today and engage in effective peacemaking and reconciliation.

Many have said that September 11 was a wake-up call—but are we awake now? Or have we gone back to business as usual? I hear a lot of talk lately about compassion, service, love, and "good-versus-evil" from leaders in our nation's capital, but I find weakness of vision and a certain insincerity in these sound bytes. I personally have found that love without wisdom is blind; wisdom without love is sterile, and can kill. And when I see how little the major enterprises of our society—big business, government, media, the military, education—have changed or are striving to transform in meaningful rather than reactive and superficial ways, I feel we have much left to learn, reassess, and transform.

The Buddha began his spiritual search twenty five hundred years ago as any warrior would: by asking tough questions and being willing to face the answers at any cost. He asked: Why do people have to suffer so much? Why is there hatred and violence in the world? Is there any escape from this condition? If there is, what is it? What are we to do?

Myself, I wonder: How has America's role in the world over the last fifty or a hundred years contributed to the problems we face today? Over the course of this year I've become increasingly uncomfortable with the knowledge that some of our aggressive, alternately imperialist and isolationist karma has come home to roost. What responsibility do we have in shaping our country's policies and how do we go about creating change? I think we need to learn a little about why some people hate us so much in order to learn how to heal that deep divisions and widening separations occurring across the globe.

Buddha taught that without any difficulties and problems, we cannot really grow in inner strength, patience, and vision. I call this the Pearl Principle: no irritation, no pearl. The Dalai Lama often says that the enemy and the adversary can be our greatest teacher, from whom we can learn patience, forbearance, humility, nonattachment, and that there are other ways to see and be in the world, as our arrogance is dispelled and we become more sensitized and even empathic towards the wishes and needs of others. We can learn to rise like a phoenix from the ashes, arising as part of a better world and a better life for one and all.

One hundred years ago, the Tibetan Dzogchen master Patrul Rinpoche lay down across a narrow mountain pass to thwart warring parties of horsemen from continuing to carry on a clan feud by raiding the adjacent valley. The young warriors had to walk their horses right over the enlightened vagabond's supine body in order to pursue their bellicose aims. Through the Lama's nonviolent witnessing, both sides were slowed down and their conflict brought to a halt. When asked how he had brought that bloody feud to an end, Patrul said: "Compassion is contagious. May all be infected by it!" This is Buddhist spiritual activism—nonviolent witnessing, putting oneself on the line.

Buddhism's long, illustrious history remains unscarred by religious warfare. Its highest ideal is the Bodhisattva Vow to deliver all beings from suffering and confusion and bring them to nirvanic peace, freedom, and enlightenment. The Bodhisattva is the ultimate social and spiritual activist. But this kind of selfless, compassionate commitment does not preclude strong, protective action on behalf of the greater good. Traditional scriptural authority backs this up, as in the case of the Buddha himself, when in a previous life as a ship's captain, he had to take the life of a murderous pirate who was about to slaughter five hundred merchants aboard his ship. Even Gandhi, the greatest advocate of *ahimsa* (nonharming) said that nonviolence can be practically applied within forceful action, as in the case of needing to forcibly restrain a violent drunk before he harms more people, or, as he said, in the case of a serial killer, one might even be forced to take a life to save lives. This is a slippery ethical principle, open to misuse, but it is also a powerful reminder of the power of nonviolent action and activism.

Spirituality today must be intelligent, strong hearted, and committed to the long-term greatest good, rather than feel-good quick fixes or mere local concerns. I would like to see more intrepid, spiritually-centered scholars, writers, and teachers speak up and provide a more muscular form of spiritual discourse. Sitting and cultivating prayerful positive attitudes is fine, but what we also need in our day is to broaden and deepen public discussion by bringing to bear process-oriented Buddhist thought and a rational understanding of impermanence, change, and interconnectedness.

The Dalai Lama has asked Western Buddhists to work against nuclear proliferation, capital punishment, and environmental exploitation, work for human rights and religious tolerance, and to teach children about peace. And we do not all need to be Buddhist masters to bring Buddhist perspectives to public discourse. As concerned citizens, we can and should take more initiative in speaking out by writing opinion pieces or letters to editors, Congress people, and other elected officials; publishing our own magazines and journals; meeting with each other, both privately and at conferences; being active in interfaith dialogue, on the internet, in volunteer and charitable organizations, and by educating ourselves about how other peoples live and worship.

But if we truly want peaceful coexistence in this world in our lifetime—and I firmly believe that we all do—we must address the violence and cruelty in our own hearts and minds. We must learn how to deal with anger and hatred and learn to soften and disarm our own hearts, as well as work in larger contexts to resolve conflicts and create peace. We need to think globally and act locally, beginning with ourselves and each other, at home and in the family, as well as at work and in the community. We need to reach out more and more, in broad, all-embracing circles of collective caring and responsibility. This is the path to a more peaceful future for all of us.

Martin Luther King Jr., who was greatly inspired and influenced by Mahatma Gandhi, said that we have only two choices today: to coexist peacefully, or to destroy ourselves. It is in our higher self-interest to pull together, if we don't want to be pulled apart.

Confronting Evil

Andrew Kimbrell

"Pure Evil," "The Faces of Evil," "Evil in the Skies"—the headlines and media coverage in the days following the September 11 terrorist attacks were rife with references to evil, and this was as it should be. As the veil of mourning lay heavily on the entire country, most Americans could only shake their heads and shudder at the enormity of what they had witnessed. "Evil" seemed the only word apt to the horror of these terrible events.

Until the recent attacks, the use of the word "evil" often met with resistance. For many it connoted an overly pejorative or judgmental mindset, and seemed redolent of outmoded taboos and attitudes. Yet, the shock and scope of the terrorist attacks jolted people into the realization that evil remains both relevant to the modern world and pertinent to our daily lives.

With the images of terror still vividly etched in our personal and collective consciousness, it is easy and tempting to project all of modern evil on to terrorists or other villainous people. At the same time, as the gravitas of the tragedy is replaced by a return to our normal lives, it is likewise tempting to let the question of evil return to the limbo into which modern ethics has sentenced it. Both reactions would signal a tragic loss of opportunity. For one of the graces that could emerge from the recent wreckage would be a new self-reflection about all evil, and especially the systemic evil in which so many of us are complicit. That reflection on, and exploration of, the nature of modern evil is essential not only for addressing the issue of terrorism and how to respond to it, but also for understanding the widening environmental and social crises that are engulfing us.

282   *Chapter 6–Andrew Kimbrell*

THE NATURE OF EVIL

Evil is an illusive concept, remaining the focus of moral, theological, and even psychological dispute. We can say, however, that evil is not simply wrongdoing or what theologians call "sin." Evil is that dysfunctional human condition which leads us into repeated patterns of wrongdoing. Under the sway of evil, wrongdoers are blinded or seduced so that they fail to understand the full consequences of their actions. Ultimately, the evil impulse is felt as so powerful and pervasive that it renders the individual powerless to avoid doing wrong in the future. Seen in this context, evil is a kind of ultimate illness that fatally erodes our sense of responsibility for, and ultimately connection to, all else.

Put another way, sin is a breach in one's relationship to others, to the creation and to God. It is an act of alienation from the other. We can, however, heal the wrong and break that alienation. This healing requires the reestablishment of the breached relationship through self-reflection, acknowledgment, and atonement (an at-one-ment). Evil is that force which seeks to make healing impossible. Evil makes sin, the alienation of one from the other, permanent. It makes the reestablishment of relationship and healing appear impossible. The bond is forever broken. That is why evil is so chilling. Its victory results in complete *diremption*, the loss of all hope of relationship, atonement, or redemption.

This dichotomy between sin and evil has extraordinary implications for human freedom. Acknowledging one's wrongdoings and choosing not to offend again (even when imperfectly realized) is the basis for gaining ethical maturity. The capability to sin, to make conscious the causes of sin, and to atone for sin, are essential for our exercise of personal freedom and our spiritual growth. Evil, on the other hand, masks sins and emasculates the sinner. It anaesthetizes the wrongdoer so he is unaware of the nature and impacts of his actions, or feels powerless to halt his actions, until it is too late. It prevents growth. Whenever evil is endemic there is a moral and ethical "developmental arrest" in a person or a society.

"HOT" EVIL

In Western culture, evil has been most often represented in personal form. A despicable villain, or perhaps "the devil himself" in human trappings, tempts a sinner, blinds him with promises, and lures him into sin, alienation, and damnation. Evil's triumph was most often reflected in an individual's spiraling descent into the "hot" sins of passion—senseless violence, cruelty, sexual promiscuity. As the events of September 11 vividly illustrate, the sins of "hot" evil are obviously still with us. Filled with hatred and perhaps misplaced religious fervor by their leaders, the terrorists committed their heinous acts. These acts and other crimes of passion obviously create enormous suffering and garner most of our collective attention and media headlines. Murders, acts of terrorism, rapes, violence, hate, and sex crimes still fascinate and rightfully repel. When confronted with such evil deeds we still wonder, with a shiver, "what could have possessed them?"

Our religious traditions seek through understanding and love to provide us with tools with which to deal with evil, "possessed" people. We are led to understand that meeting hot evil with matching hatred and violence only results in the ultimate illness of evil spreading to ever more people and leading to ever more evil acts. Martin Luther King Jr. is generally credited with the quip that "the only problem with an eye for an eye is that everyone ends up blind." We are taught not to seek revenge but rather justice, and to temper our judgment with mercy. These are difficult lessons to apply but we ignore them at our continued peril.

Most of our established religions and moral teachers devote much of their energy to addressing this personalized "hot" evil. But here we come to an enigma of modern evil. Consider that for much of the last half of the twentieth century, a nuclear arms race pushed the world to the brink of Armageddon—the unimaginable final destruction of all society and nature poised on a computer trip line. More recently, the public has been jolted by revelations of a whole new genre of global environmental threats to the biosphere itself, almost unthinkable perils to life on earth—ozone depletion, global warming, species extinction, acid rain, desertification, and deforestation. And even as the world produces ever more food and wealth, hunger and poverty increase at an astounding rate. Now close to a billion people are starving every day with many more living in poverty. Evil has never been so omnipresent as it has been over the last decades, so perilous to the earth and the very future of humanity. Yet there seem to be very few evil people. The very idea of our American society being filled with roaming masses of evil people purposefully causing hunger or ecological havoc seems somewhat comical.

"COLD" EVIL

As we meditate on the nightmares of nuclear holocaust, corporate-led globalization, and impending environmental catastrophe, we begin to unravel the enigma of modern evil. In our age of megatechnologies and massive corporate and government bureaucracies, evil no longer requires evil people to purvey it, as it did in the past. Rather evil is now primarily mediated by, and incarnated through, our "cold" technologies and technocracies. We are witnessing the "technification" of evil. Modern society has created a technological, institutional plane where "the system" effectuates evil in circumstances where individuals and their emotions or morals play no significant role. While recent events show that the "satanic" villain still is with us, passionate, feverish "hot" evil has been largely usurped by this automatic, systemic "cold" evil in which we all partake, in which we are all complicit. As M. Scott Peck notes in his *Healing Institutional Evil*, modern evil is that which "1 percent of the people cause, but in which 100 percent of us ordinary sinners participate through our every day sins. Theologian Alfred Schutze in *The Enigma of Evil*, sums up this evolution of evil in our technological times:

> [O]nly a few centuries ago evil, so-called, had to be considered pertinent to moral behavior, more specifically the backsliding or weakness of the individual. Today, it also appears in a manner detached from the individual. It shows up impersonally in arrangements and conditions of social, industrial, technical and general life that, admittedly, are created and tolerated by man. It appears anonymously as injustice, or hardship in an interpersonal realm where nobody seems directly liable or responsible. . . . It has become the grey eminence infiltrating all areas of human existence.

Unfortunately, despite the unprecedented perils it spawns, we have utterly failed to register the appropriate recognition and abhorrence of this new form of institutional evil brought on by and through our economic and technological system. Focused almost solely on "hot" evil, our religious institutions, moral leaders, and teachers rarely recognize or speak out against this cold evil which impersonally has devastated so many lives and destroyed and disfigured so much of creation. The tragic result of this failure is that technological "cold" evil flourishes, causing ever-greater ecocatastrophe and genocide, even as it remains unnamed and unaddressed.

THE ANATOMY OF COLD EVIL

A synonym for cold is the word "distant," and a vital component in the success of modern "cold" evil is the physical and psychic distance that technology creates between the wrongdoer and his deed. We have defined evil as that force which leads to wrongdoing while simultaneously hiding the sin and obscuring responsibility for it. Distancing, especially through impersonal technologies and systems, accomplishes much of this goal for cold evil.

Through technological distancing, the victim becomes little more than a computerized abstraction. During the Persian Gulf War, enemy troops and houses were viewed by pilots as so many blips on computer screens that disappeared after a "hit"—a kind of desert Nintendo. Computer scientist and author Joseph Weizenbaum noted this distancing and the irresponsibility it fosters when he critiqued a massive bombing strategy outlined by a Department of Defense "science panel" during the Vietnam War:

> These men were able to give the counsel they gave because they were operating at an enormous psychological distance from the people who would be maimed and killed by the weapons systems that would result from the ideas they communicated to their sponsors. The lesson, therefore, is that the scientist and technologist must, by acts of will and imagination, actively strive to reduce such psychological distances, to counter the forces that tend to remove him from the consequences of his actions. (*Closing the Distance* 1976)

Nuclear war perhaps best exemplifies the facelessness and technological distancing so essential to modern evil. These weapons capable of destroying life as we know it, the aptly named intercontinental ballistic missiles (ICBMs), are to be launched half a world away from their intended targets. To compound this physical and psychic distancing, and to further deflect responsibility, the missiles will not even be launched by humans but rather by technology—computers programmed to assess the threat and make the "cold" launch decision.

Modern evil's distancing is not solely a result of high-impact military technology. The behavior and nature of modern technocracies, businesses, and government organizations are equally illustrative of cold evil's distancing. Witness how corporations, now working on the global scale, routinely make calculated decisions about the risks of the products they manufacture. Typically they weigh the cost of adding important safety features to their products against the potential liability to victims and the environment and make the best "bottom line" decision for the company. More often than not safety measures lose out in this calculation. As for the people affected, they have been "distanced" into numerical units moved into profit or loss columns. The corporations decide how many "units" they can afford to have harmed or killed by their products.

The individual people involved in these decisions are not evil; I have been in many corporate law firms and boardrooms and have yet to see any "high fives" or hear shouts of satisfaction at the death, injuries, or crimes against nature these organizations cause. But that of course simply underscores the problem; the corporation is fully distanced in time and space from its actions. The pesticide company is not there, perhaps has even gone out of business, when twenty years after it has abandoned its chemical plant, local aquifers and rivers become hopelessly polluted, fish and wildlife are wiped out, and there is a fatal cancer cluster among those relying on local water supply. The tire company executives are not around to see the crash, hear the screams, or see the deaths caused by their badly made tires.

The workings of the global trade and finance organizations truly epitomize the physical and psychological distancing of cold evil. In the isolation of their first world offices, members of the World Trade Organizations and their partner financiers and economists at the World Bank and the IMF make decisions affecting hundreds of millions. This is most evident in the "cold" evil practice of what is euphemistically referred to as "structural adjustment." The IMF and World Bank have for decades loaned money at considerable interest to "developing" nations, essentially to capitalize their modernization and technification through the funding of huge, ecologically devastating, industrial projects. Not surprisingly, much of this money ended up in the hands of corrupt governments and entrepreneurs. As interest skyrocketed, many countries found themselves unable to repay these loans. To solve this repayment problem the IMF and World Bank implemented a set of "structural adjustment programs" (SAPs). These SAPs involved renegotiating a country's loan on more favorable terms if it agreed to "adjust" its policies, which meant reducing wages, lowering labor and environmental standards, slashing government spending (particularly in health, education, and welfare), and allowing increased foreign domination of the country's industries.

The effects of SAPs were devastating. Millions lost their jobs and found themselves with no access to housing, health care, or food. Spending on education in many countries declined by more than 25 percent in less than a decade. It is estimated that approximately 19,000 children die every day as a direct result of the SAPs mandated by the IMF and the World Bank. Imagine the world's response to any series of "hot" evil actions that would kill thousands of children daily. Yet the cold evil of SAPs and corporate-led globalization went without mass recognition until quite recently. To be sure, it is now generally accepted, even by the global institutions, that these SAPs have been fiscally ineffective as well as socially and environmentally devastating. But the bureaucrats simply view this decades-long regime of international deprivation and oppression as a policy "miscalculation" that requires "modification."

Cold evil's distancing is also profoundly present in those who work for corporations and other technocracies. Our minute and specialized jobs have distanced us from the morality and consequences of our collective work. Whether processing financial statements at a bank, riveting at a Boeing defense plant, litigating for a large law firm, or delivering online data to corporations, most people's work is simply a tiny cog in the great machine of production. As such we remain psychologically numbed and removed from the ultimate consequences of the collective work being done. We fall into what E. F. Schumacher terms "the sullen irresponsibility" of modern work.

Moreover even if the worker were able to somehow overcome this irresponsibility, to breach that distance and cry out against the immorality of modern production ("I reject this alienating labor, stop the machines! They are destroying nature, society, and the dignity of work!"), her employment would quickly cease. Virtually all corporations and government bureaucracies are dictatorships. These autocratic managers quickly punish any underling who would begin to demand an ethical basis for work and production. Each of us is caught, therefore, in a kind of job blackmail. We allow ourselves to be numbed by inhuman, meaningless work and fully distanced from what we actually produce. We thereby forsake responsibility for the consequences of our production system. We sell our moral birthright, all in order to "pay the bills." In this way the tremendous distancing endemic to our huge technological system has turned workers, the vast majority of us, into ethical eunuchs and unintentional criminals.

Whatever their ultimate moral and physical cost, our paychecks do allow many of us to become profligate "consumers." This, ironically enough, is termed "living the good life." The cold evil so endemic to our technological systems richly inhabits the purported "good life." We proudly bring home the new, convenient, "family-friendly" SUV without a thought as to how this polluting gas guzzler contributes to widespread respiratory illness in our children and to the catastrophic environmental devastation of global warming. We calmly munch on hamburgers without a thought as to the rainforests being destroyed for cattle grazing or the immense cruelty involved in the raising and slaughtering of these animals. We turn the computer on without thinking of the power supplied by a nearby nuclear power plant with all of its social and environmental risks. We could go through our shopping days and find that we are complicit in myriad wrongdoings brought to us by systemic evil but which we do not easily recognize because of distancing.

THE TECHNO-COCOON

Whether it be within the automobile, office cubicle, or airplane, whether we use the television, computer or telephone, we are ever surrounded and circumscribed by technologies and technocratic thinking. Our daily work usually involves being cocooned indoors in artificially lit, temperature-controlled, machine-laden office cubicles and locked into the technocratic hierarchies emblematic of corporate or bureaucratic life. As for our nonwork hours, the average American spends more than four hours a day in front of the TV and an increasing number of hours at the computer. In the transition between home and work, the majority of Americans commute alone, inside temperature-controlled cars, tuned in to their radios or stereo systems. This absorption of each individual into what I call the "techno-cocoon" is the ultimate in psychic distancing, profoundly limiting our experience and consciousness.

Techno-cocooning leads to huge segments of the population becoming "autistic" to the natural world. Nonhuman creation goes almost completely unnoticed. When nature is seen it is usually viewed on TV or glimpsed from a whizzing car, train, or plane. For the short periods when we are in nature it is usually experienced as technological "recreation" (re-creation) mediated through the roar of RVs, motorboats, jet skis, snowmobiles, and other power toys.

Our circumscription by technology has also made us "autistic" to one another, markedly eroding our social lives in recent years. Come evening time I often note the startling difference between the streets of suburban Northern Virginia where I currently live and those of the streets of Queens, New York, where I was raised more than three decades ago. During my upbringing there were people on the stoops each evening talking, kids were playing various games, babies were walked in strollers—there was a real sense of neighborhood. Now as I walk my dog each twilight through successive suburban cul de sacs, all I see are the glowing blue lights emanating from the various TVs and computers in each home, as different members of the family cocoon themselves into their favorite nighttime techno-entertainment or work. This technological isolation and collapse of community is not merely anecdotal. Author and scholar Robert D. Putnam in his aptly titled book, *Bowling Alone*, carefully documents the precipitous decline in all forms of civic participation during the last decades.

Ultimately, techno-cocooning makes impossible the "acts of will and imagination" required to defeat cold evil's psychological distancing. We passively, and with little awareness, abandon our minds and wills to the convenience, power, and amusement offered by the technological cocoon. In fact, the technological environment becomes to us as water is to a fish; we do not even consciously recognize our enclosure in the cocoon, and therefore do not realize the ongoing devastation of nature, society, or even our own spirit. As we slip into near total technological "autism," we cannot hear the great machines as they level the world's forests and dig up and destroy the earth. We cannot hear the cries of animals being abused, slaughtered, or harassed to extinction. We cannot see the suffering of our fellow humans whether they are the homeless we step over to get into cars or offices, or our own despondent family members locked into nearby, but utterly separate, cocoons. We do not even recognize the banalization and ultimate death of our own wills and imaginations as we "amuse ourselves to death" in the techno-cocoon.

All in all, the techno-cocoon provides a kind of final anatomy of cold evil, creating a continuous buffer between each person and the many horrific wrongs of our technological system, sins in which we are all complicit but now bliss-fully unaware. We sit in our various techno-cocoons fully distanced from nature and each other, yet fully entranced and engaged with the machines. The mass autism engendered by the techno-cocoon is surely unprecedented in both the scope and extent of its alienating impacts. We literally are no longer present to participate in the creation, the social world, or the spiritual world. Memory and faith become equally irrelevant. The diremption of cold evil is complete. We are deprived of the very relationships required for our healing.

RELATIONSHIP AND HEALING

I have no panacea for addressing the growing threats of cold evil, entwined as they are with so much of our daily lives in our technological society. How-ever, the first step is awareness. As we confront the terrorists' "hot" evil, we must not use the fact that the vast majority of us are not involved in this kind of evil as a vindication of our own society or our personal ethics. Rather we must avoid this trap and finally confront the cold evil with which we are com-plicit and recognize the potential catastrophic threat it represents to ourselves and Creation.

As for dealing with cold evil directly, I know that there cannot be healing or atonement without relationship. And to restore our relationships to one an-other and the natural world we must shatter the distancing so critical for cold evil. A first step could be to cease distancing ourselves as "consumers." The word "consume" means to destroy (as in a consuming fire) or waste (tuber-culosis was called consumption because it wastes away the body). We must no longer be mere consumers, destroying and wasting the natural world. We must no longer be complicit in the crimes of our industrial system. To face cold evil, we must become "creators," not consumers. We must break our techno-cocoons and truly see that each action we take in deciding which products we buy, or services we use, creates a very different future for our-selves and the earth. We must take responsibility for the consequences of how we fulfill our basic human needs.

We must also change our relationship to work. We can no longer be con-tent with mere jobs and the wage blackmail through which cold evil works. Despite the often overwhelming economic pressures, we must at least attempt to seek a vocation, a "calling," that expresses our values and fits our needs. Our work should be a "profession," a profession of our beliefs—good work whose consequences we can embrace.

Ultimately confronting cold evil requires us to begin dismantling the struc-tures and systems in which it thrives. Author Kirkpatrick Sale has urged us to reconsider the importance of "human scale." Moving toward the restoration of human scale in our social and production systems as alternatives to current global scale organizations and technologies may be the only way to permanently defeat the distancing that has been such a moral disaster for modern man.

In the memorable phrase of Father Thomas Berry, our current economic and technological system has turned all of nature from a community of subjects into a collection of objects. To restore relationship and begin healing we must again treat the living kingdom as a community of subjects, each with its own meaning and destiny, none as merely exploitable objects or means of production. Moving towards this new moral community involves nothing less than replacing the infrastructure of cold evil with technologies and human systems which are responsive to our physical and spiritual needs and the needs of the rest of the biotic community. This means evolving a means of production and social organization for which we can take true responsibility. It is a daunting, almost overwhelming task, but the alternative is to continue to live in state of cold evil, complicit in the current system's crimes and distanced from relationship and healing. This we can no longer do.

Power and Cooperation

Jonathan Schell

Following is a version of a speech given at the Tikkun Community Teach-In to Congress, June 2003.

Nothing is more important than what we as American citizens do at this absolutely critical moment. By going back into history I hope to shed some light on what I think the fundamental choice is. I happen to live six blocks from where the World Trade Center once stood. I don't say that in order to claim any special right to speak because I don't think it gives me any right. I happen to believe that it's a human entitlement, and even a responsibility, to think and reflect and act concerning events that happen far away and of which one has no direct personal experience. I say it because I want you to know that I'd be the last person to underestimate the sheer horror of what happened on September 11, or to underestimate the gravity of the danger that terrorism poses to the United States and to the world.

It was an infernal experience, and it was one that lasted far beyond the day on which it occurred, far beyond the weeks or even months after. You may recall the subterranean fires that burned on, filling the air with a kind of acrid smoke and an unmentionable odor all its own. That became a symbol in my mind of the profound disorder that had been created and unleashed in the world.

At the same time, I must say that I think our country has gone drastically off-track in its response to the crisis that began on that day. The crisis goes even deeper than anything that concerns only the United States. I believe there are moments in history when what is being decided goes far beyond the matters being discussed in the debates of the time — when the direction is being set for decades to come and sometimes even for as much as a century to come. If we look back at the twentieth century, most historians agree that the definitive moment was August 1914, when the world plunged into the First

291

World War, setting the century's course in the direction of an extreme violence of which people had no historical experience or knowledge. And the aftershocks were greater than the initial shock.

The century's first decade resembled its last decade in many respects, because both were periods of economic growth, globalization, and spreading liberalism. But at a stroke, the First World War reversed all of those tendencies, ushering in an era of depression, contraction of global trade, and repression. On the eve of the war there were two hundred divisions ready to go into battle in Europe, and when the war broke out, as the historian John Keegan says, "the submerged warrior society sprang armed through the surface of the peaceful landscape." That warrior society never went back to its barracks in the twenty-first century because in Germany and Russia, the suffering and the humiliation and the incalculable social disorganization caused by the war created conditions that made possible the rise of mass totalitarian movements. The seventy-five-year Bolshevik terror, which Aleksandr Solzhenitsyn called the "Red Wheel," rolled out of the trenches of World War I, as did its jagged counterpart, the Nazi swastika. The aggression and antagonism of these two regimes led directly to the Second World War. Political philosopher Hannah Arendt said of the period during and between the two world wars: "Nothing which was being done, no matter how stupid, no matter how many people knew and foretold the consequences, could be undone or prevented. Every event had the finality of a Last Judgment—a judgment that was passed neither by God nor by the Devil, but looked rather like the expression of some irredeemably stupid fatality."

Of course, in 1914 there were many Great Powers, as they were called in those days—five or six of them. They hadn't invented Superpowers yet. The preponderance of military force was distributed among those powers, and therefore the decision that tipped the whole world into that First World War was made by several powers.

Today, you can see that our situation is far different. The United States is the only Superpower in a unipolar world, and the military spending of the United States equals at least that of a dozen of the other top military spending nations in the world. The military force that once was distributed among several powers has now in a sense been withdrawn from them and concentrated in a single place—the arsenals of the United States. Of course, there are other countries in the world that have power that they are abusing, that have moral responsibilities and decisions to make. But when it comes to the very critical decision that we face for the twenty-first century, which is whether we are going to go back down the road of violence—as a country, first, and as a world in general—then we have to recognize that we bear an exceptional responsibility because of the tremendous power that is in American hands. I say this not to be hyperbolic about American malfeasance or virtue or responsibilities; rather, it's a realistic fact in view of the military force at our disposal.

This freakish situation is something quite new in the history of the world. And I regret to say that I think we have taken the wrong path. Our current administration has adopted a policy that relies upon force more nakedly, more explicitly, and more ambitiously than any administration in American history. We seem to have developed what properly, and again without exaggeration, can be called an imperial path. The United States, with its invasion and occupation of Iraq, has almost formally set out to reinvent imperialism for the twenty-first century. You only have to pick up the newspaper to see this. General McKiernan, who runs the military forces in Baghdad, came out after all the looting and disorder and said, "We have absolute power here." We haven't heard those words since King Louis XVI was overthrown during the French Revolution. One proconsul was put in there, General Garner, and he couldn't handle it so they yanked him out and put in Paul Bremer. He then decided, in an unfathomably reckless move, to cut off the pensions and payments to the entire former Iraqi Army. If that's not a way to make people angry at you, I don't know what is. And the result: almost every day this week there have been American casualties or British casualties in Iraq amidst a rising tide of nationalism.

This move toward imperialism is bound to fail for historical reasons, but in failing it can exact a terrible cost both in our country and around the world. Empire, among political systems, is the embodiment of force. It violates equity on a global scale. No supporter of freedom can support it. It's especially contrary to the founding principles of the United States.

Historically speaking, imperialism has rested on three foundations: the military, the economy, and politics. But the United States only enjoys unequivocal superiority in one of these areas: the military. It's true that we have tremendous economic power, but in this realm there are several equals or near-equals—the European Union, Japan, and increasingly China—none of whom is likely to bend easily to America's will. But more important is our political weakness, because in the contemporary world military force no longer translates easily into political rule, as we're now seeing in Iraq. "Covenants without swords are but words," Thomas Hobbes said centuries ago. But since then the world has learned that swords without covenants are but empty bloodshed. If you look back in history you see that an imperial power like Rome was able to convert military victories into political power, but the United States cannot do so today. In the political arena, the lesson of the anti-colonial rebellions, which occurred everywhere in the world and were successful, is that winning military victories may sometimes be easy, but building political institutions is hard. The United States today is mistrusted and disliked in many parts of the world, and if we embark on a plan of imperial domination it is our fate to be disliked still more. Can cruise missiles build nations? Does power flow from the barrel of a gun or a B-2 bomber? Can the world be ruled from thirty-five thousand feet?

Modern peoples have the will to resist and the means to do so. Imperialism without politics is a naïve imperialism. In our times force can win a battle or two, but politics is destiny. Can a nation that began its life in rebellion against the greatest empire of its time, namely the British, become an even greater empire? It can. But not if it wishes to remain a republic. Secretary of State John Quincy Adams defined the choice with precision in advising the United States not to go abroad "in search of monsters to destroy, but be the well wishers for the freedom and independence of all." He added that should the United States embark on the path of dominating others, "fundamental maxims over policy would insensibly change from liberty to force. She might become the dictatress of the world. She would no longer be the ruler of her own spirit." Our government would do well to reflect upon his words.

"Violence," Hannah Arendt said paradoxically, "can destroy power." The United States appears to be moving quickly down this path. Does our government imagine that the peoples of the world, having overthrown the great territorial empires of the twentieth century, are ready to bend the knee to an American overlord? Do they imagine that allies are willing to become subordinates? Have they forgotten that people hate to be dominated by force? History is packed with surprises, some of them appalling. The leaders of the totalitarian Soviet empire somehow had the good sense to yield up their power without unleashing the tremendous violence that was at their fingertips. But could it be the destiny of the American republic, unable to resist the allure of an imperial delusion, to flare out in a blaze of pointless mass destruction?

That sounds very extreme—but we are living in the age of nuclear weapons and other weapons of mass destruction. It is a truly outlandish situation. For one thing, we are still threatening our friend and ally, Russia, with mutual annihilation, and they are doing the same to us. It may not be the most dangerous situation of the nuclear age, but it's surely the craziest. At the same time the United States is revving up its nuclear arsenal and refastening its nuclear strategy to retarget its weapons at other countries all around the world, including Libya, Syria, China, Russia, Iran, and North Korea, according to the Bush administration's *Nuclear Posture Review*.

Yet at the same time that we not only possess but develop new weapons and strategies, we are seeking to forbid other nations from getting into the weapons of mass destruction business. Not only do we keep the weapons but we threaten to use them *first* against other countries who try to obtain them. This is the apogee of hypocrisy. But hypocrisy is the least of it; more important is that this policy is entirely unworkable. The President has one thing right—weapons of mass destruction are the greatest threat of the twenty-first century, just as they were of the twentieth. But if we don't find a workable policy to deal with this threat we are in deep trouble.

Let's reflect for a moment on how well the current policy has been working.

We had a war in Iraq in order to get rid of the weapons of mass destruction that have turned out not to be there. But the fact that they are not there is not the most important point—even if they turn out to be there, this policy is not viable. According to the president's rule book, the other two countries in the "axis of evil" (Iran and North Korea) were supposed to learn from the war against Iraq that if they got into the weapons of mass destruction business, the United States would impose a regime change on them, too. But what lesson did they actually learn? That they should build up their weapons of mass destruction. Why? Because that's the only chance they have of *deterring* the United States from attacking them. So North Korea has started building its arsenal and there's very little, or nothing, that the United States can do about it.

This North Korean policy is one that the United States should understand perfectly well because it is one that we have taught the world. In every single action, in every single policy and statement in a half a century of the nuclear age, the lesson we have taught the world is this: If you want to be safe from nuclear weapons, get nuclear weapons. That's the lesson of nuclear deterrence, and it has been the central strategy of the United States since the beginning of the Cold War.

By heading down this path, we not only fail to deal with the problem of weapons of mass destruction, we actually make the problem worse. We are heading towards a kind of nuclear anarchy, as proliferation runs unchecked (chemical and biological weapons are not going to stay in the bottle either). Our current policy strengthens the possibility that nuclear weapons will be used by or against us, or by other countries such as India and Pakistan against one another. It is entirely unacceptable. We must not hand our children a world of nuclear anarchy. We must find another path. We must move the twenty-first century away from the path of force that the twentieth took in 1914.

THE PATH TO PEACE

There is a solid foundation for a practical, realistic, and achievable path away from this unacceptable destination and towards peace. We in the United States have hugely overestimated the usefulness of force and hugely underestimated the usefulness of forms of action that do not employ violence. There is a power in this world that overmatches violence. Even as we were moving down the road of ever more extreme violence in the twentieth century, at the same time quietly, and less noticed, but no less dramatic, new forms of action were developing that hold tremendous promise for our future and that we should turn to as we ask ourselves how to proceed.

Quite frankly, I don't have a good word for this power. We use the word "nonviolence," but it's a negative word. Gandhi said that nonviolent action was the most positive, active, and energetic force in the world. Why should we have to refer to it in negative terms? Gandhi was very aware of this problem, so he held a contest back in 1905 to rename it. He said it was not passive resistance. It's not passive at all. What to call it? The winner of that contest turned out to be Gandhi, himself, and he called it *Satyagraha*, which translates into English as "soul force" or "truth force." Unfortunately that phrase hasn't really caught on. Vaclav Havel called it "living in truth" when he launched his campaign of disobedience and constructive action against the Soviet overlord. That's a slightly better phrase but still quite remote in sound and suggestion from the political world in which it had such great effect.

In the book I recently wrote, *The Unconquerable World: Power, Nonviolence and the Will of the People*, I call it "cooperative power." It's a rather colorless phrase, but one that's useful for me and that I distinguish from coercive power. Cooperative power. It's the kind of power that we generate when we work together in concert, peacefully, for common causes—as distinct from coercive power that we use against one another.

Let me offer a couple of examples of cooperative power. The first and most astonishing was the fall of the Soviet Union. The Soviet Union was a tremendous totalitarian state and empire. It had nuclear weapons, the Red Army, the KGB, all sorts of other agencies—they'd taken over every aspect of civil life. There has rarely been a state that has had more of the instruments of power in its hands. And in a world in which people believe that violence is the final arbiter in human affairs, who could imagine that the Soviet Union would no longer be with us today? Who would have thought that in 1989–1990 it would just evaporate like the morning dew? I remember the astonishment I felt when I saw the Berlin Wall coming down. The whole thing just melted away like a bad dream.

We need to reflect on that. One of those who did even before the fact was, of course, Vaclav Havel: "We introduced a new model of behavior. Don't get involved in diffuse, general, ideological polemics with the center, to whom numerous concrete causes are always being sacrificed. Fight only for those concrete causes, and fight for them unswervingly to the end." He went on to say that by "living within the lie"—which is what he contrasted "living in truth" to—"individuals confirm the system, fulfill the system, make the system, are the system." So a line of conflict was, in effect, drawn down the center of each person who was invited in the countless decisions of daily life to choose between living in truth and living in the lie. Living in truth—directly doing in your immediate surroundings what you think needs doing, saying what you think is true and needs saying, acting the way you think people should act, is a form of protest, Havel admitted, against living in the lie. So those who tried to live in truth were indeed in opposition, but that was neither all they were, nor was it the main characteristic of who they were. Because before living in truth was a protest, he said, it was an affirmation: "Individuals can be alienated from themselves only because there is something in them to alienate. The terrain of this violation is their essential existence." In other words, if the state's commands are a violation deserving of protest, then the deepest reason is that they disrupt this essential existence, this essential human integrity.

Those words might perhaps sound personal or philosophical or spiritual in a way that seems disconnected from politics, but in fact, Havel understood that this living in truth, this kind of nonviolent action, guided from within, by millions of ordinary people—in Czechoslovakia, in Poland, eventually in Russia—was actually at the center of the struggle over political power itself. Very few people understood this in 1978 when he was writing about it. "Under the orderly surface of the life of lies," he said,

> there slumbers the hidden sphere of life in its real aims, of its hidden openness to truth. The singular, explosive, incalculable political power of living within the truth resides in the fact that living openly within the truth has an ally, invisible to be sure, but omnipresent: this hidden sphere. It is from this sphere that life lived openly in truth grows; it is to this sphere that it speaks, and in it that it finds its understanding. This is where the potential for communication exists.

Who was listening at the time? Who had guessed that on the basis of this—which seemed to most people to be naïve, utopian, marginal, perhaps edifying, but not of any real-world consequence—who could imagine that here was the key to the downfall of the mighty Soviet Union?

Another example was, of course, Gandhi in India. In his many writings and in his life of thought and action he came early on to a very fundamental conclusion about the nature of political power, which turned out to hold true for the century in which he lived. He realized that not only *should* governments depend on the consent and the cooperation of the governed, but in actual fact they *did* so depend. And this held true not only for democratic governments, where you can vote the rascals out, but even for totalitarian and authoritarian regimes, as was later demonstrated in the Soviet Union. He saw that if the public, if enough people who were receiving the commands of the government, simply refused—a very tough thing to do because you could lose your life, your job, your social connections, etc.—then the government would be left barking orders into empty air and its power would come to an end. He called this noncooperation. But he realized at the same time that in addition to noncooperation there had to be a positive program. It wasn't enough just to withdraw your cooperation—you had to immediately set about building up the structures of politics, of social work, of education, and so on, to help your own people and just bypass the authorities.

The amazing fact about this sort of action, in India and in the Soviet Union, was that when people engaged in it, they developed political power. This happened with the Solidarity movement in Poland during the "self-limiting revolution." Their idea was they'd take care of society, and let the Communist Party handle government and foreign affairs in order to keep the Soviet center happy. It turned out, however, that by engaging in this massive campaign of positive action in their society they willy-nilly developed political power. I remember the day it fell into their hands in 1989, when they got all the votes in the first free elections in Poland—they were amazed. Some of them seemed almost chagrined and astonished: "Us taking positions in the government? We're in charge now?" They weren't ready for it. Even they were surprised by what they had accomplished.

I mention this because we're not dealing with a marginal fact of history. This is not some side influence of a few good and noble people whom we should admire, but who didn't have much effect on the course of history. In actual fact, every single one of the empires that was standing at the beginning of the twentieth century had fallen by the end. It was not only the British and the Soviet empires; all the empires fell. We're dealing with a very fundamental fact of human history. There are some verdicts of history that stand and the verdict against empire is one of them. There is something in this world that does not love an empire. And that's why it's a supreme folly for the United States to head down that path at this moment in history.

In conclusion, I'll quote from a passage of *The Unconquerable World*:

> Whether one calls this power cooperative power or something else, it is this that with the steady widening and deepening of the democratic spirit has over and over bent the great powers to its will. Its point of origin is the heart and mind of each ordinary person. It grows out of social work as well as political activity. In the absence of popular participation, it simply disappears. Its cheap instrument is direct action, both non-cooperative and constructive, but it is also the wellspring of the people's will in democratic nations. It is not an all-purpose mean with which any end can be pursued. It cannot be projected, for its strength declines in proportion to the distance from its source. It is a local plant rooted in home soil. It is therefore mighty on the defensive, feeble on the offensive and toxic to territorial empires, all of which in our time have died. It can be spiritual in inspiration, but doesn't have to be. Its watchwords are love and freedom.

Yet it is not just an ideal, but a real force in the world. In revolution, it is decisive. Under the name of the will of the people it has dissolved the foundations first of the monarch and aristocracy and then of totalitarianism. As opinion, it has stood in judgment over democratically elected governments. As rebellious hearts and minds it has broken the strength of great powers engaged in a superannuated imperialism. As love of country, it has fueled the universally successful movements for self-determination. Gone awry, it has fueled ethnic and national war and totalitarian rule, which soon suffocate it, though only temporarily. It now must be brought to bear on the choice between survival and annihilation. It is powerful because it sets people in motion and fixes before their eyes what they are ready to live and die for. It is dangerous for the same reason. Whether combined with violence, as in people's wars, sustained by a constitution, as in democracy, or standing alone, as in Satyagraha or living truth, it is becoming the final arbiter of the public affairs of our time, and the political bedrock of our unconquerable world.

Spiritualizing Foreign Policy

Peter Gabel

If President Bush and his advisors have their way, their military victory in Iraq will become the model for a series of future interventions—Iran, Syria, North Korea, and who knows where it will stop? As we now look at the death, destruction, hatred, and suffering that this war has generated, Peter Gabel's vision of a new approach to foreign policy is, if anything, more important than when it was written as the war began—because it gives us a model for how a peace movement steeped in the *Tikkun* approach to spiritual politics could provide a very different path for resolving and healing international conflict.

As the war in Iraq now becomes a daily reality and as the deadened-to-human-life consciousness of Bush/Cheney/Rumsfeld and the parade of the CNN generals and the killing headlines of the morning papers envelops all of us in the shadow of our fallen common humanity, we must take a deep breath and try to lift ourselves out of this shadow—not only by engaging in acts of resistance to the war but also by thinking our way out of the paradigm that accounts for war consciousness and for the deadness to human life that is married to it. This deadness both produces war consciousness and is produced by it, and it perpetuates itself over and over again from war to war, from generation to generation.

In *Tikkun* we have been trying to develop for many years now a new conception of spiritual politics that understands the world as a nexus of inherently social human beings linked to one another by more than the individualistic and material needs that have dominated prior political, economic, and social theories. We have claimed that we are each expressions of a loving energy and are animated by the desire for mutual recognition and affirmation of that loving energy—that we each long for recognition of our inherent worthiness and sacredness. We have also sought to analyze the social alienation that obscures this spiritual longing—the need to hide from the other behind masks and roles, to guard ourselves from the humiliation of a nonrecognition and rejection too painful to bear. We now know that it is this alienation of I from Thou, between I and Thou, within I and Thou, that keeps dragging us back into the shadow, and that accounts for the deadness, at the surface of the skin, in the constriction of the heart, and in the flattening of the perceptual field of the withdrawn mind's eye.

We must now apply this understanding to the development of a new conception of "foreign policy"—a term that I dislike because the Other is never "foreign." The term implies that we belong to a "we," represented by the nation-state, which is also "imaginary" to the extent that its function is partly to mask our isolation, to deny our alienation from the person next to us by insisting on our patriotic connection "in the sky." In spite of my dislike of the term, however, I will nevertheless use it here to try to help us imagine a new method of relating to the Other in the world that understands itself through the nation-state prism—keeping in mind, however, that the "foreign policy" that emerges from our vision of spiritual politics requires that we never see the Other as "foreign." Let's say that I am using "figures of speech" to communicate, but please imagine I am always keeping the quotation marks.

A foreign policy that emerges from this vision of spiritual politics understands that the present situation cannot be reduced to simple formulas that exclude spiritual understanding—the longing for authentic mutual recognition and affirmation of our fundamental humanity—that forms the basis for our vision. It's not just about oil, or about the risk of terror and weapons of mass destruction, or about "lunacy," for that matter. Rather, at the heart of our problem is a complex historical process of distortion in the relation of self to Other that *encompasses* oil, and genuine concern about terror, and even an element of lunacy if it is understood to mean the distortion itself gone out of control.

In *Tikkun*, we've often described this distortion as expressive of a historical disease of individualism and materialism, manifested in the competitive global market and in political systems that channel the frustration of the isolated individual into demonization of the Other. In the case of the Middle East, we rightly emphasize, for example, that historical dynamics dating back to the Crusades and certainly to the pre-World War I carving up of the Middle East by imperial Western powers, followed by the gradual development and expansion of globalization and capitalist markets, have contributed not only to material poverty in the Middle East but to the humiliation and degradation of entire cultures. This humiliation has contributed—sometimes with direct Western assistance because "we" perceived it to be in "our" interests—to the emergence of dictatorships and royalist antidemocratic regimes in places like Iraq and Saudi Arabia. This same humiliation of the Other's fundamental humanity has inspired the rise of fanatical, artificially connecting fundamentalisms that artificially restore a humiliated people's sense of worthiness, meaning, and purpose by glorifying the martyrdom of the suicidal killing of the humiliator, the imperial power who, degraded and fearful inside, becomes the source of the other's humiliation.

The key, as I see it, to the process of hopeful elevation, to lifting ourselves out of this System that we are all entrapped in, is to grapple with and begin to understand the meaning of *tikkun olam*, or the healing and transformation of the world. We must, with a heart that can think, grasp how the process of historical distortion and the cycle of humiliation reproduces itself as a process of "rotating paranoia." By this I mean that each cell within the distorted System or distorted nexus of human interaction—and by "cell" I mean each individual person as an existing Someone and each artificial "collective" of such persons, like "the Muslim people" or "the American people"—finds its inherent social-spiritual longing for love, recognition, and peace repeatedly short-circuited by a paranoiac fear of the Other, a fear that in any situation as complex as the current one has a long and patterned history of precisely this process, evolving pathologically like a single injured organism. On the hopeful side, we must always remember that the social-spiritual longing for love and mutual recognition is "fundamental" while fear and paranoia are not, but are rather derivative of the desire for love and recognition, expressions of the alienation of the fundamental loving desire from itself.

Thus as we analyze the current world situation and try to find a new spiritual-political way out of it, we must keenly attune ourselves to this underlying dynamic and its inherently contradictory "flow." This attunement of our thinking, this "thinking with the heart," must occur beneath the public clamor—beneath the paranoia induction of repetitions of certain key names like Saddam Hussein, or George W. Bush for that matter, which freeze our attunement with a touch of terror, carrying as they do connotations of paranoia, fear, and rage. To heal the world requires thinking, and then gradually acting, underneath this surface of the world and with a single aim: to strengthen the confidence of the longing for love and recognition as it exists across the psycho-spiritual energy field that is the interconnectedness of social space. Like the movement of paranoia and fear, this strengthening also rotates, and through this rotation elevates *itself* into existence. But because of the Devil's paranoiac power and the long history of the rotation and evolution of this paranoia, this process of rotating elevation requires our conscious assistance.

This brings us to the meaning of a new spiritual-political foreign policy. Healing the paranoiac impulse that leads to periodic outbreaks of war, violence, and killing requires an intentional process that I will call "Surrounding." "Surrounding" describes an international, transpersonal effort by the world community to simultaneously contain and reassure the herky-jerky impulse toward fear that irrationally escalates all conflict—that is, it requires both firmness in the sense that is not permissive toward violence in the Other, and love in the sense that it manifests, in its very way of being-toward-the-other, a recognition of the other's authentic humanity, even as the other resists that very recognition by throwing up a defensive wall of paranoia and engages in denunciatory words and actions toward the surrounding force.

Surrounding requires that we put up a kind of "Guard-all" shield that is as impervious as possible to the Other's denunciations, that understands they are but expressions of an individual or collective terror and anticipation of humiliation in the Other. This shield provides the basis for international empathic firmness, in which love and the capacity to recognize the Other holds its ground in spite of accusations and threats. This firmness is actually reassuring to the Other that our capacity for recognition is real and unshakeable, that we will not dissolve into counterviolence because of paranoiac shocks leveled in our direction.

The second moment of Surrounding then requires the continuing manifestation of recognition of the other's innocent authenticity and constitutes an appeal to the other's longing for recognition and affirmation, seeking to "thaw" the other's paranoia through an insistence on the real existence of the deeper interhuman bond that connects us. We must show through the quality and content of our words and actions that we understand the wounds of the past that we have mostly inherited and partly inflicted on each other—or to be more precise on our singular self-otherness or intersubjectivity—in our own lifetimes, that these wounds are mistakes, that beneath them is a longing for healing and mutual recognition, and that we no longer have any choice but to take the great opportunity forced upon us by the circumstances of modern weaponry and ecological emergency to evolve as a species and transcend the ontological immaturity that has characterized our collective existence up to the present time. This second moment of Surrounding is best understood as a manifestation of Presence that emanates outward toward the other and recognizes the other in his/her "singular universality" or unique sameness—our very selves in another form.

Surrounding, empathic firmness, thawing by manifesting Presence—these are new concepts to us. They can of course be dismissed as New Age psychobabble by our fearful inherited self-consciousness. But they are qualitative concepts meant to evoke aspects of our social being that, as I have said, exist underneath the world's noisy surface and "subtend" the entire nexus of our collective social reality. This subreality is both spiritual and political—spiritual in the sense that it exists pre-verbally in the interspace that irrevocably connects us as *inter*subjective social beings; political in the sense that as surely as the need for food and shelter, it drives the way we cocreate and govern our collective existence. Everything in human experience is spiritual/political in this sense: A line of people waiting for a bus is spiritual in the sense that in modern society it *exists* itself as a cautious manifestation of rotating anonymity; and political in the sense that it is chosen by "the people" in the line as their way of being together as a collective "no one," drawn from other infinite examples of bus lines and "lines" in general as we form them in a world of social alienation, or rather in a world where social alienation appears to have the upper hand.

But how might this international spiritual/political consciousness express itself? The first part of the answer is for us to realize that in spite of our lack of a vocabulary for it, it already has been expressing itself, in many forms, but especially through the institution of the United Nations. The United Nations is *not* only a collection of States impotently squabbling over this or that international issue without any genuine authority or power in the shadow of Real nation-states that command powerful and deadly militaries and are more or less free to act in their own self-interest. The United Nations is *also* an actual manifestation of the effort of the voice that I here speak of to manifest itself as the Unity of all Being, and to insist that we exist as this Unity, and as the collective longing of our desire to affirm this Unity. The expression "the Unity of all Being," which Michael Lerner appeals to so often, and which is so difficult to understand and act upon when we are constrained by our dominant secular mindset, expresses the beautiful and true Biblical metaphor that we are but shattered shards of light seeking to recover our awareness of our "singular universality"—that is, our ontological Truth that we exist as at once unique in our respective existences and yet manifestations of precisely the same spiritual essence, an essence that can recognize itself through love alone and that longs to recover the capacity for this recognition.

The Charter of the United Nations does not begin with the words, "We, the permanently squabbling and self-interested sovereign States of the world, form ourselves into a sort of pseudo-communal but actually alienated confederation of world nations with no real power, to accomplish little or nothing by diplomatic means, leaving the fate of the earth to the Reality of hopelessly divided national self-interests." It begins by affirming in secular language the aspiration of man and womankind toward the recovery of the Unity of all Being through the healing of our differences. And even granting cynical realism its due, it is important and helpful to understand that these high spiritual-political ideals of the Charter were at the time of their expression, following the utter catastrophes of World Wars I and II, genuinely intended by the Charter's signatories to carry this high meaning. If our preverbal hopeful longing and even conviction that we are capable in our very nature of universal love and mutual recognition, our knowledge that we are all One, unique and yet the Same, if this longing for recognition did not exist, or if it were untrue, we would have annihilated ourselves long ago. Nations would have annihilated nations as surely as our neighbor would have annihilated his brother-in-law. But just as our knowledge of our interconnectedness and our longing to recognize and affirm it underlies the noise of every event, so also this sense of our copresence, common desire, and longing partially constitutes our institutions, most nobly the United Nations.

What we might call our theoretical challenge at the present moment is to develop the language and intonation of thinking that can make this spiritual-political conception of an institution like the United Nations explicit and accessible to our common reflection. We must in a certain sense abandon or play down the internalized model that we have of the United Nations as a collection of nation-states—which reflects back to us a picture of a thing-like "entity" made up of various parts, each with its own constituency and interests—and conceive of the UN instead as the embodiment of a worldwide spiritual-political movement toward the mutual recognition of our unity. This new conception, if we are able to allow ourselves to imagine it, should grasp interventions as efforts at healing both the Other and ourselves. How, you may ask, can this possibly be relevant to a crisis like that in Iraq, in which—even assuming the totality of present circumstances are reflective of a historical distortion of Self-Other and intercultural relations—we are dealing with very dangerous nuclear, biological, and chemical weapons? It apparently is the case, for example, that Iraq has not accounted for large quantities of anthrax, nerve gas, and possibly significant quantities of pirated or purchased uranium that are in fact capable of killing large numbers of people. Putting aside all the other seemingly overwhelming issues shaping the present situation—including globalization and its impact on the region, the Israeli/Palestinian conflict, the presence of real economic interests that influence the material quality of life of millions of people, and the allegiances of each so-called "nationality" to its own interests and respective collective identity—putting all these and all other "realistic" matters aside, how can one hope by use of a spiritualized perspective to address the dangers of proliferation of weapons of mass destruction and the degree of real danger to millions of lives that these weapons pose?

The answer to this question is that preverbal and noncognitive attempts to Surround even dictators like Saddam Hussein in the manner that I am suggesting will dramatically alter even his desire to use such weapons—in part by affecting him and those around him, in part by enabling the masses of the Muslim world to feel recognized sufficiently to not support his use of these weapons and instead to try to move toward greater understanding with the real people his actions would affect. Had this approach been taken prior to the current war, we would not be seeing the enraged demonstrations in Yemen now that make the proliferation and use of these weapons more likely, and that once again rotate the paranoiac view of the Other that blocks and keeps blocking the Other's instinctive movement toward connection. Surrounding, thawing, manifesting Presence, "leaning in" toward the other in a firm but affirming-of-the-other's-humanity way, will *spontaneously* release the Other's desire for mutual recognition. This is because the underlying desire of all living beings is for precisely this recognition, and thus this desire responds spontaneously and preverbally, like an invisible precognitive force.

Indeed, the discourse of present-day diplomacy, which is not a spiritual discourse, nevertheless makes implicit reference to this spontaneous capacity whenever it speaks of "easing tensions" or of instituting "confidence-building measures." *That which is eased* is the separation from the Other, resulting from the legacy of paranoia which in each specific instance takes an historically specific form (Ireland/Britain is different from Israel/Palestine is different from United States/Iraq—but not ontologically; rather only in terms of historical and cultural specificity of the respective "forms of life" that have shaped the historically specific identity of each conflict). The *confidence* that is built in "confidence-building measures" is the commitment to recognition of the Other as equal manifestation of the Self, achieved through intercultural symbolic actions through which mutual recognition is understood to have taken place.

Of course, to repeat what I said earlier, the capacity of healing interventions to produce the spontaneous realization of desire requires symbolic action sufficiently sustained to endure all manner of paranoiac suspicion and counterreaction. It must be firm enough to endure cynicism and mistrust of every gesture—firm enough to endure the cynicism of the noise at the surface (such as media cynicism) that, because of the legacy of distortion that has produced the conviction that the Other will reject the Self and vice versa, and even attempt to exterminate the respective existence of the other, will bombard every act that manifests a healing and loving Presence. But our becoming able to "totalize" exactly these processes of mutuality in light of the distortions of our common history is what I mean by spiritualizing foreign policy.

Two recent examples in which this spiritualizing consciousness has had a dramatic effect, and that we use as models as we try to imagine ourselves lifting out of war consciousness, are the 1993 Oslo Accords—the most optimistic moment in the history of Israel/Palestinian relations in which each "in principle" agreed to recognize the other; and South Africa's Truth and Reconciliation Commission—in which the two nations of South Africa, one white and one black, sought to achieve this same mutual recognition in facing and beginning to heal an extraordinarily brutal history of domination of one by the other. From each example, we can learn how to begin to proceed down a new path, focusing our attention on methods of alleviating the stress of paranoia toward the other so that the desire for mutual recognition can emerge, *as it already wishes to do*. From each, we can develop our thought about how to make interventions in the present world situation in which the "we" that is our common humanity can Surround our terror and rage at each other, thaw the frozen rotating paranoia of our mutual antagonisms that have broken us apart, and manifest our Presence so as to move toward the peaceful existence to which all living beings aspire.

Prior to the extraordinary "breakfast diplomacy" of Oslo, the Israeli/Palestinian slice of our common humanity sat facing each other across various international tables for four decades. Each having traumatized the other, periodically through physical violence, continually through the humiliation of nonrecognition of the humanity of the other, each "side" approached the other as an agent of physical and psycho-spiritual terror. From within this wary and defensive stance, no progress could be made toward peace because true recognition of the other implied a vulnerability on the part of the self that, if not reciprocated, appeared to make the self vulnerable to psychic and perhaps physical annihilation. It is not possible to proceed toward peace in a fixed state of fracture, with the legacy of the Holocaust on one side and the imperialist occupation of the Arab world on the other, from a stance of "you go first," accompanied by a list of demands that are degrading or threatening to the other side.

In the face of that and for a complex of other reasons, in 1993 some Israelis close to then-Prime Minister Yitzak Rabin contacted Palestinian leaders close to Yasser Arafat and through a series of miracles agreed to meet in secret in Oslo, Norway, a locale that symbolized a long history of neutrality and far from the spiritual battleground of the Middle East. Under the auspices of their Norwegian hosts, the two sides met not to "negotiate" from a position of mistrust, but to talk and to walk in the green woods of Norway. Relieved of paranoiac pressure in this symbolically neutral setting, the actual persons then engaged in conversations over breakfast in which each for the first time had the opportunity to safely tell the other their story as they experienced it. And precisely because of the locale, the unofficial nature of the dialogue, the fact that it took place while sharing food in a natural surrounding, and the fact that it involved not "goals" and demands to be achieved by rationalistic and strategic conversation, but stories that revealed each side's common humanity, an extraordinary breakthrough was achieved that led to the now famous Oslo Accords, the handshake between former General and hawk Rabin and PLO fighter Arafat in front of Bill Clinton in Washington, D.C., and the very brief outpouring of hope that culminated tragically in Rabin's assassination by a right-wing Jewish settler after a peace rally in which Rabin was seen singing "Give Peace a Chance" with thousands of hopeful young Jews.

I know perfectly well that the line I have drawn here, from the initiation of Oslo to the peace rally at which Rabin was assassinated, and marking the end of that hopeful period, was not in literal, temporal reality a straight line, and also that there is more than one cynical version of the story of Oslo and its meaning. But the so-called "actual facts" as understood by the realists' after-thought misses the actual fact that what I have drawn here was a spiritual straight line, and one that might have led in a very different direction from the present tragic situation. Hunkered down in the legacy of skepticism and pain, realism can never quite see the nonlinear and atemporal openings-up of de-sire that produce the straight lines of hope in history. Nevertheless, these lines of hope remain lodged, invisible, in our historical memory and silently move the human spirit forward in spite of itself, precisely because they hold the promise of fulfilling the most essential of longings that we universally share.

The key task for us now is to reflect upon these lines of hope as they emerge and gain the knowledge *in our common conscious reflection* of the el-ements that make the development of hope possible. From Oslo, we can learn elements about time and place, about the role of informality and breaking bread, and about the capacity to tell one's painful story in an environment in which those whom we fear can hear that pain and ultimately identify with it. In that moment of identification comes the possibility of recognition that we *are* the Other and that our humanity is not inherently fractured but common; that the Other, through mutual recognition, is the source of our own comple-tion as inherently loving, social beings.

The example of South Africa provides a parallel lesson. When Nelson Mandela was in prison, he wrote that he survived his twenty-seven years there in significant part by realizing even in momentary interactions with his guards the essential goodness and humanity that resided within them. This confirmed his conviction that transcendence of even the most brutal history of domination was possible—that this transcendence in some way actually sought its own release from the compulsion to repeat its own repression through domination. When he was finally released and he and Archbishop Desmond Tutu led the overcoming of apartheid, it was this conviction that gave birth to the Truth and Reconciliation Commission, one of the great leaps forward in legal consciousness that has occurred in the development of hu-man history. As is now well-known, this process, in which some twenty-two thousand acts of apartheid-inspired cruelty were acknowledged by the (mainly) white minority perpetrators in the presence of their black victims and their families, on a daily basis and on television for all to hear across the new democratic nation of South Africa, allowed the black majority to assume power essentially without violence and retribution. If one watches the recorded proceedings of this Commission, presided over by the extraordinary moral presence of Bishop Tutu himself, one sees the healing power of the simple speaking of Truth to achieve reconciliation and break the cycle of brutality that repeats itself because the pain and suffering beneath it normally cannot be spoken without resulting in what we imagine will produce devastating guilt and humiliation.

Unlike the death penalty, which seeks to provide resolution to the suffering of victims by extermination of the dominating Other, the Truth and Reconciliation Commission provided a sufficient beginning toward the resolution of a history of suffering by the act mass acknowledgment, in which the particular perpetrators were in reality revealing the alienation of the entire white majority that had underlain the essence of apartheid domination and the entire legacy of imperialism and racism that had given rise to it. The blank statements made by this white landowner or that white policeman—blank because their confessions were often expressed without emotion as a kind of stark and factual representation of a collective truth—placed before the world its own madness, in a way that was simultaneously both monotonously repetitious and spellbinding. And instead of enacting a repetition of the cycle of violence resulting from a repetition of a denial of our common humanity, the processes of the Truth and Reconciliation Commission somehow allowed enactment to be transcended by the naming of the truth that was being denied, in which Tutu himself, as well as the victims and their families themselves, could liberate the nation by bearing witness to it.

Here again, there are many reservations one can raise about the Commission's work, but as in the case of Oslo, the reservations miss the spiritual lesson of how we must proceed to allow ourselves to evolve as an international common humanity, or "international community." On the other side of Truth, of course, is Forgiveness, which is different from freedom from accountability. Bishop Tutu's book *No Future Without Forgiveness* indicates this point in its title—that it is in mutual recognition of the truth of our history, and in forgiveness for this history, which is actually the history of what has been visited upon us as common social individuals in a social/historical common history of humanity, that *spontaneous* redemption becomes possible. I say "spontaneous" redemption because what subtends all of our historical distortions—then apartheid, today Iraq—is the desire for this mutual recognition, the desire to recognize the Other and be recognized by the Other in a precognitive relation of common Presence. That is what heals and what we mean by love.

So now we move to the present crisis. I have said that the UN should re-envision itself according to its original moment of creation, but do so before the catastrophe (that is, the next rotation of paranoia and fear that is already in the process of unfolding) rather than after it. This was the case in 1945 when the Charter was first written and its principles committed to through the act of signature. What follows is a possible spiritual-political path that the UN might have taken prior to this war and could conceivably still take, with the cooperation of the United States, as of the time of this writing.

We must begin from the starting point that the UN exists as an embodiment of common humanity seeking to recognize and return to itself, to get back in touch with its original form and intention, and to redeem itself, through actions that heal the distortions of *itself* that come before it in one particular form after another.

First, the UN Security Council, as a group constituted to be expressive of the world's effort to recognize and affirm our common humanity, should explicitly pass a resolution that reassures the people of Iraq, and the peoples of the Middle East generally, that it does not wish to engage in further acts of violence toward them, but rather seeks to insure their safety and well-being. This resolution should include provisions for significant humanitarian assistance. But in addition, the resolution should make clear *humanity's* common fear of nuclear, biological, and chemical weapons that Iraq and other nations may possess, and invite the existing Iraqi leadership to participate in a mediated dialogue about how systematically to reduce this level of fear. This must include a willingness to address the paranoiac or realistic fears that even Saddam Hussein may hold about the safety of Iraq in the face of Western weaponry, and begin a dialogue about what to do about this fear. Explicit in the design of this dialogue must be the paradox that neither side wishes to disarm in the face of the fear of the other.

One manner of conducting such a dialogue would be to have world leaders who are widely recognized to represent the highest of human ideals, such as Nelson Mandela, Mikail Gorbachev, Jimmy Carter, and Kofi Annan, along with an ecumenical group of leading religious figures, including the Pope, to convene and oversee its deliberations. These deliberations should be at least partially televised, just as the hearings of South Africa's Truth and Reconciliation Commission were, so that the process of dialogue and the emerging process of mutual recognition of one another's humanity that would be intended to emerge from it could be witnessed each day by people throughout the world.

Second, in the conduct of this dialogue, each participant should have an opportunity to state its past wounds, so that without blame, humanity as a whole, as symbolized by the United Nations convening body, could hear the suffering it has imposed upon itself. Here the entire historical legacy of the experience of each party's suffering and humiliation should be given expression—families of Americans who died on September 11 should speak to and be seen by the world via television as speaking to Iraqi families whose children have died as a result of war and economic sanctions. Here, the goal would be for our common humanity to elicit its own spontaneous compassion for the trauma and wounds we have inflicted on ourselves.

You might at first think that it makes little sense for Iraqi families to engage in such a dialogue with American families since Iraq was presumably
not responsible for the destruction of the World Trade Center and the deaths
of September 11. But understood through a spiritual-political lens, the impetus for war between America and Iraq emerges from the interrelationship of
traumatic, paranoia-inducing events and histories that are expressive of each
group's projection of the Other as a projected agent of terror and humiliation.
Expression of the experience of suffering by members of each group in a publicly televised forum, heard with compassion by the symbol of the world
community manifesting its presiding Presence, listening to the effects of its
own distortions, is one of the most powerful ways of "thawing" the carapace
of pseudo-identities that keep us locked in the rotating paranoia of the war
paradigm. Through the presence of the suffering of the Other, we "hear"
through the pain of identification how out of touch we are with ourselves,
how split from the unity of our oneness and commonality.

Third, the UN should seek to "invite," perhaps within the circular arena of
the Security Council, a mutual embrace or other expression of mutual recognition between families and across nationalistic pseudo-identities, taking care
that this is done authentically. If we remember that the desire for mutual
recognition of our common humanity—at the level of the people in our families or in the buildings in which we live as much as at the international
level—always subtends the rotating paranoia that separates us, and that this
desire for connection is capable of spontaneous emergence (think of the elevated local and world responses in the first two weeks following September
11), it is clear that a spiritual foreign policy must be one that utilizes mass
communication technologies to permit the witnessing of such spontaneous
emergence. Quiet the voice that might lead you to think this is a crazy idea,
that it is inconceivable or otherwise "unrealistic": Israeli peace activist Yitzak
Frankenthal's "Parent's Project" has already enabled such public acts of embrace and reconciliation to occur between victims of terror and occupation in
Israel/Palestine, and there is no reason why the Security Council could not
reimagine its work to emphasize public actions necessary for healing that take
account of Frankenthal's proven spiritual wisdom.

If an embrace between families is not possible or capable of being realized
with authentic spontaneity in the context of a public hearing, the presence of
this hesitancy can be valuable in itself. Merely listening, through the medium
of specific actors understood as injured and scattered shards of light, to the pain
we have inflicted on ourselves through being out-of-touch with ourselves, is
sufficient to set on course our ethical direction; and if seen though this spiritual-
political lens, the incapacity to embrace in response to an invitation to do so
points both actor and witness toward the redemptive necessity of engaging in

those acts of reconciliation, generosity, and kindness that can allow the desire for such an embrace to manifest itself eventually. It is this recognizing embrace, spontaneously pulled for in and through the suffering we have inflicted on ourselves, that we have withheld across generations because we have remained trapped in reciprocally perceiving and responding to the Other as a threat.

Fourth, UN representatives should supplement ordinary humanitarian aid with rebuilding the material infrastructure of the Middle East as a whole where such manifestations of generosity can be carried out, including postwar Iraq, no matter what the swirl of emotions, no matter what the political complexity, that such efforts will encounter. This rebuilding should especially include homes, hospitals, schools, and facilities to ensure safe drinking water and provision of food supplies. But it should also include assistance to local communities in rebuilding mosques and other locations that symbolize the historical embodiment of the region's cultural integrity. The aim here as an expression of Surrounding is to freely link acts of generosity with the transmission of recognition, and to proceed to thaw traumatized areas manifesting resistance toward participation in the activity of our common humanity in recovering contact with, and shared knowledge of, itself.

Finally, all of these activities can and should be replicated by the redemptive movements of our common humanity that exist within an increasing singular and worldwide civil society—that is, redemptive actions outside existing institutions that are already being engaged in by the millions of us whom we know make up the new, worldwide peace (not merely anti-war) movement. *We* are ordinary people committed to the recovery of our capacity to release the desire to recognize each other as the source of each other's completion. In relation to the spiritual sickness of war consciousness and the now-ancient paradigm that separates us, we are all doctors without borders. Common humanity can heal itself only by healing the Other through providing the Other with the grace of a recognition that every one of us longs for through the layer of pain and self-protection that causes us to distort who the Other actually is, and withhold ourselves from the only source of our salvation.

Earth Democracy

Vandana Shiva

Earth democracy is my vision, the basis of my activism.

Today, we are being ruled by terror and greed, fear, and insecurity. As we face the tightening control of public space by corporate globalization and militarized police states, by an economic fascism aided by political fascism, our challenge has become to reclaim our freedom and the freedom of our fellow beings. The Earth Democracy Movement takes up this challenge by advocating the creation of all-inclusive living economies that protect life on earth while providing basic needs for all.

The Earth Democracy Movement is based on two fundamental principles. The first is the continuity of all life on earth, and its right to freedom on the basis of gender, race, religion, class, and species. The second is the continuum between and indivisibility of justice, peace, and sustainability—we believe that without ecological sustainability and a just division of the earth's bounties, there can be no peace.

Corporate globalization ruptures these continuities. Because corporations establish their dominance through a divide and rule policy, corporate globalization creates competition and conflict between different species and peoples, often subjugating other species to the demands of humankind. By spreading insecurity, it transforms diversity into a set of oppositional differences, which then give rise to fundamentalisms that diminish freedom and shift our focus from sustainability and justice and peace to ethnic and religious conflict and violence.

The Earth Democracy Movement is committed to going beyond the triple crisis of economic injustice, ecological nonsustainability, and the subjugation of people and other species brought on by the growth of global capitalism. Instead, the Earth Democracy Movement provides an alternative worldview in which humans are embedded in the earth family. In this vision, we are connected to each other through love and compassion, not hatred and violence, and ecological responsibility and economic justice replace greed, consumerism, and competition as the fundamental objectives of human life.

DIVERSITY VS. MONOCULTURE

Corporate globalization embraces exclusivist monocultural modes of thinking—the belief in the necessary dominance of one species, one race, one economy, one religion. This monoculturalism is leading to the destruction of resources; the creation of monopolies over land, biodiversity, water, and food; the deepening of poverty and the exclusion of millions from their livelihoods and economic security; and the destruction of democracy, peace, and cultural diversity. It creates a negative system that provides short-run benefits to just a few. Monocultures are the result of exclusion, intolerance, and domination, and they support exclusion, intolerance, and domination. Their very presence indicates some dominant group or species and experienced coercion and loss of freedom.

The Earth Democracy Movement counters the spread of monoculturalism by transforming our minds and actions, liberating us from this dominant pattern of thought. Earth democracy recontextualises human beings as one member of the earth family (*Vasudhaiva Kutumbkam*). When the intrinsic worth and value of every life form and even human is recognized, biological diversity and cultural diversity flourish.

By replacing monocultures with diverse cultures, and replacing one-dimensional systems with multidimensional ones, the economics of scarcity can be replaced by the economy of mutually-shared abundance, the guaranteed provision of basic needs, and access to vital resources. Reembedding humans in the ecological matrix of biological and cultural diversity reopens spaces for sustainability, justice, and peace by reorganizing relationships. It also restructures constellations of power, revitalizing freedom and democracy. Gandhi's concept of *Swadeshi*—of economic freedom and economic democracy—is at the core of this vision.

THE EXCLUDED MIDDLE

Corporate globalization promotes the formation of monocultural thinking by advocating the logic of exclusion, of apartheid, of "us" and "them," of either/or. It polarizes societies and species into two camps, ignoring continuities, excluding the middle. It creates divisions and exclusions that pit the economy against ecology, development against environment, people against the planet, and people against one another in a new culture of hate.

Earth democracy fights against this polarization by reaffirming the middle that polarization excludes. We affirm the logic of "both/and," the logic of inclusion. Diversity and multifunctionality reside in the included middle; the middle is also where creativity flourishes. By embracing the included middle, Earth democracy transcends the false polarization of wild versus cultivated, nature versus culture, or even the false clash of cultures. It allows for the forest farm and the farmed forest; it recognizes that biodiversity can be preserved and also support human needs.

By embracing the logic of inclusion, Earth democracy enables us to make the mind shifts that are conducive to our meeting our needs without destroying other species. In the included middle, we can learn to improve human welfare while ensuring the welfare of all beings. This spirit of commonality is symbolized by Hindus visiting a Muslim shrine on their pilgrimage to Sabarimala, and by the Muslim singer Wasiffudin Dagar praying to the Hindu gods Durga and Shiva, keeping the ancient Dhrupad tradition alive for a composite culture. It is represented in farms rejuvenating biodiversity, and in species acting in mutuality to benefit one another. In India, we pray: "Let all beings be happy" (*Sarve Bhavantu Sukina*).

Earth democracy is not limited to protecting human beings who are privileged through class, race, gender, and religion, however. In fact, it shouldn't be limited to humans as a species. It is the democracy of all life. Since other species do not vote, cannot lobby, and have no purchasing power in the marketplace, Earth democracy creates an obligation on us as humans to take their well-being into account. As His Holiness the Dalai Lama said on his sixtieth birthday,

> All beings have a right to well-being and happiness. We have a duty to ensure their well-being.

This entails human responsibility as trustees and stewards of the planet, instead of condoning the current, dominant notion of ourselves as masters, controllers, and owners.

HUMAN RIGHTS AND RESPONSIBILITIES

Earth democracy puts responsibility at the core of our relationships with each other and with other species. Our rights flow from responsibility instead of the current, dominant paradigm that gives rights without responsibility and responsibility without rights. This separation of rights and responsibility is at the root of the ecological devastation and gender, racial, and class inequality we see all around us. Corporations that earn profits from the chemical industry, or from pollution resulting from genetically altered crops do not have to bear the burden of that pollution. These social and ecological costs are externalized and born by others who are excluded from such decisions and from their benefits.

Earth democracy is based on the idea that those who pay the price for a decision should have a say in it. Since we all rely upon the earth and pay the price for its destruction, rights to natural resources are natural rights. They are not given by states, nor can they be extinguished by them or by any other human entity, including corporations or the WTO. Earth democracy opposes corporations' current attempts to remove people's rights to land, water, and biodiversity.

By advocating natural rights and rights based on responsibilities, Earth democracy shifts the constellation of power from corporations to people, and rebalances the role and functions of the state. Earth democracy reinterprets national sovereignty, replacing political theory based on representative democracy with one based on direct democracy. Decisions that today are made by global institutions or by centralized governments would be moved to local communities.

Earth democracy would create systems of sustainable and just economics, governed by democratic and accountable organizations. Earth democracy is about maintaining life, and a society's natural right to maintain the conditions necessary to stay alive. It is about making decisions and protecting the freedoms related to everyday living—the food we eat, the clothes we wear, the water we drink. It is about creating a permanently vibrant democracy, combining economic with political and ecological democracy. Earth democracy is about creating real security, and hence the conditions of peace.

Under globalization, democracy even of the shallow representative kind is dying. Governments everywhere are betraying the mandates that brought them to power. They are centralizing authority and power, both by subverting democratic structures of constitutions and by promulgating ordinances that stifle civil liberties. The September 11 tragedy has become a convenient excuse for anti-human legislation worldwide. Politicians everywhere are turning to xenophophic and fundamentalist agendas and the fear they thrive on in order to gain votes. Economic decisions have been taken away from the nations who will have to endure them and are being made instead by largely unaccountable international groups such as the World Bank, the IMF, the WTO, and individual corporations. Old divisions between the haves and the have-nots are mutating into the "live and live-nots," as millions are robbed of their very right to stay alive. The economic apartheid between the "lives and live-nots" is being translated into what amounts to genocidal tendencies of ethnic cleansing. Democracy dies when governments no longer reflect the will of the people, but are reduced to unilateral, unaccountable instruments of corporate rule under the constellation of corporate globalization—as the Enron and Chiquita cases make so evident.

Earth democracy is a democracy that is alive. It combats these unjust and corrupt regimes through withdrawal of consent along with peaceful, nonviolent, non-cooperation. This is a reinvention of Gandhian Satyagraha (the force of truth). Through noncooperation is born real freedom and self rule (*Swaraj*).

ONE EXAMPLE: THE COMMONS

The most basic right we have as a species is survival, the right to life. Survival requires guaranteed access to resources. The commons have traditionally provided that guarantee by shifting rights and control of resources from corporate privatization and enclosures to the local communities who depend on them. Commons are neither the property of the state nor individuals. Commons are collectively-owned and community-managed resources and spaces such as rivers, ponds, forests, pastures, and air. While in the West most commons have been destroyed or encroached, in the South they still provide the sustenance base for millions. This shift from global markets to earth citizenship would shift the focus from the globalization to the localization of power, from corporations to citizens.

Privatization based on corporations' exclusive right to vital resources like water and control over biodiversity is an enclosure of the commons. When commons are privatized, it is referred to as an "enclosure," with reference to the "enclosure" movement of England that displaced peasants from the land and privatized it for the rich landlords and royalty to grow sheep for wool for the emerging industrial revolution. Many people who migrated to North America were refugees created by the enclosure of the commons. Resisting the privatization of biodiversity through Intellectual Property Rights (IPRs), the privatization of water through structural adjustment programs, and the corporatization of food and agriculture requires a combination of strategies at local, national, and global levels. It means a shift in the constellation of the power and rights of states, corporations, and citizens.

At the local and national levels, the recovery of the commons will mean the strengthening and assertion of local community rights and people's sovereign and natural rights to vital resources such as water and the preservation of biodiversity. This will mean reinvention of sovereignty, as well as a shift from states functioning on the doctrine of eminent domain to states functioning on the public trust doctrine.

At the global level, the recovery of the commons will require a movement of people fighting to keep the fundamental necessities for life beyond monopoly, ownership, and commodification. This in turn would prevent the patenting of life forms and privatization of water. These principles need to be enshrined in international law and policy, and to be backed by popular democratic pressure to reform the WTO and the World Bank. A step in the right direction would be to implement the review of TRIPs (Trade Related Intellectual Property Rights), that countries of the global south are calling for, along with an exclusion of life forms from patentability and a review of structural adjustment programs that impose export-led agricultural strategies and promote policies of water privatization. Since sovereignty, based on the doctrine of eminent domain, has become the conduit for global usurpation of communities' resources and has undermined their sovereign rights, reclaiming biodiversity and water commons must go hand in hand with reclaiming sovereignty, and redefining a new partnership between people and governments on the basis of a public trust doctrine.

Mandates to defend water and biodiversity as commons will have democratic power and substance to the extent they recognize and strengthen local communities' rights at the global level. Global commons that are not built from, or based on the authority of, locally controlled commons would be ecologically and democratically fraudulent. The idea for global commons is merely a recognition and reinforcement of local community rights.

CONCLUSION

The economic, ecological, and social crises resulting from corporate globalization invite a new way of thinking and being on this planet. We can embrace a new worldview in which compassion not greed is globalized, a new consciousness in which we are not reduced to consumers of globally-traded commodities and to narrow, fragmented, one-dimensional identities based on color, religion, or ethnicity, but can instead experience our lives as diverse beings with planetary consciousnesses, mindful and aware of what our actions may cost other humans, other species, and future generations, and connected to each other and the world in the common fabric of life.

Beginning with people's everyday actions, Earth democracy offers us the potential for changing the way governments, intergovernmental organizations, and corporations operate. It creates a new paradigm for global governance while empowering local communities, and the possibility of strengthening ecological security while improving economic security. Under Earth democracy, societies would be immune to the virus of communal hatred and fear. With earth democracy, we would be able to achieve freedom with diversity, and peace with sustainability and justice.

A Spirituality of Resistance

Roger S. Gottlieb

FINDING A PEACEFUL HEART
AND PROTECTING THE EARTH

Spiritual teachings offer us peace in place of pain. Or at least they offer us a way to accept and be at peace with the inevitable distress that comes from being alive. After my first child died at the age of two months, I went through a period of shrinking from the sight of children. Yet I liked kids and didn't want to go through life feeling envious whenever I encountered them. I asked myself what I could do. "It's simple," I realized; "when I see a child and start to feel that gnawing bitterness, I will thank God that I have eyesight to see them. Some people, after all, are blind." This was a spiritual approach: it made me a better person and made me happier. It took nothing away from anyone else, but instead increased the world's positive resources.

If we choose to follow a spiritual path, we face a dilemma. On the one hand, my awareness of the generalized suffering in the world—of the Holocaust and other genocides, and of the ecocide that threatens us all—makes me feel decidedly unpeaceful. I'd rather not be aware of them. Various forms of escape are so attractive, and seem so natural, in a world like ours. On the other hand, spiritual growth cannot be accomplished while I'm screening out the pains and dangers around me. This response will thwart my spiritual aspirations and leave me no better off than when I began. A way out of this dilemma requires that we face—and resist—that which frightens us the most.

My own search for spiritual peace began as a child. I might come upon it unexpectedly on a brilliant spring afternoon, when instead of taking the bus home from elementary school I would walk the one-and-a-half miles back to my house. Every tree, flowering bush, and blade of grass of this well-kept suburban setting seemed wonderfully, almost painfully, alive. And that almost-but-not-quite pain mixed with enough joy to float my little body back to my slightly anxious mother, home wondering why I hadn't gotten off the school bus.

As I got older I explored Mediterranean islands, hung out in tiny tribal settlements in northern Pakistan, and trekked through the Himalayas. Living as a young man with no responsibilities, far from the industrial madness that seemed to be driving everyone crazy, I discovered an ever-deeper experience of serenity: that same wonderful, almost painful, sense of being alive; a simple joy in every leaf, in the glow of stars and moon, in the touch of my lover's hand. I was also helped by psychedelic chemicals that were conducive to deep feelings of peace, belonging, and openness. Under their influence, my heart opened not just to this or that leaf or river but to the entire cosmos.

So I have known these moments, treasured them, and thanked the spirits for them. Yet at the same time there has almost always been a little voice that comes in somewhere during the experience and starts to ask painful questions. "Of course, this all feels wonderful. The world is beautiful that tree, this piece of music, your lover's breast. But what about the Others? What about the people who aren't having such a great time?"

My awareness of the Others has taken many forms. It began, I suppose, on train rides to New York from my home in White Plains. The last few miles, before the cavernous confusion of Grand Central Station, the track ran through the middle of Harlem's black ghetto. The blocks of tenements riveted me. I peered at shabbiness, dirt, laundry drying on back porches, peeled paint, tired old cars, junk-filled yards. And the people glimpsed casually from the train window against which my boy's nose was pushed seemed tired, old at any age, and beaten down.

It all made such a contrast to the brilliant green lawns on my street, my friends' immaculate split-levels. I couldn't see any reason why my family and the other kids at school should be so much better off. It seemed obvious that the people in Harlem, crammed into those ugly buildings, lacking so much that I had, didn't deserve their fate. And it was simultaneously clear that my parents, my friends, and I didn't really deserve what we had either. As I passed through Harlem for those fleeting moments, I wondered if I was right to really enjoy what I had while these other people had so much less.

I couldn't figure out what I felt about a world that was set up this way; and I didn't know how to be thoroughly at home here, full of unmixed joy at all the goodies I enjoyed, when I couldn't help but see how different it was for others.

It reminded me of those who, having been spared in a car crash which killed four acquaintances, would say, "It's a miracle that I wasn't killed."

"Some miracle," I'd think, "you weren't taken and all the Others are dead. What kind of miracle is that?"

We have feelings of peace or joy. These feelings, we want to say, prove how beautiful, how holy, the universe is. Or perhaps the feelings call up images of a more personal sense of the divine: of God the compassionate Father/Mother, of Jesus the Savior, of the Grace of Allah. The feelings then become signs of God's perfection and love, of the deep protectiveness with which a Guiding Force holds us.

For me, in between these feelings of love or serenity and the assertion of perfection and God's love, there lies an often uncrossable gap: all I know about the pain, cruelty, and injustice that permeates this life, all the suffering for which I can find no justification, rationale, or excuse.

I am concerned that to achieve spiritual peace I will have to accept what should not be accepted: that I will be told to concentrate on myself, and forget about others; or that I will be reassured that all this pain is encompassed by Forces and Realities that somehow make up for it. I cannot respond in any of these ways. I seek to live on this earth, without having to rely on promises of aid and comfort from Cosmic Forces. And I cannot forget the Others, or the threats to myself and my children. I don't see how I can accept the world, or approve of it, when these other realities are as genuine as any experiences of mystical delight or tranquillity I might have. To find a peaceful heart, I need a spirituality in which the world's unjustified pain is not denied, avoided, or forgotten. For me, the spiritual challenge is to combine moral and political commitments that direct us to respond to injustice and needless suffering with spiritual teachings about serenity and wisdom. In the act of resistance, I believe, an answer to this challenge can be found.

In *Seeking the Heart of Wisdom*, the contemporary American Buddhist teachers Joseph Goldstein and Jack Kornfield put the spiritual challenge this way:

> Wisdom replaces ignorance in our minds when we realize that happiness does not lie in the accumulation of more and more pleasant feelings, that gratifying craving does not bring us a feeling of wholeness or completion. It simply leads to more craving and more aversion. When we realize in our own experience that happiness comes not from reaching out but from letting go, not from seeking pleasurable experience but from opening in the moment to what is true, this transformation of understanding then frees the energy of compassion within us. Our minds are no longer bound up in pushing away pain or holding on to pleasure. Compassion becomes the natural response of an open heart.

The question is: what am I letting in and what am I keeping out? Isn't there a difference between letting go of my own desires, and letting go of my concern for others? Give up my own desires—for fame, higher salary, some free time, more sex—this I understand. But what would it mean to "let go" of my hope that poor people might have a better life? Or to "open my heart" to the realities of abused children or the dolphins suffocating in two-mile-long fishing nets? What might we have to screen out—and what might we have to add on top—to let go of them?

The well-known American spiritual teacher Ram Dass once said that for him the essential task of spiritual life, regardless of circumstances, is to "quiet my mind, open my heart, and relieve the suffering that I see around me." Supported by his belief that the universe is to be trusted, that it is worth our "faith," Ram Dass acts to end suffering while remaining unattached to the outcome of his actions. He writes:

> Somehow I have faith in the universe—I'm not sure where it comes from—even with all the horror and the torture and so on. This is hard to say because it's morally reprehensible to even think that the people who died in the Holocaust are, from a soul point of view, on an evolutionary path in which that experience was functional. That sounds too horrible to consider. But that's the part that isn't humanistic about the spiritual path. I have such a deep conviction about that, and it's part of what allows me to be in the presence of suffering. If somebody is suffering, even though I will do my best to relieve them, there's another part of me that trusts that the suffering is in the greater good and if I could see, I could understand.

The belief Ram Dass expresses here takes us far beyond the reality of the earth. He later admits, "certain things are not reversible—like what we're doing to the forests and species, which will disappear." In the case of the irreversibility of ecological damage it's clear that even Ram Dass' own metaphysical view cannot accommodate the slaughter of nonhuman innocents. The human-centered view that sees the entire universe as a learning ground for people is a little hard to apply to species made extinct and whole ecosystems poisoned.

What is more poignant is that this extremely intelligent and generous man admits quite candidly that the core of his teaching—the necessity to open the heart to the world's pain—depends on his belief that we (humans, anyway) are all on a cosmic trip of spiritual evolution.

The pain is real, but for the "greater good."

What would have happened, I wonder, if he had lost that faith? Would he still have opened to what was going on around him? Is it truly openness if to sustain it we have to believe that the pain is somehow justified? That, like the irritability of the teething infant or the distress of childbirth, the suffering is intimately connected to a Greater Good? Ram Dass is no escapist. He has set up foundations to help the blind and sat in rooms with dying AIDS patients.

But when we believe suffering is "all to the good," then it is damped down—as we might do to a fire burning too fast when we toss some water on it and reduce the air flow—by a metaphysics which puts it all in perspective.

Of course it takes a certain kind of deep strength to accept that the world is the way it is. Denials, avoidance, hysteria, numbness to the pain involved, we might say, are ways of not accepting the facts. That is, of not having the emotional courage to be with the dark truths of our time. But acceptance that something is going on is very different from accepting the thing itself, approving of it, or feeling that a universe in which it takes place deserves our blessing.

In place of an acceptance that is passive, or that hides from the facts, we can offer resistance. In a spirituality of resistance, evil is not avoided, wished away, or neutralized by a metaphysics that promises that it will be All Right in the End. In this spiritual realm we can fully experience the deepest of joys because we engage directly with unjust suffering by opposing it. In the act of resistance, our acceptance of cruelty, injustice, and unnecessary death is made complete—we embrace them by seeking their end. Why is resistance so powerful? Because in the act of resistance we fully engage that which frightens and depresses us the most. What we would avoid, deny, submit to, or go along with is brought into full reality. We no longer have to feel that it is too much, that we cannot tolerate a world in which it exists, or that we have to let it command our obedience. We can open our hearts in full acceptance of the world, not by telling others or ourselves that there is some cosmic meaning for all this pain, but by seeking to do something about it.

Just what is resistance?

To begin with, to resist is to oppose superior and threatening powers in a context of injustice, oppression, or violence. When we resist we cannot be neutral, or tolerantly accept that everyone's viewpoint is equally valid. When we fight back against rape, or concentration camps, or environmental ruin, the lines are drawn.

Nevertheless, while resistance means we take a stand in the face of a painful reality, it is not always clear exactly what should be done. Nor does it mean that the people we oppose are unredeemably evil (though they sometimes are). People may take part in unredeemably evil activities, even though they are more frightened, numb, or weak than they are outright ethical monsters. What resistance does mean is that I answer my students' question—"But who is to judge what is right or wrong?"—by saying, "We are; each and every one of us." We make the judgment, even though the situation may be terribly complex. We oppose the evil, even as we try to have compassion for the evildoers.

To resist is to act with the aim of lessening the collective injustice, oppression, and violence we face. We are not resisting if all we are trying to do is get the pain shifted somewhere else. Working to have the toxins stored in the next town over or buying sun block when the thinning ozone makes the sunlight dangerous—these things might be prudent or good for my health. But they do not really count as resistance to the massive forces of environmental destruction. Individual self-protection poses no threat to the powers that be, but seeks to accommodate those forces, to coexist with them.

Because the engines of environmental destruction, like many other types of evil, are strong, entrenched, and often mighty rich, and because we carry conflicting obligations, time pressures, and simple fatigue, it often seems easier or safer not to resist. Thus if we are to act, we will need to overcome the temptations of fear or laziness, of complacency and habit. These temptations, as I know very well from my own life, are continual. Unless we are in the throes of some extreme situation—the oil company at the gates of our little village, as it were; or unless we are heroes, or just plain tirelessly devoted—we will give in to those temptations.

But that is not what we always do. While the dominant social forces make it ever so easy to go along with business as usual, we may come to realize that these same forces are controlling, constraining, and limiting us. Since resistance involves throwing off limits, there can be an element of gladness, even joy, when we engage in it. Instead of conforming to the ways things are, living day to day with the gnawing feeling that something is not right, we refuse to go along. We attempt to halt or slow, if only in the most minuscule ways, the machinery of ruin. And when we do so we often experience the rush of feeling that comes from liberating the energy long buried by our suppressed awareness that we have been part of something we know to be wrong. In this light, the deep satisfaction expressed by some Jews who resisted the Nazis makes perfect sense. They chose to resist and to just that extent, no matter what the forces arrayed against them, they had become free.

In fact, the emotional and spiritual meaning of the Holocaust can be profoundly changed when we think of it not solely as the history of how the Jews were slaughtered but also of how they fought back. The images of victimization remain, but along with the piles of dead bodies we see resistance fighters. Auschwitz is identified not only with the millions who were gassed, but also with the organized network of inmates who blew up one of the crematoria. Poring over the historical record, we see that the Jews sang songs to celebrate their survival, smuggled forbidden food into the ghettos, blew up Nazi troop trains and at times expended superhuman courage and determination just to stay alive. These resistors show us that despite all the pain inflicted by violent oppression, freedom is always possible. Not freedom from the situation, but freedom within it.

In the same way, the despair engendered by environmental destruction—the self-caused cancer plagues, the dying coral reefs, the newly dangerous sunlight—can be altered by our knowledge of the people throughout the world who are resisting that destruction; and our own spiritual life can reach its most profound point when we join our energies to theirs. Our sense of the ultimate meaning of the environmental crisis may change if we see it as a time of joyful resistance, a time when we can deeply penetrate the meaning of our existence.

In the freedom of resistance comes a unique and pure happiness. It may last for only a short while before it once again gets clouded by regrets for losses, confusion over strategy, and fear for the future. But for a precious time we are at one both with ourselves and the world. Life, usually so flawed, has become perfect. Feeding the world as it has fed us, we are at that moment like a bee pollinating an apple tree, like the salmon struggling upstream against the rapids to lay its eggs, like the hawk bringing back fresh kill for its chicks, like a maple tree offering soft red buds to the warming April sunshine.

Resistance takes many forms. In any given situation, we can see that there are choices to be made: between living in denial, and living in the truth; between accepting the way things are and saying "no" to them. We can speak up, act up, share our concerns with others, give money, teach our children the truth, confront political candidates, write letters to the editor, join groups to keep indigenous peoples from being slaughtered, hug trees to protect forests from bulldozers, shut down the local polluter, nationalize the oil industry, and overthrow the government. For a start.

Consider Diana Steck, a housewife from Yukon, Pennsylvania, who confronted the relation between the chronic illnesses of her own and many of her friends' children and the nearby dump that contained chromium, cadmium, lead, arsenic, mercury, and other toxic chemicals. She struggled with condescending government officials who promised an investigation and did nothing; and health "experts" who told her she didn't know what she was talking about. Refusing to give up, she and some neighbors became a group with a name, received training in grassroots environmental politics, got arrested for sitting-in at a state office, and took over a crucial public meeting when public officials tried to dodge the issue. Friends and relatives were shocked when she was arrested or tried to stop trucks from going to the dump. But Diana had become a different person, one who wouldn't get stopped by her own fears or others' judgments. "All this," she said, referring to countless illnesses in her town, "happened for a reason. Otherwise we'd still be out here, just stupidly working and making money, oblivious to the world around us. We wouldn't be the people we are today. We wouldn't be as complete."

In my own community of Jamaica Plain, a racially and economically mixed section on Boston's southern edge, people banded together to protect our treasured Jamaica Pond: an actual lake—one-and-one-half miles around—within the city limits! The pond is bordered by a thin belt of trees and graced by sea gulls, Canadian geese, ducks, exotic-looking cormorants, snapping turtles, and imported swans. Its marvelously clear water attracts joggers, strollers, baby carriages, dog walkers, drummers on hot summer nights, old Chinese ladies doing Tai Chi, and couples of various sexual persuasions dreamily holding hands.

When you stand at the little boathouse where popsicles and popcorn are sold, you can look across the water and see the sun set over wooded hills. These hills, which border the park but are not actually part of it, were sold to a builder who wants to replace the old trees with luxury condos so that proud owners can enjoy the vista of the pond while the rest of us can view the sun setting over expensive apartments.

A local social worker spearheaded the opposition, raising four thousand signatures demanding that the local development board forbid the project and the city or state acquire the land. On the coldest night of the winter of 1998, three hundred and fifty people jammed a local church to make their voices heard—to say that this spot was not only lovely, but also sacred. Each of us at the meeting could have found something else to do that evening; could have left the effort to others; could have felt, "Oh well, you can't fight the developers." But we didn't, and in the end the project was stopped.

As we resist, we look for allies, and sometimes find them in unlikely places. Melody Chavis, a writer and community activist in Berkeley, faced a neighborhood increasingly dominated by the drug trade. She watched local kids grow up to be pushers, junkies, and gang members, and offered something better. She connected them to a local organic gardening center, where they learned to work the land with their own hands and to take deep pride in the ecological quality of what they were growing. For a number of kids the healthy connection to the soil meant a viable alternative to the polluted options that surrounded them.

Our allies can be from the neighborhood or from very far away. In an ecological age, "Love your neighbor" includes the whole world. Consider, for instance, the way international activity has been mobilized in response to the Narmada River Valley project in India. Called by critics the "world's greatest planned environmental disaster," the project envisaged 30 major, 135 medium, and 3,000 minor dams throughout central India. If completed as planned, it would displace close to 400,000 people, destroy wildlife habitat, and flood some of the last remaining tropical forest in India. As early as 1977, local opposition formed when people realized that there was in fact no land available for the local people who were to be displaced—that they would simply join the millions of other "refugees from development." During the next decade-and-a-half, opposition grew and took a variety of forms: road blockades, hunger fasts, demonstrations at state capitals, and massive gatherings at sites which were to be flooded. What is crucial here is the way a ring of international solidarity has formed around resistance to the Narmada River Valley project. Japanese environmentalists persuaded their government not to advance money to it, while American activists pressured the World Bank. In 1992, facing reports that the entire project was colored by fraud and incompetence, legislators in Finland, Sweden, and the United States asked the World Bank not to lend any more money. The International Rivers Project, located in San Francisco, organizes financial and technical aid to the continuing struggle.

Even though ozone depletion and acid rain make everyone "neighbors," we should remember that if the dam goes through, the writer and the readers of this book will not be displaced, and people in India will. We are not all affected equally by everything that takes place in the world. Martin Luther King Jr.'s claim that we are bound by an "inescapable network of mutuality, tied in a single garment of destiny" must be read in the most general of ways, or else we will paper over the differences between the drowned and the saved. Yet it is also true, I believe, that similar forces are at work in crazy dam projects, unnecessary condo building, and leaking toxic dumps. Monoculture, big money, blind indifference, and shortsighted thoughtlessness carry their weight everywhere. For that reason, resistance to one is resistance to all.

At times acts of resistance will demand everything we have. Chico Mendes was murdered for defending the rainforest and the people who live there. Ken Saro-Wiwa was hung by the Nigerian government for resisting the toxic effects of oil extraction in Nigeria—these and countless unknown others have put their time, money, energy, and even their lives on the line.

However, some acts of resistance will involve doing just a little more than we are doing already. We can make one extra phone call, toss a few more dollars towards the organization that is doing good work, not buy the chemicalized food, take the trouble to ask the office manager to use the organic bathroom cleanser. Returns on such actions won't be as grand or dramatic as those times when we manifest a greater devotion. Still, they can be essential parts both of a worldwide environmental movement and our own, most personal, spiritual life. Like a short but heartfelt prayer, a daily ten minutes of meditation, a brief reading from Psalms, each act of resistance can be a small but loving acknowledgment of our yearning to join the best within us to the best for others.

Finally, in resistance we can keep up our hope. Optimism is not always easy to hold onto, especially as we become more and more knowledgeable about what is really going on. But our knowledge should include successes as well as failures, our moments of grace as a species and culture as well as our moments of degradation. We can read of Gaviotas, a tiny Colombian village that reclaimed seemingly barren land with sustainable agriculture, democratic decision making, and an inclusive economic structure. Its windmills convert mild breezes into energy, its solar collectors work in the rain, and children's seesaws power its water pumps. In the shelter of the Caribbean pines planted as a renewable crop, an ancient rain forest is regenerating. We can marvel at the growth of the organic food industry, the resurgent forests of the American northeast, the return of the wolves to Yellowstone. We can marvel at the growth, in about a decade, of an environmental justice movement that includes groups from Texas to Massachusetts, from California to Georgia. All these examples of resistance can inspire our own. They are precious opportunities to know, as deeply as we know anything, that the environmental crisis is a time of great courage as well as great loss.

If spirituality means, among other things, moving beyond my isolated ego (and this is, indeed, the way it is frequently portrayed) then resistance is that movement. For in acts of resistance I go beyond my isolation, my self-concern, my very sense of myself as fully separate. And that sense of moving beyond my ego takes me not only into connection with the suffering Others who are human, but with the more-than-human as well I can walk over to Jamaica Pond, pat the trunk of a sugar maple tree I pass along the way and say, only half believing I won't be understood: "You and me pal—we're in this together. Best of luck to us both." I can know that my kinship with the beings of this earth is essential to who I am; and that I will not let them be wantonly destroyed without some defiance. Paradoxically, if I put some of my soul into resistance, I will occasionally be able to put down my burden of selfhood and responsibility, that searing sense that I must make it all better. There will be moments when I realize that I am merely a brief flower of mind and feeling in this vast meadow of existence. At my best I will try to be a true flower and not some plastic rose that doesn't bloom and will not wither for a hundred years. I will have offered myself to all the other flowers, to the life and health and blossoming of the rest of this garden we call the earth. Having done so I will then be able to feel the full sweetness of the springtime sun, the evening rain, and even the approach of the chill winter morning of my own natural, fitting and joyous death.

The Challenge of the Twenty-First Century

Fritjof Capra

As our [twentieth] century draws to a close, we are facing a whole series of global problems that are harming the biosphere and human life in alarming ways that may soon become irreversible. Concern with the environment is no longer one of many "single issues"; it is the context of everything else—of our lives, our businesses, our politics. The great challenge of our time is to build and nurture sustainable communities—social, cultural, and physical environments in which we can satisfy our needs and aspirations without diminishing the chances of future generations.

Since its introduction in the early 1980s, the concept of sustainability has often been distorted, coopted, and even trivialized by being used without the ecological context that gives it its proper meaning. In its correct usage, what is sustained in a sustainable community is not economic growth or development but the entire web of life on which our long-term survival depends. In other words, a sustainable community is designed in such a way that its ways of life, business, economy, physical structures, and technologies do not interfere with nature's inherent ability to sustain life. The first step in this endeavor, naturally, must be to become "ecologically literate," that is, to understand the principles of organization that ecosystems have developed to sustain the web of life. To do so, we must learn to think systemically—in terms of connectedness, context, and processes.

When systems thinking is applied to the study of the Earth Household—which is the literal meaning of "ecology"—we discover several basic principles of organization:

- that an ecosystem generates no waste, one species' waste being another species' food;
- that matter cycles continually through the web of life;

- that the energy driving these ecological cycles flows from the sun;
- that diversity increases resilience; and
- that life, from its beginning more than three billion years ago, did not take over the planet by combat but by cooperation, partnership, and networking.

The main task in the next century will be to apply our ecological knowledge and systemic thinking to the fundamental redesign of our technologies and social institutions, so as to bridge the current gap between human design and the ecologically sustainable systems of nature. Fortunately, this is already taking place. In recent years, there has been a burst of optimism about the dramatic rise of ecologically oriented design practices, in which our human purposes are carefully meshed with the larger patterns and flows of the natural world (see, for example, Paul Hawken, Amory Lovins, and Hunter Lovins' *Natural Capitalism*). In other words, ecodesign reflects the principles of organization that nature has evolved to sustain the web of life.

For example, the principle "waste equals food" means that all the products and materials manufactured by industry, as well as the wastes generated in the manufacturing processes, must eventually provide nourishment for something new. A sustainable business organization would be embedded in an "ecology of organizations," in which the waste of any one organization would be a resource for another. In such a sustainable industrial system, the total outflow of each organization—its products and wastes—would be perceived and treated as resources cycling through the system. Such "ecological clusters" of industries have recently been initiated in several parts of the world (for examples, see Gunter Pauli's *UpSizing*).

In fact, ecodesigners like William McDonough and Michael Braungart speak of two kinds of metabolism—a biological metabolism and a "technical metabolism" (as described in their article "The Next Industrial Revolution," *Atlantic Monthly*, October 1998). Things that are part of the biological metabolism—agriculture and food systems, clothing, cosmetics, and so on—should not contain persistent toxic substances. Things that go into the technical metabolism—machines, physical structures, and the like—should be kept well apart from the biological metabolism.

Eventually, all products, materials, and wastes will be either biological or "technical" nutrients. Biological nutrients will be designed to return to the ecological cycles—to be literally consumed by microorganisms and other creatures in the soil. Technical nutrients will be designed to go back into "technical cycles." This means that customers will not own these products but will merely buy their services. When they have finished with the products, the manufacturer will take them back, break them down, and use their complex materials in new products.

Today, the obstacles that stand in the way of ecological sustainability are no longer conceptual, nor technical. They lie in the dominant values of our society, and in particular in the dominant corporate values. Corporate values and choices are determined, to a large extent, by flows of information, power, and wealth in the global financial networks that shape societies today.

During the past three decades, the information technology revolution has given rise to a new type of global capitalism, which is structured around networks of financial flows. In what Manuel Castells calls "informational capitalism," the movements of capital do not follow a market logic. Rather, capital operates as if in a global casino, using information technology to scan the planet for investment opportunities and to move from one option to another in a matter of seconds. The market is twisted, manipulated, and transformed by a combination of computer-enacted strategic maneuvers and unexpected turbulences caused by the complex interactions of capital flows themselves in a highly nonlinear system.

As a result, money is almost entirely independent of production and services. Thus labor has become fragmented in its performance, organization, and collective action. At the same time, information technology has transformed the core processes of knowledge generation, economic productivity, political and military power, and media communication. As a result, presence or absence in the network is a critical source of power. The rise of this "Network Society" has thus become intertwined with rising social inequality, polarization, and social exclusion (see Manuel Castells' *The Information Age*).

At the close of this century, then, we can observe two developments that will have major impacts on the well-being and ways of life of humanity in the next century. Both of these developments have to do with networks, and both involve radically new technologies. One of them is the rise of global capitalism and the Network Society; the other is the creation of sustainable communities, involving ecoliteracy and ecodesign practices.

Whereas global capitalism is concerned with electronic networks of financial and information flows, ecoliteracy and ecodesign are concerned with ecological networks of energy and material flows. The goal of the global economy is to maximize the wealth and power of the elites in the Network Society; the goal of ecodesign to maximize the sustainability of the web of life.

These two scenarios—each involving complex networks and special advanced technologies—are currently on a collision course. The Network Society is destructive of local communities and thus inherently unsustainable. It is based on the central value of capitalism—money making for the sake of making money—at the exclusion of other values. However, human values can change; they are not natural laws. The same electronic networks of financial and informational flows *could* have other values built into them. The challenge of the twenty-first century will be to change the value system of the Network Society, so as to make it compatible with the demands of ecological sustainability.

Techno-Utopia?

Jackson Lears

In the United States, at least, utopian hope—often fired by religious faith—has been a major component of democratic social movements from antislavery to Populism to the struggle for black equality. The courage to challenge established power has often required eschatological visions of deliverance. No wonder the editors of *Tikkun* have emphasized the importance of reviving utopian thought for the renewal of progressive politics in the twenty-first century.

Yet the renovation of utopia could be a tricky project. There are problems embedded in the utopian habit of mind, difficulties that have weakened the utopian tradition from within. The dream of social perfection has often (especially in recent centuries) depended on a sentimental faith in human goodness and a universalist assumption that human needs and desires are everywhere the same—or at least everywhere assimilable to the enlightened creed of utilitarian rationality. The utopian, even at his best, falls prey to what William James called "the sentiment of rationality"—the overwhelming desire for conceptual tidiness. At his worst, as *Tikkun* contributors have frequently noted, the utopian could justify genocide in the name of the perfect world to come.

Still, the utopian impulse remains a powerful force in American public life—and probably an inevitable one, in a culture still dominated by protestant habits of mind if not protestant beliefs. For more than two centuries, a linear millenarian view of change has energized American nationalism, underscoring our allegedly crucial role in the sacred drama of world history. As millenarians became more secular, various versions of technological determinism displaced the older sense of providential order.

The latest version of techno-millennialism is the vision of a wired world now being promoted by our high-tech corporate monoculture. The celebratory perspective of Bill Gates, and of his rivals and minions too, offers us a chillingly uniform picture of whole populations happily embracing "the Web lifestyle"—whether they want to or not. Choice and determinism coexist. Apart from this confusion, what is particularly striking in this thinking is the techno-millennialists' assumption that there will simply be no one outside the Web, or at least no one worth noticing. For all their democratic rhetoric of "empowerment," cybervisionaries preserve an authoritarian streak, an addiction to market discipline. Evolve or die, says Gates.

The problem, in short, is not the absence of utopian vision but its monopoly control by the high-tech corporate elite and their publicists in the major media. Professional wise men like Thomas Friedman (in *The Lexus and the Olive Tree*) provide a balm of beneficence and inevitability to the globalization of capital. Skeptics are silenced or ignored, denied the authority of "responsible opinion."

That is why we so badly need the revival of genuinely countercultural utopianism—some alternative visions to pose against the deification of "technology" and "the market." I mean countercultural in the original sense of principled opposition to the norms of utilitarian rationality, the utopian ideology which displayed its destructive underside in the Vietnam War. It is important to distinguish this strain of protest from the caricature of countercultural politics served up almost daily by the major media—the rapid-fire montage of Nehru suits, go-go boots, and naked cavortings at Woodstock. The serious antiwar counterculture preserved a core religious dimension, a desire to rekindle some sense of the sacred amid the disenchanted landscape of American culture.

Everyone knows how quickly those larger countercultural hopes disappeared in a carnival of commodity fetishism. But the power of the original protest remains. What we need now, in my view, is a chastened utopianism: alive to the persistence of human perversity, sober in its acknowledgment of ineradicable evil, yet capable of indignation and hope—and capable, too, of addressing the millions of Americans who do not see themselves reflected in the worldview of the *Wall Street Journal*. Who knows? Maybe the fire of a utopian vision can once again inspire Americans to rise above mere money worship.

After the End of History

Julian Levinson

I found myself more truly and more strange.

— Wallace Stevens, "Tea at the Palaz of Hoon"

A long time ago in a galaxy far, far away — 1989 in the United States to be exact — a grand theory was bandied about that sought to explain the state of the world now that communism seemed to be in its final death throes. The theory, cooked up in reactionary think tanks and sent coursing through the collective national psyche, went by the ominous-sounding name of "the End of History." A convergence of Manifest Destiny and Hegelian philosophy, it asserted that if by history we mean the progressive development of social life established through conflict between opposing world views, then history in this sense had ended. In more concise words: the West had won, and it was a gosh darn good thing, too. With the end of the Cold War, the only political system left standing in the field was liberal democracy, the only ideology possessive individualism, the only economic system free market capitalism. Communism, according to the theory, had been humankind's last great effort to overthrow the dominant system and institute a new system based on a countervailing vision of human life. Now it was only a matter of time before every nation came around to embrace the basic ideals that were allegedly already in place in America, notions such as social equality, equality before the law, freedom of speech, and popular sovereignty. History as the scene of bloody revolutions and seismic cultural transformations had culminated in this, a world of nations designed as carbon copies of American democracy.

Hope, according to this view, was no mere thing with feathers. It was tangible in the collapse of the Berlin Wall. It was visible in images of people throughout the world suddenly wearing Benetton and drinking Coke. It was demonstrable according to statistics: from a grand total of three liberal democracies in 1790, the sum had risen to sixty-one by 1990, said Francis Fukuyama in *The End of History and the Last Man*. Most of all, hope in this new age was guaranteed by a singular (and cynically reductive) conception of human nature. At their core, said the voice of the End of History, humans are a bundle of basic and calculable needs. In short, they want things. And now that we've reached our superlative level of technological progress and finally hit upon the right political system, we can finally give the people what they want. Or at least make them think they're on their way to getting what they want.

Today this version of unimpeded progress cannot help but seem slightly antiquated, at least to those with enough patience to tabulate casualties. It is like looking back at the fourth act of a tragedy from the standpoint of the fifth, after the hero has been trapped by his flaw. The endgame of history, it now appears, has been interrupted by a most recalcitrant foe, the uncooperative Islamic Other. Holed up in Najaf mosques, constructing nuclear arsenals in Teheran, infiltrating our office buildings and airports, "they" have derailed the smooth transition to a new world order of pliant, structurally identical nation states. Where once we saw one nation after another turning in their authoritarian regimes and joining the free market, we now have the prospect of endless battles against radically benighted enemies who reject all things American—our political system, our products, our lifestyle. In place of the End of History, we suddenly have a new paradigm: the Clash of Civilizations. (Of course, as in Friedrich Nietzsche's eternal recurrence or Sigmund Freud's return of the repressed, it may be but an old paradigm in a new guise, with a genuflecting, Koran-waving adversary rather than a coldly calculating communist one.) Already the voices for international trade agreements and global institutions are being overpowered by less sanguine voices for strengthened security measures and a retrenchment of American patriotism. And many progressives, who were suspicious about all of this Benetton and Coke being such a good thing all along, are suddenly terrified to realize how salient their critiques of globalization and American imperialism have been.

So where do we look for hope amidst our current wreckage? What does this new arrangement have to teach us about ourselves, our politics, and the work before us? One option, available mostly to those on the right, is to cling doggedly to the idea that global uniformity modeled on American blueprints is still the ultimate destiny for the nations of the world, our current dilemmas being mere glitches in an otherwise perfect system. Another option, available to those on the left (and not wholly without merit), is to redouble our efforts at protest, saturated as we are with proof of American destructiveness. But even this response, while vital, would not necessarily generate a renewed basis for hope, I fear. And without hope, protest can become its own form of violence, merely replicating in our own neighborhoods a version of the military conflicts in the Middle East. Let us all, then, rethink our place in the march of time.

The flaw inherent in the End of History scenario—and one from which we all might learn—lies in the belief that the status quo we have arrived at is rational, that it has worked its way to the surface through an ineluctable development and that our only task is to remove the barriers to its universal extension. Whenever we worship rationality in this way, we forget that when we institute the systems according to which we live, we always act on imperfect knowledge—not just imperfect data or an imperfect understanding of causes and effects, but imperfect knowledge of our very selves and of our own deepest motives. This is a lesson that must be learned and relearned, ever and anon. In a very real sense, we are fundamentally strange even to ourselves. Something remains hidden, whether it be in the recesses of the psyche or in the ultimately mysterious surface of an external world that beckons us while simultaneously withdrawing its secret when we felt ourselves on the brink of some ultimate decoding. And so what we have contrived to produce and set in stone is mutable. Or as it says in the old Yiddish proverb: *Der mentsh trakht un got lakht* (Man proposes, God disposes). The end that we have created will end over and over again.

This is not to say that effort is irrelevant, all insight mere delusion. What it does suggest is that we tread lightly and more humbly when we sense our grandeur swelling, that we allow for, as Abraham Joshua Heschel puts it, "a mental interim, with the cultivation of a feeling for the unfamiliar." Global solidarity is a worthy goal, no doubt. But its prospects are dim when we conceptualize our role as the dispellers of a final enigma, the exporters of a final solution, either from the right or from the left. (No solution, we should know by now, should ever be considered final.) Insight must always be seen as a provisional gift from the great unknown, one that is liable to be snatched up again as soon as we overstep its province. And when it does come, it often takes the form of a question, a renewed sense of wonder in which all past certainties are suddenly insufficient.

I find hope in this, that we have once again been shown our folly. We have received notice once again that it is time return to ourselves, or to the ultimate strangeness that we inhabit and call ourselves. Instrumental reason, calculated risk, the totally administered society. These have left us marooned in repetition compulsion, desperation, and fury at the intractable other. The basis for solidarity and the prospect for hope cannot be the relentless imposition of our own design. It can only be in the willingness to bracket our grand theories and to open ourselves to the radical novelty that lies ahead. If our unknowingness can be embraced as a blessing, then hope can enter the clearing that is suddenly, strangely opened up.

Millennial Possibilities

Neale Donald Walsch

Change is inevitable and that is the only thing in life that never changes. The key question is how and who will construct the change. In the twenty-first century, the human race is going to decide that change will serve the entire human community.

In the past, we did not cast ourselves as shapers of our evolution but as witnesses to it. Consider cell phones or pagers: what could have been a wonderful change now actually enslaves us as people find that there is no place they can go to be away—their offices tell them that they must be in touch by pager or cell phone wherever they go. What is happening now is that we are choosing to play a participant's role: we are evolving in ways that we choose to evolve.

The entire human race is moving toward what Barbara Marx Hubbard calls "conscious evolution," which will involve reconstructing our major institutions—including politics, culture, spirituality, education, religion, and economics—all in ways that better reflect our grand idea of who we are and who we can become. This movement is coming not a moment too soon: if we don't act now, we may find ourselves evolving into extinction because of the unwise use of the instruments and tools that we ourselves have developed.

We are finally coming to the awareness that our society does not work. We are looking at our failures with a greater sense of impatience, and are unwilling to let these failures repeat. So, for example, we are no longer willing to be patient with an economic system which gives a tiny percentage of the world's population the ability to consume an obscene amount of the world's wealth, nor with a political system which intentionally disenfranchises a far greater number of people than it enfranchises, nor with a religious system which causes us to be afraid of the deity and of Highest Power in the universe, nor with a social system which manages to separate us from each other through class structure and categories.

These separations between us have created the mistaken notion that some of us are somehow superior to our fellows and therefore deserve to be winners at the game of life at the expense of others who we imagine really deserve to be losers. This is partly based on the notion that there is not enough for everyone. If we realized there was enough we would not have to compete with everyone and the idea of winners and losers would disappear.

What will disappear in the twenty-first century are these central and distorting cultural myths:

1. The myth of separation
2. The myth of insufficiency
3. The myth of superiority.

In their place a new awareness will emerge: that we are not separate at all, that we are all One; that there is enough for everyone if only we construct a system that allows us to share equitably; and that there is no such thing as superiority. These new awarenesses will produce a dramatic step forward towards heaven on Earth that the Highest Power has always told us could be achieved and has been trying to communicate to us from the beginning.

As our perspective changes, what was once viewed as utopian or unrealistic will be seen as possible and then realistic. What was described as utopian in the past will be seen as the product of advanced thinking by people who were giving voice to what now will become the perspective of the human race. Literature that points to a grander and better tomorrow manages consistently to find its way to the bestseller list because the world is hungry for this message—a sure and certain sign that the human race has lost patience with its past failures and is now engaged in a search for a new path.

Though I am very hopeful about the twenty-first century, the reality of change at an exponential rate is already producing social, political, and spiritual chaos in our lives. That chaos will increase in the next twenty years. But the chaos is good and will be followed by periods of advancement for the human race, now more rapid than we've ever seen before.

The chaos will be caused by those who are stuck in the traditions and mindsets of the eighteenth to twentieth centuries and who refuse to let go of their possessions and their ideas of superiority. As a result, we will find a split in the personality of human beings, between those who find comfort in this sense of superiority and those who know that we are all One.

Those who have already made this switch to a higher consciousness will feel that change is not coming fast enough. There will be lots of push and pull between those who are stuck in the past and those who feel upset that the pace of change is not quicker, and this tension is going to be very disconcerting for those whose highest desire is for serenity in their lives. It will be a time when the world badly needs spiritual healers and spiritual mentors and what I call COIs, centers of influence in the marketplace of ideas—and their task will be to be centers of peacefulness in the midst of the chaos, people who can explain what is going on and can help explain both why change is necessary and why it isn't coming faster.

From the beginning of time we've wanted nothing more deeply than to love and be loved, and yet we've put into place every cultural story, every restriction, every nuance, every rule, every tribal custom that we could imagine or construct that would tell us who and how we might love and who we might not love. Today, more and more of us are impatient with these distortions and are giving ourselves permission to find new ways to increase our capacities for love. In the new millennium, people will be more and more open to holding onto their own highest ideals as each of us will be willing to support each other in saying our deepest truths.

Index

Abraham, 124, 233
Absolute, 33
acid rain, 283, 331
adamah (land), 125
Adams, John Quincy, 294
Adenauer, Konrad, 207
Adler, H. G., 199
ad meah ve'esrim (lifespan), 149
Adorno, Theodore, 52
Advaita Vedanta, 22, 23
African Americans, 3; election of,
    248–49; slavery and, 195, 208
agape (love), 30
agnosticism: enchanted, 33
ahimsa (nonharming), 278
AIDS, 80, 254, 255, 275
AIPAC, 7
Akiva, 99
alcohol, 258
Alfer, Yossi, 232–33
All About the Baby (Tooke), 62
Allah: Grace of, 325
Allen, Woody, 104
Al Mubadra (The Initiative), 227
Alpert, Richard, 149
America: Armageddon and, 232;
    Christianity in, 39; disinvestment in,
    12; empire of, 245; imperialism of,
    293, 340; Jews in, 225; Judaism in,

143; military of, 292; mistrust of,
    293–94; Muslims in, 225;
    nationalism in, 337; nuclear weapons
    and, 294; patriotism in, 340; policies
    of, 228, 229; politics in, 262;
    religions in, 143; spirituality in, 168;
    as Superpower, 292; terrorism and,
    291
American Bar Association, 265
The American Evasion of Philosophy
    (Lerner), 250
American Jewish Committee, 5, 232–33
American Medical Association, 263,
    265
Amos, 100
ancestors: veneration of, 41
Anchor Bible, 105–6, 109
Angelus Temple, 43
anger, 74, 303
Anielewicz, Mordecai, 192
Annan, Kofi, 311
anokhi (I am), 122
anthrax, 306
anti-Christ, 230
anti-Semitism, 11, 79; criticism as, 214;
    Nazis and, 201; noses and, 91;
    threats from, 92; Zionism and, 233
apartheid, 309, 310; globalization and,
    316

Aquinas, Thomas, 230
Arafat, Yasser, 217, 236, 239, 308
Arendt, Hannah, 292, 294
aristocracy of victimhood, 178
Aristotle, 135
Armageddon, 229, 283; America and, 232
Armenia, 206
Armstrong, Karen, 38
Ashcroft, John, 24
Assembliea de Deus-Monte Sion, 39
Atman, 33
Augustine, Saint, 230
Auschwitz, 199, 328
Avodat Ellilim (idolatry), 148
Avodat Kokhavim u'Mazalot (worship of
    stars), 148
Axis of Evil, 232, 295
Ayin, 48

ba'alei teshuvah, 70
Ba'al Shem Tov, 74, 147
bagels, 84
Barak, Ehud, 239
Barocas, Carol, 177
Barocas, Harvey, 177
Barry Sisters, 72
Bauer, Yehuda, 197
Becker, Ernest, 35, 36
Beilin, Yossi, 13
Being, 122; God as, 120; mystery of,
    25; unity of, 305
Bensoussan, Aaron, 72
bereshit bara' (in the beginning God
    created), 122
Berlin, Isaiah, 37
Berlin Wall, 296, 339
Berman, Paul, 7
Bernstein, Steven, 71, 72
Berry, Thomas, 121, 290
Between Man and Man (Buber), 30
Biale, David, 64
Bible, 47; creation story of, 121–22;
    feminists and, 107
Biblical Judaism, 141
Big Bang, 127, 129

Big Crunch, 130
Binah (female womb), 136
Bin Laden, Osama, 237
biodiversity, 319
biological metabolism, 334
Blake, William, 271
Blood of Abraham, 69
Bodhisattva Vow, 278
Bolsheviks, 292
Bonhoeffer, Dietrich, 52
Boone, Pat, 108
Bosnia, 195, 206
Bourdieu, Pierre, 75–76
Bowling Alone (Putnam), 288
Bradley, Bill, 250
Brahmajñana, 23
Brahman, 22
Bratslav Hasidim, 149
Braungart, Michael, 334
Bremer, Paul, 293
Breuer, Raphael, 113
Brinkley, Alan, 247
bris, 57–58. *See also* circumcision
brit milah, 64, 66
brit periah, 66
Broszat, Martin, 196
Brothers United for Foreskins (BUFF),
    58
Browning, Christopher, 200
Brusco, Elizabeth, 43
B'tsalmeinu (in our image), 79
Buber, Martin, 29, 30, 35, 100, 101, 215
Buddhism, 25, 149, 167, 271, 277, 278;
    Dharma and, 23; impermanence and,
    154; perfections in, 26
BUFF. *See* Brothers United for
    Foreskins
bureaucracies: dictatorship of, 287
Bush, George W., 36, 225, 232, 234,
    294–95, 301, 303; Iran and, 229; Iraq
    and, 229; policy of, 246
Bushido, 51–52

Caine, Uri, 72
Calloway, Cab, 70

Calvin, John, 230
Cambodia, 197–98, 206
Campbell, Joseph, 101
Camus, Albert, 191
Canetti, Elias, 175
Canticle, 109
capital punishment, 279, 310
Carlebach, Schlomo, 73, 74
Carter, Jimmy, 311
Castells, Manuel, 335
Catholicism: sin and, 110
cell phones, 343
Center for Visionary Leadership, 169
centers of influence (COIs), 345
Chabad, 70
Chair of Elijah, 63
Chavis, Melody, 330
Chechnya, 12
Cheney, Dick, 301
children: deaths of, 1
China, 12, 294; pentecostalism in, 40
Chiquita, 319
Christ. *See* Jesus Christ
Christianity: in America, 39; Conservative, 42; Evangelicalism in, 229; Liberal, 42; mysticism in, 24; nation of, 7; virtues in, 26; Zionism in, 229, 232–33. *See also* Catholicism; pentecostalism
Christian Right, 141
cigarettes, 258
Cioran, E. M., 173
circumcision, 57–58; aesthetics of, 59–60; Judaism and, 63; morality and, 62; sexism and, 67; Torah and, 64–66
civic journalism, 268
civic professionalism, 269
Civilization and Its Discontents (Freud), 176
civil rights. *See* human rights
Clinton, Bill, 6–7, 308
Clinton, Hillary, 6–7
CNN, 301

COBE. *See* Cosmic Background Explorer satellite
Cohen, Gerson D., 109, 111, 115
COIs. *See* centers of influence
Cold Dark Matter, 129
cold evil, 283–84, 285, 289
Cold Plus Hot Dark Matter, 129
Cold War, 295
commandments, 24, 102; of Torah, 119
Commentary (magazine), 5
communism, 339
Communist Party, 298
compassion, 278
compromise, 235–37
computers, 287–88
Confucius, 271
conscious evolution, 343
consciousness, 119
consumers, 289
cooperative power, 296
Cordovero, Moses, 47
corporations, 260, 315; decision making by, 285; dictatorship of, 287; globalization and, 286; privatization and, 319; Samurai and, 51
Cosmic Background Explorer satellite (COBE), 131
cosmic background radiation, 130
cosmology: Kabbalah and, 127, 135; metaphors for, 137
The Courage to Be (Tillich), 33
Cracow, Poland, 202
creation: magnificence of, 34; story of, 121–22
creativity, 138, 271
Crusades, 302
A Cup of Tears: A Diary of the Warsaw Ghetto (Lewin), 187
Czerniakow, Adam, 185–86, 190

Dagar, Wasiffudin, 317
Dalai Lama, 22, 23, 278, 279, 317
Darby, John, 229, 234
dark matter, 128
Darwin, Charles, 120

davvenen (prayers), 148
Deak, Istvan, 198
deforestation, 283
Delbo, Charlotte, 192
democracy: globalization and, 318
Democrats, 2, 4, 248, 249
deportation: of Jews, 182
deregulation, 257
Descartes, 136
desertification, 283
devekut (cleaving to God), 24
Dharma, 23
Diamond, Malcolm, 30
Diaspora, 152, 176, 225
Diaspora Soul (Bernstein), 71
Dinkens, John, 249
dispensationalism, 229, 231, 232
Divine: nature of, 24
divorce, 258
DNA, 119
DOC. *See* Doctors Opposing
    Circumcision
doctors, 263; technology and, 266–67
Doctors Opposing Circumcision (DOC),
    58
dogma, 33, 246
Dorff, Eliott, 79
Douglas, Mary, 159
Dupré, Louis, 24
Durga, 317
Dylan, Bob, 73
The Dynamics of Faith (Tillich), 35

Earth Democracy Movement, 315
Ecclesiastes, 109
Eckhart, Meister, 48
economic parity, 271
economy: growth of, 258
Edelman, Marek, 185, 186, 191
education: inadequacy of, 14
eggs, 148
Ehrenreich, Barbara, 4
Eilberg-Schwartz, Howard, 161
Ein Sof (infinite), 47, 48, 135, 153
Einstein, Albert, 134

Eliade, Mircea, 159–60
Elijah, 218
Ellington, Duke, 76
Elohim, 47
endangerment: criticism as, 214; of
    Jews, 214; of others, 216
The End of History and the Last Man
    (Fukuyama), 340
The Enigma of Evil (Schutze), 284
Enron, 247, 319
environment, 258, 333; balance of, 271;
    damage to, 1; exploitation of, 279;
    globalization and, 261; Rapture and,
    232; reverence for, 124; SAPs and,
    286; threats to, 283
Erigena, John Scotus, 48
Eros and the Jews (Biale), 64
Essential Judaism (Robinson), 63
Esther, 152
European Maastricht Treaty, 259
euthanasia, 203
Evangelicalism, 229
evil, 281; cold, 283–84, 285, 289; hot,
    282–83; institutions and, 284; nature
    of, 282; through technology, 284
exile, 136
expediency, 37
extinction: of species, 283

FAIR, 5
faith, 34, 36
faith-based education, 36
Falk, Marcia, 106, 108
Falwell, Jerry, 232
family, 141, 142
fascists: Jews as, 215
fear, 273–74, 303
Feast of Tabernacles, 146
Feingold, Russell, 248
Feldman, Yael S., 111
feminism, 3, 157; Bible and, 107
Finkielkraut, Alain, 175–76
Fire From Heaven (Cox), 40
First Intifada, 5
flight/fight response, 271

food: distribution of, 1; hunger and, 14, 283
foreign policy, 302
forgiveness, 310
Foundation for Ethics and Meaning, 169
Frankenthal, Yitzak, 312
Frank, Thomas, 75
free markets, 259
French Revolution, 293
Freud, Sigmund, 105, 111, 176, 191, 340
Friedlander, Saul, 197
Friedman, Thomas, 338
Fukuyama, Francis, 340
fundamentalism, 38, 302–3; Christian, 40; pentecostalism and, 40

Gabel, Peter, 2, 7, 8, 301
Gad, 102, 103
Gaia, 149
galaxies, 128; evolution of, 134
Gandhi, Mahatma, 53, 278, 279, 296, 297, 316
Gaon, Sa'adya, 110
Garner, Jay, 293
Garnier, David, 59
Gates, Bill, 337–38
GATT, 259
Gaviotas, Columbia, 331–32
Gaza, 223
gefilte fish, 84, 89, 91
Genesis, 120, 134, 233; sex in, 111
Geneva Accord, 13
genocide, 183; in Armenia, 206; awareness of, 323; in Bosnia, 195, 206; in Cambodia, 197–98; of Judaism, 234; in Rwanda, 195, 197–98, 206. *See also* Holocaust
The German Catastrophe (Meinecke), 208
Ginsburg, Elliot K., 106
Gitlin, Todd, 7
Global Crossing, 247
globalization, 259, 274, 283, 302, 306, 315, 340; apartheid and, 316; of

capital, 3, 338; corporate-led, 286; democracy and, 318; environment and, 261; movement against, 2
Global Marshall Plan, 14
global warming, 103, 139, 283; SUVs and, 287
God, 22; as Being, 120; death of, 41; in exile, 136, 138; Kabbalah and, 135; in pulse, 147; relation with, 29; talk about, 169; as thing, 30; unity of, 143; as verb, 145. *See also* Allah
Goethe, Johann Wolfgang, 114
Golan Heights, 220
Goldberg, Danny, 10, 247
Goldberg, Victor, 10
Goldhagen, Daniel, 182
Goldhagen, Jonah, 202
Goldstein, Joseph, 325
Gorbachev, Mikail, 311
Gordon, Haim, 228
Gore, Al, 6
Gorenberg, Gershom, 234
goyim (non-Jews), 93, 148; as believers, 148
Graham, Franklin, 232
Grateful Dead, 73
gravity, 129
Great Powers, 292
Great Tribulation, 230, 233
Greens, 2
Grisham, John, 231
growth, 258
Guide to the Perplexed (Maimonides), 64
The Gulag Archipelago (Solzhenitsyn), 199
guns, 258
Guth, Alan, 129
Gutman, Yisrael, 185, 197, 199

Hagee, John, 233
Halacha (path of religious practice), 79, 125
ha-Lavan, David ben Abraham, 48
Haman, 152

Index

Hamas, 225; murder by, 235
Hamer, Fannie Lou, 246
Hanukkah, 146
hashgakhah pratit (specific providence), 149
Hasidism, 100, 117, 147
Havel, Vaclav, 137–38, 296–97
Hawken, Paul, 334
healing, 41; evil and, 282; of planet, 103; relationship and, 289; spiritual, 151
Healing Institutional Evil (Peck), 283
Healing Israel-Palestine (Lerner), 13
health care, 14; distribution of, 1
Hegel, George, 339
Herzl, Theodore, 64
Heschel, Abraham Joshua, 11, 53, 101, 102, 341
Hilberg, Raoul, 183, 196, 197, 200, 206
Himmelfarb, Gertrude, 249
The History of God (Armstrong), 38
hitbonenut (meditation), 148
Hitler, Adolph, 173, 179, 217
Hitler's Willing Executioners (Goldhagen, J.), 202
Hobbes, Thomas, 293
Hokhmah, 133; description of, 136; inflation theory and, 134; Kabbalah and, 135
Holiness Code, 162
Holistic Judaism: Shabbat and, 143; women and, 142
Holocaust, 139; awareness of, 323; children of, 177, 179; ghost of, 181; legacy of, 175, 179; literature of, 176; meaning of, 328; memory of, 175; perpetrators of, 196; redemption from, 185, 188
homelessness, 14, 254
homophobia, 6, 11, 79
homosexuals, 2, 3, 77; civil rights for, 80; Greeks and Romans and, 106; Torah and, 78
Hook, Sidney, 249
hot evil, 282–83

Hoyle, Fred, 129
Hubbard, Barbara Marx, 343
Hubble, Edwin, 49, 129
human rights, 226, 227, 245, 279, 317–18; erosion of, 1; for homosexuals, 80; movement for, 2. *See also* social justice
human scale, 289–90
hunger, 14, 283
Huntington, Samuel, 250
Hussein, Saddam, 12, 303, 306
Hyper-Modernity, 141–42

I Am Curious, Yellow (movie), 110
I and Thou (Buber), 29, 31
ICBMs. *See* intercontinental ballistic missiles
Idel, Moshe, 24
Iglesia Pentecostal Arce de Noe, 39
IMF. *See* International Monetary Fund
imperialism, 278; of America, 293, 340; without politics, 294
impermanence, 154
India, 295; river project in, 330
individualism, 302, 339
inflation theory, 129–32; Hokhmah and, 134
The Information Age (Castells), 335
informational capitalism, 335
The Initiative, 227
Institute for Labor and Mental Health, 4, 7
institutions: evil and, 284
Intellectual Property Rights (IPRs), 319
intercontinental ballistic missiles (ICBMs), 285
International Church of the Foursquare Gospel, 43
International Monetary Fund (IMF), 286, 318
International Rivers Project, 331
International Solidarity Movement (ISM), 227
intuitive response, 271–72
IPRs. *See* Intellectual Property Rights

Iran, 294; in Axis of Evil, 295; Bush and, 229
Iraq, 295, 301; Bush and, 229; war in, 273, 293
Isaiah, 15, 230
Islam, 224; war with, 234
ISM. *See* International Solidarity Movement
isolationism, 278
Israel, 5, 308; American Jews and, 213; criticism of, 12, 213; expansion of, 233; Jews to, 230; nationalism and, 139; ownership of, 226; self-defense of, 217
Israeli Independence Day, 223
It's a Free Country (Goldberg, D.), 247

Jackel, Eberhard, 196
Jackson, Jesse, Jr., 248
Jager, Herbert, 196
James, Henry, 112, 113
Jenkins, Jerry, 231
Jeremiah, 53, 255
Jerusalem: as holy city, 226
Jesus Christ, 167; Messianic Kingdom and, 230; Nazarene Hasidim and, 149; as Savior, 77, 325; Second Coming of, 229, 231
Jewish Caucus, 240
Jewish Fighting Organization, 185, 188, 191
Jewish Publication Society, 105–6
Jewish Renewal: A Path to Healing and Transformation (Lerner), 104
Jewish Temple: rebuilding of, 230
Jewish Theological Seminary, 80
The Jewish Woman (Adler), 157
Jews: in America, 225; as chosen people, 220; Christian proselytizing to, 233; deportation of, 182; endangerment of, 214; as fascists, 215; generation gap of, 240–41; to Israel, 230; victimization of, 218–19
The Jews of Warsaw 1939-1943 (Gutman), 199

Job, 120
John, Gospel of, 134
John of the Cross, Saint, 48
John Paul II (Pope), 92
Jong, Erica, 108
Joshua, 218
journalists, 264
Judaism, 4; in America, 143; Biblical, 141; circumcision and, 63; cleaving to God in, 22; Conservative, 139; genocide of, 234; Holistic, 142, 143; men in, 67; music and, 69–70; Orthodox, 139, 157; Rabbinic, 141; Reform, 42, 139; settler, 140; sexism and, 67; social justice and, 221; stereotypes in, 92; victimization in, 218; women in, 142, 157. *See also* Jews
Judea, 219
le juif imaginaire (imaginary Jews), 175
Jung, Carl, 156

Kabbalah, 47, 48, 49, 72, 167; cosmology and, 127, 135; God and, 135; Hokhmah and, 135; longing for, 117
Kadima Party, 13
Kafka, Franz, 178
Kagan, Yisroel Meir, 103
Kaivalyam, 22
Kanter, Rosabeth, 257
Kaplan, Chaim, 201, 209
karma, 277, 278
Karpf, Anne, 176, 177
kashrut (kosher laws), 148
Katz, Mickey, 72
kavanah (ritual intent), 155
Kazik, 193
Keegan, John, 292
Keen, Sam, 35
Kellogg, J. H., 62, 64
Keneally, Thomas, 174
Kennedy, Randy, 247
keter (crown), 136
Keter (Zohar), 72, 73

Ketuvim, 108
Khan, Nusrat Fateh Ali, 72
kibbutz, 143, 213
King, Martin Luther, Jr., 53, 240, 279, 283, 331
Kings II, 218
King, Stephen, 231
kishkehs, 100
Kissinger, Henry, 250
Klezmatics, 69
klezmer music, 70
Knitting Factory, 72
kohanim (priests' descendants), 161
Kol Ha-Ir (newspaper), 71
Kopetch, Gil, 75
Koran, 226
Kornfield, Jack, 325
kosher (pure), 124, 147
Kramer, Hilton, 249
Kristeva, Julia, 107
Kristol, William, 249, 274
Kupers, Terry, 2

labor movement, 2, 4
La Haye, Tim, 231
Lakish, Shim'on ben, 101
Lander, Shira, 165
Langbein, Hermann, 199
Lanzman, Claude, 183, 193
Lao Tzu, 149, 271
The Late Great Planet Earth (Lindsey), 231
Laumann, Ed, 61
Laurel and Hardy, 103
lawyers, 263
learned professions, 263
Leary, Timothy, 149
Leaves of Grass (Whitman), 34
Left Behind (Christian book series), 231, 232
The Left Hand of God: Taking Back Our Country from the Religious Right (Lerner), 14
Leon, Moses de, 49
leprosy, 159

Lerner, Michael, 10, 13, 38, 104, 169, 249, 272
Letters from Prison (Bonhoeffer), 52
Levi, Primo, 197, 217
Leviticus: Holiness Code of, 162; menstruation and, 158
Lewin, Abraham, 187, 189, 191
The Lexus and the Olive Tree (Friedman), 338
Libya, 294
licensing: of professionals, 264
Linde, Andre, 131–32
Lindsey, Hal, 231
listening love, 35–36
Louis XVI (King), 293
love: listening, 35–36; metaphysical, 30
Lovins, Amory, 334
Lovins, Hunter, 334
lox, 84
loyalty, 257
Luria, Isaac, 136, 153
Luther, Martin, 230

minim (believers), 148
Madonna, 70, 75, 108
The Magic Mountain (Mann), 177
Magnificence, 34, 35
Maimonides, Moses, 47–48, 64, 65, 135
mamash, 147
Mandela, Nelson, 309, 311
Manifest Destiny, 339
Mann, Thomas, 177
Maritz, Cecilia, 45
Martin Buber: Jewish Existentialist (Diamond), 30
Martyr, Justin, 230
martyrdom, 303
masturbation, 61–62
materialism, 257, 260, 302
McDonough, William, 334
McGinn, Bernard, 24
McKiernan, David, 293
McPherson, Aimee Semple, 43
meaning, 269, 271
meditation, 331

Meinecke, Friedrich, 208–9
Meir of Narbonne, 109
Mendes, Chico, 331
menstruation, 157; Leviticus and, 158
Merton, Thomas, 53, 149, 273
Messianic Age, 230
Micah, 274–75
midrash (scripture), 151
Miedzyrec, Poland, 201
mikveh (immersion), 158, 160, 162
military: of America, 292
Milky Way, 128
Millennium, 230
Minima Moralia (Adorno), 52
minorities, 2
Mizrahi music, 70, 72
mizvot (commandments), 24
Modernity, 139–41. *See also* Hyper-
    Modernity
moksa, 23
Mommsen, Hans, 196
monoculturalism, 316, 331; high-tech,
    337
monopolies, 259, 316
Mordecai, 152
Morris, Benjamin, 5
Moses, 124
Mosque of the Dome, 11
Mother Jones (magazine), 5
Mt. Zion, 230
mudras, 25
Muhammad (Prophet), 226
My Search for Absolute (Tillich),
    35–36
Mystery, 22, 24, 34–35, 35; of being, 25
mystical experience, 166
myths, 132–35, 151–52; of twenty-first
    century, 344

Na'amah, 103
Nachmon of Breslav, 99
Nader, Ralph, 247, 248
NAFTA, 259
Nahman of Bratslav, 65, 147
narcissism, 51

Narmada River Valley project, 330
The Nation (magazine), 5
nationalism: in America, 337;
    pentecostals and, 43
National Organization of Circumcision
    Information Resource Centers
    (nocirc), 58
National Organization of Restoring Men
    (NORM), 58
National Organization to Halt the Abuse
    and Routine Mutilation of Males
    (noharmm), 58
Natural Capitalism (Hawken, Lovins,
    and Lovins), 334
Nazarene Hasidim, 149
Nazis, 292; anti-Semitism and, 201;
    origins of, 208
nerve gas, 306
neshamot klaliyot (root souls), 149
Nesina, Damma ben, 101
networking, 267
Network of Spiritual Progressives, 15
Network Society, 335–36
"never again", 216–17
New Age, 52, 73, 255
New Orleans Klezmer All-Stars, 69
The New Republic (magazine), 5, 7
New Testament, 29; gods in, 33–34
Newton, Isaac, 127, 136
"The Next Industrial Revolution"
    (McDonough and Braungart),
    334
niddah (menstrual impurity), 158, 159,
    160, 161
Nietzsche, Friedrich, 340
Nigeria, 331
niggunim (melodies), 74
nihilism, 33
9/11, 14, 273, 277, 291, 312; evil and,
    281; lessons from, 245
Nintendo, 285
Nirvana, 23
nishmat kol hai (sacred breath of life),
    124
Noah, 103

Index

nocirc. *See* National Organization of Circumcision Information Resource Centers
No Future Without Forgiveness (Tutu), 310
noharmm. *See* National Organization to Halt the Abuse and Routine Mutilation of Males
non-cooperation, 298
nonviolence, 227–28, 277, 296
NORM. *See* National Organization of Restoring Men
North Korea, 294; in Axis of Evil, 295
noses, 91
Nothingness, 48
Nuclear Posture Review, 294
nuclear weapons, 279, 283, 285; America and, 294; deterrence and, 295
Nuremberg Trials, 196

Occupied Territories, 223
Ocean of Emancipation, 21, 22, 23, 26
oil, 302; in Nigeria, 331
Old Testament, 29; gods in, 33–34
opportunism, 257
oppression: resistance of, 327
Ordinary Men (Browning), 200
organic time, 146–47
Origins of the Kabbalah (Scholem), 109
Orthodox Judaism, 139; women in, 157
Oslo Peace Accord, 11, 307
The Other Side (magazine), 5
ozone, 328; depletion of, 283, 331

Pagels, Elaine, 232
Pakistan, 295
Palestinian Liberation Organization (PLO), 251
Palestinians, 11–12, 217, 219; aid for, 227; Bin Laden and, 237; compromise and, 224; frustration of, 225; as refugees, 239; subjugation of, 251
Paradigm Shift (Schachter-Shalomi), 104

paramitas (perfections), 26
paranoia, 303, 308
parenthood, 165–66
Parent's Project, 312
passive resistance, 296
Passover, 146
Pauli, Gunter, 334
Pax Americana, 274
peace: activists for, 223–24; compromise and, 235–37; Dalai Lama and, 279
Pearl Principle, 278
Peck, M. Scott, 284
penis. *See* circumcision
Pentateuch, 271
pentecostalism, 39; changes in, 43–44; fundamentalism and, 40; growth of, 39–40; as holy rollers, 43; nationalism and, 43; utopia and, 43
Penzias, Arno, 130
People in Auschwitz (Langbein), 199
Perennialism, 19, 21–22, 25
Peretz, Martin, 6
perfectionism, 155–56
Perpetrators, Victims, Bystanders (Hilberg), 200
Persian Gulf War, 284–85
Philips, Kevin, 247
philistinism, 51
Philo, 64, 65–66, 124
Piamenta, Yossi, 69
Piercy, Marge, 6
The Place Where You Are Standing is Holy (Winkler), 104
Plain Facts for Old and Young (Kellogg), 62
Plato, 132–33, 135
PLO. *See* Palestinian Liberation Organization
pluralism, 226–27
Poland, 298
The Politics of Meaning (Lerner), 14
Politics of Meaning Summit, 169
The Politics of Memory (Hilberg), 197
Pope, Marvin, 109, 110

populism, 337
Postmodernity and its Discontents
    (Bauman), 176
poverty, 14; increase in, 283
Powell, Colin, 246
praxis, 23
Presence, 307, 310
Primack, Joel R., 129, 132
Prince, 108
privatization, 257, 260; corporations
    and, 319; of water, 319–20
pro bono work, 265, 266
professionals, 263; competence of, 267;
    demoralization of, 266; ethics of,
    264, 265; licensing of, 264; privilege
    of, 268; profit-maximization and,
    264–65; public confidence in, 264.
    See also doctors; journalists; lawyers
Project for the New American Century,
    274
The Promise (movie), 239–40
Prophets, 120
Protestantism, 40
Proverbs, 109
Psalms, 109, 120
psychedelic drugs, 324
Purim, 139
purim (casting of lots), 152
Putnam, Robert D., 288

quantum field theory, 48

Rabbinical Assembly, 80
Rabbinical Assembly Law Committee,
    77, 78, 79
Rabbinic Judaism, 141
Rabbis for Human Rights in Israel, 227
Rabin, Yitzak, 308; assassination of, 309
racism, 11; Zionist, 13. *See also*
    apartheid
Radical Jewish Culture/Tzadik, 69
Ramakrishna, 148–49
Ram Dass, 149, 325
randomness, 152
Rapture, 230, 232; prediction of, 231

Reagan, Ronald, 232
rebbes (Hasidic masters), 148
Rebbe Soul, 69
RECAP. *See* RECover a Penis
RECover a Penis (RECAP), 58
Red Wheel, 292
Reggae, 70
religions, 1; in America, 143;
    disillusionment with, 41–42;
    distortion of, 19–20; emergence of,
    140; fervor of, 283; pluralism with,
    226–27; spirituality and, 101;
    tolerance of, 279; wars by, 19. *See
    also* Buddhism; Christianity; Islam
Religious Right, 3, 7
Remondino, Peter, 62
resistance, 327; freedom in, 329
Resolution for Middle East Peace, 13
Responsibility, 35–36
Reuven, 102, 103
Revelation, Book of, 231
Rich, Adrienne, 57
Richard of Saint Victor, 24–25
Ringelblum, Emmanuel, 187–88, 189
Rinpoche, Patrul, 278
Robertson, Pat, 232
Robinson, George, 63
Rogers, Carl, 38
Roman Empire, 245
Rorty, Richard, 249
Rosch, Eleanor, 20, 25
Roseanne, 70
Rose, Gillian, 174
Rotem, Simha, 193
Roth, Joel, 77, 78
Ruakh Ha'Kodesh (holy spirit), 149
Rumsfeld, Donald, 301
Russia, 12, 294; pentecostalism in, 40
Ruusbroec, Jan van, 25
Rwanda, 195, 197–98, 206

sacred narrative therapy, 151
sacrifice, 30
Sale, Kirkpatrick, 289–90
Samaria, 219

Samurai: corporations and, 51

SAPs. *See* structural adjustment
programs

sarcasm, 74

Saro-Wiwa, Ken, 331

Sartre, Jean-Paul, 181, 183

Satan, 230

satcitananda, 23

Satyagraha (force of truth), 296, 319

Saudi Arabia, 302

The Savage in Judaism (Eilberg-
Schwartz), 161

Sayre, Lewis, 62

Schachter-Shalomi, Zalman, 104

Schindler, Alexander, 6

Schindler's Arc (Keneally), 174

Schindler's List (movie), 174

Schlesinger, Arthur, Jr., 247

Scholem, Gershom, 109

Schore, Lee, 2

schtiebel, 100

Schumacher, E. F., 286

Schutze, Alfred, 284

science: disillusionment with, 41–42;
role of, 137–38. *See also* technology

Scofield Reference Bible, 231

Scott-Heron, Gil, 73

Second Coming, 229, 231

2nd Intifada, 11

Security Council, 311, 312

Seeking the Heart of Wisdom (Goldstein
and Kornfield), 325

sefirot (God's powers), 24, 118

self-actualization, 272

self-interest, 257; peace as, 279

Sellers, Peter, 104

Sephardi music, 70, 72

sephirot, 135; descriptions of, 135–36

seter (hiddenness), 152

settler Judaism, 140

Seven Noahide Laws, 148

sex: allure of, 112; danger of, 112; in
Genesis, 111; perfection in, 105;
promiscuity with, 282–83. *See also*
homosexuals; masturbation

sexism, 6, 11; circumcision and, 67;
Judaism and, 67

Shabbat: Holistic Judaism and, 143

Shaddai, 47

Shaivism, 25

Shamanism, 22, 23, 41, 100

Sharon, Ariel, 11, 13, 225, 234, 236;
invasion by, 246

Sharpton, Al, 248, 249

Shechinah (female), 220

shechitah (kosher slaughter), 124

shemitah (sabbatical year), 124

shevira (shattering), 153, 154, 156

shiurim, 73, 75

Shiva, 317

shiva (mourning), 235

shpil (game), 201

Shulamite, 106, 107, 108, 111

Shulweiss, Harold, 79

sins, 282; Catholicism and, 110; of
passion, 282–83

slavery: African Americans and, 195,
208; in Europe, 203

Sobibor, 192

social justice, 221, 271; resistance of,
327

Sojourners (magazine), 5

Solidarity, 298

Solomon, 105, 109, 111

Solzhenitsyn, Aleksandr, 199, 292

Soncino, 105–6

Song of Songs, 105–6, 110, 113–16

soul, 271–72

Souls on Fire (Wiesel), 101

South Africa, 307, 309

Southern Baptists, 233

Soviet Union: disintegration of, 257,
296. *See also* Russia

sparkpoints, 133; possibilities for, 134

Spielberg, Steven, 174

Spirit Matters (Lerner), 14

spiritual crisis, 2–3

spirituality: instant nature of, 102;
internal *vs.* external, 103–4; knowing
and, 20–21; New Age, 4;

participatory process of, 20; religion and, 101

Spock, Benjamin, 60

SS Intrepid (ship), 253

State Orthodoxy, 139, 140–41, 142

STDs, 62

Steck, Diana, 329

Steiner, George, 111

sterilization, 203

Stevens, Wallace, 339

Sting, 41

structural adjustment programs (SAPs), 286, 319, 320

Sufism, 23, 25

suicide bombing, 228, 303

sui generis (aristocracy of victimhood), 178

Sukkot, 146

sullen irresponsibility, 286

Summers, Larry, 250

Sunyata, 22; nonduality in, 23

Superpowers, 292

Surplus Powerlessness (Lerner), 14

surrounding, 303–5

survival complex, 174

survivor's guilt, 174, 216

survivor's syndrome, 174

sustainability, 333; obstacles to, 335

SUVs, 287

Swadeshi (economic freedom), 316

Swaraj (self-rule), 319

Swimme, Brian, 121

Syria, 294

Szwajger, Adina Blady, 186, 190–91, 192

Tales of Hasidim (Buber), 101

Talmud, 47, 99; charity and, 236; irony of, 174

Tanakh, 108

Tantric Buddhism, 23

Tao, 22

teachers, 264

techno-cocoon, 287–89

technology, 258; distancing with, 284; evil and, 284

tehillim (psalms), 71

television, 287–88

Teresa of Avila, 25

terrorism, 219, 237, 247, 273, 281, 283, 291, 302; of Bolsheviks, 292; occupation as, 236

Theresienstadt 1941–1945 (Adler), 199

Thich Nhat Hanh, 255–56

Thompson, Evan, 20, 25

Thurman, Howard, 149

Tiamat, 120

Tibbon, Samuel Ibn, 109, 113

Tibet, 12

tikkun, 154; as purpose, 153

Tikkun Community, 15

tikkun olam, 138, 146, 303

Tillich, Paul, 33, 35

time: organic, 146

Tooke, Robert, 62

Torah: circumcision and, 64–66; commandments of, 119; Goddess worship in, 218; homosexuals and, 78; individual and, 102; universe and, 134–35

torture, 1, 200, 201; by Israel, 217

Trade Related Intellectual Property Rights (TRIPs), 320

transcendence, 52, 138

Traverso, Enzo, 183

Treblinka, 188, 192, 201

treif (unclean), 147

The Trial (Kafka), 178

TRIPs. *See* Trade Related Intellectual Property Rights

Truth and Reconciliation Commission, 13, 307, 309, 310, 311

tsara'at (leprosy), 159

tshuvah (decision), 77

Tutu, Desmond, 309, 310

tzimtzum (withdrawal), 136, 138, 153

Ubersiedlung, 182

The Unconquerable World: Power, Nonviolence and the Will of the People (Schell), 296, 298–99

Union of American Hebrew
  Congregations, 6
United Nations, 245–46, 306
United Nations Charter, 305, 310
United Nations Conference on Racism,
  240
United Nations Security Council, 311,
  312
United States. *See* America
United Synagogue, 80
universe: expansion of, 128; harmony
  with, 146; large-scale structure of,
  128; myth of, 133–35; wrinkles in,
  130
The Universe Story (Swimme and
  Berry), 121
Upsizing (Pauli), 334
utopia, 43; hope for, 337

values, 31
Varela, Francisco, 20, 25
Vasudhaiva Kutumbkam (earth family),
  316
victim by proxy, 178
victimization: Holocaust and, 328; of
  Jews, 218–19
Villafane, Eldin, 45
violence, 217–18, 242, 295; female
  abhorrence of, 221; power and, 294;
  resistance of, 327; as sin, 282–83; of
  World War I, 292
Void, 33
Vrandenburg, George, 10
Vrandenburg, Trish, 10
vulnerability, 273–74

Wallis, Jim, 169
Wall Street Journal, 338
"War of Extermination: The Crime of
  the Wehrmacht, 1941–1945," 204
Warsaw Jewish Council, 185
WASP, 92
waste, 334
Watt, James, 232

The Way of the Boundary Crosser
  (Winkler), 102, 104
wealth: distribution of, 1, 165
Wealth and Democracy (Philips), 247
weapons of mass destruction, 294–95,
  306. *See also* anthrax; nerve gas;
  nuclear weapons
Weizenbaum, Joseph, 285
Wellston, Paul, 248
West Bank, 219, 223
Wharton, Edith, 112
Whitman, Walt, 34, 246
Wiesel, Elie, 6, 101
Wilber, Ken, 23
Wilson, Robert, 130
women: equality of, 142; Holistic
  Judaism and, 142; impurity of,
  160–61; in Orthodox Judaism, 157.
  See also menstruation
work: specialization of, 286; wage
  blackmail and, 289
World Bank, 286, 318, 320, 331
World Class (Kanter), 257
Worldcom, 247
World Court, 245–46
World Jewish Congress, 204
World Trade Organization, 286, 318,
  320; protesters of, 342
World War I, 291–92, 305
World War II, 292, 305

xenophobia, 11

Yam, 120
yeshiva (Jewish academy), 148
YHVH, 47, 120, 121, 122
Yiddishkeit, 147
Yizhak, Levi, 124
Yochai, Shim'on bar, 104
yosher (balance), 73
Young Urban Professional (yuppie), 267

Zalman, Reb, 145–49
Zel'dovich, Yacov Borisovich, 130

Zel'dovich spectrum, 130, 131
Zen of tennis, 51
zero-point energy, 48
Zionism, 64, 213; anti-Semitism and,
    233; Christian, 229, 232, 233

Zohar, 49, 72, 120
Zorn, John, 69, 71
Zoske, Joseph, 58–59
Zuckerman, Itzhak, 193
Zwingli, Ulrich, 230

About the Contributors

Mohammed Abu-Nimer is associate professor at American University's School of International Service in International Peace and Conflict Resolution, and director of their Peacebuilding and Development Institute. He is the author of numerous books, including *Peacebuilding and Nonviolence in Islamic Context: Theory and Practice*.

Rachel Adler is associate professor of modern Jewish thought and Judaism and gender at University of Southern California and the Rabbinical School at the Los Angeles campus. She is the author of many articles that have appeared in *Blackwell's Companion to Feminist Philosophy*; *Beginning Anew: A Woman's Companion to the High Holy Days*; *Contemporary Jewish Religious Thought*; *Lifecycles*; *The Jewish Condition*; and *On Being a Jewish Feminist*.

Zygmunt Bauman is emeritus professor of sociology at the University of Leeds and University of Warsaw. He is the author of more than twenty-one books, including *Work, Consumerism and the New Poor*; *Globalization: The Human Consequences*; *In Search of Politics*; *Liquid Modernity*; and *The Individualized Society*.

Daniel Berrigan is a Roman Catholic priest and renowned peace activist. A former fugitive from the FBI due to his activities opposing the Vietnam War, he is the author of *Uncommon Prayer: A Book of Psalms* and *Daniel: Under the Siege of the Divine*.

Cherie R. Brown is founder and executive director of the National Coalition Building Institute. She is the author of many books, including *Leading Diverse Communities: A How-To Guide for Moving from Healing into Action*.

Tony Campolo is professor emeritus at Eastern University and founder of the Evangelical Association for the Promotion of Education. He is the author of many books, including *Speaking My Mind*.

Fritjof Capra is a physicist and systems theorist and a founding director of the Center for Ecoliteracy. He is on the faculty of Schumacher College and the author of several international bestsellers, including *The Tao of Physics*; *The Turning Point*; *The Web of Life*; and *The Hidden Connections*.

Kim Chernin is the founder of EdgeWork Books and the author of fourteen books, including *The Girl Who Went and Saw and Came Back* and *In My Mother's House*.

Deepak Chopra is the founder and director of education at The Chopra Center for Well Being and is known worldwide for his numerous published works, including *Peace is the Way*.

Harvey Gallagher Cox is a professor of divinity at Harvard and a prolific author, including *When Jesus Came to Harvard: Making Moral Decisions Today*.

Lama Surya Das is one of the foremost Western Buddhist meditation teachers and scholars, and founder of the Western Buddhist Teachers Network. He teaches at Esalen, Open Center, Omega Institute, Interface, and at many universities in the United States and abroad. Author of numerous books, including *Letting Go of the Person You Used to Be: Lessons on Change, Loss, and Spiritual Transformation*.

Amitai Etzioni is a professor at George Washington University, where he is the director of the Institute for Communitarian Policy Studies. He is the author of twenty-four books, including *My Brother's Keeper: A Memoir and a Message* and *From Empire to Community: A New Approach to International Relations*.

Jorge N. Ferrer is an associate professor in the East-West Psychology Program at California Institute of Integral Studies. He is the author of many books, including *Revisioning Transpersonal Theory: A Participatory Vision of Human Spirituality* and *The Participatory Turn: Spirituality, Mysticism, Religious Studies*.

Estelle Frankel is a practicing psychotherapist and teacher of Jewish mysticism. She is the author of *Sacred Therapy*.

Yitzhak Frankenthal is the founder of the Parents' Circle, an organization in Israel that has united hundreds of Israeli and Palestinian bereaved parents committed to promoting reconciliation, peace, and democracy.

Peter Gabel is professor of law at New College of California, associate editor of *Tikkun*, and author of *The Bank Teller and Other Essays on the Politics of Meaning*. He has been Michael Lerner's primary intellectual partner in developing the ideas that shape the *Tikkun* community in all of its various manifestations.

Nan Fink Gefen was the founding publisher of *Tikkun* magazine and is currently the president and director of faculty of Chochmat HaLev, a Jewish spiritual leadership program in Berkeley, California.

Daniel Jonah Goldhagen is an affiliate of Harvard's Minda de Gunzburg Center for European Studies. He is the author of *Hitler's Willing Executioners: Ordinary Germans and the Holocaust* and *A Moral Reckoning: The Role of the Catholic Church in the Holocaust and Its Unfulfilled Duty of Repair*.

Roger S. Gottlieb is professor of philosophy at Worcester Polytechnic Institute and the author or editor of twelve books, including *Liberating Faith: Religious Voices for Justice, Peace, and Ecological Wisdom* and *A Spirituality of Resistance: Finding a Peaceful Heart and Protecting the Earth*.

Arthur Green is professor of Jewish thought at Brandeis University and former president of the Reconstructionist Rabbinical College. He is the author of numerous works, including *A Guide to the Zohar*.

Robert Inchausti is a professor of English at California Polytechnic State University and the author of *Thomas Merton's American Prophecy*; *The Ignorant Perfection of Ordinary People*; and *Spitwad Sutras: Classroom Teaching as Sublime Vocation*.

Andrew Kimbrell runs the Center for Food Safety as well as its parent organization, the International Center for Technology Assessment. He is the president of the Turning Point Project, director of the International Forum on Globalization, and the author of *The Fatal Harvest*; *The Human Body Shop*; and *The Masculine Mystique*.

Michael S. Kimmel is professor of sociology at SUNY–Stony Brook. He is the author of many books, including *The Gendered Society*; *Manhood in America*; and *The Handbook of Studies on Men and Masculinities*.

David C. Korten is an author, lecturer, and active member of many associations dedicated to citizen involvement and global development. Author of many books, his works include *When Corporations Rule the World* and *The Great Turning: From Empire to Earth Community*.

Lawrence L. Langer, professor emeritus of English at Simmons College, is a noted Holocaust scholar. He is the author of many works, including *Using and Abusing the Holocaust*; *Holocaust Testimonies: The Ruins of Memory; Preempting the Holocaust*; and *The Game Continues: Chess in the Art of Samuel Bak*.

Jackson Lears is professor of history at Rutgers University and editor-in-chief of the *Raritan Quarterly Review*. His publications include *Something for Nothing: Luck in America* and *Fables of Abundance: A Cultural History of Advertising in America*.

Michael Lerner is National Chair of Network of Spiritual Progressives, rabbi at Beyt Tikkun Synagogue, author of ten books, and editor of *Tikkun* magazine. His books include *The Left Hand of God: Taking Our Country Back from the Religious Right*. RabbiLerner@Tikkun.org.

Julian Levinson is an endowed professor in Jewish American studies at the University of Michigan.

Daniel C. Matt, former professor of Jewish mysticism at the Graduate Theological Union, is a leading authority on the Zohar and Kabbalah. He is the author of *The Essential Kabbalah; Zohar: The Book of Enlightenment*; *God and the Big Bang: Discovering Harmony Between Science and Spirituality*; and *Sefer ha-Zohar: The Pritzker Edition*.

Daphne Merkin is a regular contributor to *The New York Times Book Review*. Her works include *Dreaming of Hitler* and *Enchantment*.

Judith Plaskow is professor of religious studies at Manhattan College. She is cofounder, and for ten years was coeditor, of the *Journal of Feminist Studies in Religion*. She is author or editor of several works on feminist theology, including *Standing Again at Sinai: Judaism from a Feminist Perspective* and *The Coming of Lilith: Essays on Feminism, Judaism, and Sexual Ethics*.

Joel R. Primack is professor of physics at the University of California–Santa Cruz. He is the author of *The View From the Center of the Universe*, coauthored with Nancy Allen Abrams, a lawyer, writer, and former Fulbright scholar.

Or Rose teaches at Brandeis University and is the editor of *God in All Moments: Mystical and Practical Wisdom from the Hasidic Masters* and coauthor of *Abraham Joshua Heschel: Man of Spirit, Man of Action*.

Jonathan Schell, *The Nation*'s peace and disarmament correspondent, is the author of *The Unconquerable World: Power, Nonviolence, and the Will of the People* and *A Hole in the World*.

Kirk J. Schneider is a psychologist and adjunct faculty member at Saybrook Graduate School and the California Institute of Integral Studies. Dr. Schneider is president of the Existential-Humanistic Institute and the author of several books including *Rediscovery of Awe: Splendor, Mystery and the Fluid Center of Life*; *The Paradoxical Self: Toward an Understanding of Our Contradictory Nature*; and *Horror and the Holy: Wisdom-Teachings of the Monster Tale*.

Jonathan Schorsch is director of undergraduate studies and assistant professor of religion at Columbia University. His books include *Jews and Blacks in the Early Modern World* and *Jews, Judaism, Blacks and Christianity in the Early Modern Iberian Atlantic World*.

Ruth Knafo Setton is writer-in-residence for the Berman Center for Jewish Studies at Lehigh University. She is the fiction editor of *Arts and Letters*, and author of several works of fiction and poetry.

Vandana Shiva is a physicist, ecologist, activist, editor, and author of many books, including *Biopiracy: The Plunder of Nature and Knowledge* and *Stolen Harvest: The Hijacking of the Global Food Supply*.

William M. Sullivan is senior scholar at the Carnegie Foundation for the Advancement of Teaching. His works include *Work and Integrity: The Crisis and Promise of Professionalism in America* and *Habits of the Heart: Individualism and Commitment in American Life*, coauthored with Richard Madsen, Ann Swindler, Steven Tipton, and Robert Bellah.

Jim Wallis is editor-in-chief of *Sojourners* magazine. He is a regular contributor to *The New York Times, Washington Post, Los Angeles Times*, and other major newspapers. His books include *God's Politics: Why the Right Gets It Wrong and the Left Doesn't Get It*.

Neale Donald Walsch is the creator of the Conversations with God Foundation. In addition to authoring the renowned With God series, he has published sixteen other works, as well as a number of video and audio programs.

Arthur Waskow is director of the Shalom Center, and author of many books and articles, including *A Time for Every Purpose Under Heaven* and *Trees, Earth, and Torah*.

Gershon Winkler, a rabbi, is the founder and executive director of Walking Stick Foundation and author of many books.

Naomi Wolf is a bestselling author. Her works include *The Tree House: Eccentric Wisdom From My Father on How to Live, Love, and See*.